China Opens its Doors

China Opens its Doors

The Politics of Economic Transition

Jude Howell

HARVESTER WHEATSHEAF

LYNNE RIENNER PUBLISHERS

First published in Great Britain in 1993 by
Harvester Wheatsheaf
Campus 400, Maylands Avenue
Hemel Hempstead
Hertfordshire, HP2 7EZ
A division of
Simon & Schuster International Group

First published in the United States of America by
Lynne Rienner Publishers, Inc.
948 North Street, Boulder, Colorado 80302

Typeset in 10½/12pt Times
by MHL Typesetting Ltd, Coventry

Printed and bound in Great Britain by
BPCC Wheatons Ltd, Exeter

British Library Cataloguing in Publication Data

A catalogue record for this book is available from
the British Library

ISBN 0-7450-1295-7 (pbk)

Library of Congress Cataloging-in-Publication Data

Howell, Jude.
    China opens its doors: the politics of economic
transition / Jude Howell.
        p.   cm.
    Includes bibliographical references and index.
    ISBN 1-55587-480-0
    1. China — Economic policy — 1976—
    2. China — Politics and government — 1976—
    3. Amoy Special Economic Zone (Amoy, China)
    I. Title.
    HC427.92.H67 1993
    338.951'009'048 — dc20   93-2538
                                                 CIP

1 2 3 4 5   97 96 95 94 93

Contents

List of figures

List of tables

For my mother and friends

Preface

This book is the outcome of a long-standing personal and intellectual interest in China's development in the reform era. Having worked in China in the early 1980s and returned again several times since the late 1980s, I was keen to understand more about the far-reaching changes in China's economy and society. I was particularly interested in China's Open Policy which had brought not only foreign investment to China but also karaoke bars, Coca-Cola and ideas about democracy. Whilst China still maintains the rhetorical cloak of socialism, the transition towards a market economy has brought about enormous changes in the structure of society and in the state itself. The smashing of the 'iron rice bowl', the end of egalitarianism and the gradual introduction of a labour market have undermined the privileged position of the state worker. The introduction of market forces has bred a *nouveau riche* of rich peasants, traders and private entrepreneurs. The process of economic transition has reshuffled the net of winners and losers. Inevitably this has been a highly politicised process at all levels of society.

The fieldwork for this book was carried out in Xiamen SEZ, Chengdu, Beijing, Shenyang, Zhejiang province and Hong Kong. I am indebted to all those I interviewed for improving my understanding of China. I owe special thanks to the libraries of Xiamen University, University Services Centre at the Chinese University of Hong Kong, School of Oriental and African Studies in London, China—Britain Trade Group and University of East Anglia. Without financial assistance from the Nuffield Foundation and the ESRC, this book would not have been possible. Not least I am grateful to Gordon White and Bob Benewick for their comments and encouragement as well as my colleagues at the School of Development Studies, UEA, for their support over the period of writing. I hold myself entirely responsible for the views expressed in the book and any inaccuracies.

List of abbreviations

AFP	Agence France Press
AWSJ	*Asia Wall Street Journal*
BJ	Beijing
BJRV	*Beijing Review*
BYT	*Ban Yuetan*
CBR	*China Business Review*
CCP	Chinese Community Party
CCPCC	Chinese Communist Party Central Committee
CD	*China Daily*
CEI	*China Economic Information*
CITIC	China International Trust and Investment Company
CJYJ	*Caijing Yanjiu*
CM	*Chengming*
DFRB	*Dongfang Ribao*
DGB	*Dagong Bao*
DX	*Dongxiang*
EJV	Equity joint venture
ETDZ	Economic and Technological Development Zone
FBIS	Foreign Broadcasting Information Service
FDI	Foreign direct investment
FE	Far East
FEC	Foreign Exchange Certificate
FEER	*Far Eastern Economic Review*

FFPS	Fuzhou Fujian Provincial Service
FIEC	Fujian Investment Enterprises Corporation
FJJJ	*Fujian Jingji*
FJLT	*Fujian Luntan*
FJRB	*Fujian Ribao*
GD	Guangdong
GJMYWT	*Guoji Maoyi Wenti*
GJSB	*Guoji Shangbao*
GMRB	*Guangming Ribao*
GRRB	*Gongren Ribao*
GZRB	*Guangzhou Ribao*
HK	Hong Kong
HKMCED	*Hong Kong and Macao Economic Digest*
JB	*Jing Bao*
JFJB	*Jiefangjun Bao*
JFRB	*Jiefang Ribao*
JJCKB	*Jingji Cankao Bao*
JJDB	*Jingji Daobao*
JJGL	*Jingji Guanli*
JJRB	*Jingji Ribao*
JPRS	Joint Publications Research Service
JV	Joint venture
KF	*Kaifang*
LHP	*Lien Ho Pao*
LNRB	*Liaoning Ribao*
LSC	Labour Service Corporation
LW	*Liaowang*
MB	*Ming Bao*
MFN	Most favoured nation
MoFERT	Ministry of Foreign Economic Relations and Trade
NCNA	*New China News Analysis*
NFJJ	*Nanfang Jingji*
NFRB	*Nanfang Ribao*
NICs	Newly industrialised countries
PLA	People's Liberation Army
PX	*Pai Xing*
QS	*Qiushi*
Rmb	Renminbi
RMRB	*Renmin Ribao*
S	*The Standard*
SCMP	*South China Morning Post*
SEZ	Special Economic Zone
SH	Shanghai

SJJJDB	*Shijie Jingji Daobao*
SWB	Summary of World Broadcasts
TJRB	*Tianjin Ribao*
TVE	Township and village enterprise
TT	*Tang Tai*
WOFE	Wholly owned foreign enterprise
WWP	*Wen Weipo*
XB	*Xin Bao*
XH	Xinhua News Agency
XMRB	*Xiamen Ribao*
XWB	*Xinwen Bao*
YCWB	*Yangcheng Wanbao*
ZGQNJJLT	*Zhongguo Qingnian Jingji Luntan*
ZGTXS	*Zhongguo Tongxun She*
ZGXWS	Zhongguo Xinwenshe

Introduction

The year 1989 marked a watershed in development policy thinking. The crisis in Eastern Europe as well as the tragic massacre on 4 June in Tiananmen Square have discredited socialism as a viable and humane alternative to capitalism. These events have placed liberalisation, both economic and political, firmly and squarely on the development agenda.

The demise of socialism has occurred against a global background of disillusionment with the state, recession and restructuring of the world economy. This has been matched by a growing faith over the last decade in the virtues of the market. Advanced capitalist countries, centrally planned economies and so-called developing countries have enthusiastically embraced an economic strategy characterised by an increasing reliance upon market forces and a diminishing role for the state.

Although the logic for these changes differs fundamentally between capitalist and socialist countries, 'advanced' and 'developing', the surface elements of reform in countries such as China, Vietnam and the former Soviet Union share features in common with economic liberalisation packages adopted in the capitalist world. These common features include an increasing role for the private sector in the economy with a concomitant relaxation of state control over this sector; decentralisation of economic power both within the state sector and to economic units; charges to users of public goods and services; and finally, the opening up of the national economy to the international economy.

This book focuses on the politics of China opening up to the capitalist world economy.[1] China has pursued a strategy of reform and opening up for well over a decade. The death of Mao in 1976 and the subsequent downfall of the Gang of Four marked a turning-point in the post-liberation history of China. With the consolidation of Deng Xiaoping's position at the Third Plenum in December 1978, the reformist leadership ventured upon a developmental path differing radically in form and substance from that of the preceding decade. This strategy heralded a shift in economic power from the state to the market. Although China had contrary to popular opinion always maintained some trade links with the capitalist world, this was the first time since Liberation that it was to open up to the international capitalist economy on such a massive scale.

The drawing back of the bamboo curtain to the international economy has raised a host of questions of political significance. To what extent has opening up to the international capitalist economy implied a relinquishing of socialist principles such as equality and the abolition of exploitation? Who are the key proponents of the policy within the central leadership and what is their social constituency? What is the role of the Party and trade unions in enterprises with foreign investment? Who are the chief beneficiaries of the policy and what will be the response of the potential losers? How has the set of winners and losers changed with the evolution of the policy? How will opening up to the world economy affect relations between the state, labour and foreign capital? What are the consequences of the Tiananmen massacre for China's Open Policy? To what extent will economic liberalisation be accompanied by political liberalisation?

It would be overambitious even to attempt to address all of these issues in depth. The book thus homes in on two broad questions. First, to what extent is the course of the Open Policy shaped by politics? To answer this we need some understanding of the policy participants, the issues over which conflict and cooperation emerge as well as the impact of these political forces on the evolution, substance, form and goals of the policy. Second, what are the socio-political consequences of China opening up to the capitalist world economy? To what extent do they promote or impede the course of the Open Policy?

By putting the spotlight on the political dimension of the Open Policy this book hopes to enrich current analyses which have generally focused on the economic aspects of the policy.[2] Up till now there has been no systematic evolutionary account of the Open Policy. Studies of the Open Policy have tended to concentrate on specific aspects of opening up such as foreign trade, joint ventures, foreign loans and the SEZs rather than the policy as a whole.[3] Whilst the empirical and theoretical contribution of these studies has been enormous, the time has come to strengthen the political side of the story.[4] Before launching into this challenge, let us first clarify what we mean by the term Open Policy.

What is the Open Policy?

Whilst the Western press and academia refer loosely to the 'Open Door Policy', we will adopt the term 'Open Policy' throughout this book. Not only is this a direct translation from the Chinese (*kaifang zhengce*) but it also harbours fewer historico-political connotations, in particular concerning the gunboat diplomacy of the nineteenth century. The Open Policy refers to the set of policies adopted by the reformist leadership since the Third Plenum of the Eleventh Central Committee in December 1978 to promote the expansion of economic relations with the capitalist world economy. It consists of a set of subpolicies in the spheres of foreign trade, foreign direct investment and foreign borrowing.

A perusal of Chinese and Western sources on the Open Policy reveals considerable slippage in the use of the terms foreign trade, foreign direct investment and foreign borrowing. The term foreign trade has at times included joint ventures and processing and assembly arrangements whilst the term foreign direct investment has been used broadly to include compensation trade and foreign loans.[5]

In this book foreign trade refers to the international exchange of goods and services and thus excludes joint ventures. Foreign loans applies to the extension of credit by foreign governments, commercial banks or international monetary agencies. The term foreign direct investment refers to equity investment by a foreign company in production or service facilities in China. The 'foreign' companies include for example Overseas Chinese, Hong Kong/Macao, Japanese, Western European and American investment.

There are three types of enterprise with foreign investment, namely equity joint ventures, contractual joint ventures and wholly owned foreign enterprises. Whilst equity and contractual joint ventures involve varying proportions of foreign and Chinese investment, a wholly owned foreign enterprise comprises only foreign investment. The reformist leadership has given greater policy preference to equity joint ventures rather than contractual joint ventures as these involve a greater commitment on the part of the foreign investor to ensure the success of the project. They also increase the chance of technology and managerial skills transfer. Up till the late 1980s Chinese reformers restricted, however, the number and location of wholly owned foreign enterprises as these potentially allow foreigners a greater measure of control over the enterprise.

The Open Policy also embraces the set of policies adopted to manage China's Special Economic Zones (SEZs). Partly so as to contain the influence of foreign direct investment the Chinese reformers set up four SEZs in mid-1979 in Guangdong and Fujian provinces. Hainan Island joined this privileged group in 1987. These offered special incentives to foreign investors such as tax concessions, reductions in land use fees and favourable labour policies. Similar to the SEZs are the Economic Technological and Development Zones (ETDZs) set up in 14 coastal cities in April 1984 to attract technology-intensive production.[6]

The Open Policy can be distinguished both quantitatively and qualitatively from the 'isolationist' policies and practices towards the external economy adopted during the Cultural Revolution and the 'traditional' policies and practices pursued in the 1950s and to a certain extent in the Hua Guofeng era. Although we will discuss the differences in greater detail in the first chapter, the key points are as follows. First, although China has contrary to the Western media never been 'closed', the scale of foreign direct investment, borrowing and trade with the capitalist world economy has been far more extensive than at any period since the liberation of China. Second, the Open Policy has involved not only the continuation and expansion of pre-existing forms of trade and loans but also the introduction of new forms of foreign economic involvement, such as licensing, leasing, foreign direct investment and SEZs. Finally, the establishment of special economic zones and economic technological development zones reflects a *de facto* shift away from the Maoist 'supplementary' conception of the external economy towards a more implicitly 'integrative' or 'intrusive' conception of the relation between the domestic and external economy.

The politics of opening up: actors, roles and effects

Having clarified our understanding of the term Open Policy we can now return to the first of our central themes, namely, the effect of politics on the Open Policy. If we take policy to be a 'committed structure of resources', then we can see that a change in this structure can have distributive implications across the economy and society.[7] This in turn can bring about a shift in the pattern of beneficiaries, leading to conflict and cooperation as losers try to salvage what they can and potential winners try to maximise their gains. Changing policy is thus a highly politicised affair.

China's Open Policy has, along with the domestic economic reforms, significant distributive consequences for particular social and economic groups, industrial sectors, state institutions and regions. The Open Policy involves not only choices about the allocation of central economic resources but also, and indeed more importantly, the granting of particular 'rights' and 'privileges' to selected areas, sectors and social groups. The Open Policy provides opportunities and benefits for those regions, institutions and social groups granted preferential rights and privileges and bold enough to test the new entrepreneurial waters. A process of bargaining ensues between those who see their interests furthered and those who see themselves as potential losers. This conflict and cooperation not only affects the actual implementation of policy, sometimes braking its pace, sometimes steering it along unforeseen paths, but also constantly redefines the rationale, shape and content of policy.[8]

The first chapter of the book lays out the theoretical framework. It identifies the key actors involved in the drama of opening up and explores their roles in the shaping of this process. It operates with a broad conception of politics which extends beyond the macro, formal level of leaders, parties and institutions to include the mesolevel politics of intermediary organisations such as trade unions and the microlevel politics of foreign-invested enterprises.

Within the Party leaders have argued over the ideological aspects of the policy, the timing, pace and extent of opening up. Government institutions have vied with each to retain old privileges or reap new benefits. Within state bodies older, politically qualified cadres have battled against younger, technically skilled cadres to retain their positions of influence and power.[9] Alternatively, they have tried desperately to jump on the bandwagon and cash in on the opportunities offered through reform and opening up. Trade union leaders have found themselves in an ideological quandary. Party policy requires them to support opening up whilst their organisational *raison d'être* compels them to defend the interest of workers. In foreign-invested enterprises workers have welcomed the higher nominal wages but disliked the longer hours and insecure contracts. State enterprises have competed with each other for foreign investment and the numerous privileges and concessions that go with it. Envious of the growth in the SEZs and coastal cities, institutions, political leaders and individuals in the inland areas have sought either to stem the flow of the Open Policy or to extend its benefits to themselves.

This cooperation and conflict within the Party, between and within institutions, intermediary organisations, enterprises and regions in turn affects the substance, scope and indeed the trajectory of the policy. This forms the subject of the second and third chapters of the book. By tracking changes in the pace, extent, form and direction of the Open Policy, we are able to identify its evolutionary pattern from the Third Plenum in December 1978 up till the Fourteenth Party Congress of October 1992. We can best describe this pattern as a spiral consisting of a series of cycles. The cycles comprise both an upswing when decentralising policies aimed at promoting microlevel initiative in foreign economic relations get under way and a downswing when the centre reimposes its control to redress macroeconomic imbalances resulting from microlevel activity.

Each cycle moves the policy either a few steps forwards or a few steps backwards. However, each cycle leaves a residue of policies, structures and interests in its wake, which prevent a return to point zero and lay the conditions for the advance of the next cycle. In this way the Open Policy keeps moving forward. As opening up becomes more firmly established, any attempts to reverse the policy become systemically and politically more complicated.

So, the spiral nature of China's Open Policy has both an economic and a political logic. The political logic lies in the impact of the cooperation and conflict between the expectant and actual beneficiaries and losers identified in Chapter 1 upon the policy process. Economically it is the recurrent dilemma of reconciling the contradictory goals of macrolevel harmony with microlevel initiative in the context of a partially reformed economy which underpins these policy vacillations.[10]

As well as exploring the general impact of politics on the process of opening up, we also apply our analysis to the local level. The fourth chapter takes up the case of Xiamen SEZ in Fujian Province, one of the four SEZs to be set up in 1979. As the bulk of research on the SEZs has concentrated on Shenzhen SEZ this case-study charters barely traversed terrain. It considers the factors shaping the course of the policy, highlighting those specific to the area. By establishing key stages in the development of the policy, it attempts to capture the dynamic of the policy at the local level.

Socio-political impact of opening up: the state and labour

Whilst the first part of the book deals with the effect of politics on the policy process, the second part takes up the other central theme of the socio-political consequences of opening up. As the Open Policy changes the distribution of resources and power amongst individuals, social groups, institutions and regions, this implies potential changes in the social, political and institutional fabric, either intended or unforeseen. These changes in turn recondition the political environment in which the policy evolves. We concentrate our analysis on the socio-political consequences of the redistribution of power and resources for the state and labour.

As the state in China plays a key role in generating, establishing and implementing policy, the impact of opening up on the structure, operational mode and social composition of the state is clearly crucial for the future direction of the Open Policy. To the extent that the character of the state alters so as to facilitate the introduction of foreign and domestic capital, the Open Policy is likely to be pushed forwards. Given that the redefinition of the state implies winners and losers both within institutions and between institutions, this process is likely to be highly politicised, hence contributing towards the spiral dynamic of the Open Policy.

The fifth chapter thus attempts to capture the essence of these changes in the state. Not only are existing institutions adapting to suit the altered policy climate, but new institutions of a voluntary and quasi-entrepreneurial character are emerging. Institutions born out of the previous centrally planned system coexist uneasily with newly sprouting institutions adapted to cope with the needs of reform and opening up. Moreover, there is a temporary vacuum where the pace of institutional adaptation and creation falls behind the changes in the economy.

These structural changes are matched by new ways of operating. As profit becomes a leitmotiv of China's market-oriented economy, some state institutions are trying to shed their bureaucratic chains to don a more entrepreneurial garb. Central institutions are divesting power to lower levels to encourage microlevel economic initiative. Older, politically qualified cadres have to sharpen their technical and economic tools as the voices of younger technocrats become louder.

Together these changes in the structure, operational mode and social composition of the state have heralded the arrival of elements of a new market-facilitating state in China. As a result the state has a transitory, polymorphic character, betraying an uneven blend of persisting state organs associated with the command economy and nascent market-facilitating agencies. The predominance of a market-facilitating state has been greater during periods of upswing in the Open Policy whilst the web of the command state has expanded during the downswings in the Open Policy. The spiral course of institutional change thus shadows the spiral path of the Open Policy.

The opening up of China to the capitalist world economy has ramifications not only for the state but also for labour. In the sixth chapter we look at the nature of labour policy in the SEZs and foreign-invested enterprises. The establishment of foreign-invested enterprises in China raises a host of issues of political significance for labour. As China has since 1949 claimed to follow a socialist path to development, which implies *inter alia* a commitment to the interests of the working class, the introduction of foreign direct investment clearly poses an ideological and political dilemma for the Chinese state. Moreover, as the type of labour policies and practices adopted in the foreign-invested enterprises may be extended to the state-owned enterprises, the issues of equality, full employment and exploitation are of particular concern to socialist policy-makers, academics and politicians both in China and overseas.

What then has been the institutional impact of these changes on labour policy? New working conditions in foreign-invested enterprises have not only prompted changes in the methods and functions of trade unions and the Party but also in the relations between the state, labour and capital. In the SEZs newly founded Labour Service Corporations now mediate between foreign capital and the Chinese labour force. At the same time trade unions are having to adapt their structure and methods to suit the changing times. The ideological dilemma faced by trade union leaders trying to balance the representation of both the interests of workers and foreign capital has strengthened their demands for greater autonomy from the Party. The establishment of voluntary autonomous trade unions during the democracy movement of 1989 was an expression of the increasing tensions both within the trade unions and between the unions and their membership.

What lessons then can we draw from this close study of China's Open Policy? What are the implications, the risks and benefits for other socialist countries venturing upon such a path? What are the possible scenarios for China in the next century? Will it become a fully fledged member of the capitalist world economy? Or, will it always keep the door slightly closed? Will economic liberalisation in China inevitably lead to a pluralisation of the political sphere? And what are the implications of China's experience for development theory and practice?

These are some of the issues which we reflect upon in the concluding chapter. Here we weave together the strands of argument, highlighting the political essence of the policy. For a socialist country to move towards a market economy with its doors open, political factors are as crucial as economic variables. The echoes of economic liberalisation reverberate also in the halls of politics. Opening up to the capitalist world economy along with the expansion of domestic market forces leads to changes in the institutional and social fabric. This in turn reconditions the social and political environment in which opening up occurs. How far China will continue down this path is an open question. What is clear though is that to reverse this outward course would at the political level be highly problematic.

Notes

1. This book is based on research carried out in Xiamen SEZ, Fuzhou, Beijing, Shenyang, Xiaoshan and Hong Kong in the years 1987, 1988, 1990 and 1992. The case-study of Xiamen SEZ discussed in Chapter 4 is based on interviews in Chinese with Chinese officials working in foreign-invested enterprises and state-owned enterprises, officials in related state departments, foreign partners and managers in foreign-invested enterprises and academics. Since the events of Tiananmen research access has been more difficult and so China analysts have had to rely even more on secondary research. Secondary data in Chinese and English was collected in the libraries of Xiamen SEZ, University Services Centre in the Chinese University of Hong Kong, London and University of East Anglia.

   Statistical information was collated from a variety of sources so as to minimise discrepancies and lacunae. The reliability, availability and consistency of statistical data, particularly in the early years of reform, is limited, in part because of the shortage of statisticians, differing statistical methods and the political sensitivity of some information such as foreign exchange balances. Moreover, there are sometimes differences between official statistics and statistics published in internal documents to which foreigners are not granted access. Readers may find differences in statistics cited in this book compared with other sources but these do not detract from the general argument.

2. See, for example: Bucknall, 1989; Cannon, 1988; Casson, M. and Jurong Zheng, 'Western joint ventures in China', *Discussion Paper 151*, Dept. of Economics, University of Reading, March 1991: D. Chu, 1985; Goldenberg, 1988; Huang Fangyi, 1987; Kamm, 1989; Khan, 1991; Kleinberg, 1990; Kraus, 1985; Laaksonen, 1988; Lardy, 1992; Leung and Thoburn, 1991; W.H. Liu, 1986; Liu Guoguang, 1992; MacDougall, 1982; Chen Nai-Ruenn, 1986; Phillips, 1986; Pomfret, 1991; Su Wenming, 1985; Sung Yun-Wing, 1991; Vogel, 1989; Warner, 1987.

3. See note 2. Also a perusal of magazines such as *China Business Review*, *Sino-British Trade Review* and *China Trader* as well as *China's Foreign Trade*, *Beijing Review* and *Beijing Guoji Maoyi Wenti* lends credence to this. The World Bank, 1988 does examine all three aspects but from an economic perspective only.

4. For some treatment of the political aspects of the Open Policy, see: Barnett, 1981, ch. 2; Breslin, 1990; Burns, 1989; for an account of the political economy of China's SEZs, see Crane, 1990. See also Harding, 1987, ch. 6; Kokubun, 1986, pp 19—45; Lieberthal and Oksenberg, 1988; Oke, 1986; Pearson, 1991; Segal, 1990.

5. See, for example, Henley and Nyaw, 1988. According to Henley and Nyaw, p.1, foreign trade includes processing and assembly, joint ventures and wholly owned foreign enterprises whilst according to the Economic Research Centre and State Statistical Bureau of the People's Republic of China, *Almanac of China's Economy, 1984* compensation trade is included under FDI.

6. For the differences between SEZs and ETDZs, see the interview with state councillor Gu Mu, 'Policies for coastal cities' in Su Wenming, 1985.

7. See Schaffer, 1981, p. 8.

8. Other factors which may change policy include the cost of a policy, public interest in the policy, the urgency of a decision, the technicality of a policy and the international aspects of a policy (see Holmes, 1986; also Lampton discusses the impact of institutional structure, policy content, random events in Lampton, 1987).

9. A cadre is an official in an authoritative position. S/he is likely to be a Party member but not necessarily.

10. Somerville (1987) discusses a similar contradiction in the industrial reforms which likewise yields a spiral policy pattern.

1

Setting the theoretical stage

The expansion of China's economic ties with the international capitalist economy was officially endorsed as government policy at the Third Plenum of the Eleventh Central Committee in December 1978. Since then the volume of China's external trade has increased fivefold, over 41 000 foreign enterprises have agreed to invest in China and foreign debt has risen tenfold to the grand sum of US$ 52.55 billion.[1] The past decade has, however, witnessed numerous, often seemingly unexpected, changes in the pace, scope and direction of the Open Policy. The spiral character of the policy, which is the focus of the next chapter, has been a response in part to economic crises engendered by reform and opening up and in part to some of the socio-political dilemmas posed by radical transition to an open, market economy. The drawing back of the bamboo curtain has been a complex affair, characterised by conflict and cooperation and shifting alliances amongst a diversity of actors, whose interests, channels of influence and disposal of resources differ considerably.

What then are the interests of these actors? How do they seek to influence the process of opening up? How successful are they? We focus our analysis on key protagonists, namely the Party leadership, particular state institutions and regions and one of the policy recipients, namely foreign capital.[2] We begin by looking closely at the differences within the Party leadership over the Open Policy, the issues over which conflict appears and the potential impact of this on the content, pace and extent of the policy. We then turn our attention to state institutions involved in establishing and implementing the Open Policy and in particular the intra- and interinstitutional responses to opening up. Given the crucial role of foreign capital in China and the Open Policy we consider the interests of foreign investors and traders, their source of and degree of influence and the potential issues of conflict with the Chinese government at national and local levels. Finally, we consider the responses of local governments to the policy of opening up and in particular the axes of tension between coastal and inland areas.

Party leadership

The political character of the Party leadership has been an important factor in the generation and implementation of policy in China. The Party leadership in China has, contrary to popular opinion, never been a homogeneous entity. Academic analyses of China's top leadership have employed various criteria to identify and categorise different groups within the leadership. Factional models, for example, seek to identify the existence of different groupings within the leadership based on patronage networks. Tendency models, on the other hand, have identified groups within the leadership according to their supposed shared policy preferences. Other studies have identified leadership groups according to bureaucratic, institutional, personal or regional ties.[3] Although none of these models alone can define precisely the leadership groupings, they do nevertheless provide us with useful insights into the divisions within the top leadership concerning the Open Policy.

The political character of the Party leadership has affected the conception and implementation of the Open Policy in several ways. First, within the Party leadership we can locate groups of leaders sharing common views on the degree, direction and nature of China's external economic relations. We can observe this, for example, in the speeches of particular leaders, in publicised discussions between leaders at meetings and work conferences and in informal commentaries in the foreign press. Hua Guofeng's views on the external economy can, for example, be traced to the 'traditional' approach of the 1950s whilst supporters of the Gang of Four can be associated with an isolationist approach. Reformist leaders such as Deng Xiaoping and Zhao Ziyang can be linked with the more innovatory approach of the early 1960s and post-Mao era.

Although we may be able to identify different approaches within the leadership towards opening up, their influence upon the content and nature of opening up is contingent in part upon their relative power. However, gauging the relative power of different leadership groups is no easy task. This is hampered both by the methodological difficulty of measuring accurately and/or absolutely relative power and also by the secrecy surrounding intra-Party affairs within China.[4] But by carefully watching changes in the composition of key political bodies such as the Standing Committee of the Political Bureau, the Central Committee and the National People's Congress, we can identify shifts of relative power between different groups within the Party. Similarly, the frequency with which particular leaders are associated with authoritative statements about the content of the Open Policy or are addressing meetings or conferences concerned with debate about opening up indicates the relative power of leaders with competing positions on opening up. We can also observe the struggle between contending approaches to opening up in media reports of heated debates at meetings and conferences, or defensive statements by advocates of reform and opening up.

Second, leadership struggles between opposing groups linked by ideological, factional or personal ties have created uncertainty about the stability of the leadership both domestically and abroad, so dampening the pace of China's Open Policy. In the first four years following the Third Plenum, for example, the most pertinent struggle within the leadership was between the reformers led by Deng Xiaoping and the leftist 'Whateverists', centring around Hua Guofeng. Indicators of falling confidence on the part of foreign companies in the political stability of the Party leadership are statements to such effect in the foreign press, the slowing down in the signing of contracts, cancellation of contracts and delay in providing pledged capital. State officials likewise delay in signing contracts, put new projects on hold and may refrain from key decisions to do with opening up until they feel sure of whoever holds the reins at the centre.

Opposition within the Party leadership to the Open Policy may be expressed in different ways. We can see challenges to the policy in the media, in defensive statements and articles. Opponents of opening up or aspects thereof have used the mechanism of campaigns to launch their attacks, either initiating campaigns themselves or subverting campaigns to their own ends. For example, the government's attempts in 1982 to control the increase in smuggling from Hong Kong into the newly established SEZs provided an opportunity for opponents of opening up to challenge the correctness of the Open Policy. Different leadership groups or individuals may also try to promote their views by utilising their institutional power bases. Deng Liqun, for example, launched his attacks in the early 1980s from the Propaganda Department of the Central Committee, of which he was the head.

Third, differences within the dominant reformist group of leaders towards reform and opening up have, particularly since 1982, affected the specific policies adopted, the pace of implementation and the direction of opening up. We can observe these in policy statements by different leaders and in their remarks in meetings and conferences where published. Hu Yaobang and Zhao Ziyang, for example, have been the most radical proponents of the Open Policy, advocating both more rapid and extensive opening up, whilst 'moderate' reformers such as Chen Yun have adopted a more cautious approach to the pace of opening up. Then there are the more conservative reformers such as Peng Zhen, Deng Liqun and Li Xiannian who have been particularly concerned about the ideological impact of opening up.[5] From September 1985 onwards a group of 'Soviet-inclined reformers' emerged, as they favoured closer economic and political relations with the Soviet Union and Eastern bloc.[6]

It is not easy, however, to determine accurately the fissures amongst the reformers or the relative strength of different subgroups. Leadership statements may not necessarily reflect the beliefs of those leaders. The emphasis given in the media to particular leaders' views is one indicator of the relative prominence of a particular policy position. The degree to which the views of particular leaders on various aspects of the Open Policy become officially endorsed in documents and policy statements can again indicate the relative dominance of subreform groups. However, there may be occasions when the differences between the reformers over the Open Policy become subdued, so as to protect the whole policy against challenges from opposition within the Party. This was the case in 1982 when attacks upon the SEZs were virulent.

Furthermore, the boundaries between subgroups and positions of individual leaders may not be so clear. Deng Xiaoping, for example, has on various occasions expressed concern for the ideological import of the Open Policy, without however advocating greater restraint. In 1984 both Deng and Zhao Ziyang were advocating faster and greater reform. After the upheavals of 1989 Deng clearly disassociated himself from the rapid path of Zhao. Similarly, Li Peng switched from an expressed concern with 'peaceful evolution' after 1989 to allying with Deng in his calls in early 1992 for more opening up and reform. So we should treat the identification of these subgroups as a tentative but useful means of putting some order into an opaque reality.

Interinstitutional factors

Both reform and opening up have altered the balance of power between and within institutions. Some institutions have grown in importance whilst others have waned. Some have gained new policy privileges and greater decision-making autonomy, whilst others have remained tightly controlled by the centre. Within institutions, some cadres have found that their previously neglected, undervalued technical skills have now become positive assets under reform and opening up whilst others find that their political credentials are no longer enough to guarantee their career fortunes. Given the key role of state institutions in the establishment and implementation of policy in China, their responses to opening up are crucial for its success or failure.[7]

The actual and potential 'losers' have responded by obstructing, ignoring and reinterpreting policy instructions from the central leadership, whilst the beneficiaries have not only complied with policies but also expanded their scope. This inter- and intra-institutional tug-of-war has created a gulf between policy and practice, especially in the first five years of Deng's rule. Who then are the key institutional 'winners' and 'losers' under reform and opening up? How have tensions surfaced in practice? And how have these actors attempted to influence the course of the policy?

Ideological institutions

The rise to prominence of economic institutions and the concomitant demise of 'ideological' authorities, which enjoyed their heyday during the Cultural Revolution, has led to interinstitutional friction. In the process of restructuring the state to comply, *inter alia*, with the needs of the Open Policy, economic bodies such as the State Economic Commission, the Ministry of Foreign Trade and the Price Commission have eclipsed institutions dealing with ideological matters such as the Ministry of Culture and the Propaganda Department in importance. This is linked closely to the shift in orientation away from 'politics' and towards 'production' following the consolidation of Deng's power at the Third Plenum. With economics now in command, the role of ideology in the process of change takes second place. Ideological institutions find their influence both within the Party and over society under threat. The frequency of political meetings in the workplace and within educational establishments has declined considerably over the last decade, at least up till Tiananmen.[8]

Dissatisfaction amongst ideological institutions has found expression most noticeably in campaigns critical of the Open Policy and reform, linking the opening of China to cultural degradation. The Propaganda Department of the Central Committee, for example, was behind both the spiritual pollution campaign of 1983−4 and the anti-bourgeois liberalisation campaign of early 1987. These campaigns attributed the influx of drugs and pornography, the increase in prostitution and intellectual interest in 'humanism' and democracy to the Open Policy.

Light and heavy industry

The economic reforms and the Open Policy not only favour economic institutions at the expense of ideologically oriented institutions but also assign priority to particular sectors of the economy and their respective ministries. The Open Policy and reforms benefit light industry more than heavy industry, as the products of light industry find easier access to the international market. Within heavy industry emphasis has been given to the development of resources such as petroleum and coal which can earn foreign exchange through exports.

This shift in sectoral emphasis brings higher status and prestige for light industry. Whilst in the Cultural Revolution period 'steel' was taken as the key link, in the Dengist period, textiles and electronics have become the vanguard industries of the modernisation drive. In the wake of the Gulf War the electronics industry, with its dual military–civilian links, has enjoyed a further boost.[9] More importantly, these industries receive encouragement in the form of policy concessions and privileges to develop and expand, particularly if they are able to bring in scarce foreign exchange.

This sectoral shift has not proceeded smoothly, however. In the early days of opening up and reform, we find heavy industry struggling to retain its privileged position in the economy. Top cadres in related ministries soon realised, however, that the Open Policy might also be a source of golden opportunities. The so-called 'petroleum faction', comprising leaders such as Yu Qiuli and heads of petroleum and related ministries, opposed the reforms. Nevertheless, they were smart enough to welcome foreign direct investment and petroleum exports, which would further the importance of heavy industry in the economy.[10] When the cancellation of numerous projects involving imported technology in the petro-chemical, metallurgical and coal sectors was announced in early 1979, there was considerable resistance from the ministries dealing with heavy industry, which saw their potential gains under the Open Policy disappearing.[11] Along with the objections raised by foreign investors, the opposition from heavy industry led to a review of the cancellation of some of these projects.[12]

Although reform and opening up has led to tensions between light and heavy industry, both have however become increasingly concerned with the threat of foreign imports to their domestic industries. Excessive imports of cars, TV sets, fertilisers and chemical textiles have triggered complaints from the machine-building, electrical, textiles and agricultural ministries.[13] This has been reflected not only in comments and articles but also in their actual management of the technology transfer process. The Ministry of Machine-Building, for example, established a special division to monitor and approve all factory imports of equipment, including the products of Sino-foreign joint ventures in China.[14] This protectionist stance contributed to a 43 per cent decline in imports of foreign equipment in the first half of 1982 over the same period the previous year.

The army

The reforms and the Open Policy have challenged the importance not only of 'ideologically concerned' institutions but also of the military. During the Cultural Revolution the domain of the army had extended to all levels of civilian government. Even in 1983 an army officer was still acting as head in a key middle school in Sichuan province.[15] In order to curb the power of the army Deng Xiaoping not only set about gradually ousting leaders closely associated with Mao, but also reduced the numerical strength of the army.[16] Deng met with resistance in the early days from military supporters of his rival Hua Guofeng and from leaders who owed their high positions to the Cultural Revolution. Lin Biao and the Gang of Four both enjoyed a strong power base within the army. Moreover, veterans who remembered the struggle against imperialism and in particular the Anti-Japanese War were also wary about opening up to the West and Japan.

Given the sensitivity of military information in any country, it is not easy to discern the fissures of tension within this ultra-secretive institution, nor indeed to gauge their responses to particular policies. On the basis of information available in open military journals and newspapers we can observe resistance to the Open Policy from the army. In April 1981, for example, the *Liberation Army Daily* published an article strongly criticising Bai Hua's controversial story and film *Bitter Love*. Wei Guoqing, head of the General Political Department of the army and a strong opponent of Deng Xiaoping, strongly backed this condemnation. Similarly, in June 1992 the same paper referred to resentment within the army towards civilians who were becoming economically better off.[17]

Although the decline in political power of the army does not directly affect the implementation of the Open Policy — to the extent that the loyalty of the army lies with the opponents of the Open Policy — it can affect the stability of the leadership and their policies as well as the perceptions thereof. Every wise ruler knows that without the backing of the army their power rests on fragile ground. The downfall of Hu Yaobang in early 1987, one of the more radical reformers, was facilitated indirectly by his lack of support within the army. Deng's retention of his post as chairman of the Military Commission following the Thirteenth Party Congress implied a continuing mistrust of the army. The refusal of some military leaders to intervene with force in Tiananmen Square brought home abruptly the urgency of retaining command over the coercive arms of the state.[18]

Although the army as an institution has been a significant source of opposition to Deng Xiaoping, there are nevertheless sections within the army which support the reformers. The beneficiaries within the army of Deng's rise to power include both those units and individual members who fought with Deng Xiaoping before Liberation as well as the 'modernising' section within the army. Following China's humiliating defeat in Vietnam in February 1979, support within the army for modernisation through the import of military and quasi-civilian high technology has grown. The gradual conversion of military industry to civil production has provided opportunities for the army to earn foreign exchange. Moreover, attendance by top military staff at international armaments exhibitions again points to a keen interest amongst sections of the army in technologising and updating its military hardware. More recently, the Gulf War highlighted the urgency of modernising the army. The 1991 budget saw a 12 per cent increase in national defence expenditure.[19]

Tensions between institutions over their relative importance in the economy, their access to privileges and resources can influence the course of the Open Policy in several ways. Institutions losing out under opening up have not only delayed, obstructed and reinterpreted policy but also joined in the ideological assault upon the Open Policy conducted by leftist opponents in the leadership. Conversely, institutions reaping benefits under the Open Policy have kept the policy moving forward, not only by implementing new regulations but also by providing an institutional support base for the reformist leadership.

Intra-institutional factors

The process of opening up has not only created tensions between institutions but also within institutions. We can identify two distinct axes of tension within the state. The first concerns the political loyalties of cadres, political and administrative, to leaders. The second relates to the criteria for career advancement within the state.

Factional models view politics as the clash between patronage networks within the Party leadership. Patron—client ties amongst leaders and between leaders and their followers account in part for the response of particular individuals and social groups within state institutions to the Open Policy. Although there are some shortcomings to this approach, such as the difficulty in identifying the members of a particular faction and the causal relation between policy and faction, it can nevertheless provide some insights into the politics behind the Open Policy.

The clash of patronage networks within state institutions can lead to tensions, which affect the implementation of the Open Policy. Those leaders who came to power during the Cultural Revolution, particularly at the middle level of the hierarchy, will perceive their positions threatened by the radical change in leadership at the top of the government and Party. Whilst some may switch their allegiances to the reformers, others may continue to support the ideas of the Gang of Four and the older Mao.

Leaders and cadres opposed to the reformist central leadership have frequently expressed their opposition by obstructing, delaying or neglecting particular policies as well as supporting campaigns such as the spiritual pollution campaign. In Zhuhai, Shanghai and Zhejiang provinces in the early 1980s, for example, the deliberate obstruction by elements of the Party and bureaucracy of matters concerning foreign investors is symptomatic of the then underlying opposition to the Dengist reforms.[20] The low level of foreign investment up till 1984 is in part related to the predominance of opposition at middle and lower levels of institutions dealing with foreign capital.

Although Deng Xiaoping had succeeded in removing Hua Guofeng from top Party positions by the Twelfth Party Congress of September 1982, at the middle and lower levels of the Party supporters of the ultra-leftist Gang of Four and the moderate leftists, the so-called 'Whateverists', were still well entrenched.[21] Of China's 40 million Party members in 1982 40 per cent had joined during the Cultural Revolution.[22] Despite attempts over the next two years to rectify the Party at central and provincial levels, the beneficiaries of the Cultural Revolution were still being nominated for promotion. A further rectification drive in 1985 led to a reduction in the average age of top provincial Party leaders and the transfer of those ousted to advisory state bodies.

As key positions in administrative organs and state-owned enterprises have tended to be occupied by Party members, the success of Deng Xiaoping's reform programme and the Open Policy has clearly been contingent upon his ability to replace these leaders not only with technically qualified but also with politically loyal personnel.

However, attempts in 1985 and 1986 to oust leftist opponents at provincial level and below from the Party and state have contributed towards a more favourable political climate for opening up. The growing base of support within the Party and state administration for the reforms and Open Policy is an important factor in the consolidation of the Open Policy.

Apart from tensions within the state relating to divergent political loyalties, we can also find differential interests centring around the source of power and advancement. The reformist leadership has attempted to raise the technological and administrative capacity of the state. This has involved not only the promotion of technically qualified personnel to positions of authority and responsibility, but also an attempt to separate the political and economic functions of the state.[23] As a result, tensions have surfaced between 'politicocrats', that is, the political and administrative cadres who owe their positions to their political credentials and the 'technocrats', a newly emerging group of cadres whose legitimacy rests on their technical and/or professional skills. This tension between 'reds' and 'experts' has been a recurring theme in post-liberation China.

The promotion of 'experts' has been thwarted not only by cadres who stand to lose their positions of authority, which are based on their political credentials, but also by cadres who seek to retain their positions of power to gain some of the benefits of reform and opening up. Leading cadres eager to go overseas have prevented technically qualified staff from joining inspection tours with the result that inappropriate and/or poor quality technology has been introduced. The attempt to raise the technological capacity of the state has not only threatened those who owe their positions of power to political criteria but also those who enjoy seniority by virtue of age. In order to raise the technical level of its staff, thousands of students and employees have been sent overseas for training. It is unlikely that on their return, older, more experienced cadres will readily give way to these younger, but more educated technocrats. The employment of technically less competent people in foreign trade positions has in part contributed towards the duplication of imports and the introduction of unnecessary and inappropriate technology.

As well as recruiting more technically able people, the reformers have also attempted to improve the efficiency of the state by separating its economic and political functions. This has entailed simultaneously the withdrawal of political cadres from the realms of economic decision-making and the granting of greater autonomy to the managers of enterprises.

However, the failure to separate the political and economic functions of enterprises has frequently been cited as one of the main reasons for the difficulties in reforming the foreign trade system.[24] Furthermore, the continued appointment of state officials to leading positions in joint ventures has also been quoted as a factor in their management problems.[25]

Although the time-lag in training and opposition to these reforms results in unevenness in the character of the state across institutions, to the extent that reform-minded technocrats are promoted to positions of responsibility the pace of policy implementation is pushed forwards. As students return from overseas and graduates from domestic technical training programmes begin to occupy positions of power, one might predict, *ceteris paribus*, an improvement in the technical capacity of the state within the next decade. Although there have been numerous accounts of bureaucratic problems in joint ventures as well as of inappropriate technology imports, there are also success stories, which can be attributed in part to the cooperation of reform-minded Party and government officials.

Regional interests

Regional interests have played an important role in the evolution of the Open Policy. The opening up of China has favoured the development of the coastal areas, and in particular, Guandong and Fujian provinces, over the inland areas. Provincial and municipal governments have been granted privileges, policy concessions and financial support from the central coffers so as to open up. The reformers have abandoned Mao's ideological policy concern with regional inequality and drawn on the theory of comparative advantage to justify this regional shift in policy. Those areas which enjoy a comparative advantage in forming external economic relations such as coastal and urban areas, plain as opposed to mountainous areas and 'open' as compared to 'closed' cities have received special policy and financial incentives to develop. As Gu Mu, a state councillor closely involved with the Open Policy, so succintly stated at the Sixth National People's Congress Standing Committee meeting in January 1985: 'the coastal regions have easier access to foreign markets, better communications with the outside world, a certain industrial foundation and more specialised a personnel and management experience.'[26]

Whilst coastal cities can in varying degrees conduct direct trade with foreign companies and retain a greater portion of foreign exchange, which can be used to purchase imported equipment and raw materials, most inland provinces still require central approval for foreign trade and foreign direct investment contracts and are required to hand over the bulk of their foreign exchange earnings to the central government. Moreover, their distance from the coast as well as poor transportation and communication facilities combine to weaken their capacity to take advantage of any relaxations in policy regarding their foreign economic relations — at least in so far as opening up is from the seaboard. The predominance of heavy industry in the inland areas presents a hurdle in the race to open up towards the West and Japan. As a result in part of the preferential policies and central government financing, foreign direct investment has become concentrated on the coastal areas in a pattern reminiscent of pre-liberation China.

This regional pattern of development was markedly different to that of the previous two decades. From 1956 till the Third Plenum in 1978, the regional industrial strategy had, apart from some periodic variations, been to scatter industry throughout the country, concentrate certain strategic industries in inland areas and promote provincial self-sufficiency. Preferential treatment of the inland areas as reflected in their greater shares of central capital investment and fiscal subsidies was inspired by the imperative of defence, a concern with regional imbalances and a political desire to favour those areas which had supported the Communist Party during the liberation struggle.[27] The central government redistributed the industrial revenues of major coastal cities such as Shanghai to inland areas. With the advent of the reforms and Open Policy, this regional bias was reversed.

The favourable policy treatment of coastal areas in opening up has led to two sets of tensions: first, between central and coastal local governments; and second, between inland and coastal local governments. The conflict between central, inland and coastal local governments has contributed to the shaping of the content and scope of the Open Policy.

Tensions between central and local government have arisen chiefly over the degree of decentralisation of power and resources. Whilst the central government has wanted to arm local governments in the coastal areas with more privileges, concessions and decision-making power so as to accelerate and improve the process of opening up, it has at the same time become concerned with its increasing difficulty in controlling local government. Left to their own devices local governments have tended to subordinate national to local interests. The upsurge in consumer imports in mid-1985 as well as disclosures of economic corruption such as the Hainan scandal exemplify this tendency. In the Hainan scandal 89 000 vehicles were imported through the island for illegal resale to interior provinces.

The reformers are, however, acutely aware that local coastal governments and foreign trade branches are an important institutional base of support. So any attempts to reimpose macroeconomic control have a clear political dimension. The beneficiaries of these decentralisation policies have an interest in maintaining these powers and so will be reluctant to cede these newly gained privileges. Officials in the SEZs clearly resented the removal of some of their privileges following the mid-1985 foreign exchange crisis.[28] Similarly, the withdrawal of foreign exchange and importing privileges from Hainan as well as the concomitant removal of the governor, Lei Yu, in the wake of the Hainan scandal fuelled tensions between central and local governments.[29] The ensuing conflicts between central and local authorities and ministries and their branches affect in turn the ability of the central government to restore economic order. This pressure from below cushions the downswings in the cycle and provides the political fuel for the upswings.

The shift in regional priority away from inland to coastal areas has also led to considerable resentment in inland provinces.[30] The right of SEZs to retain all their foreign exchange earnings was an enormous privilege compared to other regions of China, which not only have to remit most of their foreign exchange to the centre but also have only a fixed quota assigned to them for their use. Access to foreign exchange has been a highly coveted privilege in a centrally managed foreign exchange system. Similarly, the right to import has given some enterprises and regions clear advantages in the race to modernise over those enterprises and regions burdened by the need for central government approval. The beneficiaries of these decentralisation measures, namely provincial and municipal governments in the coastal areas as well as the local branches of ministries such as foreign trade, then provide an important institutional base of support for the Open Policy.

How then do these tensions between inland and coastal areas affect the implementation of the Open Policy? The inland areas have responded in contradictory ways. On the one hand, inland officials of local government and state-owned enterprises have tried to thwart opening up. They have, for example, tried to protect their own industries against the products of both coastal regions and foreign-invested enterprises by establishing 'blockades'. Since the late 1980s they have also enhanced their own foreign exchange earnings by exporting their own products and raw materials directly rather than supplying the dependent coastal areas. Top leaders watched aghast in the late 1980s at the bitter cashmere and cotton wars which starved the coastal areas of crucial inputs.[31]

They have also lent their support to campaigns against economic crime and spiritual pollution, which have attributed negative cultural and social phenomena to the Open Policy. Some officials in the coastal provinces have indicated that they consider the attack on economic crime to reflect resentment in inland areas against the increasing coastal prosperity.[32] It is likely that criticisms raised in 1985 that the SEZs were 'feeding off' the rest of China enjoyed considerable backing from the inland provinces. These regional frictions have served to broaden the political constituency of opponents of the Open Policy.

On the other hand, the response of the inland areas to the Open Policy has not been wholly negative. Some enterprises, units and individuals in the inland areas have been quick to take advantage of the new opportunities offered by opening up and reform. The illegal resale of imported consumer goods has not been restricted to the coastal areas. In fact, many of the 85 000 vehicles involved in the Hainan scandal were destined for the inland areas. The setting up of inland provincial trading companies in the SEZs has served not only as an export outlet, hence foreign exchange earner, for inland products but also as a channel for illegal trade and speculation in foreign exchange.[33] There has been an implicit collaboration between the inland and coastal areas in taking advantage of the loopholes and inadequacies of the Open Policy, although it is the coastal areas which have benefited most from these illegal deals.

As well as cashing in on the opportunities afforded by the reforms and Open Policy, some academics and government leaders have also called for the further opening up of inland areas. Rather than opposing the Open Policy there is a lobby in the inland areas demanding the extension of preferential policies to the interior of China. This has become increasingly vocalised since the mid-1980s, by which time the regional bias and impact of the Open Policy had become explicit. One of the first indications of this was the request by 24 inland cities in 1984 for the same privileges as the 14 coastal cities. There were even demands then for the establishment of SEZs in inland areas.[34] An article published in June 1985 in a Sichuanese economic journal argued, for example, that as the hinterland is 'more in need of technology, information and funds than the coast', it should also set up SEZs.[35] This pressure from below, both in the inland and coastal areas, for further opening has been a significant factor in maintaining and pushing the policy forward.

The central leadership has responded to these rumblings in the provinces in various ways. Hardline opponents of opening up have tried to curry favour with inland areas by portraying the zones as 'parasites' feeding off the rest of China. The reformers have responded by extending privileges to the inland areas. Top leaders in favour of greater economic contact with the Soviet Union have likewise given expression to inland sentiments in national policy-making fora. From 1985 onwards we see the issue of inland—coastal relations coming explicitly onto the agenda. By 1991 it was openly incorporated into the ten-year development programme and eighth five-year plan. Although we still have much to learn about how local officials pursue local interests and affect policy outcome, we can see clearly that regional tensions created and/or exacerbated by the Open Policy have become a significant variable in the process of opening up.

Foreign capital

The course of the Open Policy has been shaped not only by institutional cooperation and conflict but also by the willingness of foreign capital to trade and invest in China. Clearly, foreign capital has a central role in the realisation of China's Open Policy. This became painstakingly obvious to the Chinese leadership in the wake of the Tiananmen massacre when foreign governments, international organisations and foreign companies froze, halted or slowed down their activities in China. Whilst the reformist leadership has sought to attract foreign capital by offering various policy concessions in taxation, wages and land use fees, it cannot, however, compel foreign capital to establish companies in China.[36] Whether or not foreign companies choose to trade or invest in China is a factor to a large extent beyond its control.

Policy-makers have from the inception of the Open Policy had to take into account the interests of foreign capital. Academic studies of the experiences of other countries in attracting foreign direct investment, articles in the foreign press concerning foreign companies' reactions to the Open Policy as well as investigations by ministerial research departments into the experiences of existing foreign-invested enterprises have all shaped leaders' perceptions of the needs of foreign investors. Similarly, statements by reformist leaders underlining the continuation of the Open Policy during the readjustment of the economy between 1979 and 1982 and various ideological campaigns betray an awareness of the 'political risk' factor in foreign direct investment.

The importance of taking the interests of foreign capital into account has increased not only because of the growing presence of foreign-invested enterprises in China but also because of the perception amongst reformers that particular policies have failed to attract the desired level, scale and type of foreign direct investment. It is this disappointment amongst reformist leaders, particularly the radical reformers, with the pace of opening up that has provided a significant impetus to further changes in the policy favourable to the foreign investors. As the level of actual foreign direct investment in China has gradually increased, reaching almost US$ 23 billion in early 1992, the influence of foreign capital on the content of policy has risen.[37]

The interest of foreign capital in China will vary, however, according to sector, national source, time horizons and the existence of alternative markets. In the short term the foreign partner may be mainly interested in creating goodwill for future operations. In the long term the motives may vary according to the national source of the foreign investor. The chief investors in China since 1978 have been Hong Kong, the USA, Western Europe and Japan, with Taiwan growing in importance since 1988 (see Table 1.1). Hong Kong companies are keen to transfer the labour-intensive processes of their textile and electronics production to China so as to move further up the product cycle into more technically sophisticated production as well as to bypass textile quotas.[38] As 1997 approaches small-scale investors are concerned to secure an economic niche in their future homeland whilst capitalist giants like Jardine and Matheson are already shifting out of Hong Kong to tax havens such as Bermuda.

Table 1.1 National source of foreign direct investment in China: 1985−9

Total	Percent (100)
Hong Kong/Macao	61.5
Japan	12.8
USA	11.2
Taiwan	7.6
United Kingdom	1.1
France	0.9
Italy	0.7
Singapore	0.6
Others	3.6

Source: Khan, 1991, p. 44.

For US and European companies the lure of the 1-billion market is particularly relevant, whilst the abundance of coal and mineral ores as well as the potential availability of oil have been key factors drawing Japanese capital to China.[39] However, the recent collapse of the Soviet Union and East European socialist states has deflected the attention of European companies in particular away from China towards markets nearer home where cultural differences are also less apparent. For Taiwanese investors the cheap source of labour and the large market, as well as the securing of an economic investment in a possibly reunified China, are of particular interest.

However, the interests of foreign capital may not necessarily accord with those of the Chinese government or at the microlevel with those of the Chinese enterprise entering a joint venture. The primary objective of the Chinese partner in establishing joint ventures may include one or several of the following: the introduction of foreign technology and management expertise, increases in foreign exchange through export earnings and a supplementary source of capital. The objectives may vary as the 'Chinese partner' in joint ventures may be one or several partners with converging and/or competing interests. The 'Chinese partner' frequently incorporates a government financing body such as the newly founded quasi-state Investment and Trust Corporation and a local factory. The interests of the Chinese partners may vary, with each partner attaching different priority to the above-specified goals. Moreover, these goals may also change over time. Following the foreign exchange crisis in mid-1985 Chinese partners became increasingly concerned that the joint ventures increase foreign exchange earnings through exports.

At the macrolevel the Chinese government has been keen to attract foreign capital from Hong Kong/Macao, Overseas Chinese and more recently Taiwanese. It has even given greater incentives to these investors. The focus on these countries has been politically informed by the prospect of eventual reunification. The realisation, however, that Hong Kong/Macao and Taiwanese companies invest primarily in commercial, non-productive, low-technology projects yielding quick profits has in turn prompted policy-makers to seek ways to encourage European, American and Japanese investment. The dissatisfaction of the reformist leadership with the pattern of foreign direct investment since 1979 has increased the weight accorded to the interests of foreign investors, particularly from the USA, Japan and Western Europe.

These differences in motive are the source of some of the tensions between the Chinese and foreign partners during contract negotiation. These tensions have surfaced in issues such as the proportion of domestic sales, the repatriation of foreign exchange earnings, the transfer of technology, marketing and localisation of inputs.[40] Furthermore, at the factory level, tensions between foreign capital, the Party and trade unions over labour issues have affected the attractiveness of China as an investment site to foreign investors. Moreover, the inadequacy of existing policies relating to foreign economic relations, fluctuations in policy as well as inconsistencies in their implementation have not instilled the confidence of foreign investors in the overall foreign direct investment climate. The immaturity of the legislative framework, institutions and fluctuations in policy have also been important factors precluding greater investment by Japanese, European and American companies in China. Political instability, and in particular the upheavals during 1989, have made foreign investors even more cautious of investing large sums in China.

Although foreign capital is crucial to the realisation of the Open Policy, it is not directly involved in the policy-making process. The extent to which it can influence the content, scope and pace of the Open Policy depends upon a variety of factors such as its relative importance in terms of level of investment in the Chinese economy, national and local, its relative importance to the Chinese government in policy strategy terms, the official and unofficial channels available for presenting its views and relations between its government and the Chinese government. Of course one of the difficulties in foreign capital presenting its interests is that, as already pointed out, it is neither monolithic nor is it a wholly cooperative group. Whilst foreign companies may share a common interest in improving the terms and conditions under which they trade and invest in China, foreign firms are as much in competition with each other as with domestic producers. However, we can detect common patterns of behaviour on the part of individual foreign companies to promote their interests. Over the past decade there have been a number of instances when foreign companies on a national and even cross-national basis have jointly put forward their views to the Chinese government.

How then can foreign capital influence the course of the Open Policy? The most extreme negative influence would be simply not to trade or invest in China at all. In the immediate aftermath of Tiananmen, China experienced to its horror the power of foreign companies to withhold and withdraw capital. The freezing of loans from foreign governments and international agencies shocked the Chinese government even more and made it acutely aware of the dangers of indebtedness to global institutions.

The slow rate and small scale of foreign investment in the first five years of China's Open Policy can also be interpreted as an indirect influence of foreign capital upon the Open Policy. Disappointed in the level, source and sectoral nature of foreign direct investment, reformist leaders not only expanded the Open Policy in 1984, but also tried hard to improve the legislative framework.

Apart from the indirect power of withholding investment, absolutely or relatively, foreign capital has at the microlevel attempted to influence policy through informal and formal channels. Informally, foreign investors can pass on their grievances and views to their Chinese partners and colleagues.[41] To the extent that these get transmitted to higher authorities and put onto the agenda, foreign capital can bear some influence. Local-level authorities also have formal contact with foreign investors. This may be on special festive occasions or at specially convened meetings. These official meetings provide opportunities for foreign capital to present its interests.

Since 1987 the Chinese government has experimented with setting up liaison-type state bodies to coordinate the management of foreign-invested enterprises, to mediate between foreign investors and other state bodies and to resolve disputes. Foreign companies may also seek the help of their own governments in trying to change policy to their favour. Whether or not foreign capital can influence policy content through these formal and informal channels depends as much on the willingness and indeed ability of the Chinese leaders to make further concessions and themselves to influence microlevel activity.

A more direct, though less common, method of interest expression by foreign capital has been the joint presentation of demands to the Chinese government. This was the case in early 1986 when 12 foreign managers of relatively successful joint ventures met with central leaders dealing with foreign investment issues to present their problems and propose solutions.[42] In view of the sudden drop in foreign direct investment in the first six months of 1986, the urgency of meeting some of the requirements of foreign investors in order ultimately to achieve modernisation became paramount. This confrontation with organised foreign capital led to the promulgation of the 22 Articles which granted further incentives to foreign investors such as reductions in taxes, wages and land use fees. Although greater concessions were made, foreign investors still doubted whether they would actually be implemented.[43]

The year 1986 thus marked an important turning-point in the political processes underlying the Open Policy. Whilst up till then the central government had attempted to anticipate and incorporate some of the potential interests of foreign capital, in 1986 the situation was reversed, with foreign capital demanding the incorporation of its interests into the policy-making process. Foreign-invested enterprises, which were the concrete creations of the policy and as such the 'objects' of policy, had begun to articulate their demands collectively and as such had transformed into the 'subjects' of the policy. The political isolation of China after Tiananmen strengthened further the hand of foreign capital.

Before looking more closely at how the interests located above combine to influence the course of the Open Policy, we should first give some attention to the economic context within which these political forces operate. As there is a considerable literature on various aspects of reform and opening up, we will refer only to the most salient points.[44]

Economic context

The most salient economic factor in the opening of China has been the recurring dilemma of balancing the contradictory goals of microlevel dynamism and macrolevel stability in a partially reformed economy. To encourage microlevel initiative the reformers have decentralised some control over economic decision-making. The ensuing economic disorder has led in turn to the reimposition of central control by administrative means over the economy. With microlevel dynamism stifled, the economy has then begun to stagnate. In response the reformers have embarked again upon a round of decentralisation (see Figure 1.1). Liu Guoguang, a well-known Chinese economist, described this reform phenomenon as a 'cycle of relaxation−disorganisation−restriction−stagnation'.[45] Liu's prescription was to reform at a slower pace and to combine market and plan.

What then are the mechanics of this decentralisation cycle in relation to opening up? The reformist leadership decentralises in varying degrees some authority over foreign exchange and foreign trade management to branches of ministries, provincial and municipal governments and some enterprises. This decentralisation of authority has, however, ambiguous results. On the one hand, it increases the contact between provincial and municipal trading companies and some enterprises and their foreign suppliers and customers. This raises awareness about quality and packaging standards demanded in the international market as well as international prices.

On the other hand, the decentralisation of foreign trade and foreign exchange management also has unintended, negative consequences which affect the implementation of foreign trade reforms. For example, the extension of these privileges to other provinces in 1984 led to an enormous upsurge in imports of luxury consumer goods such as cars, TVs and fridges. Exports did not, however, increase simultaneously. With enterprises enjoying the right to export directly to foreign companies, foreign trade companies began to have difficulties maintaining supplies of export goods. In 1984, for example, the supply of certain types of cloth to Foreign Trade Bureaux fell by between 30 per cent and 50 per cent.[46] As a result, not only were these bureaux not able to meet the terms of contracts, affecting their credibility abroad, but the enterprises acquired a larger amount of foreign exchange which lay outside the control of trade authorities. This in turn contributed to the loss of central government control over foreign trade and foreign exchange earnings and reserves.

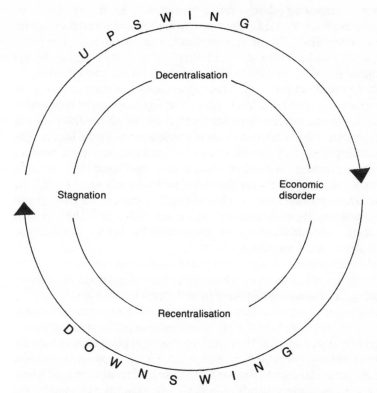

Figure 1.1 The economic dynamic of the Open Policy cycle

Decentralisation engenders cut-throat competition amongst enterprises and foreign trade companies and between foreign trade organs in different provinces, leading to significant economic losses in foreign trade. The outcome in 1984 was a foreign trade deficit of US$ 1.2 billion and a fall in foreign exchange reserves from US$ 16.6 billion in November to US$ 14.4 billion in the first quarter of 1985.[47]

By decentralising the use of foreign trade and foreign exchange management central government forfeits control over the rate of foreign exchange expenditure as well as the category of goods imported. Moreover, cadres at both provincial, municipal and county levels take this opportunity to increase both the earnings of their localities as well as their own private income. The most publicised example of such corruption concerned the Hainan scandal.

Due to the immaturity of parametric controls and the lack of mechanisms to deal with imbalances brought about by the market, the central government responds by reimposing administrative restrictions. So in early 1985 the central government restricted imports and withdrew the foreign exchange privileges of the SEZs. These recentralisation measures lead, however, to a new set of problems for the Open Policy. With their foreign exchange wings clipped the SEZs find themselves unable to finance capital construction projects already in progress. Trade agreements and contracts for joint ventures cannot be honoured. Joint ventures selling a portion of their goods on the domestic market in return for foreign exchange suddenly do not receive payments. Newly imposed import restrictions on inputs for foreign-invested enterprises stall the fulfilment of licensing and joint venture agreements. Foreign investors then begin to lose confidence in the stability of the Open Policy. To continue the example, by the autumn of 1985 the economic situation in the zones had become so dire that central government relaxed foreign exchange restrictions in the zones again.[48] This cycle of centralisation—decentralisation—recentralisation has been a key factor in the spiral dynamic of the Open Policy.

As well as this tension between micro- and macroeconomic goals, contradictions in the specific aims of the Open Policy have also caused fluctuations in the policy. By expanding the scale of its foreign economic relations the reformist leadership hoped to accelerate the pace of modernisation through introducing advanced technology and managerial expertise and increasing its foreign exchange earnings. However, there is an implicit tension between the desire to increase imports of technology, which can be attained relatively quickly and the preference to finance these through export earnings, which cannot be increased immediately. Similarly, the benefits expected by the reformers from foreign direct investment, such as increasing exports, introducing advanced technology and managerial skills, cannot be achieved simultaneously. The acquisition and absorption of advanced technology and managerial skills are long-term ventures whilst export earnings can be achieved fairly rapidly through labour-intensive, export-oriented processing and assembly.

Contradictions in the economic and political objectives of the Open Policy have also influenced the way the policy has unfolded. As well as renegotiating its position in the international political arena, which had been mitigated during the isolationist period of the Cultural Revolution, the reformist leadership also saw the Open Policy, and in particular the SEZs, as a means to facilitate the process of reunification with Taiwan, Hong Kong and Macao. By attempting to create 'state capitalism' in these zones and living and business conditions similar to those in Hong Kong, China sought to realise in practice the principle of 'one country, two systems'. However, whilst the inflow of capital from Hong Kong/Macao and Taiwan might accord with the political objectives of the Open Policy, this source of foreign capital is less likely to introduce either advanced technology or capital-intensive forms of investment.

Apart from these contradictions in the goals of the Open Policy, features of the economic context such as the shortage of foreign exchange, the inconvertibility of the local currency and also the unevenness of domestic economic reforms have likewise shaped the evolutionary trajectory of the Open Policy. The inconvertibility of the Chinese currency has affected the attractiveness of China as an investment site to foreign companies.[49] It has also prompted the emergence of a parallel market in foreign exchange. Three currencies now operate in the SEZs, particularly in Shenzhen, namely the Hong Kong dollar, the Chinese yuan and Foreign Exchange Certificates. This parallel market in foreign exchange reduces the foreign exchange earnings of the state as individuals, enterprises and state organs fail to report and/or retain their overseas earnings so as to speculate in foreign exchange. The situation has been compounded by an overvalued exchange rate and partial price reform.

The Open Policy has not only been affected by various unintended economic consequences but also by the nature, direction and implementation of other domestic economic reforms. Changes in macroeconomic policy as well as attempts to reform particular aspects of the economy have not only led to changes in the track of the Open Policy but also affected the success of foreign trade reforms.[50]

The interpretation of changes in domestic economic policy as indicative of about-turns in the Open Policy has reverberations upon the overall foreign investment climate in China. For example, periodic readjustment policies, such as in 1979−82, which seek to cut back on the level of investment, have raised doubts amongst foreign traders and investors about the continuation of the Open Policy and the prospects for trade and foreign direct investment in China. Conversely, decentralisation measures may also be interpreted to apply to foreign economic relations, so enhancing foreign investors' confidence in the business climate.

The partial and uneven nature of domestic economic reforms as well as the failure to coordinate the two sets of reforms have also constrained the process of opening up. As the Open Policy has evolved, the mutual interdependence of domestic economic reforms and reforms in the foreign trade system has become a subject of increasing concern amongst policy-makers and academics. This has been most salient with regard to the price reforms.

Due to the partial nature of price reforms the attempt to increase export earnings by making import and export enterprises responsible for their own profits and losses has not met with success. The higher prices commanded by some products on the domestic market have made factories and trading companies reluctant to export their products. Moreover, without reforms of the domestic price system, the mobilisation of resources through price signals to different sectors of the economy, and in particular to export production, cannot be achieved. Partial price reforms have made factories unwilling to engage in export despite the granting of other incentives.[51] So due to the unevenness of the price reforms non-price foreign trade reforms such as increasing the financial accountability of foreign trade companies have tended to flounder.

Inflation brought about by reforms in the price system has affected both foreign trade performance and foreign direct investment policy. Removal of price subsidies on food, clothing and some grains as well as the mushrooming of private markets has, by raising the costs of these goods, also led to demands for wage increases. Moreover, higher nominal wages in foreign-invested enterprises, particularly in the SEZs, have in turn fuelled the rise in prices, stimulating demands for higher wages. The perception amongst policy-makers of the need to keep labour costs low and retain China's comparative advantage lay behind the proposed reductions in wages in the 22 Articles to improve foreign investment issued in October 1986.

The rapid growth in both imports and exports and in particular the rise in manufactured exports have been significant indicators of the success of the Open Policy, thus serving to push the policy forward. However, the unintended economic consequences of opening up, such as the loss of central control over foreign trade and the emergence of parallel markets in imports and foreign exchange, have led to the reimposition of central control. This cycle of decentralisation—disorder—recentralisation—stagnation is a key feature of the economic context within which the Open Policy has to proceed.

Politics and economics create a spiral path

We have seen how within the party there are divisions over not only whether or not to reform and open up but also how much, how fast, in what direction and to what extent. We have observed how different social, regional and political interests respond to the challenges of reform and opening and how this conflict and cooperation influences the policy-making process. We have also seen how the economic context of partial reform as well as the economic consequences of opening up structure the policy options open to Party leaders. What then has been the combined effect of these political and economic factors upon the Open Policy?

If we examine the evolution of the Open Policy since 1978, we find a spiral pattern of development (see Figure 1.2). This spiral consists of a number of cycles. Each cycle in turn is composed of an upswing and a downswing. In the upswings we can observe policy innovation, the introduction of more open policies, a more rapid pace of establishment

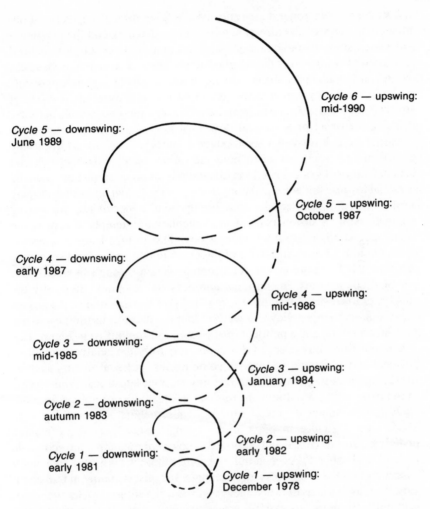

Figure 1.2 The six cycles of the Open Policy

and implementation. Conversely, in the policy downswings we find a slowing down in implementation, more restrictive policies and a less favourable political climate for opening. However, the downswings are never sufficiently strong to undo what has already been started. So rather than a recurring return to the pre-1978 situation we find an incremental, spiral evolution of the policy.

This spiral dynamic is a product of both a political and economic logic. During cyclical upswings socio-political forces with an interest in more opening cooperate to push the policy forward. Periods when the advocates of opening up are strongest are reflected in a faster pace of implementation, attempts to broaden the direction of opening up and extend the privileges and concessions to other areas and institutions. However, this central relaxation of control over the microeconomy leads to economic imbalances or, in Liu Guoguang's terms, 'disorganisation'. At this point opponents of the Open Policy and reform cash in on this economic crisis. Central government then reimposes restrictions over microeconomic activity, marking the onset of a cyclical downswing.

During these downswings socio-political forces with an interest in curbing the Open Policy cooperate to hold the policy back. Factional ties and personal networks of connections (the ubiquitous *guanxi*), institutional and personal loyalties, ideological convictions and personal ambitions all play a role in this process. Periods when the opponents of opening up are waxing are matched by a slower pace of implementation, attempts to restrict the areas opened up and to limit concessions. This in turn leads to a period of stagnation. Leaders in favour of the Open Policy and reform start once again to call for more and faster opening. Again through factional ties, personal connections, institutional and personal loyalties, they rally the support of lower-level institutions, regional governments and social groups benefiting from this policy. So we find that the decentralisation cycle has both an economic and a political momentum, as exemplified in Figure 1.3.

It is not easy, however, to determine precisely the relative weight of political and economic factors. In some cycles, political factors such as the leadership struggle between the reformers, ultra-leftists and Whateverists in the early 1980s are dominant in shaping the course of policy. In other cycles, economic crises may be the key cause behind a downswing as in 1985. The difficulty in pinpointing a single cause for policy change underlines the theoretical and empirical problem of separating the economic and political spheres. As economics becomes more in command, we might expect politics to become less important in a socialist economy in transition. However, as marketisation and the growth of a private sector alter the socio-economic structure, provoking a new array of socio-economic interests and tensions, and ideological differences within the leadership continue to prevail, politics continues to influence the policy process.

Of course these cycles cannot be neatly separated nor can their upswings and downswings be precisely determined. We find that even during downswings in the Open Policy reformers are able to push through regulations establishing the policy. Similarly, even in upswings we find that some aspects of opening up may be under central control and vulnerable to attack. It is not a simple case of stop-and-go. The boundaries within and between cycles are often blurred. But as the Open Policy becomes more deeply entrenched and China continues to open up, it becomes increasingly difficult for the leadership to pull the tide back to the pre-1978

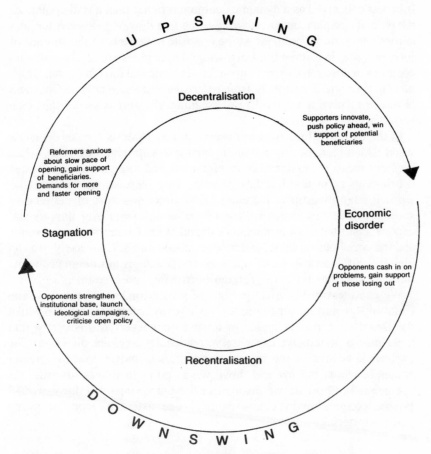

Figure 1.3 Political and economic dynamic of the Open Policy cycle

days. As certain sectors and areas of China become more interlocked into the international economy, so too does the web of beneficiaries expand. Going back becomes economically and politically more risky.

How then can we identify these cycles? How do we know if the Open Policy is in an upswing or a downswing? How do we know if China is becoming more or less open? Let us first clarify our understanding of openness and then consider possible indicators of upswings and downswings.

Openness

Openness is a difficult concept to define, let alone measure precisely.[52]

It is best conceived as a dynamic continuum rather than a static point. At the pole of complete openness we have the free flow of goods and services across international borders. At the opposite pole we have the absence of foreign trade, investment or borrowing. These poles are ideals in that all countries impose some barriers upon foreign trade and foreign capital, whilst no countries withdraw totally from external economic relations. Openness is thus a relative term, used most meaningfully across time rather than across space.

In the case of China we can observe moves towards greater openness when China increases its economic relations with other countries, when it adopts measures to liberalise foreign trade and foreign exchange, when it brings its economic legislation in line with international practice and when foreign investment increases. Economic indicators of the relative success of these measures will be the value and volume of imports and exports, contribution of exports to GNP and of foreign investment to exports and industrial output value, and foreign indebtedness. Conversely, we can identify shifts towards lesser openness in reductions in foreign economic links, restrictions on trade, foreign borrowing and investment.

We can identify historical periods of greater or lesser openness. The Cultural Revolution, for example, was a period of greater closure whilst the Dengist reform era is one of greater openness.[53] Moreover, within these macro periods we can observe tendencies in either direction. The cyclical upswings of the reform period reflect moves towards greater openness whilst the cyclical downswings point to moves towards less openness. But how do we distinguish these upswings and downswings? We draw on five key indicators, namely, pace, extent, direction, form and policy clustering.

Pace

In tracking the course of the Open Policy we find that there are periods when the process of implementation is proceeding rapidly and periods when it is slow. We can identify these changes in pace from the following. First, they follow in response to calls from central government leaders for a faster pace of opening up, or alternatively, for a slowing down of the policy. Such exhortations are often accompanied by pleas to remove 'bureaucratic obstacles' and to quicken the approval time for contracts with foreign trading and investment companies. Conversely, calls for a slower pace are often matched by pleas for a more 'cautious' approach. Visits from central government leaders to local levels can be used to reinforce policy statements regarding the need to 'speed up' or 'slow down'.

Second, these appeals from Party leaders are then translated into actual changes in the pace of implementation. We can observe this in references to the length in the time needed to approve contracts. These may either be perceived as overly long periods or stated intentions to reduce the time. Increases in the volume and value of foreign trade, borrowing and particularly investment each year can also indicate changes in the pace of policy implementation. Moreover, the passing of new legislation strengthens the confidence of investors and so hastens the pace of implementation. Of course it is important to remember that policy implementation may lag behind or indeed anticipate policy rhetoric.

Extent

This refers to the regional and institutional spread of the Open Policy. An expansion of the Open Policy is mirrored in the granting of special privileges and concessions to more areas in China to increase their foreign economic relations. For example, the decision in 1984 to extend the Open Policy to 14 coastal cities would represent an expansion of the Open Policy. Similarly, the granting of concessions and incentives to more institutions, such as foreign trade companies or exporting enterprises would also represent an expansion of the Open Policy. A reduction in the extent of the Open Policy refers to a contraction of these special privileges and concessions to particular areas or institutions.

Direction

A change in the direction of the Open Policy refers to the external regional target of opening up, that is, the part of the world to which the Chinese government seeks to open up. We can observe desired changes in the direction of policy in the statement of leaders calling for greater external economic relations with particular countries or regions. For example, from the mid-1980s we see some top leaders calling for increased economic links with the Soviet Union and Eastern Europe. Following Tiananmen we can observe top leaders calling for greater economic ties with the Third World. Also, we can see certain countries being offered special incentives to trade or invest with China. In the last three years, for example, special tax incentives have been offered to Taiwanese capital to invest or trade with China. A willingness to maximise rather than limit trading and investment partners would represent a more open approach.

Form

Form refers to the means through which opening up is to proceed; broadly, to forms such as foreign direct investment, foreign trade and foreign borrowing. More specifically, it refers to forms of trade such as barter trade, compensation trade and monetary trade. As regards foreign direct investment, it may refer to equity joint ventures, wholly owned foreign enterprises, SEZs or bonded zones. In foreign borrowing it might include commercial loans or government loans. A greater diversity of forms would indicate more openness whilst a restricted range of forms would indicate greater closure. In the isolationist period, for example, foreign direct investment was banned, foreign trade took mainly the form of barter trade and foreign borrowing was limited to government loans.

Policy clusters

We can posit two general clusters of policy, conducive to either 'greater' or 'lesser' openness. If we consider a policy change to be both a change in statement of intent and an actual change in practice, then by noting shifts in policy declarations and actual practice we can observe changes in the policy process. Broadly speaking, policies associated with greater openness seek a quicker pace and greater regional and institutional extent of opening up, a diversity of forms and a wider range of partners. Policies conducive to less openness can be associated with a slower pace, narrower extent, restricted forms and fewer external partners. Cyclical upswings will feature a more open policy cluster. Cyclical downswings will feature a cluster of less open policies. These clusters are summarised in Table 1.2.

However, this is clearly a rough approximation to reality as policy indicators of greater or lesser opening may coexist. For example, a decentralisation of the right to approve foreign trade contracts may coexist with a recentralisation of the rights to retain foreign exchange earnings. Alternatively, the introduction of new legislation favourable to foreign investors may coincide with restrictions on the autonomy of the SEZs. To the extent that a greater number of the policies within each category combine, then we can observe a general upward swing in the process of opening up. Conversely, to the extent that a greater number of 'less open' policies co-occur, we can witness a general downswing in the process of opening up.

These upswings and downswings in turn reflect the relative strengths of advocates and opponents of opening up. When privileges and concessions are extended to regions and institutions, that is, when the net of beneficiaries expands, we find the pro-Open Policy within the leadership gaining force. Conversely, when a less open policy cluster predominates in a downswing, we find that the opponents of opening up have gathered force.

These upswings and downswings in the policy also become reflected in the levels of foreign trade, investment and borrowing. As the Open Policy becomes more institutionalised, the baseline of levels of external economic relations rises, that is, although the downswing in the process of opening

Table 1.2 Policy clusters

Greater opening	Lesser opening
Decentralisation of: (a) rights to approve foreign trade, foreign investment, foreign borrowing contracts (b) rights to retain and use own foreign exchange earnings (c) rights to engage in import and export	Recentralisation of: (a) rights to approve foreign trade, foreign investment, foreign borrowing contracts (b) rights to retain and use own foreign exchange earnings (c) rights to engage in import and export
Extension of (a–c) to areas over and above experimental sites, e.g. new SEZs, 14 coastal cities	Restriction of (a–c) to limited areas
Increase concessions to already open areas	Decrease concessions offered to already open areas
Expansion of external economic relations to more regions/countries, e.g. USSR	Limits on countries to which China will open up
Institutionalisation of Open Policy, i.e. introduction of new laws and regulations at national and provincial levels in line with international practice	Delays in establishing Open Policy
Innovation in forms of Open Policy, e.g. SEZs, leasing, industrial parks	Delays in going ahead with new ideas
Easing up of restrictions on imports, especially materials used in export processing	Imposition of restrictions on imports
Tax and sales incentives to foreign investors, e.g. domestic sales	Restrictions on tax and sales incentives to foreign investors, e.g. domestic sales
New contracts, projects	Project cancellations and delays
Membership of new international bodies, e.g. joins UN, Asian Development Bank	Restrictions on membership, e.g. post-Tiananmen

up may lead to a slowing down of this process and a contraction of foreign trade and investment, the actual levels of trade and investment do not return to the original point. In this situation we can then talk about an expansion of the cycle. If a downswing in the policy takes levels of foreign trade and investment down to below their level in the preceding cycle, then we can talk about a contraction of the cycle.

Conclusion

The process of opening up involves a cast of actors from the higher reaches of the Party and the state to the lower levels of government and society. Certain sections of the economy, state and society have stood to win during the course of this process. Although it is difficult to define neatly the continuum of winners and losers as these may change over time and some may both win and lose, we find that the chief beneficiaries under opening up have been economic institutions, light industry, provincial and municipal authorities, ministerial branches, the modernising section of the army, some enterprises, especially in coastal areas, and technocratic cadres. The major losers are ideological institutions, some sections of heavy industry, some sections of the army, some central ministries, inland areas and politicocratic cadres. As the Open Policy becomes more deeply entrenched, the web of beneficiaries expands.

These 'winners' and 'losers' provide the social constituency of support for the reformers and their opponents within the central leadership. The 'losers' resist the Open Policy by deliberately delaying, obstructing and reinterpreting policy. The winners cooperate in the implementation of policy and provide the social base for maintenance and extension of the Open Policy.

This conflict and cooperation becomes more intense as the contradictions in the reformers' goals of microlevel dynamism and macrolevel stability become periodically apparent. Although decentralisation of some authority to lower-level authorities, branches and some enterprises facilitates the process of opening up, it also leads to imbalances in foreign trade. In response the reformist leadership reimposes central administrative control over the economy, which in turn adversely affects the foreign investment climate. With the restoration of balance in the economy, the reformers then embark upon a new round of decentralisation.

These contradictions in the economic goals of the reformist leadership also have a crucial political dimension. Decentralisation of authority over foreign economic relations means greater power and more resources for lower-level authorities, branches and enterprises. The Open Policy creates its own web of interests, repainting the political landscape. These new beneficiaries are reluctant willingly to cede their newly acquired privileges. Moreover, they also form the socio-political support base of the reformers. Recentralisation becomes politically complex and the central government encounters greater difficulties in withdrawing powers from lower levels.

The reformist leadership thus faces a political and economic dilemma. If it decentralises, it forfeits economic control, but if it recentralises, it stifles local initiative. Moreover, if it decentralises, it expands the web of beneficiaries, whilst if it recentralises, it forfeits some of its political support. As the opposition has tended to capitalise on the periods of economic crisis, the maintenance of this base of support is even more crucial. However, pressure from a burgeoning constellation of actors aware of the interests to be maintained or gained not only restrains the central leadership from rolling the policy back to its starting-point but also propels it forward.

It is this political and economic tension between the pursuit of particularist and general interests and between the desire for microlevel dynamism and macrolevel stability that has been the crucial dynamic in shaping the Open Policy. Hence we find that the trajectory of the Open Policy is not a recurrent series of cycles but a spiral of expanding cycles. Each cycle draws the bamboo curtain open further. This spiral trajectory forms the central theme of the next two chapters.

Notes

1. Xinhua News Agency, Beijing (XH, BJ) 2.8.1991 in SWB/FE/W0196 A/2 11.9.1991; XH, 28.10.1992 in SWB/FE/W0255 A/2 4.11.1992; ZGTXS, Beijing in SWB/FE/W0225 A/8 8.4.1992.
2. For a detailed exposition of the range of actors involved in the Open Policy and the stages at which they become involved, see Howell, 1989, pp. 9–11 and pp. 66–7.
·3. On factional models, see Nathan, 1973; and Pye, 1981. On tendency models, see Oksenberg and Goldstein, 1974. See also Ferdinand, 1990 and Goodman, 1989; and Barnett, 1985. See Harding's 1984 analysis for a discussion of different leadership models and the problems in establishing causal relations in policy-making.
4. Lukes, 1972.
5. See Dittmer, 1990 and Barnett, 1992 for further discussion of the attitudes of different leaders to political and economic reform.
6. The rise of this group can be traced back to the Party conference held in September 1985 when Deng Xiaoping ousted several leaders in the army, government and Party who had risen to prominence during the Cultural Revolution.
7. Policy establishment refers to the process whereby policy is 'legitimised, authorised and institutionalised'. See Schaffer, 1981.
8. Personal communication.
9. ZGTXS/Hong Kong 20.3.1991 in SWB/FE/1027/B2/2 22.3.1991.
10. See Bachmann, 1986, also Shirk, 1985, p. 207. Both the Ministry of Coal and the State Capital Construction Commission headed by Gu Mu expressed their desire for increases in exports as early as 1976 (XH, BJ 14.11.1971 in FBIS 22.11.1976 E11–13 and Beijing Radio 14.11.1976 in FBIS 15.11.1976 E13–15).
11. Clarke, 1981.
12. See XH, BJ 18.3.1981 in FBIS 19.3.1981 D1; *The Times* 7.4.1981; XH, BJ 23.9.1981 in FBIS 23.9.1981 K2.
13. RMRB 11.2.1981 in FBIS 17.2.1981 L7; GZRB 10.12.1981 FBIS pp. 76–8; RMRB 22.4.1982.
14. The machine-building industry had been expanding at almost 20 per cent a year between the 1950s and 1970s and thus was keen to retain its monopoly and growth rate (see Shirk, 1985, p. 206).

15. Personal experience.
16. PLA troops have been cut by a quarter since reform began.
17. See Ladany, 1988, p. 438; and JFJB 3.6.1992 in SWB/FE/1418/B2/1 27.6.1992.
18. Since Tiananmen military top personnel have been reshuffled. See Jencks, 1991.
19. China Central TV, Beijing in SWB/FE/1033 C1/1 29.3.91.
20. For example, Xu Qihao, the Vice-Governor of Zhejiang province attributed the low level of FDI in the province to the 'conservative policies of some cadres' (CD, 18.6.1983, p. 2).
21. This was highlighted by Hu Yaobang in his report to Congress (see Ladany, 1988, p. 455). The 'Whateverists' adhered to the principle that 'whatever Mao said' must be followed. Probable Whateverists were Wu De, Ji Dengkui, Chen Xilian and Wang Dongxing.
22. See Ladany, 1988, p. 468: RMRB 29.10.1982.
23. Whereas in the Maoist period recruitment to administrative and political positions within the state was primarily according to the 'redness' of the character, with the shift in emphasis onto the development of the productive forces in the Dengist period, the criterion for state employment and Party membership has switched from 'red' to 'expert'. There has thus been a deliberate policy to encourage the promotion of the young, educated and technically competent to positions of responsibility.
24. See Zheng Tuobin, 1987, p. 33.
25. See RMRB 29.8.1986 in SWB/FE/8359 C1/2.
26. XH, BJ 17.1.1985 in FBIS 23.1.1985 K5−14.
27. The Chinese Communist Party faced the most significant opposition from coastal city areas of China in the 1920s and 1930s (see Shirk, 1985, p. 210).
28. JJRB 22.2.1986 in FBIS 5.3.1986; and JJRB 6.9.1986 in FBIS 11.9.1986.
29. For a discussion of Lei Yu's removal and the politics underlying the appointment of key political figures in the SEZs, see HK, CM, no. 130, 1.8.1988, pp. 24−5 in FBIS 12.9.1988.
30. Although one can infer from the statements of leaders and commentaries in Chinese newspapers that there is growing resentment in the inland areas over the bias in the Open Policy towards the coastal areas, it is much more difficult to determine precisely how these regional sentiments feed into the policy process. Personal ties between provincial and central leaders as well as forums such as national work conferences attended by provincial leaders provide some of the channels for the expression of regional interests. For further references on regionalism see also Goodman, 1989 and Ferdinand, 1990.
31. XH 19.2.1991 in SWB/FE/0995/B2/5 13.2.91.
32. See Shirk, 1985, p. 214.
33. The SEZs were alleged in mid-1982 to be selling their foreign exchange at profitable rates to interior provinces, see HK, MB 6.7.1982 in SWB/FE/7073 C/3 6.7.1981.
34. See JJRB 3.6.1985 in FBIS 12.6.1985.
35. Li Chongyi, 'Strategic choices for inland provinces in opening up to the outside' in *South West Development*, 1987, 3, pp. 35−7; and personal communication.

36. For an overview of the different investment and taxation incentives offered by China (and other countries) see Khan, 1991, app. 4, pp. 39—42.
37. XH 30.1.1992 in SWB/FE/1293 C1/3 1.2.1992.
38. See P. Sillitoe, 'Seeking a new style' in FEER 4.4.1985, pp. 49—50 and L. do Rosario, FEER 1.8.1985, p. 26.
39. In a study of 11 US firms, it was found that the prospect of serving China's market rather than obtaining a particular energy or mineral resource had been the primary motive in entering China. See Daniels *et al.*, 1985, p. 48.
40. See Howell, 1989, ch. 6 and 'The myth of autonomy: the foreign enterprise in China', ch. 7 in Smith, C. and Thompson, P., *Labour in Transition: the labour process in Eastern Europe and China* (Routledge: London, 1992).
41. Personal communication from various foreign investors in Xiamen.
42. See *Financial Times* 12.6.1986.
43. See Shaanxi People's Broadcasting Station 25.11.1986 in SWB/FE/8428 BII/13.
44. See note 2.
45. JJCKB BJ 21.1.1991 in SWB/FE/0993 B2/5 11.2.1991.
46. See HK,SCMP 3.10.1984 in FBIS 4.10.1984; and XH 31.10.1984 in SWB/FE/7794 BII/B.
47. See AWSJ 1.10.1985.
48. See 'How Europe goes to work in E. Asia' in FEER 22.8.1985, pp. 66—8.
49. See HK S 13.5.1985.
50. See SJJJDB 7.10.1985 in FBIS 28.10.1985.
51. See RMRB 20.4.1983, p. 1 in FBIS 21.4.1983.
52. See Papageorgiou *et al*, 1991.
53. RMRB 24.2.1992 in SWB/FE/1315 B2/1 27.2.1992: 'There was a time before the Third Plenary session . . . when . . . independence and self-reliance was pitted against opening up to the outside world and when the introduction of advanced western technology was regarded as slavish comprador philosophy . . . .' 'With the strategic policy of opening up to the outside world . . . our country has shifted from a closed economy to an open one.'

2

Spiralling outwards. Part A: 1978-86

We begin our exploration by stepping back into the past. We examine China's external economic relations from the Opium Wars of the 1840s to the consolidation of Deng Xiaoping's position at the Third Plenum in December 1978. We then trace the cycles in the evolution of the Open Policy from December 1978 up till the Fourteenth Party Congress of October 1992, drawing attention to the economic and political factors shaping each cycle. For a chronological account of the key events in the evolution of the Open Policy, see the Appendix at the end of the book. Altogether the Open Policy has passed through five cycles of development and is currently in its sixth. Each cycle has taken the policy further and deeper. By the time of the political and economic crises of 1989 China was already too linked to the international economy to shun the West. Sanctions bit hard. Reluctant to reform politically the reformers have made every effort at the economic level to induce foreign capital back to China.

Gunboats, opium and concessions

In the early nineteenth century China's external economic relations consisted mainly of trade in tea and silk with foreign merchants located within the confines of Guangzhou.[1] This economic seclusion was abruptly ended in the early 1840s with the arrival of British gunboats. The Treaty of Nanjing in 1842 allowed foreigners to trade in the new treaty ports of Shanghai,

Fuzhou, Amoy, Ningbo and the newly ceded Hong Kong.[2] By 1913 the number of treaty ports in operation had risen to 48, though many of these were only 'ports of call'. Within these treaty ports foreigners enjoyed extra-territoriality and certain tax incentives.[3] This system continued up till the Second World War when foreign powers relinquished their privileges.

Although trade was the dominant economic link between China and the outside, the opening of the treaty ports in 1842 also stimulated the growth of foreign investment, particularly in coastal shipping and coal-mining. However, it was not until the defeat of China in 1894 by the Japanese and the subsequent signing of the Treaty of Shimonoseki that factories could be erected in the treaty ports.[4] The preferential terms secured by the Japanese then sparked off a wave of demands by the other foreign powers for exclusive rights in their spheres of influence.[5]

By the late 1920s the impact of foreign investment on certain sectors of the economy was already apparent. In 1928 foreign-owned mines produced 81.7 per cent of the coal extracted with modern equipment in China.[6] Furthermore, 98 per cent of all railroads in China were by 1927 either foreign-owned or controlled via foreign loans.[7] This skewed sectoral distribution of foreign investment clearly reflected the political and economic ambitions of the foreign powers. Japanese and Russian investment in the railways in Manchuria, for example, exemplify well the politico-strategic dimensions of foreign investment.[8]

China's external economic relations were not only sectorally skewed but also geographically uneven. In 1931, for example, over one-half of foreign investment was located in Shanghai and another third in Manchuria.[9] The orientation of manufacturing towards the needs of foreign traders as well as the concentration of factories in enclaves along the east coast created few linkages with the rest of the economy. Moreover, the Japanese occupation of Manchuria in 1931 served to constrain the potential spillover effects of its economic development onto the rest of China.[10]

Although the development of transport and other infrastructural facilities through foreign investment laid the foundations for indigenous industrialis-ation, the privileged treatment accorded to foreign investors in the various unequal treaties, coupled with their financial prowess, superior technology and managerial expertise gave foreigners a strong competitive edge over local industry.[11] Certain sectors of the traditional handicrafts industry, such as cotton spinning, suffered from foreign competition.

Although foreign competition weakened certain industries, it also stimulated some local Chinese enterprises, particularly in textiles and foodstuffs.[12] By 1933 90 per cent of factories were Chinese-owned, although most of these were small-scale, non-mechanised and devoted to the traditional products of the handicraft sector.[13]

At the political level the alliance of merchants, landlords and compradors

with foreign interests served to inhibit the emergence of a strong industrialis-
ation process led by a progressive bourgeoisie.[14] Furthermore, successive
political and military defeats by imperialist powers with the subsequent
granting of economic and administrative privileges had weakened the ability
of the state to mobilise national resources for development. The attempts
by the Nationalist Party to unify the country and rid China of its semi-
colonial yoke were continually thwarted by Japanese military incursions
culminating in the onset of the Sino-Japanese War in 1937 which severely
disrupted the course of foreign investment and trade.[15] China's external
economic relations thus evolved within the context of unequal treaties, extra-
territoriality and interimperialistic rivalry.

Whilst up till 1949 the pattern of China's external economic relations
reflected its historical international subordination and concomitant weak
state, in the post-independence era three distinct policy approaches towards
external economic relations can be identified, namely the 'traditional',
'reformist' and 'isolationist' approaches. These vary according to the pace,
rationale, direction, form and extent of opening up.

The traditional approach predominated during the decade of the 1950s
and more recently in the Hua Guofeng era. US hostility towards China
for both the nature of its political system and its involvement in the Korean
War severely restricted the extent and direction of China's foreign economic
relations. The imposition of trade embargoes by the USA and its Western
allies led China to 'tilt' to the USSR for help in reconstruction. In the 1950s
the Soviet Union supplied China with US$ 1.35 billion of equipment for
130 Soviet plants, which was paid for with agricultural products, minerals
and light manufactures.[16] With the relaxation of West European trade
restrictions to China in the late 1950s, imports of machinery and technology
from Western Europe increased somewhat.[17] Nevertheless, foreign trade
continued to be dominated by the USSR and Eastern Europe.

During the 1950s China adopted the Soviet system of foreign trade
characterised by central planning, large-scale turnkey plant imports in the
heavy industrial sector and payment in kind. In the light of China's recent
semi-colonial past the newly formed government was concerned to balance
its trade with each country and restrain the level of foreign borrowing.
Foreign investment was not tolerated, although the Soviet Union operated
four equity joint ventures up till 1954 in Xinjiang and Dalian.[18]

The disastrous consequences of the Great Leap Forward coupled with
the withdrawal of Soviet political and economic support led to the adoption
of a series of reforms to restore the economy in the early 1960s and a
concomitant reformist approach towards foreign economic relations. This
was paralleled by a shift in the direction, rationale and forms of trade.
Although China continued to import from the Soviet Union at a sharply
reduced rate, attention was now focused increasingly on Western Europe

and Japan.[19] Due to the drop in food crop production in the early 1960s foodstuffs replaced capital goods as the chief import item.[20]

The need to tap alternative sources of capital led to a relaxation in attitude towards foreign investment. In the early 1960s Overseas Chinese Investment Corporations were set up in 11 provinces and districts to draw private investment into state enterprises.[21] Moreover, increased trade with Western Europe and Japan requiring payment in foreign exchange meant that China entered into deferred payment arrangements — effectively, forms of short-term credit. This tempo of reform activity was dampened, however, by the onset of the Cultural Revolution in 1966.

The political and economic turmoil of the Cultural Revolution coupled with the supremacy of ideology over economic affairs and the emphasis on 'self-reliance' resulted in an isolationist approach towards China's external economic relations. Technology imports were castigated as 'servility to things foreign', whilst exports were portrayed as a form of 'national betrayal'.[22] Whilst foreign investment was completely outlawed, foreign trade continued, but on a much smaller scale, with the West, Japan and the USSR.[23]

The death of Lin Biao in 1971 followed by the visit to China of Nixon in 1972 marked the start of another period of reformist influence on external economic relations. Not only did China resume its trade with the USA but it also expanded its imports of technology from Japan and the West, particularly in the steel and chemical industries.[24] Moreover, the increase in trade with the West and Japan entailed a relaxation in attitude towards foreign borrowing. Around 60 per cent of China's complete plant imports during this period were financed by deferred payments.[25]

However, a renewed upsurge of activity by the so-called Gang of Four in the first part of 1974 and again during the campaign against Deng Xiaoping in 1976 led to the resumption of an isolationist approach towards the external economy. Of particular concern was the payment of complete plant imports with the export of petroleum and raw materials. Indeed the Gang of Four were later accused of having sabotaged oil exports in 1976.[26] This renewed challenge to foreign trade from within the leadership had a dampening effect on any enthusiasm to enter into further long-term agreements.[27]

The death of China's 'great helmsman' in September 1976 followed by the appointment of Hua Guofeng a month later as Mao's apparent 'chosen' successor signalled the start of a new phase in China's foreign economic relations, harbouring elements of both the traditional and reformist approaches. Aware of the yawning technological and economic gulf between China and the neighbouring newly industrialised countries (NICs) of South Korea, Taiwan, Singapore and Hong Kong, and worse still its historic rival, Japan, Hua Guofeng set about devising measures to reform the economy, including a reappraisal of the role of foreign technology. The success of the 1976 autumn export commodities fair in Guangzhou coupled with criticisms of the Gang of Four's isolationist trade policies contributed towards the emergence of a more favourable foreign trade climate.

In the Hua Guofeng era the expansion of China's foreign economic activity was conceived principally as a resumption and extension of practices common in the 1950s and early 1960s. The role of foreign trade in the economy was supplementary, serving to fill in technological gaps or meet limited supply. Moreover, as in the 1950s priority was to be given to imports for heavy industry, such as steel, petro-chemicals and machinery, mineral and oil-prospecting, which would be financed through export production.[28]

Compared to the traditional policies of the 1950s, Hua Guofeng was prepared to tolerate a higher level of foreign borrowing, in part for reasons of economic expediency and in part because of the growing influence of leaders such as Deng Xiaoping. However, there was still considerable controversy over foreign borrowing, linked partly to the issue of self-reliance. This was reflected in the contradictory statements of leaders in 1977 and 1978.[29] Whilst the reformers were pressing for greater amounts of and more diverse forms of credit, supporters of Hua Guofeng wanted only a moderate increase in foreign loans, if any.

Although the controversy over foreign loans continued throughout 1978, the pressure to finance the large-scale import of technology required by Hua Guofeng's grandiose plans pushed China into accepting loans sooner than anticipated. In February 1978 Hua Guofeng had outlined a broad strategy for China's economic development over the next seven years, whereby foreign trade, aid and credit would play a key role in the economy. As in the 1950s, this plan was to hinge crucially on the large-scale import of technology and equipment, particularly in heavy industry.

Shortly after the announcement of Hua Guofeng's plan China signed trade pacts with the EEC and Japan. Whilst the EEC trade pact served chiefly to lubricate political relations between China and the EEC, the long-term trade agreement with Japan was of far greater economic significance as it entailed changes in policy towards both the export of oil and foreign credit.[30] According to this agreement China agreed to sell coal and oil in return for technology and plants, marking a radical break from the Gang of Four's proclaimed antipathy towards the sale of China's raw materials.[31]

By mid-1978 the influence of the reformers on policy towards China's external economic relations had grown significantly. In June 1978 Vice-Premier Li Xiannian, who had the previous year denied any role for foreign borrowing, stated that China might consider a British bank loan. Six months later China signed an agreement with 10 British banks for US$ 1.2 billion worth of ECGD-backed credit.

The influence of the reformers was apparent not only in the relaxation of policy towards foreign loans but also in the attempt to diversify sources of finance by drawing on Overseas Chinese capital. In May 1978 the special retail stores for Overseas Chinese were reopened and the Overseas Chinese Investment Corporations reestablished.[32] The chief instigator of this policy change was none other than Deng Xiaoping, who as early as September 1977 had called for the issue of Overseas Chinese affairs to be put on the agenda.[33] Underlying this change in policy towards Overseas Chinese was not only an economic logic but also an implicit political rationale. Creating favourable conditions for Overseas Chinese would ease the process of eventual reunification with Hong Kong, Macao and Taiwan.

As well as putting Overseas Chinese Affairs onto the policy agenda, the reformers were also pushing for the introduction of new forms of external cooperation such as joint production, joint equity ventures and buy-back agreements.[34] From references in the Chinese press to Soviet–foreign joint companies, concessions and foreign technical assistance it was apparent that discussions were taking place within the leadership on potential forms of foreign economic activity.[35] By the end of 1978 China had drawn up several contracts with firms establishing joint-stock companies.[36]

The influence of reformist leaders also underpinned the mounting criticism against the adequacy of technology imports to promote modernisation. From August onwards articles began to appear in the press reporting the poor results in some projects using imported equipment. The lack of staff training, the negative attitude of some leaders as well as the overall lack of experience in arranging such imports had led in some cases to a failure either to employ or absorb that technology.[37] At the same time these articles highlighted the positive aspects of management techniques in capitalist enterprises.[38] The experience of Hua Guofeng's ambitious import plans underlined the importance of introducing not only foreign technology but also foreign management expertise.

These seeds of innovation which were being sown from mid-1978 onwards reflected the growing influence of reformist leaders, such as Deng Xiaoping, Bo Yibo and Zhao Ziyang within the leadership. However, it was not until the consolidation of Deng's political position at the Third Plenum in December 1978 and the concomitant downfall of Hua Guofeng that these ideas could really flower.

Cycle 1 — period of innovation: December 1978 to 1981

Whilst in the Hua Guofeng era the substance of foreign economic activity was reminiscent of the 1950s and early 1960s, the consolidation of Deng Xiaoping's power in December 1978 marked the onset of a more innovatory and exploratory policy. A spate of policy innovation was the key feature of the upswing in the first cycle of the Open Policy. Continuing imbalances in the economy as well as mounting opposition to the SEZs led, however, to a downswing in early 1981.

Changes in the political context facilitated this innovative upswing. By appointing more 'reform-minded' and innovating persons such as Zhao Ziyang and Yao Yilin to positions of authority in 1979 Deng Xiaoping was able to strengthen his power base in the central government.[39] Moreover, the normalisation of Sino-US relations and the conclusion of the Sino-Japanese Peace and Friendship Treaty at the end of 1978 paved the way for an extension of trade relations with the USA and Japan.[40]

This shift in the political context permitted changes in China's policy regarding both its domestic and external economy. At the domestic level there was a switch in priority from investment in heavy industry to investment in light industry and agriculture. Within heavy industry there was to be a drastic readjustment of capital investment away from steel towards projects that would earn foreign exchange such as coal and oil.

At the external level there was to be a large-scale expansion of China's foreign economic relations, in particular with the West and Japan, as well as innovations in the type of activity, contrasting starkly both with the isolationist tendencies of the Gang of Four and the more mundane approach of Hua Guofeng. The pace and scale of the Open Policy was constrained, however, by the immediate economic context. The impending rise in China's trade deficit following Hua Guofeng's 'Great Leap Outward' (see Table 2.1) as well as the continuing infrastructural, technical and managerial constraints on the absorption of foreign technology induced the reformers to follow a more cautious step-by-step approach, using imported equipment to supplement what China already had.[41]

These constraints led initially to a reversal of Hua Guofeng's policy of large-scale imports and in particular to the cancellation of numerous steel plant deals.[42] In February 1979 22 contracts with Japanese firms for equipment worth US$ 2.6 billion were suspended. The construction of the controversial Baoshan Steel Mill in Shanghai was to continue, however. Similarly, numerous Western projects such as British power-stations and Dutch port renovation, were completely dropped by mid-1979.

Whilst initially the new leadership sought to control foreign exchange expenditure through central administrative means, it at the same time decentralised control and innovated in the spheres of foreign trade, foreign borrowing and foreign direct investment. It introduced new forms of trade such as compensation trade and processing and assembly. Although experiments in processing and assembly arrangements were, in fact, already underway in 1978, they received increasing emphasis after the Third Plenum.[43] By the end of 1979 Guangdong had signed over 800 compensation trade agreements, the bulk of these with Hong Kong companies.[44]

Table 2.1   China's foreign trade balance: 1976 to July 1992

Year	Exports	Imports	Trade balance (US$ 1 billion)
1976	6.85	6.58	+ 0.27
1977	7.59	7.21	+ 0.38
1978	9.75	10.89	− 1.14
1979	13.66	15.67	− 2.01
1980	18.12	20.02	− 1.90
1981	22.01	22.02	− 0.01
1982	22.32	19.29	+ 3.04
1983	22.23	21.39	+ 0.84
1984	26.14	27.41	− 1.27
1985	27.35	42.25	−14.90
1986	30.94	42.90	−11.96
1987	39.44	43.22	− 3.78
1988	47.52	55.28	− 7.76
1989	52.54	59.14	− 6.60
1990	62.09	53.55	+ 8.54
1991	71.91	63.79	+ 8.12
July 1992	39.87	23.59	+16.28

Sources: Compiled from *Statistical Yearbook of China 1991* (in Chinese), p. 615; SWB/FE/W0214/A/8 22.1.92; SWB/FE/1477/B2/2 4.9.92. (NB. Figures pre-1979 are from the Ministry of Foreign Trade; figures post-1980 are from Customs statistics).

As well as introducing new forms of trade activity, the reformist leadership also began to reform the foreign trade system. They expanded old methods of trading and promoted ideas fostered in the 1970s such as export-commodity bases. Having used Beijing, Shanghai and Tianjin in 1979 as experimental sites for foreign trade reform, the reformers then extended this experience in 1980 to Guangdong province. They set up specialised import/export corporations combining industry and foreign trade so as to forge direct links between production and marketing. In addition, they granted greater autonomy in foreign economic activities to some prefectures and counties and to the foreign trade branches of central foreign trade departments.[45]

Administrative decentralisation of foreign trade authority was matched by a regional extension of powers. In April 1980, the State Council approved the opening of eight ports on the Yangtse River to foreign trade.[46] Previously, all exports were handled through sea-ports, each specialising in particular commodities.

The more innovatory climate encouraged the reformist leadership to relax its attitude towards foreign loans. In March 1979 Li Qiang, Minister of Foreign Trade, indicated that China would accept foreign loans. In the same month China linked the honouring of large plant deals with Japan to financing, and in particular, to a shift from cash to deferred payments, signalling a greater willingness to borrow from abroad.[47] From early 1979 China was also courting numerous international monetary and financial agencies such as the Asian Development Bank with a view to obtaining foreign loans. In April 1980 China succeeded in joining the IMF and World Bank. The acceptance of loans from international organisations and governments of the West and Japan not only marked a radical break in previous practice but also placed China in the category of an aid receiver. Reluctant to make great use of commercial bank loans, China had nevertheless by 1979 drawn almost US$ 10 billion in such loans, over one-third of total credit in this period.[48]

The upswing in this first cycle witnessed not only a diversification of foreign trade activity and expansion of foreign loans but also the introduction of foreign direct investment from capitalist countries for the first time since Liberation. In a speech to Hong Kong businesspeople in mid-December 1978, Li Qiang revealed the reformers' intentions:

> Not long ago we still had two important 'forbidden zones' in our dealings with other countries. First, we would not accept government-to-government loans. We would accept only commercial loans between banks. This has since changed. Second we would not consider foreign investment. Recently we have decided to break down these 'forbidden zones'.[49]

During his trips to Western Europe in 1979, Rong Yiren, Vice-Chairman of the All-China Federation of Industry and Commerce, discussed the possibility of foreign direct investment. Academic journals began to carry articles on the advantages of foreign direct investment over foreign loans, arguing in particular that the former would facilitate the absorption of foreign technology and management techniques and promote the international marketing of products.[50] In June 1979 Hua Guofeng referred to the possibility of joint production with capitalist enterprises as a means to promote the development of the domestic economy.[51] A month later China's first law on Sino-foreign joint ventures came into effect.[52]

Although the law was loosely defined, it nevertheless marked the official sanctioning of foreign direct investment in China. The law guaranteed the legal protection of the foreign companies' investment, stipulated a minimum foreign capital investment of 25 per cent and permitted the remittance of net profits overseas via the Bank of China.[53] The Chinese side would retain control over the joint ventures by allowing only Chinese to act as chairperson of the board of directors.

A more radical break with the past was promised when both Rong Yiren and Gu Mu referred to the possibility of China permitting foreign companies with 100 per cent ownership, that is, 'wholly owned foreign enterprises'.[54]

Previously this would have been perceived as a threat to China's sovereignty as full ownership meant full control. Similarly, the proposal to export Chinese labour overseas again marked a radical turnabout from previous policy.

The promulgation of the law on Sino-foreign joint ventures in July 1979 was paralleled by two other important milestones in China's Open Policy. The first of these concerned the regional distribution of power. Both Guangdong and Fujian provinces were granted 'special policies and flexible measures' in managing their external economic activities. This had in fact already been under discussion in the latter part of 1978 as preparations for the establishment of the Fujian Investment Enterprises Corporation were then already under way.[55]

The second concerned the designation of selected areas in Fujian and Guangdong provinces as special zones open to foreign direct investment. The first export-processing zone to be established was in fact in Shekou in January 1979.[56] Although inspiration for the idea of SEZs probably came from a variety of sources, accounts attributing the proposal to Wu Nansheng, later head of the Administrative Committee for the SEZs of Guangdong province, suggest that there was a provincial support base for this subpolicy.[57]

Further evidence of local support for the idea of SEZs was reflected in the discussion concerning the precise location of the other zones, which continued over the next six months. Whilst Wu Nansheng favoured Shantou over Shenzhen, which he argued lacked labour, the Guangdong Party proposed that all of the province should become a zone.[58] This suggested considerable local interest in the expansion of foreign economic relations, engendering a process of bargaining between the province and centre over the regional limits to the scope of the policy. In March 1979 both Baoan and Zhuhai county were granted municipality status, marking a preliminary step towards the creation of zones in these counties.[59] At the same time the Fujian authorities expressed interest in establishing a special zone.

Interestingly, the reformers did not choose any of China's provincial capitals as SEZs. This reflected partly an unwillingness to let the provincial capitals have too much autonomy too soon. Similarly, the option of Shanghai was also on the agenda.[60] Given the importance of Shanghai's contribution to the national budget there was strong central opposition to losing this golden egg. However, 13 years later during his southern trip in early 1992 Deng Xiaoping expressed his regret at not having included Shanghai.[61]

Although Deng Xiaoping endorsed these various proposals in April 1979, he nevertheless underlined that the zones would have to be self-financing and thus primarily a concern of the provincial government. After this meeting Gu Mu, head of the State Capital Construction Commission and

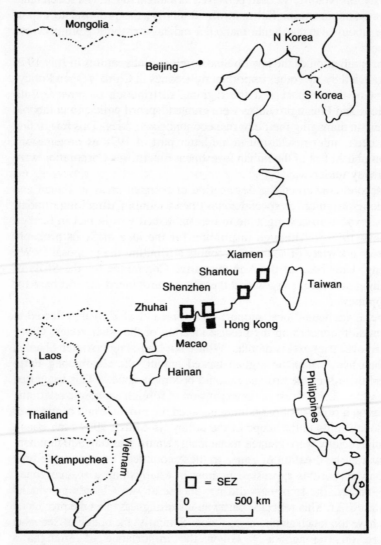

Figure 2.1   China's four SEZs, 1979–86 (Source: *National Westminster Bank Quarterly Review*, Feb. 1986, p. 41)

state councillor, led a working party to Guangdong and Fujian to examine the various options. In July 1979 the central government announced that SEZs would be established in Shenzhen, Zhuhai, Shantou and Xiamen (see Figure 2.1). As indicated later by Gu Mu, these would not only invite joint ventures and wholly owned foreign enterprises to set up but also adopt more liberal economic policies than in the interior, though the content of these policies was not specified clearly.[62]

The process of establishing the policies concerning the SEZ proceeded over the next two years. In November 1979 Shenzhen achieved municipal status. At the end of that year the Guangdong government drew up draft regulations for the establishment of two SEZs.[63] These regulations not only covered aspects of labour and organisational management but also included details on the contract periods and profit taxes of companies operating in the SEZs which had been of concern to foreign investors since the promulgation of the Sino-foreign joint venture law. However, it was not until September 1980 that Guangdong issued the first statute concerning SEZs.[64] The delay was probably in part because of controversy over granting preferential conditions to foreign companies.

Pressures from different regional interests within Guangdong province to become the beneficiaries of the SEZ policy also infused the processes of policy generation and establishment during this upswing. Although the central government had declared certain areas special zones, the actual areas referred to were still subject to different interpretations throughout the year, reflecting pressure from below to extend the scope of the policy. For example, it was apparent from an article published in March 1980 that 'some' interpreted the whole of Shenzhen and Zhuhai to be 'Special Economic Zones' whilst 'others' thought that any areas engaging in compensation trade or assembly and processing would also become 'special zones'.[65] This confusion was in part due to both Hong Kong/Macao businesspeople wishing to make the most of the lack of clarity as well as local level enterprises and authorities seeking to cash in quickly on this opportunity.

Provincial interests led to a broader interpretation not only of the scope of the SEZs but also of their functions. This was reflected in the change in terminology used to describe these areas. Up till August 1980 they were officially referred to as 'Special Export Zones'. However, from October 1979 onwards the term 'Special Economic Zone' had been slipping into use at the provincial level.[66] In March 1980, Sun Ru, member of the Guangdong Political Consultative Conference and President of the Guangdong Society of Economics, used the term 'Special Economic Zone' more precisely to refer to a specially designated area open to various forms of foreign direct investment and trade and employing a new administrative system.[67]

This change in terminology served both to underline the comprehensive character of the zone, distinguishing it from the narrower export-processing zone, and also to highlight the fact that it was economically special but politically no different from the rest of China.[68] The use of the term 'SEZ' in provincial and national regulations in April and August 1980 respectively reflected its official acceptance.[69]

The coining of the term SEZ by provincial theorists as well as its broader connotations were further indications of the level of provincial initiative and support in the initial stages of the zones. In fact, up till mid-1981 the centre considered the SEZs to be primarily the concern of the provincial government. It was theorists from Guangdong rather than from the centre who initially parried ideological attacks upon the SEZs relating to their compatibility with traditional Marxist principles, and in particular the inevitable exploitation of labour inherent in capitalist enterprises.[70]

Policy innovation was the key feature of this upswing from 1978 to early 1981. The official sanctioning of joint ventures in mid-1979, the establishment of four SEZs and the expansion of foreign loans were all major breaks with previous practice. The change in central leadership as well as support from particular regions hoping to benefit from the policy provided a favourable political context for the generation and implementation of these new policies. This flurry of policy innovation was dampened, however, by continuing imbalances in the economy as well as mounting opposition to the Open Policy and domestic reforms. Of particular concern to the reformers was the persisting shortage of foreign exchange, despite the fall in the foreign trade deficit from US\$ 2 billion in 1979 to US\$ 1.9 billion in 1980 (see Table 2.1). The cycle then took a downward turn with a subsequent shrinking of policy generation and implementation and the reassertion of central control.

This downswing in the Open Policy started with a new round of project cancellations in February 1981, affecting Japanese, German and US companies.[71] This was also partly an expression of China's anger at Japan for agreeing to build Baoshan Steel Mill knowing that the land was unsuitable. In March there were indications of a further seven cancellations of large-scale projects involving again both Japanese and German investment.[72] Moreover, Ji Chongwei, a member of the Import/Export Commission and the Foreign Investment Control Commission, proposed that the number of new projects be reduced over the next four years due to China's lack of funds. At the same time import restrictions on luxury items such as cars and TV sets were introduced, reflecting a growing concern about the impact of Japanese car imports on local car production. In April 1981 the centre issued new directives to increase central control over exports.[73]

This concern with foreign exchange led to a more selective approach in the use of foreign capital. Foreign capital was to be deployed in the energy, communications and light industrial sectors. There was a shift away from the construction of new plants to the transformation of existing enterprises with imported technology. Moreover, large-scale projects would be financed by long-term low interest or interest-free loans. The reformers emphasised the need to plan and conduct feasibility studies before the signing of contracts.[74] They also encouraged greater use of international financial practices such as deferred payments and purchasers' credit.

This downswing in the first cycle was reinforced by the emerging wave of criticism in mid-1981 against the SEZs sponsored by leftist opponents of reform and opening up. In the period between the Third Plenum of 1978 and the Sixth Plenary Session in June 1981 the struggle between the 'reformers', those aligned to Deng Xiaoping, and the 'Whateverists' and 'ultra-leftists' was particularly intense. The Whateverists, who swore allegiance to Maoist principles, were associated with Hua Guofeng. The ultra-leftists or 'Cultural Revolutionists', were linked to leaders such as Wang Dongxing, were less repentant about the excesses of the Cultural Revolution and saw the reformers as pursuing the much hated 'capitalist road'. With the gradual ousting of the ultra-leftists and Whateverists from key positions within the Party, differences within the dominant group of leaders, namely the reformers, over the Open Policy also began to increase in importance.[75]

Reports of widespread smuggling in the coastal provinces of Guangdong, Fujian and Zhejiang provided the occasion for these differences amongst the reformers to surface.[76] Prominent in the attack upon economic crime in August 1981 was Peng Zhen, who since February 1979 was in charge of the Politico-Legal Committee of the Central Committee and also head of the Legal Commission of the National People's Congress. At this point it was difficult to determine where Peng Zhen's loyalties lay. His appointment to the Politico-Legal Committee suggests that he enjoyed the favour of the reformers.[77] However, when Ye Jianying retreated to the south in early 1981, in part to avoid submitting his resignation in line with Hua Guofeng, he asked Peng Zhen to take care of military affairs.[78]

Following an anti-smuggling conference convened by the State Council in August 1981 central government began to take a closer interest in the affairs of these provinces, which appeared to be slipping out of central control.[79] Criticism gradually began to focus on Shenzhen, which had allegedly become a major channel for smuggling between Hong Kong and the interior of China. As a result the development of the zones became an issue of national concern. These ideological campaigns against crime and smuggling were in turn used by the Whateverists and ultra-leftists, whose formal positions of power were gradually being eroded, indirectly to challenge the reformers.

The continuing struggle between the reformers, and the Whateverists and ultra-leftists was resolved by the end of the year. In January 1982 Chen Yun commented that the 'SEZs could be continued, but the experience must be summed up and reviewed continually'.[80] As Chen Yun favoured a cautious approach to reform and opening up with an emphasis on planning his comment also marked the dominant climate of thought amongst the reformers. With this statement the reformers reflected their continuing commitment to the SEZs, signalling the onset of a new cycle of the Open Policy.

Cycle 2 — Pushing ahead, but not too fast: 1982–3

Whilst Chen Yun's comment on the SEZs marked a victory for the reformers, it nevertheless portended a slower pace of policy implementation. The upswing in this second cycle from early 1982 up till the autumn of 1983 witnessed further changes in the pace and extent of the Open Policy. However, the continuing controversy over the SEZs surfaced once more in the form of an ideological attack upon the SEZs in the autumn of 1983, triggering a downswing in the policy.

The upswing in this cycle began with further proposals for the regional decentralisation of authority over foreign economic relations. In February 1982 the State Council discussed a plan to grant greater autonomy to 11 provinces, cities and autonomous regions over imports, customs duties, foreign exchange, interest-rate concessions on loans and investment projects.[81]

It was during this upswing that the regional direction of the Open Policy also became more explicit. As coastal areas were purported to enjoy a comparative advantage in foreign trade, they were the place to concentrate foreign capital. The proposals to make Shanghai into a SEZ and possibly Hainan reflected this emerging regional strategy. Although Shanghai did not become a SEZ, it was, however, along with Chongqing granted greater autonomy in its foreign trade and in approving foreign technology and equipment. This in turn reflected an attempt by top leaders to appease those in Shanghai and the centre who may have envisaged a more prominent role for Shanghai in opening up.

Whilst this regional decentralisation of foreign trade authority implied that the Open Policy was continuing to move forward, the ongoing struggle within the leadership over the SEZ policy simultaneously braked the implementation of this aspect of the Open Policy. In the course of the year central leaders made frequent visits to the zones to monitor developments more closely. In March 1982 cadres in Shenzhen attended a self-criticism meeting to discuss the spread of corruption and 'bourgeois thought'.[82]

During this time the press abounded with articles on the causal links between the Open Policy and economic crime, reflecting intense divisions within the leadership over the Open Policy.[83] Advocates of such links portrayed the zones as 'breeding grounds' for economic crime. Although Peng Zhen had initiated the attack upon economic crime, the ultra-leftists and Whateverists soon appropriated and deflected the campaign.

This, then, provided the context for a more general challenge to the SEZ concept itself. Would the zones become 'new colonies' similar to the treaty ports in pre-liberation China? Whilst some of the reformers may also have shared these doubts, as reflected in the report on the zones published in September 1982, uniting to preserve the Open Policy became imperative. So the reformers hit back with press articles denying any direct links between economic crime and the Open Policy. Arguments concerning the impact of imported consumer goods on domestic industry, particularly machine-building and chemicals, provided further ammunition in the attack on the SEZs.[84] This suggested that sectors of heavy industry which were losing out under the reforms and Open Policy had joined in the attacks led by leftist groups aligned to Hua Guofeng and the Gang of Four.

By July 1982 the tension between provincial and central government came to a head, when Guangdong province was rebuffed for mismanaging its foreign exchange and signing contracts with foreigners which were 'unfavourable to the state'.[85] The final blow came when central government prohibited Guangdong from opening up any more zones, referring to Hainan Island, which had already in December 1981 been granted greater powers. This marked the end of a short-lived upswing. Guangdong's wings were clipped again. The whole concept of SEZs was now seriously in question. The imposition of customs duties on raw materials imported for export processing in July 1982 as well as the withdrawal of the power of lower levels to export a large number of goods also signalled tighter central government control over the external economy.

This backlash against the SEZs as well as the spate of project cancellations in 1981 not only put a brake on the extension of the SEZ concept but also shook foreign investors' confidence in the stability of the Open Policy.[86] At the same time other forms of foreign economic activity also came under attack from ultra-leftist groups and supporters of Hua Guofeng. They condemned processing and assembly as only benefiting foreigners and criticised foreign direct investment for failing to develop China's international marketing skills.[87] They claimed greater flexibility in foreign trade had disrupted the flow of 'normal' trade in Guangdong.[88]

In September 1982 the results of the investigation into Zhuhai and Shenzhen by the State Council Economic Research Centre were published revealing intense divisions of opinion over the zones. The key issues which divided the reformers from their opponents were first, whether or not the SEZs were potential concession areas and colonies, and second, whether the zones necessarily gave rise to economic corruption.[89] If the first were true, then China's national sovereignty was at stake, whilst if the second were true, then the continuation of the SEZs was under threat. However, the conclusions of the report signalled a victory for the reformers. The report called for a more flexible system of economic management, greater administrative powers for the enterprises in the zones and greater autonomy for the leaders of the SEZs *vis-à-vis* central government.

The proposals made in September 1982 following the investigation of the zones indicated not only that the reformist leadership had gained the upper hand but also that certain subgroups within the reformers had triumphed.[90] More moderate reformers such as Chen Yun, who had urged caution early on in the year as well as those conservative reformers concerned with the ideological aspects of the zones, such as Deng Liqun, found themselves overshadowed by more radical reformers such as Deng Xiaoping who wanted to innovate and push ahead with opening up. These struggles within the leadership undermined foreign investors' confidence in the stability of the Open Policy, which affected the pace of contract negotiation.[91]

These proposals also marked a turning-point in the functional role of the zones. The zones were to serve not only as a means for learning about the international capitalist economy but also as a test-site for potential reforms in the domestic economy. This in turn bolstered the legitimacy of the zones as they now fell under the ambit of the overall reform programme. This linking of the SEZs to domestic reform was of significance not only for the SEZs but also for the overall relationship between China's foreign economic relations and the domestic economy. It meant a shift away from the 'supplementary' approach which conceived of China's foreign economic relations as additional and extraneous to the domestic economy to an 'integral' approach which envisaged a closer functional relationship between foreign economic activity and the domestic economy. It also indirectly acknowledged that the concentration of foreign direct investment in the zones would require adjustments in the immediate economic and institutional environment. In the wake of this report the SEZs began in the next two months not only to offer special incentives in taxation, land leases, rent and wages to attract foreign direct investment but also to reform their economic management system.[92]

By early 1983 the storm over the SEZs had abated somewhat. Articles critical of the SEZs continued, however, to surface throughout the year criticising various aspects of the SEZ and Open Policy.[93] In February 1983 Hu Yaobang, one of the chief supporters of the Open Policy, visited Shenzhen and outlined the future direction of the zone.[94] His visit not only suggested continuing central government support but also that the pro-Open Policy leaders were gaining ground.

In the next few months the evolution of the Open Policy continued to make further advances. Two proposals in particular suggested that the SEZs were still considered a viable means of opening up. First, in March 1983 plans were revealed to develop a SEZ in Shanghai.[95] Second, around the same time a proposal was submitted to the National People's Congress to make Hainan a first-level government instead of falling under Guangdong, suggesting that Hainan too was being considered as a potential SEZ.[96]

Throughout 1983 new policies extending the privileges enjoyed by joint ventures were generated and established. Eager to attract more investment from nearby Hong Kong and Overseas Chinese the reformers had to relax their requirement for 100 per cent export-oriented joint ventures and high technology. In April 1983 joint ventures in Shenzhen were permitted to sell some of their products domestically.[97] Up till then China had been adamant that joint ventures should export all of their products. In September 1983 the centre lifted duties imposed on joint ventures importing raw materials and components used in export production.[98] Moreover, there were indications that Shenzhen was planning even more preferential policies for joint ventures.[99]

There was also a relaxation in attitude towards wholly owned foreign enterprises. In September 1983 it was announced that wholly owned foreign enterprises in SEZs could set up enterprises on a trial basis in some provinces, municipalities and autonomous regions.[100] However, as joint ventures began to come into operation and greater privileges were extended to them over the year, rumblings of discontent amongst state-owned enterprises increased as they saw not only their products threatened by the often superior products of joint ventures but also priority given to joint ventures in terms of loans, taxation and other costs.[101]

China continued to borrow from abroad, accepting loans from the World Bank and IDA for periods up to 20 and 50 years respectively.[102] This was for China a particularly long-term commitment, as of the US$ 10.8 billion borrowed between 1978 and 1982, US$ 7.1 billion had already been repaid.[103]

The consolidation of the Open Policy in the first half of 1983 was to face another setback prompted by both economic and political factors. Concern about future imbalances in the economy due to decentralisation led in mid-1983 to the reimposition of central control over investment spending, affecting in turn the management of technology imports.[104] At the same time, however, Shanghai and Tianjin were granted greater decision-making power on a trial basis for importing technology for medium and small enterprises.

This downswing in the Open Policy was accelerated with the launch of the spiritual pollution campaign in October 1983. As well as attacking intellectuals for promoting ideas of humanism and socialist alienation, the campaign attributed the influx of pornography, speculation, smuggling, Western bourgeois thought and the revival of 'decadent practices' such as prostitution and superstition to the influence of the Open Policy. Once again the SEZs became the subject of an attack. Deng Xiaoping encouraged political and military reformist leaders, both 'conservative' and 'radical', to visit the zones in the course of 1983 and report their impressions.

The chief promoter of the campaign was none other than Peng Zhen who had also instigated the drive against economic crime. It seemed that Peng Zhen was seeking to establish his own power base within the coercive arms of the state and the National People's Congress. In June 1983 at the Sixth People's Congress Peng Zhen replaced Ye Jianying as head of the Standing Committee. Four of the new subcommittees were headed by those who had lost their positions of power at the Twelfth Party Congress.[105] The conflict between Deng Xiaoping and Peng Zhen surfaced at the Second Central Committee Plenum in October 1983.[106] Ten days after the plenum Peng Zhen addressed an extraordinary meeting on the subject of 'spiritual pollution' calling for a document to be published on this issue. Although the idea for the campaign probably originated with Peng Zhen, the actual management of the campaign fell upon the conservative Deng Liqun who was head of the Propaganda Department of the Central Committee.

The spiritual pollution campaign highlighted divisions within the reformist leadership over the pace and forms of the Open Policy. The existence of two or possibly three main groupings within the reformist leadership became increasingly evident. On the one hand, there were the 'radical' reformers such as Deng Xiaoping, Hu Yaobang and Zhao Ziyang, who favoured a more rapid pace of opening up, further regional expansion of the Open Policy and greater innovation and diversity in the forms of external economic relations. On the other hand, there were the 'conservative' reformers such as Peng Zhen, Deng Liqun and Li Xiannian, who were particularly concerned about the ideological impact of the Open Policy. They favoured greater restraint in the pace and scale of opening up, harked back to the 'Golden 50s' and were sceptical about the SEZs. Then there were the 'moderate' reformers such as Chen Yun, who advocated a more cautious pace of opening up for reasons of economic balance. These took a more positive view than the conservatives towards the SEZs, but wanted a clear role for planning. In Chen Yun's terms, they wanted 'the bird firmly in the cage'.[107]

General public weariness with such ideological campaigns as well as the excesses of leftist cadres at lower levels undermined, however, the potential thrust of this campaign. Institutions benefiting from opening up and reform resisted the campaign. In December 1983 the State Science and Technological Committee, for example, held that 'spiritual pollution' should not be discussed in the fields of science and technology.[108]

Although the spiritual pollution campaign had by mid-1984 almost completely petered out, being confined anyway in that year to the field of culture, it had nevertheless served to reinforce existing doubts about the correctness of Deng's reform programme, and in particular, the Open Policy. Moreover, it made foreign investors increasingly anxious about the political stability of the leadership. Fearing that the campaign marked the onset of a Second Cultural Revolution, several foreign investors withdrew their contracts.[109]

The attack upon economic crime and the spiritual pollution campaign affected not only foreigners' perceptions of the political stability of China but also domestic confidence in the stability of the leadership. This in turn delayed the negotiation of some contracts involving foreign trade and foreign direct investment as well as production in some foreign-invested enterprises. As lower-level officials became concerned about the outcome and potential implications of such campaigns and, more importantly, the potential impact on their own future positions, they became reluctant to sign contracts or take any other major decisions.

These intense struggles within the leadership between 1979 and 1984 account in part for the low level of foreign direct investment (see Table 2.2). Moreover, the small quantity of Japanese investment in China relates not only to their more general prediliction for trade but also to their lack of confidence in the stability of the leadership. The slow progress in the SEZs in these early years is also partly due to the impact of these two ideological assaults.

Up till this point neither Deng Xiaoping nor Chen Yun had inspected the zones. The tide of controversy over the zones was finally quelled when Deng Xiaoping visited the SEZs in January 1984, paving the way for a new cycle in the evolution of the Open Policy.

Compared to the spate of policy innovation in the first cycle between 1979 and 1981 the controversy over the SEZs constrained the pace of policy innovation and implementation. The reassertion of central control over provincial initiatives reflected the more cautious approach towards the SEZs. The call for more reforms in the report on the SEZs in September 1982 led to further advances in the Open Policy. By the autumn of 1983, however, concern for the impending foreign trade deficit as well as the launch of the spiritual pollution campaign led to a downturn in the policy cycle.

Cycle 3 — Striding ahead: 1984–6

The third cycle of the Open Policy from early 1984 to mid-1986 witnessed the rapid extension and deepening of both the reforms and the Open Policy. The fast tempo of the upswing led, however, in mid-1985 to serious imbalances in the economy. The subsequent reimposition of central control heralded another downswing in the Open Policy.

By personally visiting the zones and commenting positively on their performance, Deng Xiaoping not only endorsed the 'correctness' of

Table 2.2 Cumulative foreign direct investment in China by type: 1979 to September 1992

Type	1979–82	79–83	79–84	79–85	79–86	79–87	79–88	79–89	79–90	79–91	79–92
EJV											
No. of agreements	83	190	931	2,304	3,235	4,630	8,530	12,189	16,280	na	na
FDI pledged ($m)	128	316	1,376	3,405	4,780	6,730	9,863	12,522	15,226	na	na
FDI realised ($m)	103	177	431	1,010	1,814	3,299	5,274	7,311	9,197	na	na
CJV											
No. of agreements	792	1,123	2,212	3,823	4,405	5,194	6,815	7,994	9,311	na	na
FDI pledged ($m)	2,726	3,230	5,437	8,933	10,291	11,574	13,198	14,281	15,535	na	na
FDI realised ($m)	292	530	995	1,580	2,373	2,992	3,771	4,522	5,195	na	na
WOFE											
No. of agreements	33	48	74	120	128	174	584	1,515	3,375	na	na
FDI pledged ($m)	367	371	470	515	535	1,006	1,487	3,140	5,583	na	na
FDI realised ($m)	40	68	82	100	116	140	366	737	1,420	na	na
JOINT OIL DEVELOP.											
No. of agreements	13	31	31	35	41	44	49	59	64	na	na
FDI pledged ($m)	1,392	2,423	2,423	2,782	2,863	2,868	2,927	3,130	3,324	na	na
FDI realised ($m)	486	782	1,302	1,782	2,042	2,225	2,437	2,669	2,913	na	na
Total											
No. of agreements	921	1,392	3,248	6,321	7,819	10,052	15,988	21,767	29,040	41,320	69,230
FDI pledged ($m)	4,613	6,340	10,706	16,635	19,469	23,178	28,475	34,073	40,668	45,038	na
FDI realised ($m)	921	1,557	2,810	4,466	6,369	8,680	11,873	15,264	18,750	na	na

Note: na = not available.

Sources: Compiled from: Chen, Nai-Ruenn, 1986, p. 8; Khan, 1991; 1989–90: *Statistical Yearbook of China 1991* (in Chinese), p. 629; *Foreign Economic Trade Yearbook of China 1991* (in Chinese); XH in SWB/FE/W0256 A/1 11.11.92.

the policy to establish SEZs at the national level, but also encouraged leaders at the provincial level to push ahead with reforms.[110] Two major proposals came out of his visit: first, that the Open Policy be extended to 14 coastal cities and Hainan Island; and second, that Xiamen SEZ be widened to cover the whole of the island.

In April 1984 the State Council convened a forum at which these two major proposals were, after much heated discussion, agreed upon (see Figure 2.2).[111] Some of these 14 cities would set up mini-SEZs called 'Economic and Technological Development Zones' (ETDZs) which would grant preferential treatment to joint ventures and wholly owned foreign enterprises, though less than that in the SEZs.[112] These would concentrate on the development of knowledge and technology-intensive enterprises.

Foreign capital was to be channelled towards the transformation of existing enterprises and the creation of small- to medium-scale enterprises requiring little investment and yielding quick results. This shift in policy away from new large-scale projects reflected the reluctance of central government to provide any funds for the coastal cities. As emphasised by Zhao Ziyang, the opening up of the coastal cities would have to rely on policies rather than central funds.[113] The meeting also called for a relaxation in taxation and marketing policies for foreign-invested enterprises.

In the course of the year the details of these proposals were worked out. The coastal cities were granted certain privileges concerning the approval of foreign direct investment, taxation and foreign trade which were still less than the SEZs but greater than the inland areas.[114] An order of priority emerged with the SEZs granted the most privileges with regard to their foreign economic relations, followed by the ETDZs, the coastal cities and finally certain inland areas. Restrictions on domestic sales of joint ventures were eased. This was also significant as it meant that China was increasingly willing to trade its domestic market for the acquisition of foreign technology. As Gu Mu put it: 'We can allow them [foreign businesses] to take 30%, 50%, even 100% provided the technology is what we need and geared to the production of what we lack.'[115] The resulting domestic competition might also serve as an impetus to state-owned enterprises to improve their efficiency.

The forum not only gave the go-ahead to a regional extension of the policy but also reinforced the concept of the SEZ as an experimental site for economic reforms which might later be applied to the rest of the economy. Particular attention was paid to the case of Shekou industrial zone, which was claimed to have carried out 'an adventurous attempt in reform'.[116] With this official impetus Shenzhen introduced three reforms in its economic management system in July 1984 and by October was considering further reforms in its management and wage system.[117] Like

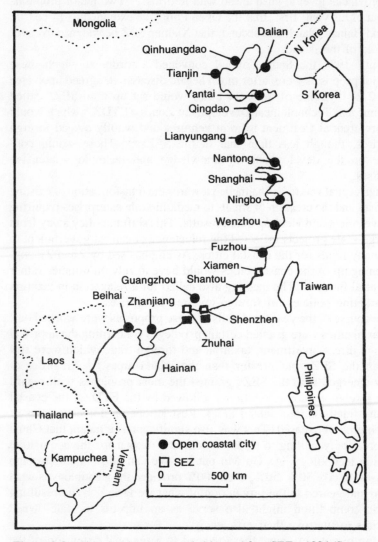

Figure 2.2 China's 14 open coastal cities and four SEZs, 1984 (Source: *National Westminster Bank Quarterly Review*, Feb. 1986, p. 41)

the SEZs, the 14 coastal cities were also to function both as 'windows' to the outside and as models of reform.

The choice of 14 cities on the coast betrayed again the implicit regional bias in the Open Policy. Dissatisfaction was, however, already brewing

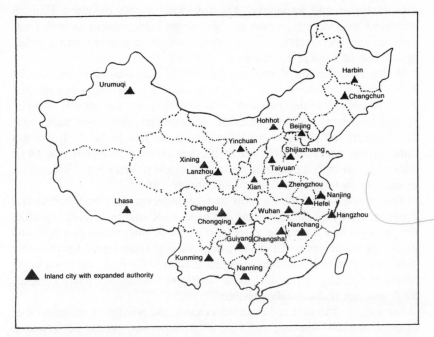

Figure 2.3 24 inland cities with expanded authority, 1984 (Source: *China Business Review*, Nov.–Dec. 1984, p. 15)

in the inland areas which perceived themselves as becoming increasingly marginalised in the race for modernisation. In response to this resentment central government granted 24 inland cities the right to some incentives to attract foreign direct investment (see Figure 2.3).[118] Moreover, in October Wuhan won provincial status in economic management with limited privileges regarding foreign direct investment.[119]

The official endorsement of the SEZ policy as well as the opening up of the 14 coastal cities created a climate in the first half of 1984 which was favourable to further reforms in the foreign trade system. In August 1984 Chen Muhua, Minister of Foreign Economic Relations and Trade announced various reforms in the foreign trade system, which were to come into force from January 1985.[120] The nature of these reforms was similar in principle to reforms advocated for other sectors of the economy. They signified the continuing intermeshing of China's Open Policy with domestic economic policy. These included the separation of 'government from enterprise', the delegation of foreign trade authority to lower levels and the introduction of an import/export agency system, whereby foreign trade companies would act as agents for handling the imports and exports of manufacturers and importers. The following month the State Council approved the decentralisation of the foreign trade system to both local governments and enterprises.[121] Exporters would be able to retain a higher proportion of foreign exchange.

Whilst the expansion of the Open Policy to 14 coastal cities became official policy in April 1984, other issues were also coming onto the policy agenda. First, the concept of the 'free port', which at this point was not well defined, filtered into the Open Policy rhetoric. In particular, there were indications that Xiamen and Hainan Island might become 'free ports'.[122] It was not until almost one year later that it became publicly revealed that Deng Xiaoping had in fact proposed certain free-port policies for Xiamen SEZ in his speech to senior leaders in February 1984.[123]

The introduction of the free-port concept, however ill defined, had several implications for the SEZs. On the one hand, as Xiamen was already a SEZ, the proposal that it become a free port might be interpreted as a rejection of the appropriateness of the Shenzhen model to other areas. On the other hand, the 'free-port' concept might have been yet another variation in the forms of opening up, which could be adopted where the more complex SEZ was not immediately feasible.

Second, Gu Mu referred in an interview to the possibility of more cities in the hinterland opening up, depending, however, on the performance of the coastal cities.[124] Here we can discern possible pressure from the inland areas to extend the scope of the Open Policy.

The wind of innovation continued into 1985. The year opened with Gu Mu announcing a further regional extension of the Open Policy to four large regions, namely, the Pearl River Delta, Yangtse Delta, Liaoning Peninsula and Jiaodong Peninsula in Shandong.[125] This was amended, however, to the opening of 'three golden triangles', namely, the Yangtse, Pearl and South Fujian Deltas (see Figure 2.4).[126]

Whilst no reason was given for shelving Liaoning Peninsula, that this area came onto the policy agenda reflected an emerging desire to open up in the direction of the Soviet Union and Eastern Europe. Quan Shuren, Governor of Liaoning, referred in the 1985 provincial plan to the likelihood of increased trade with the Soviet Union and Eastern Europe.[127] Again we can detect particular regional interests in an extension of the Open Policy towards the Eastern bloc. However, continuing strains on the relations between China and the USSR inhibited any rapid innovations in their economic relations at this point.

This proposal to extend the Open Policy to Liaoning pointed also to the potential emergence of a Soviet lobby within the leadership.[128] In consolidating his power-base within the top party leadership Deng Xiaoping had quietly encouraged octogenarian leaders to retire and actively promoted 'younger' leaders in their 50s and 60s. Many of these 'middle-aged' leaders,

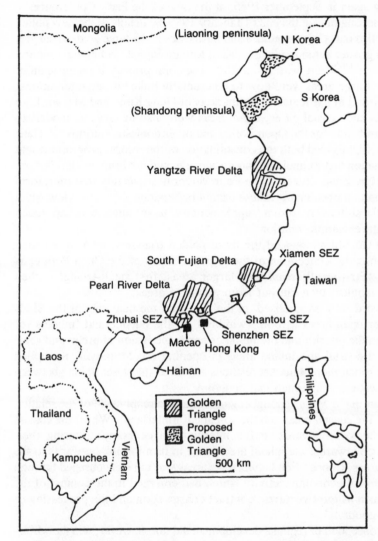

Figure 2.4 China's three golden triangles, 1985 (Source: Compiled by author)

such as Qiao Shi and Li Peng, received their training in the Soviet Union and Eastern Europe. These Soviet-trained leaders were probably wary of the role of market forces in the economy. They would thus support reformers such as Chen Yun, and even Peng Zhen, who would advocate greater caution in reform and opening up. Moreover, they might be sympathetic to closer economic ties with the Soviet Union. Gu Mu took up the theme of opening Liaoning again in September 1985, at the time of the Party Conference.[129]

At a meeting held at the end of January 1985 the details of the new policy were spelled out. Cities, counties and businesses in the three golden triangles received greater autonomy in the use of foreign capital, technology imports and exports.[130] There was also a shift in sectoral priority from agriculture to trade. Large areas were now to be crucially linked to the international economy and in particular to the markets of Hong Kong and Macao. Like the SEZs and coastal cities, these areas were also to serve as models to the rest of China for the Open Policy and other domestic reforms.[131] Their dual role highlighted both the consolidation of the reform programme and the realisation that technology imports alone would not bring modernisation. As stated by Zhao Ziyang: 'The Four Modernisations rely first on reform and second on opening up. These cannot be separated.'[132] This view again reflected a shift away from a 'supplementary' to an 'integrative' approach to foreign economic relations.

When Gu Mu announced the three golden triangles, he also revealed a much broader conception of the regional extent of the Open Policy, as seen in: 'First small areas, then larger areas, first small triangles, then larger triangles; then fan out from points to areas.'[133]

The word 'fan' symbolised on the one hand the dual role of the SEZs and other open areas as both 'windows' to the outside and 'models' of reform to the interior and on the other hand, the fusion of urban and rural areas and coastal and inland areas in opening up. Moreover, it implied a deeper penetration of market relations as well as the closer linking between the domestic and international economy.

Implicit in Gu Mu's announcement was also a reappraisal of the relation between the coastal areas and the so-called 'hinterland'. Whilst the coastal regions looked outwards to the international economy, filtering their experience inwards, the inland areas were in turn to look outwards to the coastal areas. Cooperation between the areas was to be encouraged through new forms of economic activity which had emerged in the context of the SEZs, such as joint ventures, contract construction and the processing of foreign goods.[134]

This conception of regional development did not, however, win the wholehearted favour of the inland areas. In the course of the year, several articles appeared calling for SEZs in the hinterland and for greater autonomy in foreign economic relations for inland areas.[135] Moreover, the SEZs, which continued to suffer problems, were also facing stiff competition from the newly opened coastal cities.

Although significant advances had been made in the Open Policy since the visit by Deng to the SEZs in early 1984, the SEZs nevertheless continued to be a source of simmering controversy. Hints of latent opposition were revealed in April 1985 when the China People's Political Consultative Conference referred to Shenzhen as an 'aberration'.[136] In response reformist leaders continued publicly to express their confidence in the permanency of the Open Policy. In May 1985 Zhao Ziyang indicated that any future changes in the Open Policy would be in the direction of further opening up. This optimism concerning the Open Policy was quelled, however, by the strains in the economy in mid-1985, which signalled a downswing in this cycle of the Open Policy.

Once again the reformist leadership confronted the dilemma of decentralisation stimulating microeconomic initiative but leading also to macroeconomic imbalances. The decentralisation of foreign trade and the loosening of foreign exchange controls had led to the duplication of technology imports, the inappropriate use of foreign exchange for the purchase of luxury consumer goods and a staggering foreign trade deficit (see Table 2.1). Moreover, the disclosure in March of the Hainan scandal highlighted the loss of central control over foreign trade. The distortions engendered by the free rein given to local authorities put a brake on any further extension of the Open Policy.

Opponents of reform and opening up cashed in on this macroeconomic disorder to renew their assault upon the zones. The contradictions between the political goal of reunification and the economic goal of acquiring advanced technology were now visible in the pattern of foreign direct investment. Although most foreign investment came from Hong Kong and Macao, which complied with the political aim of the Open Policy, the type of companies set up were mainly in the service sector, small-scale and labour- rather than technology-intensive. Yet the credibility of the concept of 'one country, two systems', hence the attractiveness of reunification, hinged crucially on the economic success of the SEZs.

Similarly, the difficulty of rapidly increasing exports as well as attracting large-scale foreign capital meant that the construction of Shenzhen continued to depend, in Vice-Premier Yao Yilin's words, on 'state blood transfusions'. Moreover, Shenzhen was allegedly earning more money from illegal domestic sales than from sales abroad.[137] Deng Xiaoping's comment that the SEZs were in fact 'only an experiment' did little to instil confidence in the zones.

In response to these events, the reformist leadership tightened central control over foreign economic relations, especially in the SEZs. In July 1985 the State Council imposed new customs duties on luxury consumer goods such as vehicles and TVs in order to control the illegal resale of these commodities on the domestic market at inflated prices.[138] There was also a recentralisation of foreign trade and foreign exchange management. The zones forfeited their privileges concerning foreign exchange retention, domestic sales, foreign direct investment and foreign trade as well as central financial support.[139] The State Council, rather than the provincial government, replaced the dynamic Liang Xiang as mayor of Shenzhen with the more cautious Li Hao, member of the State Economic Commission.

In the same month Gu Mu announced to a Japanese delegation that 10 of the 14 cities opened in April 1984 would be 'frozen' whilst efforts would be concentrated on the development of Shanghai, Tianjin, Dalian and Guangzhou.[140] Whilst Gu Mu claimed the freeze would be 'temporary' reports from Hong Kong suggested that it might be longer-term.

Although the reimposition of central control over foreign trade, foreign exchange and the SEZs as well as the reduction in the number of coastal cities put a brake on the pace of the Open Policy, it in no way implied a full retreat. Despite these apparent setbacks it was announced that Xiamen SEZ would adopt certain free-port policies.[141] Moreover, the renewed attack upon Shenzhen may have been to deflect attention from Hainan, which the reformers were hoping later to turn into a SEZ. Although Liang Xiang was replaced as mayor of Shenzhen, he still retained his post as Party secretary and later became governor of Hainan. In September, in fact, Deng Xiaoping referred to the SEZs as 'a successful experiment'.[142]

Similarly, the reduction in the number of open coastal cities was not a rejection of the 'open coastal city' concept itself nor of ETDZs, but a comment on the *pace* of opening up. At this stage the controversy over the Open Policy reflected mainly the differences between the 'moderate' and 'radical' reformers over the pace and extent of opening up. As stated later in the year by Gu Mu: 'Things were developing too fast and time is needed to consider and rationalise.'[143]

Moreover, central leaders continued publicly to confirm the continuity of the Open Policy.[144] In September 1985 Gu Mu referred again to the possible opening up of Jiaodong and Liaoning Peninsulas as coastal economic zones.[145] Confidence in the Open Policy was such that Gu Mu was able to reveal a longer-term plan to open up a coastal belt extending from north to south, sowing the seeds for Zhao Ziyang's coastal development strategy announced in 1987.[146]

Whatever the reason behind Deng's comments, they were nevertheless an acknowledgement of the serious economic problems in the SEZs, such as the coexistence of several currencies, the inappropriate use of foreign exchange and the low level of foreign direct investment. Hostility towards the zones continued to be expressed throughout the year.

In order to allay the continuing concern about the SEZs after Deng Xiaoping's statement in mid-1985, Gu Mu held a meeting of senior officials from the State Council, SEZs and coastal cities in Guangzhou at the end of the year.[147] Whilst affirming the success of the SEZs, the meeting also called for greater efforts to improve the infrastructure, legislation and investment environment as well as pressing ahead with reform. Official confirmation of the success of the zones thus indicated that the SEZ policy would continue, though strict central control over China's foreign trade and foreign exchange would be maintained.

Whilst the reimposition of central control over foreign trade as well as the devaluation of the renminbi (Rmb) in early 1986 sharply reduced China's foreign trade deficit, the adverse effect on the level of foreign direct investment was becoming increasingly apparent. In the first half of 1986 foreign direct investment fell to 20 per cent compared to the same period in 1985, whilst foreign loans had doubled. Although central government continued to maintain a tight control over the economy in the first half of 1986, the more stable economic situation allowed the reformers to revise the strategy of the zones, devise new reforms in the foreign trade system and work out new concessions to foreign investors.

In early 1986 central financial support to the SEZs was resumed, indicating not only the inability of the zones to extricate themselves economically, but also continued central government support for them.[148] In order to control the use of foreign exchange, in April 1986 the central authorities reduced the regional allocation of exchange.[149] It was clear that the SEZs and coastal cities resented the removal of many of their privileges, which in their eyes had rendered their conditions no different to those of other parts of China.[150]

At the same time further reforms in the foreign trade system were urged, whilst maintaining tight control over foreign trade. In January 1986 the Foreign Trade Ministry called for the separation of trading companies from Party and governmental organs.[151] Party and government cadres were not permitted to work both in trade companies and in Party and government institutions. The growing foreign trade deficit, due in part to the drop in the price of coal and oil, pressurised China, however, to make further cuts in its imports and in particular on Japanese consumer goods.[152] At the same time the Ministry of Foreign Economic Relations and Trade set about reasserting its control over the vast array of foreign trade companies which had sprung up under decentralisation.[153]

The need to reform the foreign exchange management system as a prelude to further reforms in foreign trade came increasingly under discussion.[154] In May 1986 Zheng Tuobin, Minister of Foreign Trade, indicated in an interview that further reforms in the foreign trade system, including exchange rates, would be introduced later in the year.[155] However, after several trips throughout China, Zheng Tuobin concluded that the slow pace of domestic economic reforms was a significant constraint upon any future reforms in foreign trade. The fate of domestic economic reform and reforms in the foreign trade system were thus crucially interlocked.

As the reformers planned to double the level of imports through foreign direct investment in the Seventh five-year plan (1986–90), improvements in the overall investment climate became urgent. In January 1986 the State Council approved the extension of the period of operation of joint ventures from 30 to 50 years.[156] This committed China to at least half a century of opening up. It also approved further concessions to joint ventures on domestic sales.[157] In addition, discussion was underway on a law which would provide a variety of means for joint ventures to solve the foreign exchange problems.[158]

There was also a reassessment of the attitude towards wholly owned foreign enterprises. Whilst priority had previously been shown towards joint ventures and in particular to equity joint ventures, there was now some discussion about whether the restrictions on wholly owned foreign enterprises should be relaxed.[159] The drafting of a law on wholly owned foreign enterprises, seven years after the official acceptance of foreign direct investment, marked an important step in the improvement of foreign economic legislation and formed part of a series of measures adopted throughout 1986 to attract more foreign capital.[160]

The growing awareness of the adverse effect of central control over foreign trade and foreign exchange upon foreign direct investment as reflected in the discussions during the first half of 1986 prompted a new round of policy generation in August 1986, signalling the onset of a new cycle. The period from early 1984 to mid-1986 was marked by the regional expansion and deepening of the Open Policy. The decentralisation of foreign trade and foreign exchange as well as the impact of other domestic economic reforms led to serious imbalances in the economy. In order to restore order the reformers reasserted central control over foreign trade and foreign exchange management. However, this had a deleterious effect upon foreign direct investment which the reformers were keen to encourage in the seventh five-year plan. Although the central government continued to retain control over foreign trade and foreign exchange in the first half of 1986, serious discussion on foreign trade reforms and ways to improve the investment climate were taking place. This paved the way towards a new cycle in the Open Policy which was to expand China's foreign economic relations even further.

Notes

1. King, 1969, p. 15.
2. Amoy refers to the current city of Xiamen in Fujian province.
3. Hou, 1965, pp. 104–5.
4. King, 1969, p. 54.
5. Cheng, 1978, p. 9.
6. ibid., pp. 40–1; moreover, almost one-half of shipping capacity was accounted for by British investment.

7. Hou, 1965, p. 127.
8. ibid., pp. 18–20, p. 64; the trade imperative to foreign investment was also a key determinant of the scope of foreign investment. In 1931, for example, whilst only 16.5 per cent of foreign investment was in manufacturing, 25 per cent was in transport, 21 per cent in import and export trade and 9.5 per cent in banking and finance (see Remer, 1968, p. 186).
9. Dernberger, 1975.
10. ibid., pp. 38–9.
11. Cheng, 1978, p. 41. Local industry was not only deprived of tariff and other forms of protection but also was required to pay much higher levies on the interior sales of their products.
12. Cowan, 1964, pp. 117–20.
13. Dernberger, 1975, p. 41.
14. Lasek, 1983, p. 51.
15. Cheng, 1978, p. 43.
16. MacDougall, 1982, p. 152.
17. Imports of machinery and transportation equipment from EEC countries were worth US$ 50 million in 1958 compared with US$ 4.5 million in 1955. See de Keijzer, 1977, p. 11.
18. Brown, 1986, p. 59.
19. For example, whilst between 1960 and 1964 imports of machinery and transportation equipment from non-communist countries increased from US$ 49.6 million to US$ 61.3 million, imports from the communist bloc dropped from US$ 790 million to US$ 101 million. See de Keijzer, 1977, p. 15, table 1.
20. For example, between 1956 and 1960 foodstuffs accounted for around only 5 per cent of total imports from non-communist countries. This increased to around 50 per cent from 1961 to 1963. See Eckstein, 1966.
21. Kraus, 1985.
22. SH, JFRB 15.1.1979, p. 2 in FBIS 12.2.1979 E10–11; Guangzhou Provincial Service 15.11.1976 in FBIS 16.11.1976 E12; Guangzhou Provincial Service 22.11.1976 in FBIS 24.11.1976 H5; Beijing New China News Analysis (NCNA) 10.12.1976 in FBIS Daily Report China 15.12.1976 E7–8; Beijing Radio Service 22.1.1977 in FBIS 24.1.1977.
23. de Keijzer, 1977, p. 1.
24. See Hajime, 1976, pp. 37–78. Japan was China's largest trading partner during this period, followed by Hong Kong and the USA (see Howe, 1978, pp. 153–4).
25. Denny and Suris, 1977, p. 18.
26. ibid., p. 20; also NCNA 13.1.1977 in FBIS 14.1.1977 E5.
27. Denny and Suris, 1977, p. 18.
28. HK, AFP 2.11.1976 in FBIS 3.11.1976 E13. Also by December 1976 it had become clear that the expansion of China's foreign economic relations was constrained by both the shortage of foreign exchange and the low level of productive capacity. The amount of China's imports would thus be contingent upon its forex resources and level of exports (see Li Qiang's comment

to the French employers' delegation in Hong Kong Agence France Presse 5.11.1976).

29. For example, in October 1977 the West German Foreign Minister, H.D. Genscher, was informed that China would accept performance guarantees, a form of bank deposit equal in value to the intended purchases of equipment (see MacDougall, 1982, p. 156).

30. The agreement was for eight years involving the purchase of US$ 7−8 billion worth of technology and equipment over the first five years.

31. See Beijing NCNA 13.1.1977 in FBIS 14.1.1977 E1 for examples of the Gang of Four's views on foreign trade.

32. HK, AFP 16.8.1978 in FBIS 18.8.1978 E1.

33. NCNA 3.1.1978 in FBIS 3.1.1978 E10−12.

34. MacDougall, 1982, p. 160.

35. GMRB 18.8.1978, p. 4 in FBIS 24.8.1979 E1.

36. HK, SCMP 28.12.1978 in FBIS 28.12.1978 E17−18. Indications that changes might occur were apparent in November 1978 when a French trade mission to China was informed that China was ready to accept foreign direct investment (see HK, AFP 17.11.1978 in FBIS 17.11.1978 E11).

37. RMRB 19.10.1978 in FBIS 27.10.1978 E25−6.

38. GMRB 6.9.1978 in FBIS 6.9.1978 E2−3; RMRB 19.10.1978 in FBIS 27.10.1978 E25−6; RMRB 25.8.1978 in FBIS 28.8.1978 E1.

39. Chen Yun and Bo Yibo, who had steered China's economy back on course in the late 1950s, both became vice-premiers in June 1979. Yao Yilin had worked in foreign trade and commerce before the Cultural Revolution. He also became director of the General Office of the CCPCC in January 1979. Chen Yun, Li Xiannian and Yao Yilin all took up key positions in the newly founded Finance and Economic Commission.

40. XH, BJ 1.1.1979 in FBIS 2.1.1979 E3−4.

41. In a talk with Hong Kong businesspeople Li Qiang, Minister of Foreign Trade, said: 'What we lack we can import. What we have in surplus we can export.' Reported in HK, DGB 21.12.1978, p. 19 in FBIS 21.12.1978 N1.

42. Kyodo News Agency, Japan 2.4.1979 in FBIS 4.4.1979 L4.

43. Beijing NCNA 7.6.1978 in FBIS 7.6.1978 E1.

44. HK, SCMP 18.12.1979, p. 1 in FBIS 14.1.1980 p. 56.

45. HK, JJDB no. 22 4.6.1980, pp. 25−7 in FBIS 19.8.1980, p. 78; in July Guangdong Foreign Trade Corporation was established to manage and organise foreign trade in Guangdong. Of the 885 export commodities managed by the provincial foreign trade system, 700 were handed over to branch corporations.

46. These were Zhanjiang, Nantong, Nanjing, Wuhu (Anhui), Jiujiang (Jiangxi), Wuhan, Chenglingji (Hunan), Chongqing Wugang (Sichuan) (see XH 17.4.1980).

47. MacDougall, 1982, pp. 165−6.

48. ibid., p. 165, see table 2.

49. HK, DGB 21.12.1978 in FBIS 21.12.1978 N1.

50. HK, CM 1.7.1979 in FBIS JPRS 14.8.1979, pp. 11–12; and 23.2.1979; BJ, JJGL no. 4, April 1979 in FBIS 19.7.1979, p. 102.
51. XH, BJ 20.6.1979 in FBIS 21.6.1979 L7.
52. XH, BJ 27.6.1979 in FBIS 28.6.1979 L1.
53. ibid. It was soon realised that the promulgation of the joint venture law was but the first step in a series of legislative measures that would have to be enacted to manage the introduction of foreign direct investment in China. In an interview with Hong Kong reporters, Rong Yiren, Vice-Chairman of the CPPCC and General Manager of CITIC, indicated that laws on taxation, patents, company and labour would also be required (see HK, DGB 31.8.1979, p. 1).
54. See HK, SCMP 10.11.1979; Li Xiannian also suggested to a visiting Japanese delegation that wholly owned foreign enterprises might be permitted in specially designated areas in China (see Hong Kong Wen Wei Po (HK, WWP) 9.3.1980).
55. XH, BJ 11.5.1979 in FBIS 30.8.1979, p. 56.
56. Chu, 1986, p. 24.
57. Wu Nansheng apparently proposed setting up a special area for foreign direct investment at Shantou like the export processing zone in Taiwan during his visit to Guangdong after the Third Plenum (see Leung, 1986 p. 9). Others maintain that Ye Fei, then minister of transport, suggested to the China Merchants' Steam Navigation Company (CMSNC) that it develop export processing activities at Shekou whilst other accounts imply that the initiative came from the CMSN itself (see Chan, Chen and Chin, 1986 p. 88).
58. Chu, 1986, p. 22.
59. ibid.
60. See *Zhongguo dui guangdong gongzuo zhishi huibian 1979–82* (Annals of Central Government Work Directives to Guangdong).
61. See HK, JB in SWB/FE/1351/B2 9.4.1992.
62. HK, WWP 9.3.1980 in FBIS 2.4.1980 pp. 46–55. Some of the policies mentioned by Gu Mu included lower taxes and land fees than in Hong Kong, duty-free imports and exports and the establishment of special labour policies and institutions.
63. HK, WWP 26.12.1979 in FBIS 25.1.1980, p. 32.
64. ibid.
65. HK, WWP 9.3.1980 in FBIS 2.4.1980, pp. 46–55.
66. HK, WWP 26.12.1979 in FBIS 25.1.1980, p. 32.
67. HK, WWP 9.3.1980 in FBIS 2.4.1980, pp. 46–55.
68. Chu, 1986, p. 22.
69. HK, WWP 8.3.1980 in FBIS 7.4.1980, p. 15.
70. Sun Ru, in defence of the SEZs, referred to the experience of the USSR in the 1920s, underlined the necessity for a less-developed economy to deploy foreign capital and indicated that China would tolerate a certain degree of exploitation in order to reap the benefits (ibid.).
71. *The Times* 2.2.1981; *The Observer* 1.3.1981.
72. *The Observer* 1.3.1981.

78 *China opens its doors*

73. Somerville, 1987, p. 184.
74. RMRB 6.11.1981 in SWB/FE/6888/BII/1.
75. There was already evidence of existing differences as witnessed in the project cancellations of 1981 (see Kokubun, 1986).
76. Chan *et al.*, 1986, p. 96.
77. However, it was not certain at this point how close he was to Deng Xiaoping.
78. HK, DX no. 33 16.6.1981 in FBIS 25.6.1981 W2−5.
79. Chan *et al.*, 1986, p. 96.
80. ibid.
81. The 11 provinces, cities and autonomous regions are Guangdong, Fujian, Shanghai, Tianjin, Beijing, Liaoning, Hebei, Shandong, Jiangsu, Zhejiang and Guangxi (see FEER 26.2.1982).
82. Chan *et al.*, 1986, p. 96.
83. See, for example, RMRB 13.5.1982 in FBIS 14.5.1982 K1.
84. XH 15.4.1982 in FBIS 19.4.1982 K3 and RMRB 24.4.1982 in FBIS 26.4.1982 K3.
85. HK, MB 6.7.1982 in SWB/FE/7073/C/3.
86. HK, MB 17.7.1982 in FBIS 4.8.1982.
87. RMRB 20.8.1982 in FBIS 27.8.1982.
88. HK, MB 18.10.1982 in SWB/FE/7162/BII/8.
89. RMRB 13.9.1982 in SWB/FE/7145/C/4.
90. However, as pointed out by Hu Yaobang in his report to the Congress, supporters of Lin Biao and the Gang of Four continued to hold leading positions (Ladany, 1988, p. 455); also 7 of the 27 members of the Politburo were active in the military, which has been one of the main bastions of opposition to Deng.
91. See HK, MB 17.7.1982, p. 3 in FBIS 4.8.1982.
92. HK, WWP 4.10.1982 in FBIS 13.10.1982; Chan *et al.*, 1986, p. 99.
93. HK, MB 18.10.1982 in SWB/FE/7162/BII/8.
94. Guangdong People's Broadcasting Station 27.2.1983 in SWB/FE/7271/BII/1.
95. JJRB 16.3.1983 in SWB/FE/7294/C/10.
96. NCNA 22.3.1983 in SWB/FE/7291/C1/2.
97. NCNA 8.4.1983 in SWB/FE/7306/BII/5.
98. In September 1983 this was extended also to export-oriented factories (XH 14.9.1983 in FBIS 15.9.1983 K17).
99. Guangdong People's Broadcasting Station 6.6.1983 in FBIS 8.6.1983 P1.
100. XH 27.9.1983 in SWB/FE/7452/C/1.
101. RMRB 14.5.1983 in FBIS 18.5.1983 K9.
102. XH 21.4.1983, p.1 in SWB/FE/W1234/A/7.
103. XH 11.5.1983 in FBIS 16.5.1983 K9.
104. JJRB 11.5.1983 in SWB/FE/W1241/A/11; XH, BJ 23.8.1983 in FBIS 24.8.1983 K6−7.
105. Peng Chong joined the Legal Commission; Wang Renzhong went to the Finance and Economic Commission; Geng Biao joined the Foreign Affairs Commission and Ye Fei went to the Overseas Chinese Commission (see Ladany, 1988, p. 464).

106. See Ladany, 1988, p. 467.

107. ibid., p. 457.

108. ibid., p. 470.

109. At a meeting on spiritual pollution, Zhao Ziyang announced that Japan had withdrawn more than one hundred contracts for fear of the effects of the campaign (see HK, CM 1.4.84). For further details of this campaign, see Schram, 1984.

110. HK, CM 1.3.1984.

111. XH 6.4.1984 in FBIS 9.4.1984 K7.

112. For differences between SEZs and ETDZs see Guangzhou Kaifang 8.9.1986 pp. 27–9 in FBIS 15.1.1982. Also it should be noted that these new zones have been variously translated as 'technical', 'technological' and 'technology' zones. Here, the term 'technological' is used.

113. Nanfang Ribao (NFRB) 11.6.1984, p.2 in FBIS 18.6.1984 K1.

114. The 14 open cities were not however treated equally. For example, Shanghai and Tianjin enjoyed the right to approve independently projects involving investment of up to US\$ 30 million. Other coastal cities could approve investment projects involving only US\$ 10 million or US\$ 15 million of total investment, depending on the economic conditions in each city (see CBR, May–June 1984, p. 17).

115. Quoted from HK, WWP 14.12.1984, p. 3 in FBIS 17.12.1984 W2.

116. Quoted by Yan Gang, general director for the construction of Shekou in NFRB 11.6.1984 in FBIS 18.6.1984 K1.

117. YCWB 27.7.1984 in FBIS 3.8.1984 P2; Guangdong 11.10.1984 in FBIS 15.10.1984 P1.

118. However, these rights differed between the 24 inland cities. For example, Bank of China branches in Shanghai and Tianjin could approve foreign exchange loans to Chinese and Sino-foreign JVs up to US\$ 10 million. In other cities the limit was US\$ 5 million or even US\$ 3 million.

119. XH 26.10.1984 in FBIS 29.10.1984 P5.

120. Beijing People's Broadcasting Station 19.8.1984 in FBIS 24.8.1984 K4.

121. CD 14.10.1984, p. 1 in FBIS 16.10.1984 K11.

122. HK, WWP 14.2.1984, p. 3 in FBIS 17.12.1984 W2.

123. HK, XWB 3.1.1985 in SWB/FE/7841/BII/1.

124. HK, WWP 14.12.1984, p. 3 in FBIS 17.12.1984 W2.

125. HK, SCMP 4.1.1985, p. 1 in FBIS 4.1.1985 W3.

126. NCNA 24.2.1985 in SWB/FE/7886/BII/6.

127. XH 13.5.1985 in FBIS 15.5.1985.

128. HK, SCMP 4.1.1985 in FBIS 4.1.1985.

129. SJJJDB 8.7.1985 in SWB FE/8031/BII/4 16.8.1985.

130. Following his inspection tour of Guangdong and Jiangsu provinces Zhao Ziyang proposed that all counties and cities in the Pearl Delta set up local companies to trade directly with Hong Kong and Macao (HK, WWP 15.1.1985 in SWB/FE/7853/BII/9).

131. XH 31.1.1985 in FBIS 1.2.1985 K10. In fact, during his inspection tour Zhao Ziyang underlined the role of the SEZs as experimental sites for

domestic reform. In particular, he referred to the price reform and capital construction reforms which had already become official policy (HK, WWP 15.1.1985 in SWB/FE/78753/BII/9).

132. LW no. 8, 25.2.1985 carries the article, 'A new situation in China's opening up to world' which reports Zhao Ziyang as making this point in a speech at the January forum on the three golden triangles.

133. NCNA 24.2.1985 in SWB/FE/7886/BII/6.

134. JJGL 5.4.1985.

135. HK, SCMP 7.3.1985 in FBIS 7.3.1985; JJRB 3.6.1985; Ban Yuetan 25.8.1985 in FBIS 12.9.1985 K7; LW 23.9.1985 in FBIS 17.10.85 K1.

136. HK, S 18.6.1985.

137. See HK, MB 25.4.1985 for effects of decentralisation of foreign trade.

138. XH 14.7.1985.

139. HK, WWP 26.1.1986 in SWB/FE/8169/C1/1.

140. HK, S 17.7.1985 in FBIS 17.7.1985 W1.

141. NCNA 23.7.1985 in SWB/FE/8017/BII/17.

142. ZGXWS 16.9.1985 in FBIS 16.9.1985 K12.

143. LW 23.9.1985 in FBIS 17.10.1985 K1.

144. HK, WWP 7.7.1985 in SWB/FE/8000/BII/3; LW 5.8.1985 in SWB/FE/8037/BII/1.

145. SJJJDB 8.7.1985 in SWB/FE/8031/BII/4 16.8.1985.

146. KF 8.9.1985 in SWB/FE/8081/C/1 and SJJJDB 6.10.1986 in FBIS 12.1.1987, p. 23.

147. HK, CM 1.1.1986 in FBIS 7.1.1986 W1.

148. ibid.

149. HK, SCMP 10.3.1986 in FBIS 11.3.1986 W4.

150. JJRB 22.2.1986 in FBIS 5.3.1986 P1; JJRB 6.9.1986 in FBIS 11.9.1986 K4.

151. GJSB 16.1.1986 in SWB/FE/8182/C/3.

152. HK, CM 1.1.1986 in FBIS 7.1.1986 W1; XH 22.1.1986 in FBIS 23.1.1986 K8; HK, SCMP 26.2.1986 in FBIS 27.2.1986 W3.

153. GJSB 16.1.1986 in SWB/FE/8182/C3.

154. TJ, ZGQNJJLT 25.4.1986 in FBIS 4.3.1987.

155. BYT 25.5.1986 in SWB/FE/8282/C1/1.

156. XH 24.1.1986 in FBIS 27.1.1986 K5.

157. ibid.; XH 29.1.1986.

158. HK, WWP 15.1.1986 in FBIS 9.4.1986 W1.

159. GJSB 5.6.1986 in FBIS 19.6.1986 K9; HK, SCMP 9.4.1986 in FBIS 9.4.1986 W1.

160. HK, WWP 17.4.1986 in FBIS 25.4.1986 W6; for example, in May Shenzhen drew up draft regulations for further tax concessions to joint ventures and wholly owned foreign enterprises (HK, SCMP 19.5.1986).

3

Spiralling onwards. Part B: mid-1986 to 1992

Cycle 4 — moving ahead, but not too fast: mid-1986—1987

Having reduced somewhat the size of the trade deficit and halted the fall in foreign exchange reserves, a more favourable climate prevailed for another round of policy innovation. At a meeting with foreign investors and bankers in August 1986 Zhao Ziyang disclosed that more concessions might be offered to foreign investors.[1] Plans were also underway to facilitate loans to export-oriented, productive foreign-invested enterprises which introduced advanced technology.[2]

The urgency of increasing the level of foreign capital also led to a further relaxation in the management of foreign borrowing. In August the State Council granted nine 'window institutions' the right to handle the business of raising funds abroad.[3] China also increased its use of commercial loans, with the result that foreign loans reached their highest level in 1986.[4]

As well as relaxing central control over foreign borrowing, further concessions to foreign investors were also proposed. In October 1986 the State Council promulgated 22 new regulations, granting foreign investors more incentives. The key elements of the proposals were a reduction in wages, land and other costs as well as further tax concessions for foreign-invested enterprises engaged in export, introducing advanced technology and/or reinvesting their profits in China. Several provinces thereupon issued their own sets of regulations.[5] Around the same time reforms in China's foreign exchange structure were also announced.[6]

There were also indications that the SEZs were returning to favour. Xue Muqiao, a well-known Chinese economist, suggested that the SEZs in particular should be granted more power.[7] Import restrictions on cars were lifted in Hainan, implying that the situation was now under control.[8] The proposal to set up a SEZ in Wuhan also reflected a more positive attitude towards SEZs.[9] Confidence in the stability of the Open Policy was also strong when Deng Xiaoping announced to a US delegation that the Open Policy would last through the next century.[10]

The onset of a new cycle in the evolution of the Open Policy was marked not only by major concessions to foreign investors but also by the revelation of a further regional expansion of the Open Policy. One of the key protagonists of this view at the national level was Ji Chongwei who stated: 'If we truly want to open up every corner of China, we must further open up China's North West, North East and other border areas.'[11]

The meaning of Ji Chongwei's statement was clear. China was now to expand economic relations with the USSR and East Europe. Trade between the Soviet Union and China had already increased from US\$ 200 million in 1981 to US\$ 2 billion in 1985. Moreover, in 1986 Vice-Premier Yao Yilin visited the Soviet Union and concluded agreements which would increase the volume of trade between the two countries to US\$ 30 billion. In December 1986 an article was published in the provincial paper outlining a plan to develop Liaoning as an export-oriented zone, indicating a revival of Gu Mu's proposal in 1985 to open this area.[12] This reaffirmed the existence of not only specific regional interests in the direction of trade but also a pro-Soviet lobby within the top leadership.

Underlying this policy shift was not only a desire to increase trade with the Soviet Union but also to gain easier access to Europe's market. It was argued that whilst shipping goods from China to Europe required 50 days, by land only half the time was required.[13] Moreover, China's continuing trade deficit with Japan meant that China was keen to diversify its sources of capital. By strengthening its economic relations with the Soviet Union, China would also be able to drive a wedge between the USA and USSR in the future.

By 1987 the situation had improved again with the number of foreign direct investment agreements signed rising 50 per cent to 2233 with a total pledged investment of US\$ 3.7 billion (see Table 3.1). Although the 22 regulations encouraged foreign direct investment, there were still doubts, however, amongst foreign investors whether they would be properly implemented at the local level.[14]

The shift in attitude towards wholly owned foreign enterprises as signalled in the new piece of legislation was further reinforced in early 1987 when

Table 3.1 Annual foreign direct investment in China by type: 1979 to September 1992

Type	1979–82	1983	1984	1985	1986	1987	1988	1989	1990	1991	1992
EJV											
No. of agreements	83	107	741	1,412	892	1,395	3,900	3,659	4,091	na	na
FDI pledged ($m)	128	188	1,060	2,029	1,375	1,950	3,133	2,659	2,704	na	na
FDI realised ($m)	103	74	254	579	804	1,485	1,975	2,037	1,886	na	na
CJV											
No. of agreements	792	331	1,089	1,611	582	789	1,621	1,179	1,317	na	na
FDI pledged ($m)	2,726	504	2,207	3,496	1,358	1,283	1,624	1,083	1,254	na	na
FDI realised ($m)	292	238	465	585	793	619	779	751	673	na	na
WOFE											
No. of agreements	33	15	26	46	18	46	410	931	1,860	na	na
FDI pledged ($m)	367	4	99	45	20	471	481	1,653	2,443	na	na
FDI realised ($m)	40	28	14	12	16	24	226	371	683	na	na
JOINT OIL DEVELOP.											
No. of agreements	13	18	0	4	6	3	5	10	5	na	na
FDI pledged ($m)	1,392	1,031	0	359	81	5	59	203	194	na	na
FDI realised ($m)	486	296	520	480	260	183	212	232	244	na	na
Total											
No. of agreements	921	471	1,856	3,073	1,498	2,233	5,936	5,779	7,273	12,280	28,000
FDI pledged ($m)	4,613	1,727	2,366	5,929	2,834	3,709	5,297	5,559	6,596	4,370	na
FDI realised ($m)	921	636	1,253	1,656	1,873	2,311	3,193	3,391	3,486	na	na

Note: na = not available.

Sources: Compiled from: Chen, Nai-Ruenn, 1986, p. 8; Khan, 1991; 1989–90: *Statistical Yearbook of China 1991* (in Chinese), p. 629; *Foreign Economic Trade Yearbook of China 1991* (in Chinese); XH in SWB/FE/W0256 A/1 11.11.92.

the decentralisation of the authority to approve wholly owned enterprises to provincial-level authorities came onto the agenda.[15] Legislation for wholly owned foreign enterprises covering taxation, labour, import/export was still required, whilst a law for contractual joint ventures had yet to be drafted. The increase in international commercial loans continued into 1987. In January there was a further decentralisation of authority over foreign borrowing when the Bank of China revealed that some local branches would also be permitted to raise funds on the international market.[16]

This upswing in the policy cycle was braked, however, by mounting concern over the economy and the launch of the anti-bourgeois liberalisation campaign in early 1987. This in turn shook the confidence of foreign investors and government officials in the political stability of China.[17] At the same time there were indications of a further tightening of central control over the economy, particularly investment expenditure, suggesting that the previous attempts at restoring economic order had not been sufficiently effective.[18] There were reports of cuts in credit to Chinese buyers and withdrawal of projects for review. Foreign exchange reserves were rumoured to be critically low and some foreign companies reported delays in payment for equipment.[19] Moreover, in an interview with a French envoy, Li Peng warned 'you must be psychologically prepared for some projects to be rejected or restudied'.[20]

Tensions between the conservative, moderate and radical reformers over the pace and extent of reform and opening up had been brewing since the summer of 1986. Although the policy advances in foreign borrowing and foreign direct investment indicated that the radical reformers retained the upper hand, the conservatives were still pressing for restraint. The issuing of the spiritual civilisation resolution at the Sixth Plenum of the Twelfth Central Committee in September coupled with the outbreak of the student demonstrations in December 1986 provided the opportunity for the hardline conservatives, such as Peng Zhen and Deng Liqun, to hit back at the radical reformers. By attributing the calls for democracy and a multi-party system as well as the apparent increase in crime to 'excessive Westernisation', the conservatives were able through the anti-bourgeois liberalisation campaign to attack the Open Policy.

Similar to the spiritual pollution campaign, this campaign linked the spread of Western ideas such as 'bourgeois democracy' and 'unhealthy practices' such as gambling, prostitution and corruption to the opening up to the West. Student demonstrations calling for democracy in the winter of 1986 as well as demands by some intellectuals for a multi-party system not only were of concern to the less radical reformers but also highlighted the political contradictions of the Open Policy. The anti-bourgeois liberalisation campaign was again linked to Peng Zhen and Deng Liqun, who now headed propaganda affairs in the National People's Congress.

Since the demise of the spiritual pollution campaign, Peng Zhen had sought through other means to constrain the pace of opening up and reform. At the People's Congress in May 1984 he stated that the Standing Committee of the People's Congress was above the State Council. Moreover, in order to increase his influence over foreign economic relations, Peng Zhen proposed not only that the People's Congress should have a larger role in China's international economic relations, but also that a new Ministry of State Security dealing with external espionage should be established. Following the Third Central Committee plenum in October 1984 Peng Zhen addressed an informal meeting of members of the National People's Congress, stating that the policies proposed at the Plenum were only valid if codified in law.[21] By insisting on the need to legislate policy, he sought to undermine the legitimacy of Deng's reform programme and the Open Policy.

At the same time, however, supporters of the Open Policy confirmed its continuity and stability. Gu Mu maintained that the reformers were still in control and that the negative impact of the campaign was less than imagined.[22] According to Gu Mu one of the major problems was that China had not opened sufficiently. Moreover, he indicated that the SEZs would continue to take the lead in the Open Policy. Attention was now to be concentrated on ensuring the implementation of existing policies and the improvement of the operation of joint ventures.[23] In line with this, 12 supplementary regulations for encouraging foreign direct investment were issued in March 1987.[24]

Although it was not feared that the anti-bourgeois liberalisation campaign signalled a second Cultural Revolution, there were nevertheless doubts both at home and abroad about the stability of the reformist leadership.[25] Provincial and municipal cadres were also hesitant in taking any major decisions, particularly as the balance of power might shift in the approaching Thirteenth Party Congress.

By the spring of 1987 the effects of the anti-bourgeois liberalisation campaign had abated. The reformers felt confident enough to express their intentions to open even further. In a meeting with the US Secretary of Commerce, Rong Yiren, chairperson of China International Trust and Investment Company, revealed that China's Open Policy would be 'maintained and expanded'.[26] In August 1987 it was revealed that Hainan Island would not only acquire provincial status but would also become a SEZ.[27] Moreover, it was to adopt even more liberal policies than in other parts of China. This change was to come into force from 1988.

As well as the regional expansion of the Open Policy, restrictions on domestic sales were relaxed further in October 1987. Newly opened foreign-invested enterprises and those facing foreign exchange imbalances were permitted to sell part of their products on the domestic market.[28] At the same time Shenzhen proceeded with further reforms.[29]

Whilst the reformers granted more concessions to foreign investors, they still maintained central control over foreign trade. The urgent need to develop exports led, however, to the generation of some new foreign trade policies in early 1987. This included, first, the granting of preferential policies for the construction of national sectoral export commodity bases, and in particular for the machinery and electronics industry, which were considered crucial for the realisation of the Seventh five-year plan.[30]

Second, a contract responsibility system was proposed. The Ministry of Foreign Economic Relations and Trade would sign contracts stipulating export and cost quotas with its subordinate companies which in turn would sign contracts with provincial branches and so on. This would, however, strengthen central control over foreign trade. Third, an import/export licence system was introduced to simplify procedures.[31] Central control over foreign trade continued to be tight compared to the decentralisation heyday of 1984.

This policy towards foreign trade contrasted starkly with the advances made in foreign direct investment policy in 1987. The reason for this difference lies with the domestic economic reforms. It had become increasingly apparent in the past three years that the success of any reforms in the foreign trade system would be contingent upon further reforms in the domestic economic system, particularly regarding the enterprise and price system.

Before forging ahead with further trade reforms, the reformers aimed first to restore order in foreign trade and await the outcome of the Thirteenth Party Congress. Also wary of the outcome of this congress, Chinese officials involved in foreign economic relations took a cautious, risk-minimising approach to their work. Nevertheless, 1987 did witness an increase in the level of foreign direct investment and an improvement in the foreign trade deficit.

Cycle 5 — riding high, falling fast: 1987 to mid-1990

The further consolidation of the reformers' position at the Thirteenth Party Congress signalled the onset of a new cycle in the evolution of the Open Policy. Plans to deepen and extend the process of opening up quickly became apparent. For example, at the end of the year it was announced that 'inland' SEZs would be set up along the Yangtse River and in Jiangxi province.[32] Hainan was to become a province and Guangdong and Fujian provinces were to become experimental areas for overall reform.[33]

As well as pushing inwards the Open Policy was also to spread lengthways along the coast. In early 1988 Zhao Ziyang revealed his coastal development strategy which aimed at opening the whole coastal strip to the international capitalist economy. Although the inland areas were also to enjoy some privileges in their foreign economic relations, they were to play a less direct role in the external economy. Frontier cities formed the 'second line' in the opening up process and in cooperation with the inland cities were to target neighbouring Eastern Europe and the Soviet Union.[34] This revealed a firm commitment to stronger economic links with its former socialist adversaries.

One of the first inland cities to take advantage of this upswing was Wuhan. In June 1988 the mayor of Wuhan announced at a press conference that Wuhan would adopt the same open policies as the 14 coastal cities.[35] Beijing too won new privileges in foreign trade and investment, putting it on a par with coastal cities.[36] Competition to attract foreign capital was intensifying as towns along the coast hurried to set up processing zones for foreign companies regardless of local conditions.[37]

Reassured of a favourable climate foreign investors seized the opportunity to set up new businesses. In the first four months of 1988 1061 foreign-invested enterprises registered, over three times the number in the same period of 1987.[38] Taiwanese investment also took off from early 1988. More contracts were signed then than over the previous five years.[39] Plans were afoot to improve the legislative framework to attract more foreign investors. There were indications that new preferential policies were in line, covering tax, land use fees and labour and that foreign investors might be allowed to chair joint venture boards.[40] In May 1988 the State Council approved new regulations governing the hiring rights of joint ventures.[41] Symptomatic of this forward movement was the approval given to China's first private joint venture in Dongguan, Guangdong. Zhang Jijian, owner of six factories, received permission to set up a joint venture with a Hong Kong firm.[42]

In this wave of optimism the central government granted Hainan more special policies, giving it greater decision-making powers in theory than any other province or SEZ.[43] More innovation came in July when the central government issued new regulations granting Taiwanese investors special privileges.[44] In the same month Shenzhen set up a new form of investment, namely a bonded industrial zone.[45] Shen Jueren, Vice-Minister of Foreign Economic Relations and Trade, also announced new regulations which would further decentralise foreign trade, facilitate barter trade with the Soviet Union and Eastern Europe and increase the power of coastal areas to approve foreign investment.[46] However, the centre was well aware of the threat foreign enterprises could pose to local industry. So to increase exports and protect local industry it introduced new regulations restricting joint venture domestic sales in July. In October 1988 the Ministry of Foreign Economic Relations and Trade again indicated that plans were afoot to improve the legislative framework of foreign investment.

There were hints that local governments would be allowed to approve cooperative projects worth less than US$ 30 million.[47]

Greater flexibility in the banking sphere also became possible. The Bank of China increased its foreign currency loan quota to support export production in the coastal areas.[48] At a symposium on international finance held in May 1988, there was a discussion about allowing foreign banks to operate in coastal cities.[49] In June 1988 the Bank of China gave foreign banks permission to conduct business in Rmb in the SEZs, again another step towards improving investment conditions.[50]

Despite these policy overtures to deepen and expand the Open Policy there were already signs that the economy was facing increasing difficulties. By mid-1988 the state administration of currency control was sounding warning bells. The foreign debt was growing too fast for comfort.[51] Moreover, the situation was likely to worsen once central and local foreign trade departments were separated. Chinese academics predicted that the debt repayment rate would rise from 10 per cent to 15 per cent in the 1990s, well below the internationally recognised danger line of 20 per cent, but nevertheless troubling to a leadership which was always anxious about the implications of heavy indebtedness.[52] By November 1988 private commercial debt had risen to US$ 5.02 billion, 40 per cent more than at the beginning of the year.[53] A burgeoning trade deficit with the USA and Japan added to the anxieties of top leaders.[54]

The decentralisation of foreign trade and foreign exchange management had taken its toll. In 1988 alone over 2000 foreign trade enterprises were authorised to engage in foreign trade.[55] Moreover, township and village enterprises, which were developed to deal with the problem of rural surplus labour, were also becoming increasingly active in the export economy, highlighting again the gradual intermeshing of the processes of domestic reform and opening up.[56] The proliferation of companies and enterprises engaged in foreign trade had led once again to a loss of central control. Moreover, the dual price system along with decentralisation provided opportunities for state cadres to line their own private purses. Corruption continued to be an unwelcome thorn in the side of the Party. In September 1988 Li Hao, City Party Secretary of Shenzhen, drew attention to the abuse of power amongst Party and state cadres and called for new measures to be drawn up to crack down on this.[57] Similar concerns were expressed at the Second Plenum of the Hainan Provincial CCP Committee.[58] These difficulties in the economy provided an ideal opportunity for the conservatives to voice their dissatisfaction with the pace and trend of opening up and reform.

Alarmed by this burgeoning foreign debt and growing bilateral trade deficit the Minister of Foreign Economic Relations and Trade, Zheng Tuobin, announced in October 1988 five measures to strengthen central control over the foreign trade sector. This marked the onset of the downswing in the fifth cycle. The measures included reining in so-called 'briefcase companies', restoring order over the procurement of export commodities, managing more strictly the issuing of licences and planning of foreign trade, promoting an agency system and improving import controls. At a national conference on foreign trade planning in October 1988 Vice-Premier Tian Jiyun again reiterated the urgency of strengthening central control over foreign trade enterprises and those cities with preferential foreign trade powers.[59] In the same month the State Council decided to withdraw the prefential foreign exchange retention rates of the SEZs, allowing them to retain only 80 per cent like the rest of the country.[60] This tightening of central control over the localities was paralleled by the onset of a rectification campaign within the domestic economic sphere.

It was against this background of growing difficulties in the domestic and external economy, that Huan Xian, member of the National People's Congress and Director of the State Council's International Studies Centre, published an article criticising Zhao Ziyang's coastal development strategy.[61] One month later an article in the *People's Daily* betrayed worrying doubts within the leadership about the appropriateness of the coastal development strategy during a period of rectification.[62] Concern was also expressed over rapid price rises as regions and enterprises competed furiously to capture domestic inputs in short supply. Reform and opening up were put on hold again as the reformers tried to reassert macroeconomic control over the economy.

To allay the fears of foreign investors Tian Jiyun stated clearly at a China People's Political Consultative Conference forum on opening up held in early December that the Open Policy was a 'basic policy that would not change'.[63] Moreover, along with Zhao Ziyang he urged foreign investors to set up not only more joint ventures but also more wholly owned foreign enterprises, reflecting less suspicion on the part of the reformers about this form of investment.[64] Although almost 6000 foreign-invested enterprises involving over US$ 5.2 billion were agreed in 1988, the last quarter saw a fall in foreign investment as rectification got underway.[65] China's top tax official hinted at corporate income tax reductions of at least 17 per cent in the hope of staving off a further decline.[66]

Radical reformers such as Zhao Ziyang fought back to keep the process of opening up on the go. During the spring festival of 1989 Zhao visited Shenzhen SEZ. His positive endorsement of Shenzhen's potential for further reform and opening up consoled local officials who, having lost their foreign exchange retention privileges, had begun to doubt the future of Shenzhen.[67]

Attempts to bring foreign trade under control continued into the next year with the ban of imported cigarettes and alcohol.[68] Plans were afoot to rectify 5000 enterprises engaged in import and export. However, the prospects for improving exports looked grim as quality remained a problem and the rate of contract implementation dropped.[69]

The overheating of the domestic economy, rising inflation and growing discontent with state corruption soon translated into the political sphere. The death of Hu Yaobang in April 1989 sparked a wave of student protest. Hu in particular had been a prominent advocate of intellectual freedom and political reform. He had supported protests in December 1986 and was forced to resign in January 1987. This was followed by the statutory 4 May student demonstrations which snowballed into calls for political reform, an end to economic corruption and inflation.[70] The unrest soon spread to the provincial cities. The students were joined by workers and clerical staff. The streets of China's major cities seethed with discontent. As the students marched into Tiananmen Square, set up their tents and went on hunger strike, the eyes of the world focused on the upheaval in China. The massacre of 4 June shocked the world. Horrified by accounts of thousands killed Western governments and donor agencies imposed economic sanctions on what was now described as the brutal Dengist regime. Foreign loans were frozen, diplomatic exchanges halted and new projects cancelled.

The political crisis of 1989 witnessed major changes in leadership at central and local levels over the next two years as cadres close to Zhao Ziyang were ousted from leading positions. Zhao, one of the key protagonists of the Open Policy, was now under house arrest. The Governor of Hainan, Liang Xiang, also an innovating reformer and staunch supporter of opening up, was replaced in September by his deputy secretary, Liu Jianfeng, fuelling doubts amongst foreign investors about the stability of the government and continuity of the Open Policy and reforms.[71] Liang Xiang had sent a telegram urging the State Council to talk with the student strikers; he was ousted on the charges of embezzlement and nepotism.[72] In July 1990 Xu Shijie, Party Secretary of Hainan, was replaced by Deng Hongxun from Jiangsu. Xu had apparently been close to Zhao Ziyang.[73] In January 1990 Yuan Geng, the chairperson of China Merchants' Steamship Navigation Company of Shekou, was dismissed. Shekou was for long held up as the pioneer of reform and opening up. Open criticism of the Shekou model reflected not only a direct attack upon Zhao Ziyang but also underlying divisions within the leadership over the Open Policy.[74] With the radical Zhao now out of the way the stage was free for a virulent assault upon the Open Policy.

The Propaganda Department, a well-known conservative stronghold, launched yet another anti-bourgeois liberalisation campaign.[75] At the same time public security hunted out those who had participated in the demonstrations. Dissidents were imprisoned. Students were sent to work in the countryside and to participate in military training. As news filtered out about the persecution of dissidents China's human rights record became a key issue in international relations. The tanks in Tiananmen and the subsequent wave of persecution served to isolate China politically.

The Tiananmen massacre also meant a further loss of legitimacy for the Party. According to a report issued by the CCP Central Commission for Discipline Inspection over two years later, almost 800 000 party members had been involved in the political turmoil.[76] Moreover, between May and July 1989 around 90 000 party members throughout the country tried to leave the party; 8000 party cadres also submitted their resignations. The report also stated that almost a third of party organisations had not been able to carry on their normal organisational work since 1989.[77]

The imposition of economic sanctions along with perceptions of China as politically unstable took its toll upon the economy. According to the World Bank the growth rate of foreign direct investment came to only 5.7 per cent in 1989, compared to 42.8 per cent in 1988 and 30.9 per cent in 1987.[78] In the last quarter of 1989 foreign direct investment fell by 43 per cent compared to the same period the previous year.[79] The slowdown in investment from the USA and Japan was more dramatic than that of Taiwan.[80]

Existing enterprises continued to operate, however. Chinese official sources claim that 85 per cent of foreign-invested enterprises were operating normally in the immediate aftermath of Tiananmen.[81] But rectification was exacerbating the operations of some foreign-invested enterprises as working funds became harder to obtain, leading the Bank of China to increase its foreign exchange loans to foreign-invested enterprises in early 1990.[82]

Particularly hard hit was Guangdong province, which was home to over half of China's foreign-invested enterprises. Moreover, these enterprises accounted for 35 per cent of the province's exports. Guangdong also relied on foreign commercial banks for over 30 per cent of its hard currency funds.[83] Rectification had already brought about the closure by mid-1989 of 600 import and export companies in Guangdong province, as well as 100 Guangdong companies operating in Hong Kong and Macao.[84] One month after the massacre around 900 foreign engineers, technicians and management personnel had been withdrawn from Guangdong, affecting over 400 enterprises.[85] Contracts were halted, negotiations suspended and loans withdrawn. Uncertain of the political climate foreign investors were hesitant to invest more money in China. The Japanese Rinnai Corporation, for example, postponed a technical aid contract with Guangdong because of the uncertainties of the political and economic situation.[86]

With foreign loans frozen China had to dig into its own foreign exchange reserves to finance projects and imports. Increasing exports became an even more urgent task. Rectification of foreign trade companies continued over the year. In November 1989 the Ministry of Foreign Economic Relations and Trade proposed a further tightening up of these companies to the State Council. Exports managed to hover 5 per cent above the 1988 figure but were still a concern to the leadership as debt repayments became due in the 1990s.[87] The situation could have been worse had foreign industrial and commercial interests also refused to trade with China.

The situation in Guangdong became so dire that a national meeting was held in May 1990. The deputy director of Guangdong Foreign Economic Relations and Trade Commission revealed that almost half of foreign-invested enterprises in the province were losing money and around one-fifth of such enterprises had closed down over the past decade.[88] The withholding of loans from international financial organisations continued to aggravate the crisis. Hainan province also suffered a setback. The first half of 1990 saw a 70 per cent fall in the number of new contracts signed and in the amount of foreign investment absorbed.[89] The vice-governor attributed this to international sanctions, rectification and the shift in focus towards Pudong in Shanghai.[90] Moreover, rectification had led to the closure of over one-third of enterprises on Hainan Island.[91] Continuing controversy over the grand Yangpu project in Hainan delayed its approval. In particular the granting of a 70-year lease to the Japanese consortium to develop Yangpu brought the issue of sovereignty onto the agenda of the National People's Congress in 1989. Zhuhai SEZ also saw a fall in exports and trade in 1989 as well as the closure of one-third of its factories.[92]

In the first six months of 1990 the contractual value of new foreign-invested enterprises fell 22 per cent compared to the same period in 1989.[93] Nevertheless, there was an outstanding increase in wholly owned foreign enterprises. By April 1990 over 1879 such enterprises had registered involving US$ 5.06 billion of contracted investment. Over half of these had been approved in 1989, exceeding the total of the previous years.[94] This reflected both a recognition of the difficulties in running joint ventures, as well as a relaxation of attitude towards full foreign ownership particularly given the hostile international context.

How then did the reformers respond to the negative impact of international sanctions? First, the need to increase exports and cut imports became even more imperative. Devaluation of the Rmb in 1989 was an obvious measure to take. Second, aware of the intensifying global competition for foreign investment, improvements in the foreign investment legislative framework continued. Work on a new joint venture law planned for the spring went ahead. This included a pledge not to expropriate joint ventures, which was aimed not only at improving the long-term investment climate but also at allaying any short-term fears about the situation in China.[95] The National

People's Congress also hoped to speed up the drafting of other legislation concerning foreign trade, maritime law and foreign exchange.[96] New preferential policies to encourage foreign investment in Shantou SEZ were introduced in early 1990.[97]

Third, the post-Tiananmen leadership continued to affirm their commitment to reform and opening up. Politics and economics were separate affairs. At a National Conference on the SEZs held in February 1990, for example, Li Peng called for greater use of market forces in the SEZs than the rest of the country.[98] However, his reference to combining this with a planned economy reflected a far less radical approach than that of his adversary Zhao Ziyang.

Fourth, international sanctions made the Chinese leadership painfully aware of the dangers of 'tilting' too much in one direction. This hard lesson prompted China to diversify its trade links further and indeed to rethink its regional strategy of opening up. In early 1990 the State Council outlined an 'all-round open strategy' which identified three main regions for opening up: the Pearl River Delta, which would target Southeast Asia and Hong Kong, the Bohai area and the north-west centring on Xinjiang, which would target the Soviet Union and the Middle East.[99] Western rejection had led China to cultivate more and closer economic and diplomatic ties with neighbouring countries and the Third World and to accelerate links with Eastern Europe and the Soviet Union. In 1990 China restored relations with both Indonesia and Singapore.

Particularly interesting was the switch in focus away from the SEZs towards Shanghai. The downfall of the radical Zhao had vindicated the doubts long expressed by conservative and moderate reformers about go-ahead Guangdong and Fujian and their SEZs. Chen Yun had indeed never set foot in Shenzhen. The growing autonomy and economic leverage of these two provinces was a crucial concern of central leaders who were keen to maintain political stability, national unity and macroeconomic control. Moreover, the very economic success of Guangdong and Fujian meant that the centre could now squeeze them through taxation and allow Shanghai to flourish. Li Peng followed his visit to the SEZs with a trip to Shanghai in April 1990. There he announced plans to let Shanghai enjoy investment incentives enjoyed previously only by Shenzhen and Xiamen.[100] Pudong was to become a free port and financial centre on a par with Hong Kong.

Officials in the SEZs were anxious, however, that Shanghai fever would mark the end of their privileges and prosperity.[101] The economy of the SEZs had already been hard hit by the rectification policies. At the National Work Conference on SEZs held in February 1990 the Shenzhen government pushed for more privileges from the central government, and in particular, the opening up of the border with Hong Kong.[102] Central leaders, however, introduced more controls at the conference, limiting bank credit and requiring the SEZs to pass on more revenue to the centre.[103] Pressure from Shenzhen for further opening continued. In March Shenzhen submitted a plan for approval to the State Council to set up a bonded industrial area and a duty-free raw materials market and to expand the securities market.[104] In March and April the State Council circulated a draft of the eighth five-year plan to the provinces. Proposals to curb the financial powers of the provinces angered lower level officials.[105] This added to the anxieties of cadres in the zones.

This central backing for Pudong had significant implications not only for the position of the older SEZs but in particular for the development of Hainan SEZ. Despite calls from Hainan officials for greater central investment the central government remained insistent that Hainan rely on policies to attract foreign capital.[106] Central concern over sovereignty with regard to contracting land to foreigners now fell into the background. Hainan officials clearly felt that Hainan was losing out in its development to Pudong.[107]

By June 1990 the developmental significance of Pudong and Shanghai was becoming increasingly clear. In a speech made to foreign guests, Vice-Premier Yao Yilin pointed to a new phase in the Open Policy. Whilst the first decade of reform and opening up had focused on Guangdong and Fujian, the next decade was to centre on Pudong.[108] This attention from the centre was eagerly coveted by local officials. In July 1990 the Vice-Mayor of Shanghai, Huang Ju, proclaimed the city's pivotal role in economic restructuring. He likened the relationship between Shanghai and China to that of Hong Kong and Guangdong. Moreover, Shanghai would concentrate on secondary and tertiary industries whilst the zones would focus on labour-intensive production.[109] Yet at the National Work Conference in February 1990 Li Peng had urged the SEZs to focus on technology- rather than labour-intensive industry.[110] In August the Bank of China provided a US$ 200 million loan for capital construction in Pudong over the next two years.[111] Underlying this central focus on Pudong was the intention to open up China even further.[112]

Rectification and international sanctions led to stagnation in the economy. Restrictions on credit as well as a fall in consumer demand had a negative impact on industrial growth rates. Inflation was nevertheless getting under control, falling from 18.5 per cent in 1988 to 2.1 per cent in 1990.[113] Ironically China was able to bring its foreign trade back into balance as exports grew proportionately to imports (see Table 2.1). Technology import contracts in 1990 were half what they were in 1989.[114] By mid-1990 China was already enjoying a trade surplus. The worst period of rectification from the second half of 1989 to the first half of 1990 was now over. Inflation was still a potential threat and the budget looked as though it could lurch into deficit again early on in the year.[115] As the medicine of rectification began to take effect and sanctions against China began gradually to relax in mid-1990 the Chinese leadership became bolder again in reform and opening up, but not without some struggles as we shall see in the next cycle.

Cycle 6 — on track again: mid-1990 to 1992

The final cycle in China's Open Policy was triggered by the relaxation of international economic sanctions from mid-1990 onwards as well as the overall improvement in the economy as a result of rectification. This then provided a favourable and more secure context within which to push ahead with further policy changes. By this time imports were beginning to pick up, foreign investment was increasing and exports continued to rise.[116] The Taiwanese government took a more relaxed approach to mainland investment, issuing a list in July of 2000 product categories suitable for investment in China.[117] In September a central work conference announced satisfaction with the impact of rectification, marking an end to this period of austerity. By the end of 1990 China had a trade surplus of US$ 8.54 billion, the first since 1984. Moreover foreign exchange reserves had increased from US$ 17 billion in 1989 to US$ 26 billion in 1990.[118] Also symptomatic of this upturn was a rapid increase in China's foreign debt, especially in the last quarter of 1990.[119] Similarly, 7273 foreign investment contracts were approved in 1990, worth a total of US$ 6.6 billion.

With this more favourable political and economic climate the reformers were able to develop the Open Policy further. The elaboration of the eighth five-year plan and ten-year development programme provided the opportunity for a revitalisation of reform and opening up. The ten-year development programme promised a further regional expansion of the Open Policy. Whilst the fifth cycle focused on the coastal strategy, this final cycle extended the process of opening up to the inland frontiers of China. International political isolation had underlined the importance of keeping on good terms with neighbours and in fact served to accelerate these economic linkages. Some inland cities and areas on the borders would be selected as 'windows', a metaphor first used for the SEZs.[120] This process was in fact already underway, illustrating how policy formulation is often pre-empted in practice. In September 1990 Xingang economic zone in Liaoning province opened to foreign investors.

The SEZ and ETDZ forms were used to initiate this regional expansion. At the end of 1990 a new SEZ in Suifenhe, Heilongjiang opened, strengthening ties with the Soviet Union and North Korea.[121] Hubei was also setting up an ETDZ in Gedian, near Wuhan, to attract foreign capital.[122] In February Guangxi set up the first Overseas Chinese investment zone in Nanning, giving preferential policies to Overseas Chinese, Taiwan, Hong Kong and Macao.[123] In April the State Council approved 26 new high tech development zones bringing the total to 38.[124]

In June 1991 the central government approved a plan to set up an export outlet in Yunnan and an economic development zone on the border. By turning to Burma and Southeast Asia Yunnan could export industrial goods whereas if it oriented itself to the West it would only be able to export raw materials.[125] In July 1991 three cities in Heilongjiang were designated special open-door market zones to facilitate economic and trade links with East Siberia. These cities would receive preferential policies to promote trade and investment as in the SEZs.[126]

At the same time, however, centre—local relations were becoming increasingly fraught. The attempt to curb the financial powers of provinces in the draft eighth five-year plan had led to fierce resistance from provincial officials. When called to Beijing in September 1990, a group of leaders headed by the governor of Guangdong protested at this attempt at recentralisation and demanded more reforms. They succeeded in getting some revisions into the draft.[127] Officials from the zone were clearly worried by the central emphasis on Pudong. So during his visit to Shenzhen in November 1990 Jiang Zemin affirmed that the policy of SEZs was correct and should be continued.[128]

However, at the Seventh Plenary Session in December 1990 the central leadership continued to call for a recentralisation of financial power as state revenue had fallen to 18 per cent of GNP compared to 30 per cent before.[129] The gradual expansion of the private and individual sectors over the last decade along with greater financial powers to regional governments and some enterprises was now seriously beginning to undermine the economic base of the central state. Moreover, localities were providing their own preferential incentives to foreign capital.[130] In February it was announced that Ye Yuanping would leave his post as governor of Guangdong. By transferring him to Beijing to become vice-chair of the China People's Political Consultative Conference, it was hoped to weaken the autonomy of Guangdong.[131]

The ten-year development programme also gave the green light to a further restructuring of the foreign trade system. This included the implementation of the agency and contract systems and the abolition of subsidies on export commodities, implying a reduction in state control over foreign trade.[132] The introduction of a unified foreign exchange retention system according to commodity and not region was deliberately aimed, however, at curbing the foreign exchange privileges of local governments, trade companies and enterprises, and in particular the SEZs. Similarly, the call for restrictions on the import of consumer goods in the eighth five-year plan was an attempt to clamp down on irrational imports and in particular the spending habits of the localities.[133] These reforms were also aimed at bringing the foreign trade system more in line with international practice so that China could enter GATT.[134]

The Ministry of Foreign Economic Relations and Trade also approved the opening of more foreign trade ports. In February 1991 11 new foreign trade ports opened on the borders with Mongolia, Soviet Union and Laos, bringing the total to 150.[135] Two more ports in Fujian and Guangxi were also under discussion.[136]

The Gulf War brought home to the reformers and the military once again the significance of high-tech modern warfare. The eighth five-year plan included a 12 per cent increase in defence expenditure in 1991 with more funds promised over the five years.[137] Although this was in part to placate the army, it was also a response to the rapidly changing international situation. Top priority was accorded to developing the electronics industry, which can serve both civilian and military purposes.[138] Moreover, in March 1991 Li Peng changed the order of the 'four modernisations' putting science and technology in first place.[139] Modernising China and in particular its defence capability was more important than ever.

Although the post-Tiananmen leadership had consistently maintained its commitment to reform and opening up, the Seventh Plenary Session at the end of 1990 provided the opportunity for those seeking more reform to push for this. Yuan Mu, for example, stressed that China must open up 'without hesitation' and that China would be 'hopeless without the Open Policy'.[140] Li Peng was now calling for deeper reform and more opening. With the economy now back on course Deng Xiaoping was manouevring behind the scenes to weaken the hold of the conservatives over the Party and state and hasten the process of reform.

Deng Xiaoping now sought the help of Li Peng and Jiang Zemin, urging them to 'pay more attention to the economy'. This reference to the economy rather than ideology pointed to increasing tensions between the conservatives and the reformers. The conservatives had taken full advantage of the 1989 upheavals. As this political crisis had called for a strengthening of ideological and political control, the conservatives felt vindicated in their emphasis on ideology.

The CCP had also to act against the corruption both within its own corridors of power and within society. The CCP needed a 'clean image' more than ever. Throughout 1990 and early 1991 the reformers tried desperately to purge corruption openly and legitimise itself morally before the masses. The Mao craze which was sweeping parts of China in early 1991 symbolised both the loss of legitimacy of the Party and the ideological and spiritual vacuum amongst youth. In Guangdong and Shenzhen there were reports of Mao portraits being hung in shops, hotels and businesses.

Taxi drivers in Liaoning province hung miniature Mao portraits from their car windows.[141] Conservatives such as Deng Liqun made use of this Mao craze indirectly to challenge the nature of opening up. By interpreting this craze as a celebration of the 'golden 1950s' when the economy was sound, officials honest and relations between people were harmonious, they were implying that radical reform had contributed to ideological and moral degeneration.[142] Deng, however, sought the legitimisation of the Party in terms of the performance of the economy.

The struggles within the leadership intensified during the year. The key divisions regarding the Open Policy were between the conservatives, who emphasised ideology and restraint, the moderates, who advocated a slower pace of opening up and reform with a definite role for the plan, and again the 'radical reformers' who wanted to push ahead with market reform but without tampering too much with the political system. Deng Xiaoping was skilfully switching camp again from the moderates towards the radicals. The influence of former 'radical reformers' such as Zhao Ziyang who advocated substantial political reform as well was still greatly subdued. However, continuing references in the press to discussions about the possible return of Zhao Ziyang suggested that at least at the economic level Zhao's ideas were still treated seriously.[143]

A boost for the radical reformers came with the reappearance of Hu Qili at the National People's Congress Session in March 1991.[144] In April Zhu Rongji, Party Secretary of Shanghai and Zou Jiahua became vice-premiers, both of whom had lost their posts after Tiananmen. The appointment of Zhu in particular served to strengthen the hand of the more radical reformers. Qian Qichen became a state councillor.[145] Some older leaders stepped down. Zheng Tuobin, for example, who had pioneered many of the reforms in foreign trade was replaced by a Li Peng nominee, Li Lanqing.[146] There were also rumours that Ye Xueping, a strong supporter of reform and opening up in Guangdong might replace Li Xiannian.[147]

The struggle within the leadership was also mirrored in the discussion of whether or not to rehabilitate Zhao Ziyang. Deng Xiaoping was trying to have the Zhao issue resolved at the Fourteenth Party Congress in October 1992. Chen Yun and Deng Liqun were still opposed to any rehabilitation of Zhao. It was rumoured in the Hong Kong press that Deng Liqun and Wang Zhen had been discrediting Zhao Ziyang in their speeches in the provinces, referring to him as a 'bourgeois agent'. At a theoretical symposium held in August the conservative Hu Qiaomu referred to the 'pro-American faction' within the party and society.[148] Both Deng Liqun and Gao Di, well-known conservatives, were present at this symposium.

The reemergence of the self-reliance debate also reflected ongoing struggle within the leadership. Those in favour of more reform countered the juxtaposition of self-reliance and Open Policy in the media. In his speech at the National People's Congress on 25 March 1991 Li Peng reportedly said: 'The policy of self-reliance does not contradict with the open policy . . . Opening up to the outside world and making use of foreign technology, experience and capital will be conducive to . . . China's . . . self-reliance.'[149] These sentiments were echoed by Yuan Mu, Director of the Policy Research Office of the State Council, at a meeting with over 60 foreign experts at the end of May 1991 in Beijing. In his words: 'opening to the outside world will enhance self-reliance, and . . . being more self-reliant will make it easier to introduce advanced technology and use funds from foreign countries.'[150]

Both the self-reliance issue and the Mao craze pointed to the strengthening of the conservatives. Clearly Deng Xiaoping was concerned about their growing influence which could endanger reform and opening up, but he was also aware of the need for some ideological control. At a theoretical study group meeting of the provincial CCP committee, participants said that Hainan was a socialist SEZ and not a political or cultural special zone, an argument reminiscent of the heated controversy over the zones in the mid-1980s. It was therefore important to develop spiritual civilisation as well.[151] Moreover, Deng was now pushing the issue of the abolition of the Central Advisory Commission onto the agenda. The Central Advisory Commission had become a bastion of opposition to further reform. Deng was keen to sweep this out of the way and promote younger people to positions in the Party and state.

In the first quarter of 1991 central leaders toured the provinces with the message that reform and opening up were very much on the agenda. The predominance of the conservatives in the aftermath of Tiananmen had also led to doubts amongst the masses about the continuity of reform and opening up. Chinese farmers who had prospered well under the agricultural reforms still needed reassurance that the tide of reform would continue. Moreover, the current focus on Shanghai still caused considerable anxiety and confusion in the zones about their role and status in the economy. So in early January Yang Shangkun visited Guangdong before going on to Shanghai for the spring festival.[152] In late February Song Jian and Li Ruihuan both made separate trips to Hainan whilst Bo Yibo visited Shenzhen.[153] The appointment of Xu Jingan, a reformer close to Zhao Ziyang, as head of the Shenzhen Municipal Commission for Restructuring the Economy reflected the continued commitment of Shenzhen to reform. It also showed the difficulty the hardliners had in purging the Party of all Zhao's supporters.

The following month Wang Zhen visited Shenzhen, then Xiamen and Fuzhou whilst Peng Zhen visited Shanghai.[154] Chen Yun's visit to Shanghai in May did little to allay the fears of officials in the zones, however, as he had not once set foot in Shenzhen.[155] Reassured somewhat by these central visits, the SEZs forged ahead with establishing more open policies.

In April the Hainan government began to draw up regulations to attract Taiwanese investment.[156] Shenzhen planned to adopt dual-line customs control and to set up two bonded zones.[157] Zou Jiahua visited Hainan in May 1991.[158] The same month Hainan opened a foreign exchange swap centre, bringing the total number of centres set up in China since 1988 to 1990.[159]

As well as visiting the zones, central leaders also ventured on long journeys to the border areas to endorse and promote opening up. In February, for example, Qiao Shi went to Yunnan to encourage trade links with Southeast Asia, reassuring them of the continuity of reform and opening up.[160] With the easing of relations with Taiwan, top leaders encouraged lower levels to favour Taiwanese investment. In May, for example, Vice-Premier Wu Xueqian and Wang Zhaoguo, director of the State Council Taiwan Office, went to Liaoning in part to encourage more Taiwanese investment.[161]

Although China's relations with the West had improved since mid-1990, top leaders continued to emphasise relations with the Third World.[162] Similarly, China continued to consolidate its links with the Soviet Union and Eastern Europe over the coming six months. In March 1991 the Soviet Deputy Premier went to China and signed a Sino-Soviet economic cooperation protocol, the first since the two countries switched from a clearing agreement to cash trade.[163] China agreed to give US$ 700 million in aid to the Soviet Union in return for arms.[164] In early April the Soviet Foreign Minister visited China. The following month the Soviet Defence Minister met Li Peng in China, reflecting China's continuing attempts to secure military cooperation from the Soviet Union after Tiananmen.[165] On 15 May Li Peng met Gorbachev in Moscow and could claim to be the highest Chinese official to visit the Soviet Union since 1957.[166] He also called upon the Ministers of Defence, Foreign Affairs and Foreign Trade.[167] The Soviet Union proposed a five-sided conference between the USSR, China, Japan, India and the USA to start a dialogue on the Asia-Pacific region.[168] During the same month an agreement for the first Sino-Soviet joint venture in China, a flax textile mill in Beijing, was signed.[169] In July 1991 Inner Mongolia opened four cities to direct border trade with the Soviet Union and passed regulations for foreign direct investment.[170]

Relations with Japan were almost back on an even keel. Moreover, Western rejection had encouraged China to consider more seriously its geostrategic role. In February 1991 China's Foreign Minister was proposing a new East Asian economic sphere with China and Japan at its core.[171]

Although sanctions against China had eased considerably by early 1991, relations with the USA and some Western countries were still not fully back to normal. When Western foreign ministers came, they still used the opportunity to reproach China on its poor human rights record. The United States were, however, the most reluctant to renew their relationships unconditionally. Signs of a turnround came in November 1990 when James Baker, Secretary of State, invited Qian Qichen to the USA. In March 1991 Zeng Tao became the first National People's Congress delegate to visit the USA since Tiananmen.[172] Throughout 1991 a fierce debate was raging between the State Department and Congress as to whether or not to grant China Most Favoured Nation (MFN) status. The US Congress had four major grievances: first, the issue of human rights and treatment of political prisoners after Tiananmen; second, the matter of exports of arms which might be used for nuclear purposes, particularly to its Arab foes; third, the question of intellectual property rights; and finally the question of Tibet.

China saw the sensitive matter of human rights as well as the issue of Tibet as an infringement on its own sovereignty. China was none too pleased when President Bush met the Dalai Lama at the White House on 17 April.[173] Moreover, it was very concerned by what it saw as attempts by the USA to destabilise the country through a policy of 'peaceful evolution'. The unrest in Eastern Europe, both politically and economically, provided the Chinese leadership with a taste of the potential outcomes of destabilisation and instability.

In its bargaining over MFN status the USA pointed to its huge imbalance in trade with China. In 1990 the USA had a trade deficit of US$ 10.4 billion with China.[174] China, however, argued that this deficit was in part the result of different methods of calculating trade volumes. Moreover, China's imports from the USA had inevitably fallen following the imposition of trade sanctions. The US exposure of the export of labour camp products was aimed at pressurising China into concessions in the negotiations.[175]

The arrival of Britain's Foreign Secretary, Douglas Hurd, in early April was a major landmark in the restoration of Sino-British relations.[176] Hurd's visit was followed shortly by the Japanese Foreign Minister.[177] In July 1991 China and Britain signed a memorandum on Hong Kong airport, ending a major bone of contention between the two sides.[178]

With Li Peng's visit to Moscow relations between China and the USA became more fraught. The USA was worried that China would forge a close alliance with the Soviet Union. On 28 May, shortly after Jiang's Moscow visit, President Bush suggested renewing China's MFN status to Congress but still insisted on blocking high-tech exports to China because of their continued export of missiles.[179] The rapid changes in the international political order, the collapse of state socialism in Eastern Europe as well as the perceived threat of peaceful evolution from the USA encouraged China to bolster its links with remaining socialist countries. By June 1991 China was proposing a new socialist alliance circle between China, the USSR, North Korea, Mongolia and Vietnam.[180] Jiang Zemin had already visited the USSR, North Korea and Vietnam during the year.[181]

The relaxation of international sanctions, commitment to open further and the more favourable economic context boosted the confidence of foreign investors. In the first half of 1991 China had approved 5028 new foreign direct investment projects, 80 per cent more than the same time the previous year. Over a quarter were wholly owned foreign enterprises.[182] By this time China had over 30 000 foreign-invested enterprises, of which half were in production.[183] The trade volume continued to increase and exports still exceeded imports. However, the Ministry of Foreign Economic Relations and Trade still exerted tight control over foreign trade. By June 1991 923 out of 2140 foreign trade companies no longer had the right to trade.[184]

On the domestic front enterprises continued to borrow too much and there was a danger of overheating. Since 1991 there had been a rapid increase in the scale of capital construction. Debt chains were a key concern of the government. In June 1991 the State Council issued an emergency circular to localities to curb the institutional import of non-productive items such as cars, which would now require provincial approval.[185] Moreover, China suffered its worst floods for a century in August 1991. Those affected blamed the Party for neglecting the irrigation system in its reforms.[186]

The failure of the short-lived anti-Gorbachev coup in August 1991 shook the Chinese leadership. The socialist camp was shrinking further and China was in danger of becoming even more ideologically and politically isolated. Social and ethnic unrest in the neighbouring Soviet Union threatened to fuel demands not only for political reform but also for greater autonomy for China's ethnic minorities. In the run up to the seventieth anniversary of the CCP in July 1991 several 'counter-revolutionary incidents' in Beijing including sabotage and death threats on leaders were reported in the Hong Kong press.[187] The public security bureau knew of at least 60 underground organisations operating in Beijing. Following the coup the Political Bureau issued 'five adherences and five oppositions' which included opposition to multi-partyism, a parliamentary system and socialist democratisation.[188] Fearing a similar venture by the PLA the Party reaffirmed its absolute leadership over the army.

The coup provided the conservatives with an opportunity to lash back. For the conservatives the failed coup reflected the success of the US attempt at 'peaceful evolution'. Ideological counter attack was therefore now crucial in preventing a similar development in China. The conservative, He Jingzhi, Deputy Director of the Central Propaganda Department and acting Culture Minister proclaimed that the ideological field was the main arena of struggle between peaceful evolution and opposition to it.[189]

The struggle within the leadership intensified over the next three months. The conservatives went so far as to challenge the basic idea of reform and opening up. In September the conservative-leaning newspaper *Guangming Ribao* printed an article arguing that it was necessary to distinguish between capitalism and socialism in approaching reform and the Open Policy.[190] The implication was that the reformers, and in particular Deng Xiaoping, were leading China along a capitalist path of development. At the same time the conservatives increased their attacks upon Zhao Ziyang from their institutional bases of the Central Advisory Commision, Central Propaganda Department and Beijing Municipal Party. They also put increasing pressure on Li Ruihuan, who was in charge of ideological work in the Political Bureau, to leave. On 26 August 1991 Jiang Zemin announced that Hu Qiaomu, a well-known conservative, would join the Political Bureau and Secretariat, paving the way for Li Ruihuan's resignation.[191]

The military coup in the Soviet Union also undermined Deng Xiaoping's plans to abolish the conservative stronghold, the Central Advisory Commission. Chen Yun now persuasively argued that allowing veterans to remain in power would prevent such a coup happening in China.[192]

The conservatives were going too far, however, in their exploitation of the coup. Deng Xiaoping was concerned by their stranglehold over the media. The Hong Kong press reported that Deng Xiaoping had to go south to the Shanghai press to promote his ideas of reform and opening up. In 1965 Mao too had to head for Shanghai to get his ideas published. In September 1991 at the CCP Central Work Conference, Deng spoke out against this emphasis on opposing peaceful evolution which was nothing less than an implicit attack on reform. He informally met with Li Peng, Song Ping and Qiao Shi to bolster support around Jiang Zemin.[193] Jiang Zemin also criticised the *People's Daily*'s emphasis on peaceful evolution at this conference and called for this issue not to be discussed below provincial level.[194]

The following month Deng Xiaoping instructed Jiang Zemin and Yang Shangkun to tell the Propaganda Department to tone down their ideological work against 'peaceful evolution'.[195] The conservatives were apparently even using terminology common during the Cultural Revolution. So both Yang and Jiang publicly expressed their concern about the recent lack of articles on reform and opening up. At the same time Deng Xiaoping developed his 'new cat theory' to challenge the conservatives' implicit accusation of adopting a capitalist line. This theory argued that neither should socialism be identified with planning nor capitalism with the market. This debate was redundant. The commodity economy could exist within socialism and planning could, and indeed did, operate within capitalism.

To contain the potential impact of the conservatives' ardent ideological attacks, Deng Xiaoping stated repeatedly that the issue of peaceful evolution should be kept within the Party's top echelon.[196] With the conservatives gaining ground after the coup attempt, it was even more important that the market reformers reassured both the international community and its own populace that reform and opening up were still on the agenda. At a central work conference in late September, a China People's Political Consultative Conference meeting in October 1991 and during his visit to Guangdong's SEZs Li Peng reiterated that China must reform and open up more.[197] His national day speech also called for greater reform and more opening up.[198] Following this, top leaders made pertinent visits to coastal areas to encourage a faster pace of opening. In October 1991, for example, Li Peng visited Shenzhen whilst Zhu Rongji went back to Shanghai for a visit.[199] Qiao Shi went to Hainan and Tian Jiyun went to inspect the economic zones in Guangdong.[200] With the foreign press and diplomats, the reformers argued that the Soviet coup would only have a 'small impact' on China as the circumstances of the two countries were quite different. At the Eighth Plenary Session of the CCP Central Committee in late November Deng Xiaoping and allies gained the upper hand when economic construction rather than opposing peaceful evolution was taken as the main task.[201]

Despite the continuing struggle within the leadership China continued to open. The government was quick to recognise diplomatically and maintain trade links with the newly emerging countries of the former Soviet Union. In September 1991 China began to adopt transitional measures to expand border and barter trade with these new countries.[202]

Moreover, regional expansion of the Open Policy continued. In October 1991 it was announced that Shantou SEZ would be expanded to cover the whole city.[203] The State Council approved three more free-trade zones in Tianjin and Shenzhen in 1991.[204] There were also indications that a further two free-trade zones would be set up in Guangzhou and Dalian in the near future. These free-trade zones would enjoy even more flexible policies than SEZs. In the same month a further 14 cities and counties were opened to foreigners bringing the total to 747.[205]

Central–local relations were still strained. In September 1991 the State Council issued a circular calling for greater control over investment in fixed assets.[206] The SEZs were demanding more legislative autonomy. The central government had still not ratified the legislative position of Futian bonded industrial zone set up in 1988. As a result foreign investors were reluctant to commit any capital and the zone had to rely on domestic bank loans to start construction.[207] Shenzhen city demanded that the 'special policies and flexible measures' be turned into laws. Shenzhen's legislation required the approval of Guangdong People's Congress. But in 11 years Guangdong had only authorised 17 economic rules. Although Shenzhen had set up an elected People's Congress in December 1990, it was still waiting to be granted legislative powers. Shenzhen City had 84 draft legal rules in the pipeline for the next three years. This highlighted not only the tension between the zones who wanted to push ahead faster and the centre who wanted to retain control, but also the lag between institutional and economic reform.

This battle for greater local power was also fuelled by the persisting fear that Shanghai would take over the SEZs' privileged position. That this fear was still alive was implicit in Li Peng's speech during his visit to Xiamen in December when he stressed that the opening of Pudong did not mean the downgrading of Guangdong.[208] He also said that Guangdong could continue to develop 'relying mainly on its own strength'.[209] The SEZs and many other areas had responded to this focus on Pudong by intensely competing to provide preferential terms to attract foreign capital.[210]

The failure of the Soviet coup and the subsequent abrupt emergence of a new international order underlined further the importance of maintaining and restoring relations with the West. In September 1991 the British Prime Minister, John Major, and his Foreign Secretary, Douglas Hurd, visited Beijing, raising again the issue of human rights.[211] This marked a new phase in Sino-British bilateral relations, signalling the restoration and expansion of relations after Tianamen.[212]

By September China was beginning to make some concessions to end the dispute with the USA. Wang Zhen, as President of the China Association for International Friendly Contacts said that Sino-US relations could be restored and normalised.[213] Around the same time an official from the Ministry of Foreign Economic Relations and Trade said that China was against the export of labour camp goods.[214] The attitudes of some re-formers to former dissidents had already begun to mellow. In July Wan Li, Deng Xiaoping and Jiang Zemin all gave their open support to rehabilitating dissidents, encouraging units to reemploy them and letting students return to their studies.[215] In October in Paris Qian Qichen met the US Secretary of State, James Baker, who said that relations should be normalised.[216] However, the USA continued to put pressure on China with an investigation into their trade practices and particularly the use of other countries' quotas for the export of their goods.

In October the Ministry of Foreign Economic Relations and Trade expressed its dissatisfaction with the US decision on 10 October to start the Section 301 investigation.[217] The visit of James Baker to China in mid-November marked the end of the ban on senior-level exchange with the USA.[218] Qian Qichen of course asked Baker to lift sanctions against China. Baker noted the positive cooperation of China in the Gulf War, Cambodia and arms control in the Middle East. November also saw the normalisation of Sino-Vietnamese relations with new bilateral accords signed.[219]

The issue of MFN status still remained unresolved by the end of the year. In mid-December the USA had unilaterally suspended further talks. The Seventh Round of Negotiations with the USA over intellectual property rights began on 21 December.[220] By this time Deng Xiaoping was advocating a more flexible approach to the USA. It was reported in the Hong Kong press that Deng Xiaoping advised members of the Political Bureau

Standing Committee in private that some compromises should be made in US-Sino relations and that China should give people more human rights.[221] The conservative Wang Zhen was outraged by this and accused Deng of advocating peaceful evolution. At the Eighth Plenary Session a report about Zhao was given. He was accused of encouraging bourgeois liberalisation, of being corrupt and being responsible for overheating. He was thus not permitted to take on any new jobs.[222]

By November 1991 the domestic economy was facing difficulties. An emergency State Council circular was released calling for a reduction in state expenditure. It instructed localities and departments to cut down on meetings and celebrations.[223] The National Financial Work Conference also pointed to a worsening financial deficit.[224] The continuing budget problems encouraged Chen Yun to call for restraint in the economy in December. According to a Hong Kong report Chen Yun advocated a proportion of 8:2 of plan/market.[225] Chen Yun was also concerned that many places were setting up various types of zones, but without conditions.

Reform of the foreign trade system continued apace. In November 1991 the State Council announced cuts in import tariffs for 225 different kinds of commodities including raw and processed materials from January 1992.[226] In the same month the Dongming trade outlet to the former Soviet Union was opened.[227] Moreover, at a national work meeting in November the Ministry of Foreign Economic Relations and Trade, the China Council for the Promotion of Investment and Trade and other organisations amended the regulations on country of origin of exports to bring these in line with international practice.[228] Similarly, the decision to publicise 17 internal documents on foreign trade was a further attempt to approximate international conventions. In December an export adjustment fund was set up and exporters of light industrial products were allowed to retain 20 per cent of their foreign exchange.[229]

By the end of the year China had agreed to a record number of 12 280 foreign-invested enterprises, bringing the total to 41 800.[230] Well over a third of these were wholly owned. That year foreign-invested enterprises accounted for almost 17 per cent of total exports, a record number.[231] Over 17 000 foreign-invested enterprises were in operation, involving US$ 23 billion of actual investment.[232] In 1991 Taiwan became China's third largest investor, overtaking Japan.[233]

With the Fourteenth Party Congress approaching the struggle within the leadership was intensifying. At the Eighth Plenary Session of the Central Advisory Commission in January 1992 Chen Yun expounded his 'six points of view and opinions' which included calls for opposition to peaceful evolution, cautious economic reform and stress on Marxist credentials for party leaders.[234] There were reports in the Hong Kong press that members of the Central Advisory Commission had written a letter in January condemning the SEZs, denouncing them as 'hotbeds for peaceful evolution'.[235] Deng Xiaoping and allies warned of the dangers of 'formalism', an implicit attack on the ideological manouevring of the Propaganda Department. The rhetoric of the reformers switched for the first time since Tiananmen from merely asserting that reform and opening up would continue to urging more opening up and reform. Deng was throwing down the gauntlet to his conservative adversaries.

Deng Xiaoping set off in the New Year to inspect the zones with the dual aims of promoting faster reform and opening up and consolidating his support in the south. He visited Shenzhen, Zhuhai, Gongbei and Shanghai. Deng Xiaoping affirmed the continuation of reform and opening up for the next 100 years. Reported statements by Deng such as 'we have to introduce more foreign-invested enterprises and not be afraid to do so' and 'we must adopt capitalism's strong points' reveal a determination to speed up the process of reform and opening up.[236] He urged Shenzhen to become the 'fifth little tiger' within the next 20 years.[237] Deng Xiaoping also revealed his regret in not making Shanghai a SEZ back in 1979 as well: 'One of my major errors was not to include Shanghai when setting up the four special economic zones.'[238] These sentiments were echoed by Yang Shangkun during his visit to Shanghai in February: 'Our line of reform and opening to the outside will not change and cannot change. We should still further the reform; open wider to the outside world; attract more foreign funds; import more advanced technologies ....'[239] Deng Xiaoping described foreign-invested enterprises as a 'useful supplement to China's socialist economy'.[240] The word 'supplement' has here a different function to its usage in the traditional approach to the Open Policy. Deng uses it here to downplay the power that conservatives attribute to foreign enterprises in their attacks upon opening up. Moreover, Deng reaffirmed the socialist nature of the SEZs, pointing out that foreign enterprises account for only one-fourth of the economy in the zones.

In addition to calls for more and faster reform there was also a subtle turnround in the attitude to political reform. Following the downfall of Zhao Ziyang, who had been the key advocate of political reform, discussion of any major change in the political system was not on the agenda. From the autumn of 1991 onwards we find increasingly open comments that economic and politics were inseparable. During his trip to Shenzhen in January Qiao Shi apparently called for SEZs to take the lead in political reform: 'Our special zones are SEZs. But economics cannot be separated from politics, as economic reform will inevitably involve some political factors. Therefore, reform of political structure also needs to be launched in the SEZs before other parts of the country.'[241] The crisis of Tiananmen had highlighted the contradiction between the existing political system and the changing economic base. Enough time had passed since then for the reformers to seek some solutions to this structural gap. Perceiving the need for some change, moderate and radical reformers were keener to be in control of this than to let China slip into chaos again. By discussing 'multi-party cooperation', 'socialist democracy' they tried to appropriate and adapt the language of the democracy activists in an attempt to affect some minimal change. With the handover of Hong Kong only five years away, the reformers were keen to have a more acceptable image.

At the enlarged meeting of the Political Bureau on 12 February Jiang Zemin relayed the content of Deng Xiaoping's speech during his southern trip. Various versions and interpretations of this speech appeared in the press, reflecting the ongoing struggle between the conservatives and Deng supporters. In March his speech finally appeared as Document Number Two.

As Document Two filtered downwards, top reformist leaders as well as provincial and subprovincial leaders began to echo its sentiments. Up till then the conservatives had been obstructing the relaying of the document and distorting the content of Deng's remarks.[242] Southern provincial leaders had begun in any case openly to support this call to accelerate reform and opening up immediately after Deng Xiaoping's visit. In February Li Hao, Party Secretary of Shenzhen, reiterated the idea of building a 'socialist Hong Kong' in Shenzhen whilst the Guangdong government began to draw up plans for further reform and opening.[243]

Vice-Premier Tian Jiyun during his visit to Zhuhai in April was reported to have described the speeding up of reform and opening as 'an irreversible trend'.[244] The following month in an inspection tour of Dalian President Yang Shangkun stated that 'development is simply out of the question under a closed-door policy'.[245] Leading academics such as Ma Hong called for more and faster opening.[246] Provincial leaders from Sichuan, Yunnan, Gansu, Inner Mongolia, Shandong, for example, openly called for more reform and opening. In his government work report the deputy of Guangdong, Ren Zhongyi went so far as to blame the central leadership for constraining the reform process as seen in the following:

> The primary and key problem lies not in the lower but in the upper level. Looking at Guandong, the masses of cadres all have a strong and pressing desire to broaden opening up, deepen reform and speed the pace of economic construction . . . In a word they feel that the superior level is not broad-minded enough and is conservative in its thinking.[247]

The Provincial Governor of Hainan, Liu Jianfeng, called for building a 'socialist Hong Kong' in Hainan.[248]

The opponents of further opening up and reform did not hesitate to take up the gauntlet. They launched their attack once again within the ideological domain. Their criticisms surfaced in newspapers they controlled, such as *Renmin Ribao* and *Guangming Ribao*, and in statements issued by key ideological institutions such as the Ministry of Culture, Ministry of Radio, Film and TV, Central Party School and the Propaganda Department of the Central Committee. Deng Xiaoping was forced to seek publication of his views in the south, first in Shanghai's *Jiefang Bao* and then in *Shenzhen Tequ Bao*.

At the ideological level the struggle was manifested in two issues, namely, the 'one centre' theory and the SEZs. Whilst Deng Xiaoping emphasised 'one centre, two basic points' where the one centre referred to the economy, Chen Yun was reported to be calling for 'two centres', the second centre being the domain of ideology.[249] The familiar conservative critique of the zones, namely that they were forms of capitalism, sources of corruption and heralded the return of the imperialists came out into the open again. They condemned the development of Yangpu in Hainan as 'a traitorous act'.[250]

The reformers parried these veiled and open attacks in three ways. First, they tried to gain control of the ideological institutions. Thus Qin Chuan, the former director of *Renmin Ribao*, sharply criticised Gao Di from late December onwards for using the newspaper to advance the views of conservatives, such as the debate about whether reform is socialist or capitalist.[251] By April Gao Di's fate was sealed and he was forced to step down as director. There were rumours that other conservative leaders in these ideological institutions, in particular Wang Renzhi, head of the CCP Propaganda Department, He Jingzhi, Acting Culture Minister and Ai Zhisheng, Minister of Radio, Film and Television would soon be ousted from their positions.[252] A Hong Kong paper reported that in April arch-conservative Deng Liqun had written to the Political Bureau complaining that the Party School and major newspapers were rejecting his articles.[253] The battle in the media was now in full swing.

Second, they underlined the necessity of opening up and reform for modernisation and development. A closed economy would be detrimental to economic growth and leave China lagging way behind its neighbours. The following excerpt from an editorial in *Renmin Ribao* — which was now under the influence of the reformers — in April 1992 illustrates this well:

> Only by opening to the outside world can we broaden our vision, see the entire world, look closely at ourselves, and enhance our sense of urgency and responsibility ... Only by opening to the outside world can we import capital and technology and introduce to our country talented people and advanced management experience to make up for our deficiency. If

the pace of reform and opening is not accelerated, we will be unable to speed up the overall development of the national economy.[254]

The reformers refuted any necessary link between corruption and the process of reform and opening up. For example, a Hong Kong newspaper reported Vice-Premier Tian Jiyun stating the following at the Guangzhou Trade Fair in May: 'We should not attribute corruption and other disgusting phenomena to reform and opening up, because in the closed-up areas there also exist corrupt and uncivilised phenomena.'[255]

Third, they tried to undermine the influence of the conservatives within the military. Acutely aware of the need for support from the army pro-Deng military leaders such as Yang Baibing, half-brother of Yang Shangkun, began in earnest to lobby top army personnel. This task was not an easy one given the decision at the December 1991 Central Military Commission Conference to make further cuts in troop size.[256] This had angered many of the 100 000 military officers who were in line to lose their jobs and in particular the preferential retirement conditions they would enjoy. At a crucial meeting of top military leaders in Zhuhai in late January Yang Shang Kun called for support for reform, linking this to the modernisation of the army. From March till the end of June 1992 the Central Military Commission organised a series of visits of army generals and officers to the SEZs.[257] By April the military newspaper *Jiefangjun Bao* was openly supporting Deng Xiaoping's 'one centre' theory and advocating faster economic reform and opening up. The following quote from an article in this paper illustrates well the shift away from anti-peaceful evolution rhetoric:

> If we stick the label of capitalism on and oppose every means and method once employed by capitalist countries, we will become as ridiculous as those who considered and destroyed as a bourgeois railway the railway left by the Tsar after the October Revolution.[258]

In June military leaders delivered a report to the Central Military Commission and Political Bureau affirming the SEZ model, opposing leftism and calling for the professionalisation of the army.[259]

The struggle between the conservatives and reformers intensified in the run-up to the Party Congress. Deng Xiaoping met with Chen Yun in April and July in an attempt to win him over. During his visit to Shanghai in May Chen Yun openly endorsed the development of Pudong. However, he continued to hold deep-seated reservations about the zones, and had serious doubts about an increased role for the market. He referred frequently to keeping 'the bird' (the market) safely in 'the cage' (the plan). He was also anxious about the potential loss of central control as provinces competed with each other for foreign capital.[260] There was also the danger that growing interprovincial rivalry might split China along ethnic lines, as had happened in the former Soviet Union. The death of Li Xiannian on 21 June removed one possible conservative candidate for the Central Committee. In an attempt to spur on the pace of reform and opening up Jiang Zemin made a key speech to the Central Party School on 9 June calling for the implementation of Deng Xiaoping's remarks.[261]

By the summer the reformers had secured their grip over these ideological institutions. The Ministry of Culture was urging more reform. The ban on films such as *Judou* and *Raise the Red Chinese Lantern* was lifted. *Guangming Ribao* was publishing articles extolling the virtues of capitalism and arguing that socialism and a market economy were compatible.[262] However, the Shenzhen stock riots in September provided a welcome opportunity for the conservatives to criticise the zones. Chen Yun called for a summing up of the SEZ experience, particulary with regard to corruption within the Party and government.[263] Whilst top reformers were clearly concerned about these riots, they saw them as the 'price to pay' for reform and the Open Policy rather than as a reason to reverse the policy.

As the reformers increasingly gained the upper hand in this leadership contest, they continued to push through policies which were indicative of greater opening, preparing the way for a Congress victory. At the world economic forum in Davos in February Li Peng promised more changes in the management of imports 'so as to meet universally accepted rules of international trade'.[264] In March there were rumours that the coastal areas would get back the preferential policies which had been withdrawn during the period of rectification.[265] South Korea and China signed a non-governmental trade agreement. In April the border gates along the Sino-Vietnamese border opened. In May Xinjiang provincial government announced plans to set up a SEZ aimed at Central Asia whilst the Tibetan local government promised to open more than one-third of its border counties to border trade.

In June Central Document Number Four was circulated to Party members. This document contained a proposal by Tian Jiyun for a further expansion of the Open Policy. In particular, it suggested the opening up of border areas and the setting up of SEZs in border regions, the extension of policies previously enjoyed by the coastal open cities to key cities in the Yangtze Valley as well as to the capitals of inland provinces and regions.[266]

A major change in foreign direct investment policy came in July 1992 when the Ministry of Foreign Economic Relations and Trade announced that foreign businesspeople could invest in all sectors of the economy including previously 'forbidden areas' such as insurance, finance and ocean shipping.[267] Furthermore, there was to be no limit on the lifespan or on the amount of foreign investment in foreign-invested enterprises. Foreign shareholders could now become chair of the board of directors. In September the oil fields in the Tarim Basin in Xinjiang province were opened to foreign investment, reversing the previous policy of restricting foreign exploration to coastal fields. In mid-October Liu Minxue, Director of the State Administration for Industry and Commerce, announced plans to decentralise further the administration of foreign-invested enterprises to provincial and city authorities.[268]

China continued to bring its foreign trade system in line with GATT regulations. In June the Ministry of Foreign Economic Relations and Trade announced further plans to reduce commodities requiring import/export licences, to abolish internal management documents, to liberalise foreign exchange rates and to introduce anti-dumping and foreign trade legislation.[269] The next month the General Administration of Customs announced plans for free-trade zones in numerous coastal cities.[270]

In the first half of 1992 over 17 000 foreign investment contracts had been approved, with pledged foreign capital of US$ 18 billion.[271] China now boasted over 60 000 Sino-foreign joint ventures. The trade volume continued to increase in the run-up to the Congress with imports outpacing exports by 6 per cent.[272] By September 1992 border trade had doubled over 1991 to US$ 1,186 million.[273] China had in 1992 alone opened up 13 border cities, 4 cities along the Yangtze River and 19 provincial capitals.[274]

Official commitment to another 100 years of reform and opening up had given a boost to the economy. By mid-June GNP was growing at a rate of 10 per cent, 4 per cent above target whilst industrial growth had reached 18.2 per cent in June.[275] State investment in fixed assets had grown by over 30 per cent compared with the same period in 1991.[276] In the light of this the State Council proposed revising the planned economic growth rate of the eighth five-year plan upwards from 6 per cent to 10 per cent.[277] Zhu Senlin, Governor of Guangdong, even called for two-digit growth if Guangdong was to overtake the 'four little dragons'.[278]

Relations between the USA and China eased somewhat in early 1992. In February the USA lifted the ban on high-tech exports to China which had been operating since June the previous year. At the end of the month the US House of Representatives adopted a bill on conditional extension of China's MFN status. By the middle of the year, however, tension was increasing again as the USA passed the Chinese Student Protection Act in June.[279] Relations deteriorated over the course of the next three months as the USA first sold 150 F-16 fighter planes to Taiwan and then passed the Hong Kong Policy Act, which China saw as an interference in its affairs.[280] In retaliation to the sale China temporarily withdrew from the arms talks on the Middle East and the USA responded by threatening not to support China's application to join GATT.[281] However, the signing of the market access memorandum between China and the USA and confirmation of US support for GATT membership eased relations before the crucial start of the Party Congress.[282]

At the same time China was ensuring friendly ties with the newly emerging countries in the former Soviet Union. The shadow of sanctions still hung over the reformers, who continued in 1992 to broaden and diversify economic and diplomatic relations. At a foreign trade work meeting in January 1992 Tian Jiyun urged the expansion of markets in developing countries, the former Soviet Union and Eastern Europe.[283] Preparations were underway in May for the visit of the Japanese Emperor after the Party Congress. On 24 August China and South Korea announced the normalisation of their relations. South Korea was now China's fourth largest trading partner.[284]

In this growing atmosphere of confidence indications of a new theory on the economy to be adopted at the Fourteenth Party Congress began to surface. At a forum on deepening rural reform held on 1 June the well-known economist Du Rensheng called for the realisation of the 'socialist market economy' in rural areas.[285] A Hong Kong newspaper reported Jiang Zemin as referring in his speech to the Central Party School on 9 June to the 'socialist market economic structure'.[286] In July the Institute of World Observation sponsored a seminar on the 'new structure of the socialist market economy' which was attended by many well-known economic theorists including as Du Rensheng, Dong Fureng and Lin Zili.[287] The term 'socialist market economy' continued to crop up in theoretical debate in the run-up to the Congress. At the same time writers and literary critics spoke out boldly against leftism and for a liberation of the arts.[288] Well-known figures in the cultural scene such as ex-cultural minister and writer Wang Meng who had fallen out of official favour over Tiananmen, as well as former *People's Daily* editor, Wang Ruoshui, began to appear again in the press.[289] A few days before the Congress the CCPCC agreed to end the examination and investigation into Zhao Ziyang.[290]

The long-awaited Fourteenth Party Congress finally took place from 12 October till 18 October. This congress was a major landmark in the process of reform and opening up. As well as providing the opportunity for a significant personnel reshuffle, it also marked a victory for the radical reformers who were seeking a bolder move towards the market. What then were the key changes at this congress?

Three new faces joined the Political Bureau Standing Committee, namely, Zhu Rongji, General Liu Huaqing and Hu Jintao. The dynamic Zhu Rongji, a well-known advocate of faster and deeper opening up and reform, had served a successful three years in Shanghai and was currently Director of the State Council's new Economic and Trade Office. His expected appointment as first vice-premier to the State Council at the next National People's Congress is widely seen as a preparatory post for taking over the premiership from Li Peng. Pundits were surprised somewhat at the appointment of General Liu Huaqing rather than Yang Baibing. Yang Baibing lost both his posts as Secretary General of the Central Military Commission and Director of the PLA's General Political Department but became a member of the Political Bureau. His elder half-brother Yang Shangkun retired from both the Political Bureau and the vice-chairmanship of the Central Military Commission. General Liu is a professional military person. He is likely to promote the modernisation of the army, which will involve streamlining of personnel, updating of weaponry and hence the need for further opening. Liu has played a key role in the recent development of Sino-Russian military relations. Hu Jintao is a rather unknown quantity who has made his mark within the Communist Youth League and Tibet. He is considered a reformer but by not being so well known he may pose less of a threat to the conservatives.

The numbers of military represented on the Central Committee increased from 16.5 per cent on the previous committee to 23.2 per cent, reflecting the continued importance of the military to the radical reformers.[291] Gao Di, He Jingzhi and Wang Renzhi all lost their places on the Central Committee as had been in the pipeline. However, Hua Guofeng, Shao Huaze, editor of the *People's Daily* and Ai Zhisheng, Broadcasting Minister, remained on the Committee. Some reformers, such as Yan Mingfu, chief of the United Front and Rui Xing, ex-secretariat member, who were both allied to Zhao Ziyang, lost their seats. So we can expect the struggle between the radical market reformers and conservatives to continue over the next five years.

Over half of the 309 new full and alternate members on the Central Committee were relatively young, with the average age being 56.3 years. Most of the members had tertiary education and professional training, reflecting the increasing importance of technocrats as compared with politic-ocrats. The number of regional representatives on the Central Committee also increased, reflecting the growing economic importance of the provinces. Five provincial and municipal party committee secretaries from Beijing, Shanghai, Tianjin, Guangdong and Shandong were elected to the Political Bureau.

The reformers succeeded in closing down the lair of the conservatives, the Central Advisory Commission. No sentence was passed on Zhao Ziyang, signalling again a victory for the reformers. Contrary to rumours in the foreign press none of the so-called 'princelings', that is, the children of top cadres such as Chen Yuan, son of Chen Yun or Deng Nan, daughter of Deng Xiaoping, were voted onto the Central Committee, reflecting again the desire to maintain a 'clean' image for the Party.

In terms of policy the insertion of Deng Xiaoping's theory of socialism with Chinese characteristics and the Party's basic line of 'one central task and two basic points' into the constitution marked a victory for the Dengist strategy of reform and opening up. The official introduction of the idea of a 'socialist market economy' marked a decisive shift away from the plan towards the market as well as a commitment to further opening. In this new socialist market economy public ownership was to be the mainstay of the economy whilst the individual, private and foreign sectors were to serve as 'supplements'.[292] As stated previously whilst the word 'supplement' had resonances with the traditional approach to opening up, it was also used to counter the conservative attempt to link opening up with a loss of national sovereignty.

As regards political reform there was no major change. In fact the idea of a separation between the Party and government which Zhao Ziyang put forward at the last congress in 1987 was not even mooted. This reluctance to carry out any fundamental political reform is in tune with the constant references to the NICs and in particular to Singapore. The reformers attribute the success of these countries to their adoption of a market economy matched by an authoritarian political system.[293]

In brief, the Fourteenth Party Congress officially endorsed a further round of reform and opening. Increasing reliance on the market, a faster pace of change as well as an expansion of the Open Policy were features characteristic of the radical programme associated with Zhao Ziyang and Hu Yaobang. Apart from reform of the state administration there were no plans for a fundamental change of the political system. Over the next five years we can expect to see foreign investment spreading to inland and border areas, and greater trade links in all directions as well as more foreign borrowing.

Conclusion

These last two chapters set out to trace the evolution of the Open Policy over the 14 years since the Third Plenum in December 1978 and consider the theoretical implications of these empirical findings for our understanding of the policy process in China. We found that the Open Policy had followed a spiral path, consisting of six key cycles. Each of these cycles involved changes in policy form, rationale, extent and direction. Each cycle led to the further extension and deepening of the Open Policy. The spiral dynamic of the Open Policy has both a political and economic logic. Differences within the top leadership over the pace, goals and extent of the Open Policy as well as the collision of institutional and social interests have significantly affected the course of the policy. Economic crises inspired in part by decentralisation have required rapid leadership responses, with further consequences for opening up. At the same time they have provided golden opportunities for opponents to launch their attacks.

With the Fourteenth Party Congress now behind them the more radical economic reformers can push ahead with their ambitious plans to steer China towards a socialist market economy. In doing so they will face the problems of an overheating economy, inflation and declining state revenues. Increasing income differentials between state, individual and private sectors, as well as a growing army of unemployed as enterprise reform gets underway, will pose crucial problems of social unrest. The pace of opening will quicken over the coming years. The geographical spread of foreign investment and trade will continue to expand whilst local governments and enterprises will acquire more powers in managing foreign economic relations on their doorsteps. As more areas compete for foreign investment, we can expect the management of this Open Policy to become increasingly complex and more difficult for the central leadership to hold on course. The increasing economic power of border areas as well as the weaving of cross-border links with common ethnic groups may fuel demands for greater regional autonomy and contribute to ongoing ethnic unrest. The fear of 'splittism' in areas such as Xinjiang and Tibet will be a continuing concern for central leaders. The question of succession as the gerontocracy gradually passes away will have an important bearing on the future course of opening up.

Notes

1. These would be in the spheres of wages and land rents, particularly to enterprises exporting or reinvesting in China or using their profits to purchase Chinese goods for export (XH 7.8.1986 in SWB/FE/8334/BII/1).
2. ZGXWS 15.8.1986 in FBIS 29.8.1986 K19; XH 7.8.1986 in SWB/FE/8334/BII/1; XH 9.10.1986 in SWB/FE/W1415/A/10.
3. HK, ZGXWS 23.12.1986.
4. In 1986 they reached US$ 6.93 billion (XH 23.1.1987 in FBIS 28.1.1987 K/6).
5. For example, Guangdong, ZGXWS 14.10.1986 in SWB/FE/8384/BII/3, Liaoning, XH 17.10.1986; Shandong, ZGXWS 22.10.1986 in FBIS 6.1.1987, p. 88; Hubei, ZGXWS 14.10.1986 in SWB/FE/8384/BII/3; Yunnan People's Broadcasting Station 30.12.1986 in FBIS 23.1.1987, p. 35.
6. HK, MB 2.10.1986 in SWB/FE/8384/BII/1.
7. HK, MB 4.10.1986 in SWB/FE/8384/BII/1.
8. ZGXWS 26.11.1986 in SWB/FE/8431/C1/2.
9. ZGXWS 14.12.1986 in FBIS 23.1.1987.
10. XH 14.11.1986 in SWB/FE/8417/BII/1.
11. SJJJDB 6.10.1986 in FBIS 12.1.1987.

12. LNRB 18.12.1986 in FBIS 19.3.1987.
13. SJJJDB 6.10.1986 in FBIS 12.1.1987.
14. Shaanxi People's Broadcasting Station 25.11.1986 in SWB/FE/8428/BII/13; HK, ZGXWS 19.12.1986 in FBIS 12.1.1987.
15. HK, SCMP 30.4.1987 in FBIS 1.5.1987 K9.
16. XH 12.1.1987 in FBIS 4.3.1987.
17. HK, SCMP 26.2.1987 in FBIS 26.2.1987 K22.
18. FJRB 19.2.1987 and 22.2.1987.
19. HK, SCMP 30.4.1987 in FBIS 26.2.1987 K22.
20. HK, SCMP 26.2.1987 in FBIS 26.2.1987 K22.
21. See Ladany, 1988, p. 485.
22. HK, DGB 11.2.1987 in FBIS 23.3.1987, pp. 35−6.
23. ibid.
24. XH 10.1.1987 in FBIS 25.2.1987 p. 61.
25. Chanda, N. 'What's going on there? in FEER 5.2.1987, p. 14 and E. Salem, 'Shadow of a doubt' in FEER 5.2.1987, pp. 48−9.
26. XH, BJ 7.5.1987 in FBIS 6.6.1987, p. 66.
27. HK, WWP 9.8.1987 in SWB/FE/8643/BII/8.
28. XH 29.10.1987 in SWB/FE/W1466/A/1.
29. SJJJDB 26.10.1987 in SWB/FE/8723/BII/3.
30. RMRB 3.1.1987 in FBIS 20.3.1987, pp. 32−4; XH BJ 12.3.1987 in FBIS 10.4.1987, p. 11.
31. XH 2.12.1986 in FBIS 6.1.1987 p. 106.
32. Hubei People's Broadcasting Station 5.12.1987 in SWB/FE/W005/A/9; XH 19.12.1987 in SWB/FE/244/41.
33. Li Hao 'The path of reform and opening up has become increasingly broader', NFRB 7.11.88 in FBIS 88/218/27.
34. XH 19.7.1988 in SWB/FE/W0036/A/1.
35. XH 6.6.1988 in FBIS 88/107/42.
36. XH 25.5.1988 in FBIS 88/103/43.
37. RMRB 25.6.1988 in SWB/FE/0197/B2/3; for example, Shenyang 14.5.1988 XH in FBIS 88/095/70; 16.5.1988 XH in FBIS 88/095/49.
38. CD 23.5.1988.
39. XH 3.9.1988 in SWB/FE/W0043/A/5.
40. CD 23.5.1988.
41. XH 18.5.1988 in FBIS 88/101/30.
42. XH 1.7.1988 in FBIS 88/128/57.
43. CD 3.6.1988; BJRV 2.5.1988.
44. Khan, 1991, p. 10.
45. HK, SCMP 18.7.1988 in FBIS 88/138/45, BJRV 2.5.1988.
46. XH 3.7.1988 in FBIS 88/132/44.
47. CD 19.10.1988.
48. XH 30.5.1988 in FBIS 88/105/47.
49. ZGXWS 22.5.1988 in FBIS 88/103/27.
50. CEI 22.6.1988 in FBIS 88/120/29.
51. XH 22.7.1988 in FBIS 88/142/55.

52. XH 2.8.1988 in FBIS 88/149/34.
53. XH 9.1.1989 in SWB/FE/W0061/A/7.
54. XH 18.10.1988 in SWB/FE/W0049/A/1.
55. XH 26.7.1989 in SWB/FE/0522/B2/3.
56. On contribution of TVEs to export production see XH, BJ 14.5.1991 in SWB/FE/W0181/A/5 29.5.1991; XH, BJ 4.8.1991 in SWB/FE/W0192/A/2 14.8.1991; and XH, BJ 23.11.1991 in SWB/FE/W0208/A/1 4.12.1991 (in the seventh five-year plan rural enterprises accounted for 30 per cent of net increase in foreign exchange earnings). Also see Zweig, 1991.
57. HK, ZGXWS 23.9.1988 in FBIS 88/188/67.
58. Hainan People's Broadcasting Station 17.10.1988 in FBIS 88/202/48.
59. XH 8.10.1988 in SWB/FE/0281/B2/1.
60. HK, WWP 15.10.1988 in SWB/FE/0286/B2/5.
61. Kyodo News Agency, Japan 2.10.1988 in FBIS 88/191/23.
62. RMRB 19.11.1988 in SWB/FE/0335/B2/5.
63. RMRB 2.12.1988, p. 1 in FBIS 88/234/30.
64. XH 3.12.1988 and XH 31.5.1990 in FBIS 90/106/31.
65. RMRB 2.1.1989 SWB/FE/W0061/A6.
66. HK, SCMP 7.11.1988 in FBIS 88/215/49.
67. HK, WWP 9.2.1989 in SWB/FE/0382/B2/1.
68. XH 20.2.1989 in SWB/FE/W0065/i.
69. XH 21.8.1989 in SWB/FE/W0091/i.
70. Much has now been written on the 1989 democracy movement. Some starters are listed here: Cheng Chu-yuan, 1990; Han Minzhu, 1990; Yasheng Huang, 1990; Saich, T., The Beijing People's Movement of 1989', Social Movements Studies Research Seminar, Draft Paper Sinologisch Instituut, Leiden 30.10.1989, pp. 1–38; Bachman and Yang, 1991.
71. ZGXWS 14.9.1989 in SWB/FE/0563/B1/2; ZGXWS 16.10.1989 in SWB/FE/0593/B2/7; Hainan 28.11.1989 in SWB/FE/W0108/A/1.
72. HK, SCMP 24.3.1990 in FBIS 90/058/36.
73. HK, SCMP 7.7.1990 in FBIS /90/131/54.
74. HK, MB 13.1.1990 in SWB/FE/0666/B2/7.
75. XH 26.7.1989 in SWB/FE/0522/B2/3.
76. HK, CM 1.7.1991 in SWB/FE/1116 B2/5 5.7.1991.
77. ibid. in SWB/FE/1116 B2/6 5.7.1991.
78. Khan, 1991, p. 9.
79. ibid., p. 12.
80. ibid.
81. RMRB 19.11.1989 in SWB/FE/0622/B2/8.
82. XH 15.5.1990 in FBIS 90/096/40.
83. XH 31.5.1990 in FBIS 90/106/31.
84. Guangdong radio 29.7.1989 in SWB/FE/0522/B2/3.
85. HK, MB 18.8.1989 in SWB/FE/W0092/A/1.
86. Kyodo News Agency, Japan 5.9.1989 in SWB/FE/W0094/i.
87. HK, WWP 7.2.1990 in SWB/FE/0684/B2/5.
88. XH 31.5.1990 in FBIS 90/106/31.

89. HK, SCMP 19.7.1990 in FBIS 90/139/45; HK, MB 18.7.1990 in SWB/FE/W0139/A10.
90. HK, SCMP 19.7.1990 in FBIS 90/139/45.
91. HK, SCMP 24.3.1990 in FBIS 90/058/36.
92. HK, MB 7.1.1990 in SWB/FE/W011/A/6.
93. XH 23.7.1990 in SWB/FE/W0139/A/11.
94. XH 31.5.1990 in FBIS 90/106/31.
95. XH 4.1.1990 in FBIS 90/004/31.
96. XH 9.12.1989 in SWB/FE/0638/B2/7.
97. ZGXWS 16.1.1990 in SWB/FE/W0113/A/5.
98. XH 9.2.1990 in SWB/FE/0688/B2/1.
99. HK, WWP 22.1.1990 in SWB/FE/0671/B2/5.
100. HK, SCMP 24.4.1990 in FBIS 90/085/73.
101. JJRB 25.12.1989 in FBIS 90/030/16.
102. HK, S 12.1.1990 in FBIS 90/031/16.
103. HK, S 28.2.1990 in FBIS 90/042/38.
104. CD 21.3.1990 in FBIS 90/058/35.
105. HK, MB 3.1.1991 in SWB/FE/0966/B2/1 10.1.1991.
106. HK, JJDB 25.6.1990 in FBIS 90/124/44.
107. HK, MB 18.7.1990 in SWB/FE/W0139/A/10.
108. ZGXWS 6.6.1990 in SWB/FE/0785/B2/3.
109. HK, SCMP 20.7.1990 FBIS 90/140/47.
110. XH 9.2.1990 in SWB/FE/W0116/A/6.
111. XH 18.8.1990 in SWB/FE/W0143/A/6.
112. ZGXWS 6.6.1990 in SWB/FE/W0134A/3.
113. XH, BJ 14.6.1991 in SWB/FE/1100/C1/1 17.6.1991.
114. XH, BJ 9.5.1991 in SWB/FE/1069/A1/2 11.5.1991.
115. XH, BJ 14.1.1991 in SWB/FE/W0163/A/1 23.1.1991; 27.3.1991 i.
116. RMRB BJ 24.1.1991 in SWB/FE/0980/C1/1 26.1.1991; XH, BJ 27.12.1990 in SWB/FE/W0161/A/1 9.1.1991; XH, BJ 27.12.1990 in SWB/FE/W0161/A/2; XH, BJ 9.1.1991 in SWB/FE/W0162/A/6 16.1.1991.
117. Khan, 1991, p. 13.
118. XH, BJ 2.9.1991 in SWB/FE/W0196/A/1 11.9.1991.
119. XH, BJ 24.2.1991 in SWB/FE/W0169/A/9 6.3.1991.
120. XH, BJ 1.4.1991 in SWB/FE/1041/C1/1 9.4.1991.
121. Heilong Jiang radio 31.12.1990 in SWB/FE/W061 A/11 9.1.1991.
122. XH, BJ 5.1.1991 in SWB/FE/W0162/A/6 16.1.1992.
123. XH, BJ 8.2.1991 in SWB/FE/W0167/A/3 20.2.1991.
124. XH, BJ 1.4.1991 in SWB/FE/1036/B2/3 3.4.1991.
125. HK, WWP 31.5.1991 in SWB/FE/1089/B2/5 4.6.1991.
126. Kyodo News Agency, 22.6.1991 in SWB/FE/W0186/A/3 3.7.1991.
127. HK, MB 3.1.1991 in SWB/FE/0966/B2/1 10.1.1991; HK, MB 29.1.1991 in SWB/FE/0893/B2/2 30.1.1991.
128. XH 26.11.1990 in SWB/FE/0933/B2/1.
129. HK, WWP 31.12.1990 in SWB/FE/0959/B2/2 1.1.1991.
130. XH, BJ 21.1.1991 in SWB/FE/0977/B2/5 23.1.1991.

131. HK, MB 22.2.1991 in SWB/FE/1007/B2/6 27.2.1991.
132. XH, BJ 23.1.1991 in SWB/FE/0980/C1/1 26.1.1991.
133. XH, BJ 28.1.1991 in SWB/FE/0984/C1/20 31.1.1991.
134. Beijing TV 30.3.1991 in SWB/FE/1035/C1/3 2.4.1991.
135. XH, BJ 26.2.1991 in SWB/FE/108/B2/2 28.2.1991.
136. XH, BJ 25.2.1991 in SWB/FE/1008/B2/2 28.2.1991.
137. XH, BJ 26.3.1991 in SWB/FE/1032/C1/1 28.3.1991.
138. XH, BJ 30.3.1991 in SWB/FE/1035/C1/2 2.4.1991.
139. HK, WWP 12.3.1991 in SWB/FE/1020/B2/4 14.3.1991.
140. JFRB, 15.1.1991 in SWB/FE/0975/B2/4 21.1.1991.
141. In October 1992 you could still see Mao portraits in taxis in Shenyang and Beijing, personal observation.
142. HK, ZGTWS 11.2.1991 in SWB/FE/0997/B2/10 15.2.1991.
143. See Dittmer, 1990.
144. HK, WWP 26.3.1991 in SWB/FE/1032/C1/4-5 28.3.1991.
145. XH, BJ 8.4.1991 in SWB/FE/1042/C1/1 10.4.1991 — lists members of State Council.
146. Li was a mere 58 years old, had trained in the Soviet Union and had been deputy mayor of Tianjin in 1983, see XH, BJ 28.12.1990 in SWB/FE/0959/C1/5 1.1.1991.
147. HK, DGB 10.4.1991 in SWB/FE/1044/C1/7 12.4.1991.
148. HK, JB 5.8.1991 in SWB/FE/1147/B2/2 10.8.1991.
149. Beijing People's Broadcasting Station 25.3.1991 in SWB/FE/1031/C1/7 27.3.1991.
150. XH, BJ 30.5.1991 in SWB/FE/1089/B2/6 4.6.1991.
151. Haikou People's Broadcasting Station 8.7.1991 in SWB/FE/1123/B2/5 13.7.1991.
152. XH, BJ 15.2.1991 in SWB/FE/0999/B2/3 18.2.1991.
153. Haikou People's Broadcasting Station 20.2.1991 in SWB/FE/1003/B2/1 22.2.1991.
154. XH, BJ 22.3.1991 in SWB/FE/1030/B2/1 26.3.1991 ; XH, BJ 14.3.1991 in SWB/FE/1023/B2/5 18.3.1991.
155. XH, BJ 15.5.1991 in SWB/FE/1075/B2/2 18.5.1991.
156. XH, BJ 29.3.1991 in SWB/FE/1036/C1/4 3.4.1991.
157. XH, BJ 9.4.1991 in SWB/FE/1047/B2/4 16.4.1991.
158. XH, BJ 2.5.1991 in SWB/FE/1065/B2/5 7.5.1991.
159. XH, BJ 24.4.1991 in SB/FE/W0178/A/3 8.5.1991.
160. XH, BJ 17.12.1991 in SWB/FE/1000/B2/1 19.2.1991.
161. XH, BJ 30.4.1991 in SWB/FE/1061/B2/2 2.5.1991.
162. Beijing People's Broadcasting Station 27.3.1991 in SWB/FE/1033/C1/1 29.3.91.
163. Tass 21.3.1991 in SWB/FE/1029/A2/1 25.3.1991.
164. Beijing People's Broadcasting Station 27.3.1991 in SWB/FE/1033/C1/1 29.3.1991.
165. XH, BJ 7.5.1991 in SWB/FE/1067/A2/1 9.5.1991.

166. XH, BJ 10.5.1991 in SWB/FE/1069/A2/1 11.5.1991.
167. SWB/FE/1073 i 16.5.1991.
168. SWB/SU/1074 C1/1 17.5.1991.
169. XH, BJ 25.5.1991 in SWB/FE/W0183/A/4 12.6.1991.
170. XH, BJ 9.7.1991 in SWB/FE/W0188/A/6 17.7.1991.
171. SWB/FE/1028 i 23.3.1991.
172. XH, BJ 22.3.1991 in SWB/FE/1030/A1/1 26.3.1991.
173. HK, WWP 19.4.1991 in SWB/FE/1052/A1/1 22.4.1991.
174. XH, BJ 9.5.1991 in SWB/FE/1069/A1/2 11.5.1991.
175. Beijing People's Broadcasting Station 7.5.1991 in SWB/FE/1068/A1/1 10.5.1991.
176. ZGXWS BJ 2.4.1991 in SWB/FE/1038/A1/2 5.4.1991.
177. SWB/FE/1040 i 8.4.1991.
178. XH, BJ 4.7.1991 in SWB/FE/1117/A3/1 6.7.1991.
179. XH, BJ 28.5.1991 in SWB/FE/1084/A1/2 29.5.1991.
180. HK, JB 10.6.1991 in SWB/FE/1091/C1/1 6.6.1991.
181. HK, CM 1.8.1991 in SWB/FE/1140/A3/1 2.8.1991.
182. XH, BJ FE/W0190/A/1 31.7.1991.
183. XH, BJ 7.11.1991 in SWB/FE/W026/A/8 20.11.1991.
184. HK, ZGTWS in SWB/FE/1111/C2/2 29.6.1991.
185. XH, BJ 23.6.1991 in SWB/FE/1108/B2/1 26.6.1991.
186. HK, CM 1.8.1991 in SWB/FE/1140/B2/4 2.8.1991.
187. HK, CM 1.7.1991 in SWB/FE/1116/B2/5 5.7.1991.
188. HK, MB 29.8.1991 in SWB/FE/1182/B2/4 20.9.1991.
189. RMRB BJ 20.8.1991 in SWB/FE1161/B2/3 27.8.1991.
190. GMRB 13.8.1991 in SWB/FE/1172/B2/6 9.9.1991.
191. HK, CM 1.10.1991 in SWB/FE/1196/B2/7 7.10.1991.
192. HK, JB 5.9.1991 in SWB/FE/1182/B2/4 20.9.1991.
193. HK, JB 5.1.1991 in SWB/FE/1277/B2/1 14.1.1992.
194. GMRB 12.1.1992 in SWB/FE/1297/B2/1 6.2.92.
195. HK, MB 8.10.1991 in SWB/FE/1199/B2/1 10.10.1991.
196. HK, PX 1.12.1991 in SWB/FE/1251/B2/4 10.12.1991.
197. XH, BJ 9.10.1991 in SWB/FE/1210/C1/1 23.10.1991; XH, BJ 12.10.1991 in SWB/FE/1203/B2/5 15.10.1991.
198. XH, BJ 30.9.1991 in SWB/FE/1193/C1/1 31.10.1991.
199. XH, BJ 12.10.1991 in SWB/FE/1203/B2/5 15.10.1991; and XH, BJ 15.10.1991 in SWB/FE/1205/B2/3 17.10.1991.
200. RMRB BJ 11.10.1991 in SWB/FE/B2/1 23.10.1991.
201. HK, JB 5.1.1992 in SWB/FE/1280/B2/1 17.1.1992.
202. HK, ZGTWS 24.9.1991 in SWB/FE/1188/B2/5 27.9.91. Also in mid-September China established diplomatic ties with Latvia. See XH, BJ 12.9.1991 in SWB/FE/1177/A2/1 27.9.1991 b2/5.
203. HK, DB 9.10.1991 in SWB/FE/1207/B2/6 19.10.1991.
204. XH, BJ 4.11.1991 in SWB/FE/1222/B2/6 6.11.1991.
205. XH, BJ 18.11.1991 in SWB/FE/1233/B2/7 19.11.1991.

206. XH, BJ 28.8.1991 in SWB/FE/11662/B2/2 2.9.1991.
207. HK, ZGTWS 28.11.1991 in SWB/FE/1248/B2/1 6.12.1991.
208. HK, JJDB 9.12.1991 in SWB/FE/1259/B2/6 19.12.1991.
209. ibid.
210. HK, ZGTWS 30.8.1991 in SWB/FE/172/B2/5 9.9.1991.
211. ZGXWS BJ 29.8.1991 in SWB/FE/1166/A1/1 2.9.1991.
212. XH, BJ 4.9.1991 in SWB/FE/1170/A/3 6.9.1991.
213. XH, BJ 18.9.1991 in SWB/FE/1183/A1/1 21.9.1991.
214. XH 19.9.1991 in SWB/FE/1184/A1/2 23.9.1991.
215. JB 5.9.1991 in SWB/FE/1182/B2/3 20.9.1991.
216. XH, BJ 23.10.1991 in SWB/FE/1212/A1/2 25.10.1991.
217. XH, BJ 11.10.1991 in SWB/FE/1202/A1/1 14.10.1991.
218. HK, WWP 14/15.11.1991 in SWB/FE/1231/A1/1 16.11.1991.
219. In November 1991 the German economic minister became the first minister to visit China since Tiananmen but came armed with a list of imprisoned dissidents. See XH, BJ 4.11.1991 in SWB/FE/1222/A1/1 6.11.1991.
220. XH, BJ 24.12.1991 in SWB/FE/1266/A1/1 31.12.1991.
221. TT, HK 15.12.1991 in SWB/FE/1265/B2/4 19.12.1991.
222. ibid. in SWB/FE/1262/B2/5 23.12.1991.
223. XH, BJ 8.11.1991 in SWB/FE/1227/B2/1 12.11.1991.
224. XH 9.12.1991 in SWB/FE/1253/B2/1 12.12.1991.
225. HK, JB 5.12.1991 in SWB/FE/1254/B2/2 13.12.1991.
226. XH, BJ 11.11.1991 in SWB/FE/W0206/A/8 20.11.1991.
227. XH, BJ 8.12.1991 in SWB/FE/1252/A1/1 11.12.1991.
228. XH, BJ 14.11.1991 in SWB/FE/1232/B2/4 18.11.1991.
229. HK, JJDB 9.12.1991 in SWB/FE/1258/B2/10 18.12.1991.
230. XH, BJ 28.11.1991 in SWB/FE/W0210/A/5 18.12.1991.
231. XH, BJ 17.1.1992 in SWB/FE/W0215/A/6 29.1.1992.
232. Kyodo News Agency, Japan 31.1.1992 in SWB/FE/1293/C1/3 1.2.1992.
233. ZGTWS BJ 27.3.1992 in SWB/FE/W0225/A/8 8.4.1992.
234. BYT 25.11.1991 in SWB/FE/1271/B2/1 7.1.1992.
235. HK, MB 6.3.1992 in SWB/FE/1328/B2/3 13.3.1992. Other reports suggest 32 members — Kyodo radio, Japan 9.3.1992 in SWB/FE/1325/B2/1 10.3.1992.
236. HK, MB 14.2.1992 in SWB/FE/1306/B2/4 17.2.1992 and HK, WWP 18.2.1992 in SWB/FE/1310/B2/4 21.2.1992.
237. HK, MB 21.1.1992 in SWB/FE/1286/B2/1 24.1.1992.
238. HK, MB 7.3.1992 in SWB/FE/1328/B2/3 13.3.1992.
239. XH, BJ 14.2.1991 in SWB/FE/1306/B2/1 17.2.1992.
240. HK, GJJ 16.3.1992 in SWB/FE/1333/B2/3 19.3.1992.
241. HK, MB 19.4.1992 in SWB/FE/1360/B2/5 21.4.1992.
242. HK, MB 7.3.1992 in SWB/FE/1328/B2/2 13.3.1992.
243. HK, MB 23.2.1992 in SWB/FE/1316/B2/3 28.2.1992.
244. HK, DGB 19.4.1992 in SWB/FE/1360/B2/3 21.4.1992.
245. XH 5.5.1992 in SWB/FE/1375/B2/1 8.5.1992.
246. XH 23.3.1992 in SWB/FE/1342/C2/2 30.3.1992.

247. NFRB 28.3.1992 in SWB/FE/1361/B2/3 22.4.1992.
248. Hainan People's Broadcasting System 8.4.1992 in SWB/FE/1355/B2/8 14.4.1992.
249. HK, CM 1.3.1992 in SWB/FE/1328/B2/4 13.3.1992.
250. HK, JJDB 23.3.1992 in SWB/FE/1341/C2/3 28.3.1992.
251. HK, JJDB 28.4.1992 in SWB/FE/1371/B2/1 4.5.1992.
252. HK, DFRB 25.3.1992 in SWB/FE/1340/B2/4 27.3.1992.
253. HK, CM 1.6.1992 in SWB/FE/1409/B2/4 17.6.1992.
254. XH 27.4.1992 in SWB/FE/1368/B2/1 30.4.1992.
255. HK, MB 4.5.1992 in SWB/FE/1375/B2/2 8.5.1992.
256. HK, CM 1.3.1992 in SWB/FE/1322/B2/2 6.3.1992.
257. HK, MB 11.3.1992 in SWB/FE/1333/B2/5 19.3.1992.
258. JFJB 25.3.1992 in SWB/FE/1366/B2/5 28.4.1992.
259. HK, TT 15.6.1992 in SWB/FE/1420/B2/6 30.6.1992.
260. HK, XB 12.5.1992 in SWB/FE/1385/B2/1 20.5.1992.
261. HK, CM 1.7.1992 in SWB/FE/1429/B2/7 10.7.1992.
262. GMRB 1.8.1992 in SWB/FE/1465/B2/5 21.8.1992.
263. HK, MB 1.9.1992 in SWB/FE/1482/B2/2 10.9.1992.
264. XH, BJ 30.1.1992 in SWB/FE/1293 C1/2 1.2.1992.
265. HK, WWP 9.3.1992 in SWB/FE/1326/B2/4 11.3.1992.
266. HK, DGB 12.6.1992 in SWB/FE/1406/B2/1 13.6.1992.
267. ZGXWS 24.7.1992 in SWB/FE/1445/B2/5 29.7.1992.
268. XH 15.10.1992 in SWB/FE/1519/B2/1 23.10.1992.
269. JJDB, BJ 22.6.1992 in SWB/FE/W0238/A/6 8.7.1992.
270. XH 21.6.1992 in SWB/FE/W0238/A/5 8.7.1992.
271. ZGTXS, HK 19.10.1992 in SWB/FE/W0255/A/3 4.11.1992.
272. XH 7.7.1992 in SWB/FE/W0240/A/3 22.7.1992.
273. XH 7.10.1992 in SWB/FE/W0252/A/5 14.10.1992.
274. XH 4.9.1992 in SWB/FE1480/B2/1 8.9.1992.
275. JJDB, HK 17.8.1992 in SWB/FE/W0246/A/2 2.9.1992.
276. QS 1.8.1992 in SWB/FE/W0249/C1/1 23.9.1992.
277. XH 16.7.1992 in SWB/FE/1435/B2/1 17.7.1992.
278. ZGTWS, HK 15.7.1992 in SWB/FE/1436/C2/2 18.7.1992.
279. XH 8.6.1992 in SWB/FE/1403/A1/2 10.6.1992.
280. XH 3.9.1992 in SWB/FE/1478/A1/1 5.9.1992.
281. XH 16.9.1992 in SWB/FE/1489/A2/1 18.9.1992.
282. XH 11.10.1992 in SWB/FE/1509/i 12.10.1992.
283. XH, BJ 24.12.1991 in SWB/FE/1267 B2/5 1.1.1992.
284. Seoul TV 30.9.1992 in SWB/FE/1501/A2/2 2.10.1992.
285. ZGXWS 2.6.1992 in SWB/FE/1404/B2/3 11.6.1992.
286. HK, DGB 23.7.1992 in SWB/FE/1446/B2/1 30.7.1992. However, the XH 14.6.1992 report of his speech does not mention this (see SWB/FE/1408/B2/1 16.6.1992).
287. ZGTWS, BJ 6.7.1992 in SWB/FE/1438/B2/3 21.7.1992.
288. HK, WWP 16.10.1992 in SWB/FE/1517/B2/8 21.10.1992.

289. XH 19.9.1992 in SWB/FE/1499/B2/1 30.9.1992 and Gittings, J. in *The Guardian*, 17.6.1992.
290. XH 9.10.1992 in SWB/FE/1509/B2/1 12.10.1992.
291. Tai Ming Cheung, 'Back to the front' in FEER 29.10.1992, p. 15.
292. XH 14.10.1992 in SWB/FE/1514/B2/2 17.10.1992.
293. In the late 1980s there was a lively debate within Chinese academic circles about the relationship between authoritarianism and economic development. See Rosen and Zou, 1992.

4

The dynamics of the Open Policy in Xiamen SEZ

Given the regional and cultural diversity of China as well as its huge economy, the process of opening up will inevitably vary accordingly. Having tracked the dynamics of the Open Policy in general, we now focus our attention more narrowly on the local level. We have chosen as our site of investigation Xiamen SEZ, a coastal city in Fujian province. Whilst scholars and journalists have poured into Shenzhen SEZ, Xiamen has escaped the glare of the academic limelight. As a result research and reporting on Xiamen has been far less extensive or systematic.[1] In traversing this barely charted terrain we hope to lend specificity to our overall analysis.

Since the opening of Xiamen (Amoy) under the Treaty of Nanjing in 1842 the main form of foreign economic activity has been foreign trade. After Liberation the Fujian Overseas Chinese Investment Company was set up to attract investment. Up till its abolition in 1965 this company had set up 47 Overseas Chinese enterprises in the province, drawing Y80 million in investment. Military aggression from Taiwan during the post-liberation period not only impeded the extension of foreign economic ties but also inhibited domestic economic development in Fujian province. Treated as part of China's front line, the state, both centrally and locally, invested little in either the infrastructure or industry.[2]

In the post-Mao period the reformers selected Fujian province, along with Guangdong province, as a major base for the development of the Open Policy. As such, Fujian received special privileges to attract foreign capital.

125

Since 1979 Fujian province has experimented with a plethora of economic forms such as a SEZ, the open coastal city of Fuzhou, an ETDZ, the large open area of the 'South Fujian golden triangle', bonded industrial zones and Taiwanese investment zones. It has also has engaged in different types of economic arrangements such as compensation trade, leasing, financial joint ventures and floating bonds overseas. Xiamen SEZ in particular offers the most favourable conditions to foreign investors in Fujian.

The Open Policy in Fujian has unfolded along a spiral path similar to that at the national level. Both political and economic factors have contributed to the periodic fluctuations in policy. We can identify a similar conjuncture of interests as at the national level. Differences within the political leadership, inter- and intra-institutional fissures and regional interests have combined to jostle the policy along. However, the course of the Open Policy in Fujian also had its own distinctive features. The political struggle within the provincial government took longer to resolve than at the national level, thus holding back the pace of change in the early 1980s. Tensions between Taiwan and China have also constrained the development of trade and investment whilst Overseas Chinese connections have positively influenced opening up. We will first explore in greater detail the disparate interests involved in the opening up of Fujian province and then consider their combined impact on the process of opening up.

National and provincial leadership

The consolidation of Deng Xiaoping's position at the Third Plenum in December 1978 was a crucial factor in the expansion of China's foreign economic relations. Similarly, leadership struggles in Fujian province have also been important determinants in the course of the Open Policy. In fact the continuing dominance of a less reform-minded provincial leadership up till mid-1981 contributed towards the slow pace of policy implementation in Fujian compared to nearby Guangdong.

The provincial government of Fujian was up till mid-1981 led by Ma Xingyuan, a member of the so-called Shanxi clique. This group consisted of political cadres sent from Shanxi in the late 1950s to work in Fujian province.[3] Although Ma Xingyuan and other members of the Shanxi clique probably welcomed some changes, they nevertheless took a cautious approach to reform and opening up. References by these leaders to 'class struggle' indicate that they favoured a Maoist approach to the economy, but not as radical as during the '10 dark years'.

The differences in approach to the Open Policy amongst these provincial leaders became apparent during a meeting on foreign economic relations in early October 1981. Ma Xingyuan revealed a conservative stance, calling for caution and restraint, as seen in: 'In our economic activities with foreign countries, we should be bold and active on the one hand and careful and cautious on the other.'[4] Although it is difficult to determine exactly the policy preferences of these leaders, it is likely that they favoured a restoration of the *status quo* of the late 1950s.

Xiang Nan, who was a protégé of Hu Yaobang, and Hu Ping were, however, intent on a more rapid pace of implementation. Although the appointment of Hu Ping and Xiang Nan as vice-governor and provincial chief in late 1981 weakened the position of Ma Xingyuan, the predominance of the Shanxi clique in the provincial Party Central Committee was still a potential source of opposition to any too radical changes.[5] The influence of the Shanxi clique in the provincial government was a crucial factor in the slow pace of policy implementation in the early years (see Table 4.1). The appointment of Hu Ping as governor of Fujian in January 1983 provided a further impetus to the Open Policy.[6] Moreover, the reorganisation of the provincial leadership in the spring of 1983 strengthened the position of the reformers.[7]

As well as the consolidation of the reformers at the local level, support from central leaders has accelerated the pace of policy implementation in Fujian province. In particular, Deng Xiaoping's visit to Xiamen SEZ in early 1984 was a significant factor in the subsequent spate of policy innovation and the dramatic increase in the level of foreign direct investment (see Table 4.1). Moreover, central leaders have also fed into the formulation of development strategies for the zone. Deng Xiaoping, for example, expressed a keen interest in the adoption of 'free-port' policies in Xiamen whilst Zhao Ziyang gave emphasis to the introduction of high-tech industry into the zone.

Open central government support for the zones as well as the promotion of reform-minded leaders at the local level may have pushed the Open Policy forward, but opposition to opening up and reforms at both national and local levels have also been significant constraints. The Shanxi clique, for example, which also had factional ties at the central level, continued to exert its influence on policy affairs. Taking advantage of the economic crisis in mid-1985 as well as revelations of local economic corruption, the Shanxi clique launched an attack upon Xiang Nan and the Open Policy. In particular they accused Xiang Nan of 'engaging in the colonial economy' and claimed that the province's renowned Sino-Japanese joint venture Fujian—Hitachi was 'controlled by the Japanese imperial army'.[8] The pressure from the central Shanxi clique led in early 1986 to the dismissal of Xiang Nan. He was replaced by the more moderate reformer, Chen Guangyi, from Gansu province. Although Hu Ping was still at the helm, this shake-up in the political context dampened official enthusiasm for the Open Policy and contributed towards the downswing in the third cycle.

Table 4.1 Annual foreign direct investment in Xiamen SEZ: 1980 to June 1992 (US$m)

Type	1980–3	1984	1985	1986	1987	1988	1989	1990	1991	1992
EJV										
No. of agreements	10	51	69	26	31	87	55	36	na	na
Agreed investment	73.34	205.82	310.94	47.13	77.00	226.18	92.00	48.61	na	na
Agreed FDI	22.81	87.39	150.17	22.60	35.00	56.88	47.00	21.67	na	na
Realised FDI	0.20	30.85	62.74	30.73	na	36.01	na	na	na	na
CJV										
No. of agreements	13	30	30	3	6	14	10	31	na	na
Agreed investment	14.15	74.21	92.94	4.00	6.30	11.60	4.50	112.70	na	na
Agreed FDI	10.05	47.76	87.45	3.38	3.18	8.36	4.00	97.37	na	na
Realised FDI	4.10	8.27	9.07	2.14	na	1.92	na	na	na	na
WOFE										
No. of agreements	1	5	6	5	13	79	136	195	na	na
Agreed investment	4.20	14.52	4.40	1.60	18.50	124.33	463.00	354.00	na	na
Agreed FDI	4.20	14.52	4.40	1.60	18.5	90.40	463.00	334.32	na	na
Realised FDI	3.45	1.32	1.47	1.59	na	10.03	na	na	na	na
Total										
No. of agreements	24	86	105	34	50	180	201	262	213	133
Agreed investment	91.69	294.55	408.28	52.73	101.80	362.11	559.50	515.31	586.00	na
Agreed FDI	37.06	149.67	242.02	27.58	56.68	155.64	514.00	453.36	520.00	na
Realised FDI	7.75	40.44	73.28	34.46	17.53	479.60	129.80	72.73	na	na

Note: na = not available.
Sources: Xiamen Statistics Bureau, Interview, 1987; *Xiamen Statistical Yearbook 1989 and 1990* (in Chinese), pp. 361 and 328 respectively; *Almanac of Xiamen SEZ* (in Chinese), 1991, p. 290; *Fujian Statistics Yearbook 1987* (in Chinese), p. 344; *Fujian Economic Yearbook 1988* (in Chinese), p. 681; *Collection of Statistical Material on the Open Coastal Cities, SEZs, Unified Planned Towns, 1989 and 1990* (in Chinese), pp. 105–10/p. 112; XMRB 8.1.92; XH in SWB/FE/W0239/A/6 15.7.1992.

Apart from the Shanxi clique, those within the provincial and municipal leadership who owed their positions to the Cultural Revolution and so expected to lose out under the reforms were likely to oppose the changes in policy. Moreover, those who enjoyed personal ties with particular leaders would also be likely to support any opposition to change in the *status quo*.

Opposition to the Open Policy has found expression both nationally and locally in the domain of ideology. The ideological themes recurring in the debates on the Open Policy in the local press in 1981 centred around the issues of self-reliance and imperialism.[9] With the launch of the campaign against economic crime the focus shifted to the causal links between the Open Policy and smuggling. In the autumn of 1983 the key themes taken up by the opposition concerned 'spiritual pollution'. By early 1987 the focus was on the evils of 'bourgeois liberalisation'. After Tiananmen the leitmotiv was anti-peaceful evolution. The thrust of all of these campaigns was in the ideological sphere where the reformers were weakest.

The influence of the opposition was not confined to the provincial leadership. With the extension of the Open Policy to the rest of Xiamen Island, the arena of conflict between the supporters and opponents of the policy has also widened. The reformist attack upon the opposition in 1984 spread out to rural areas. Local leaders or 'peasant secretaries' who felt that negotiations with foreign investors took too much time were castigated for ignoring the Open Policy.[10] This was interpreted as indicative of 'leftist' influence and the long period of the closed-door policy. Articles in the provincial newspaper stressed the need to 'liberate thought' and 'overcome leftist influence'. Cadres in Quanzhou, Longxi district and Jinjiang county in particular became the subject of criticism in the press.[11] However, some villages in Jinjiang county had taken the initiative and sent people to Shenzhen to negotiate projects.[12]

Struggles within national and provincial leadership have unabashedly shaped the course of opening up. As the Open Policy became more the order of the day, the need for political change at lower levels became more urgent. Similarly, as the reformers consolidated their position at the local level, the conditions for opening up improved. Let us now look at the institutional interests affecting the Open Policy.

Institutional factors

As at the national level we can identify particular inter- and intra-institutional interests at work. Of particular relevance in the case of Fujian province are the army, ideological institutions and tensions between cadres. Let us look at each of these in turn.

Army

As certain sections of the army have been a bastion of opposition to the Open Policy at the national level, it is not surprising that the army has played a similar role at the local level, particularly as Fujian hosts a substantial army population. Up till 1978 Fujian province and Xiamen in particular were part of China's front line against Taiwan. As a result, the army came to hold a significant position in government, land control and the economy.

The plan to construct a SEZ at Huli district in Xiamen and the later extension of the zone to cover the whole island entailed substantial material and political losses for the army. The construction of the SEZ as well as areas for tourism required the acquisition of land either under military control or near to military areas.[13] The army and the relevant departments of the government formed a leadership group to assess the strategic utility of certain military areas and buildings and decided which could be converted for civilian use, which abandoned and which should remain within the control of the army.

The army was destined to lose not only land but also their command over other basic resources such as food, water and electricity. Clearly, the development of a large industrial area with the capacity to hold 200 factories would make considerable demands on the city's electricity and water resources. Furthermore, both the labour required to construct that area as well as the future labour force employed in the factories would require guaranteed food supplies. The necessity to resolve this conflict with the army led to a meeting between the Municipal Food Company, the Commerce Bureau, the Water and Electricity Department and the army. Although they guaranteed the needs of the army in their coastal defence work, it was nevertheless clear that the priority of the army as a customer to these agencies had dropped in favour of productive enterprises.[14]

The general overhauling of the army at the national level facilitated the decline in its importance and prioritised position. Not only was the army being streamlined, but it was also expected, like productive enterprises, to be accountable for its budget. This then provided a favourable context for the municipal government to negotiate with the army. The construction of Huli industrial district as well as the opening of tourist areas heralded a potential conflict over local resources and in particular, between the army and local government.

Although explicit evidence is not always available, it would be safe to assume that the army has played a key role in some of the expressions of opposition to the Open Policy in Xiamen since 1980. During his visit to Xiamen in June 1982, Xiang Nan, the provincial Party chief, called for coordination and cooperation in carrying out the Open Policy.[15] The following report of his visit betrays some of the axes of political tension: 'This means that we should carry out properly the unity between the army and government, the army and civilians, between the local cadres and cadres from outside and between the cadres and the masses.'[16]

This suggests first, that the army was a major source of opposition to the policy; second, that there was growing friction between local cadres and cadres recruited from outside the city. Furthermore, references to the Cultural Revolution and 'bourgeois factionalism' suggest that the 'disunity' was linked both to ideological differences and the need to redress grievances stemming from that period.

Although there was resistance within the army to the Open Policy and reforms, there were nevertheless sections of the army supporting the new policies. On the same day as the above quote, the political department of the army published an article in defence of the Open Policy. The following extract exemplifies underlying divisions within the army: 'There are some people who have used the Open Policy to commit economic crimes, this does not imply that there is a problem with the policy itself.'[17] Sections of the army in favour of the reforms and the Open Policy include those keen to modernise the army, those who had suffered during the Cultural Revolution and veterans of the pre-independence struggle who had fought with Deng Xiaoping.

Ideological institutions

As at the national level, ideological institutions such as the provincial Propaganda Department have played a key role in the campaigns directed against the Open Policy. At the same time as the second provincial anti-smuggling conference in September 1981, for example, the Propaganda Department held a provincial meeting of its directors, urging them to criticise 'bourgeois liberalisation'.[18] The use of this term not only suggested the influence of leftists but also indicated the forging of causal links between opening up and economic crime. The Propaganda Department was also prominent in the anti-bourgeois liberalisation campaign in early 1987.[19]

Following Deng Xiaoping's visit in February 1984 particular institutions were singled out where the weight of opposition had thwarted the implementation of the policy. These included governmental departments such as industry and commerce, customs, planning, finance, taxation and banking, and intermediary institutions such as Xiamen SEZ United Development Company.[20] Deng realised the urgency of securing the support of these particular institutions to speed the process of opening up.

Intra-institutional interests

Different configurations of interests within institutions have also shaped the course of the Open Policy. As mentioned previously, during his visit to Xiamen in June 1982, Xiang Nan called not only for greater unity between the army and government but also amongst cadres.[21] There are three aspects to this conflict amongst the cadres. First, in order to improve the institutional capacity of the local state, the provincial government has not only provided training for existing cadres, but also 'imported' cadres from outside the province to meet immediate needs. In 1984 Huli Management Committee recruited 260 specialised, technical cadres from Beijing, Shanghai, Tianjin and Nanjing, some of whom took up positions as managers and supervisors in joint ventures.[22] However, there was probably resentment from local cadres that cadres from 'outside' were occupying important positions in the zone administration, particularly as these received better payment for taking up their positions.

Second, those cadres appointed from outside are likely to be supporters of the Open Policy, possibly with factional ties to central reformist leaders. The arrival of such cadres would have made the future political demise of existing cadres, particularly those opposed to the policy and reforms, more imminent.

Third, the cadres from the outside were likely also to be more technically and professionally qualified. In 1983, for example, only 5 per cent of employees in the municipal trade bureau of Xiamen had any specialisation in foreign trade.[23] This tension between 'technocratic' and 'politicocratic' cadres was also significant amongst Fujian cadres, particularly as the new opportunities for training increased the importance and number of technocratic cadres.

Although, for a variety of reasons, there was an institutional network of opposition to the Open Policy and reforms, there was also a considerable base of institutional and popular support for the Open Policy. Xiang Nan's reference to the 'disunity between cadres and the masses' betrays this. The implication here was that there was conflict between the 'masses' who wanted to push forward the Open Policy because they could see immediate benefits to themselves and the 'cadres' who tried to obstruct the policy because they saw a threat to their positions. We can also interepret it to refer to those with Overseas Chinese connections who wanted to establish economic links but were thwarted in their efforts by particular cadres.[24]

Regional interests

The Open Policy has decentralised some authority and granted special rights in foreign economic relations to lower-level authorities, branches and enterprises in particular parts of Fujian. This has led to competition between different regions in Fujian province to become the recipients of the policy. This pressure from below has been an important factor pushing the policy forward, contributing towards the cyclical upswings.

The choice of a site for the SEZ revealed competitive tensions between the northern capital of Fuzhou and the southern light industrial base of Xiamen. Given that none of the SEZs were located in provincial capitals, it was clear that the centre was from early on wary of the provinces becoming too powerful. It was not until early 1984 when Fuzhou became one of the celebrated 14 coastal cities, that some of Fuzhou's ambitions could be met. However, it still enjoyed fewer privileges than Xiamen. Moreover, the granting of greater autonomy to Xiamen in early 1984 also meant that Fuzhou lost some of its control over Xiamen.

As well as tensions betweeen the provincial capital of Fuzhou and Xiamen SEZ, it was also apparent from early on that there were pressures from other areas in South Fujian to appropriate the benefits of the Open Policy. Demands by local enterprises and authorities for greater authority in foreign trade revealed considerable local support for opening up. As early as 1980 some enterprises in counties demanded greater autonomy from the trading companies. Similarly, in the autumn of 1984 Quanzhou also pressed the provincial government for greater inclusion in the scope of the Open Policy. The tendency of some provincial leaders such as Hu Ping to give central government policy statements a broader interpretation pointed to pressure from below to widen the net of beneficiaries. This support from below was also seen in the rapid spread of processing and assembly deals in Quanzhou and Jinjiang county, areas with strong Overseas Chinese connections. As a result, policy formulation concerning the scope of the Open Policy tended to lag behind practice.

Although the opening up of the South Fujian golden triangle in 1985 had extended some of the privileges of the Open Policy to Zhangzhou and Quanzhou and surrounding counties, some central and regional leaders were becoming increasingly concerned about the regional implications of the Open Policy.[25] At the national level Li Xiannian had drawn attention to the growing regional disparities between coastal and inland areas, whilst at the local level Hu Ping and Chen Guangyi highlighted the expanding gap between the coastal and mountainous areas in Fujian province. To redress this regional imbalance as well as to meet the demands from the mountainous areas which saw themselves losing out, the provincial government extended some authority over foreign economic relations to these areas.

Whilst the strong local support for the Open Policy in Fujian province has been a significant factor sustaining the policies during downswings and pushing it forward during upswings, it has also contributed, however, to the occasional derailment of the policy. As at the national level, there have been instances of cadres taking advantage of the loopholes in the Open Policy to engage in smuggling and the illegal resale of imported goods. Moreover, the low level of training of cadres involved in foreign economic relations resulted in both opportunities being missed and losses being made. A local newspaper reported the following incident: 'A Hong Kong business-person went to a district in Jinjiang County and asked about the different grades of ginger and their prices. The cadre was dumbstruck and unable to give an answer.'[26]

Although the decentralisation of some authority to municipal, district and county authorities unleashed local initiative, it also contributed towards the foreign trade deficit in Fujian province in mid-1985 (see Tables 4.2 and 4.3). As the Open Policy has spun its own web of regional and institutional interests, efforts by the local government to tighten control over the economy then face both an economic and a political challenge. Although the broad regional base of support carries the policy forward, it also makes retrenchment increasingly difficult, as evidenced in the renewed attempts in early 1987 to cut investment expenditure. It is this political tension between the national and provincial attempts to restore control over the economy and the pressure from below to continue the policy that has contributed towards the spiral pattern of the Open Policy. By 1987 local academics were already discussing the stifling effect of continuing central and provincial authority over the SEZ. An article in *Fujian Jingji* (Fujian Economy) called for greater authority for the local Xiamen SEZ office in managing the zone.[27]

Table 4.2 Foreign trade balance in Fujian province: 1977–90

Year	Trade volume (US$m)	Exports (US$m)	Imports (US$m)	Balance (US$m)
1977	139.46	129.19	10.27	+ 118.92
1978	202.60	190.14	12.46	+ 177.68
1979	274.01	246.49	27.52	+ 218.97
1980	505.43	363.66	141.77	+ 221.89
1981	565.25	398.18	167.07	+ 231.11
1982	516.74	379.13	137.61	+ 241.52
1983	599.18	394.70	204.48	+ 190.22
1984	693.81	423.72	270.09	+ 153.63
1985	1,116.92	491.48	625.44	− 133.96
1986	893.74	578.54	315.20	+ 263.34
1987	1,341.22	849.33	499.33	+ 357.44
1988	2,195.26	1,405.74	789.52	+ 616.22
1989	2,397.02	1,661.71	735.31	+ 926.40
1990	3,171.37	2,238.13	933.24	+1,304.89

Source: *Fujian Statistical Yearbook 1991* (in Chinese), p. 309.

Table 4.3 Foreign trade balance in Xiamen SEZ: 1980–90

Year	Trade volume (US$m)	Exports (US$m)	Imports (US$m)	Balance (US$m)
1980	141.00	140.00	1.15	+138.85
1981	151.27	131.12	20.15	+110.97
1982	147.21	124.02	23.19	+100.83
1983	139.86	123.81	16.05	+107.76
1984	303.83	127.22	176.61	− 49.39
1985	443.97	165.00	279.00	−114.00
1986	443.96	165.27	278.69	−113.42
1987	415.76	261.07	154.69	+106.38
1988*	1,364.80	574.04	790.76	−216.72
1989*	1,356.34	704.53	651.81	+ 52.72
1990*	2,017.29	960.97	1,056.32	− 95.35

* Figures for 1988–90 do not match in official and non-official sources. Official sources indicate positive balances in years 1988, 1989 and 1990.
Sources: Compiled from *Almanac of Xiamen SEZ 1986*, p. 94 and p. 396; *Xiamen Statistical Yearbook 1989*, p. 368; *Almanac of Xiamen SEZ 1991*, pp. 288–9; *Collection of Statistical Materials on the Open Coastal Cities, SEZs and Unified Planned Towns 1989 and 1990*, pp. 102–3 and pp. 106–7; *Xiamen Statistical Yearbook 1991*, pp. 288–9; Zhang Fengqing, 1987, pp. 16–18; *China's SEZs Annals 1990*, pp. 497–9.

Economic factors

The trajectory of the Open Policy has both an economic and a political logic. The most salient economic factor has, as at the national level, been the contradictions in the reformist leadership's dual aspirations of microlevel initiative and macrolevel balance. The decentralisation of some authority over foreign trade and foreign direct investment to municipal, district and county authorities and some enterprises has led, as at the national level, to a rapid increase in imports, particularly of consumer goods, as well as the inappropriate use of foreign exchange. This culminated in a substantial foreign trade deficit and the doubling of Fujian's foreign debt within a year. At the same time exports could not be increased rapidly enough, whilst imported production lines required constant supplies of imported materials.[28]

In order to stem the tide of imports and control the illegal circulation of foreign exchange, the Provincial Party Committee introduced new measures to improve exports, foreign trade and foreign exchange management and control the quotas for foreign exchange use at subprovincial levels.[29] However, the administrative tightening of control over foreign exchange led not only to a decline in the volume of trade but also in the ability of Chinese enterprises to obtain loans to set up joint ventures.[30]

This recentralisation of control over foreign trade and foreign exchange led to a decline in foreign direct investment in Xiamen SEZ in 1986. The number of contracts for foreign direct investment signed fell from 105 in 1985 to 34 in 1986 (see Table 4.1). This was partly because of the effects of the foreign exchange crisis of the previous year and partly because of the mounting dissatisfaction of foreign investors with the investment climate. However, with the issue of the 22 Articles encouraging foreign direct investment in October 1986, the level of foreign direct investment improved again over the next year.[31] As at the national level, there has also been a cycle of decentralisation and recentralisation, which has been the primary economic cause of the Open Policy spiral.

The fluctuations in the Open Policy can also be linked to the contradictions in the specific economic goals of the Open Policy for Xiamen SEZ. The desire to use the SEZ to introduce advanced technology conflicts, however, with the political goal of reunification with Taiwan. Although over 80 per cent of foreign direct investment in Xiamen came from Hong Kong and Taiwan, as in Shenzhen, the bulk of this was in small-scale, non-productive enterprises (see Tables 4.4 and 4.5). Moreover, as most of the joint ventures were oriented to the domestic market up till the mid-1980s, their contribution to export earnings was less than anticipated. Awareness of the failure of the policies to achieve some of their objectives led to a reappraisal in early 1986 of the strategies and specific measures adopted in the zones. Emphasis was given to ensuring better selection of projects, particularly those involving export production and the introduction of high-tech industry.

Table 4.4　National source of foreign direct investment in Xiamen SEZ: 1980—9

Country	No. of projects		%	Total FDI (US$m)	%
Hong Kong/Macao	382		56.5	804	65.5
Taiwan	175	(227*)	25.5	216	17.6
Singapore	43		6.0	57	4.6
USA	26		4.0	43	3.5
Japan	19		3.0	43	3.5
Philippines	17		2.5	32	2.6
W. Germany	3		0.4	14	1.1
Jordan	2		0.2	14	1.1
Others	13		1.9	4	0.3
Total	676		100.0	1,227	100.0

* Bracketed figure refers to Taiwanese investment via other national enterprises. This is probably an underestimate as it is difficult to identify this form of Taiwanese investment.
Source: *Almanac of Xiamen SEZ 1990* (in Chinese), p. 329.

Table 4.5 Sectoral breakdown of foreign direct investment in Xiamen SEZ: 1980−9

	Projects		%	%	FDI (US$m)		%	%
	1980−5	1980−9	1980−5	1980−9	1980−5	1980−9	1980−5	1980−9
Industry	92	478	54.5	70.7	111	737	43.5	60.1
Agriculture	9	36	5.3	5.3	5	36	2.0	3.0
Transport & comms	5	14	3.0	2.1	3	8	1.1	0.7
Construction	24	21	14.2	3.1	18	7	7.1	0.6
Commerce	17	28	10.0	4.1	17	13	6.7	1.1
Real estate	11	91	6.5	13.5	20	331	7.8	27.0
Other	11	8	6.5	1.2	81	93	31.8	7.5
Total	169	676	100.0	100.0	255	1,227	100.0	100.0

Source: *Almanac of Xiamen SEZ 1990* (in Chinese), p. 329 and *1986*, p. 93.

Apart from the contradictory nature of these goals, the constant vacillation in the stated policy objectives of Xiamen SEZ has also made the interpretation of the policies not only more difficult but also more vulnerable to distortion. The confusion over policy goals accounts in part for the predominance of small-scale, non-productive enterprises which yield quick results. Moreover, the economic imbalances engendered through decentralisation have also led to a change in emphasis on particular goals. The need to deal with the foreign exchange crisis of mid-1985, for example, placed primacy on the goal of increasing export earnings in 1986.

As well as the contradictions in economic goals, features of the economic context have also shaped the course of the Open Policy. The shortage of funds for the development of Xiamen SEZ has been a significant constraint on the improvement of the foreign direct investment climate. As Fujian province received little central state funding prior to 1978, the task of infrastructural development was formidable. Moreover, as Deng Xiaoping had stressed that the zones were to rely on 'special policies' rather than central funds, the burden on the provincial government was even greater. Nevertheless some central government funding has been provided.[32] These funding constraints have encouraged Fujian to innovate in the field of foreign borrowing. Fujian province was the first province in China to issue bonds overseas. Since then it has repeatedly raised money through overseas bond issues.

The shortage of foreign exchange was linked not only to the administrative system of foreign exchange allocation, but also to the inconvertibility of the Rmb. The existence of three currencies in the zone, namely Hong Kong dollar, Foreign Exchange Certificates and Rmb has encouraged, *inter alia*, the hoarding of foreign exchange. Holders of foreign exchange would delay in depositing it in the Bank of China so as to buy and resell imported goods and engage in speculation.[33] The illegal use of foreign exchange led to a fall of 65 per cent in the quantity of Overseas Chinese remittances from US$ 33.43 million in 1980 to US$ 11.46 million in 1984.[34]

The contradiction between the dual goals of microlevel dynamism and macrolevel balance has, as at the national level, been a prominent factor in the spiral of the Open Policy in Xiamen SEZ. Furthermore, contradictions and vacillation in the specific objectives of the zone as well as features of the economic context have also shaped the course of the Open Policy.

Cycle 1 — getting going: 1979–1981

Six months after the offical endorsement of the Open Policy the State Council issued a document granting Fujian and Guangdong provinces 'special policies and flexible measures' to open up. It was already apparent in the latter part of 1978 when preparations for the establishment of Fujian Investment Enterprises Corporation (FIEC) were underway, that the opening up of Fujian province was on the agenda. The shift in policy towards Taiwan facilitated this process. In December 1978 the Standing Committee of the National People's Congress called for economic ties with Taiwan as well as a halt to the daily bombing of Quemoy Island, a Taiwanese island lying opposite Xiamen.[35]

But why was Fujian chosen as a site to experiment with the Open Policy? The decision to grant Fujian province special privileges in its foreign economic relations as well as the later establishment of a SEZ in Xiamen was guided primarily by politico-economic considerations linked to reunification with Taiwan and the cultivation of links with Overseas Chinese.

The desire for reunification with Hong Kong, Macao and Taiwan was a dominant factor not only in the Open Policy but also in the geographical location of three of the SEZs. Xiamen, Shenzhen and Zhuhai SEZs all lie opposite areas which have been historically severed from mainland China. Xiamen faces Taiwan, Shenzhen borders on Hong Kong and Zhuhai lies next to Macao (see Figure 2.1). Although Shantou does not lie directly opposite any of these areas, it is nevertheless relatively close to Hong Kong and is also home to many Overseas Chinese. These SEZs would then serve explicitly as 'windows for advanced technology and advanced managerial methods' but also implicitly as 'windows for exemplifying the principle of "one country, two systems"'.[36] We can see this underlying political rationale for Xiamen SEZ in the following extract from a provincial newspaper: 'Making the SEZ a success, will not only be beneficial to the promotion of the construction of our socialist modernisation, but also has an important meaning for the reunification of Taiwan with the motherland.'[37]

Fujian's overseas connections also made it a suitable target for the Open Policy. There are currently over six million Overseas Chinese in more than 90 countries who have their roots in Fujian province. As Fujian province is a coastal area and particularly poor, especially in the inland mountainous areas, emigration over the last few centuries has been quite substantial. Fujian is, next to Guangdong province, the second largest home to Overseas Chinese.

But why were these overseas connections so important? First, by opening up Fujian province the capital resources of the Overseas Chinese could be utilised both in the construction of the zone and in the economic development of the province, so saving scarce domestic resources. Second, by relying initially more on Overseas Chinese investment, the 'Chinese' face of foreign investment might make the adoption of the Open Policy more palatable to opponents who harboured 'anti-foreign' sentiments. Third, the initial investments of Overseas Chinese would serve as a 'buffer stock' until the investment climate proved sufficiently attractive to other sources of foreign investment. Fourth, by expanding economic links with the Overseas Chinese community, China could influence current thinking within both those communities and their host countries towards China. The cultivation of a pro-China lobby in the Overseas Chinese communities could serve to pressurise foreign governments, such as the USA, to recognise only China as the 'true representative of the Chinese people'. This would contribute indirectly through external channels to the process of reunification.

One of the special privileges granted to Fujian province included the right to establish a SEZ. We can trace the origins of this idea to a number of sources, both central and local. Seeing that Guangdong had already established an export-processing zone in Shekou in January 1979 and was considering two more zones in Bao'an and Zhuhai counties, the Fujian authorities also began by March of that year to express an interest in establishing a zone, indicating support from below for the SEZ policy.

Whilst the selection of Fujian province as a base for the Open Policy was the outcome of central decision-making processes, the choice of Xiamen as a locus for the SEZ involved a broader base of participants, including provincial and municipal leaders and researchers. The selection of a site for the SEZ turned out to be a highly politicised process. As with any policy change the distribution of resources, and in particular the granting of special privileges, embodies 'political choices'. The vacillations in the proposed location of the SEZ in Fujian province reflected these conflicts. Up till the final decision to locate the SEZ in Huli district of Xiamen three potential sites had been proposed, namely Langqi Island near Fuzhou, the capital of Fujian province, Xinglin district near Xiamen and Huli district near Xiamen (see Figure 4.1). Initially, only the first two options were under

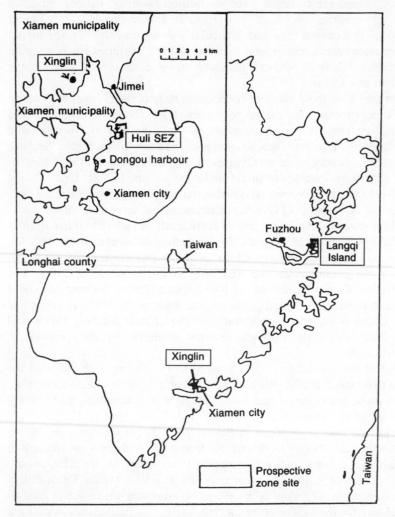

Figure 4.1   Potential zone sites in Fujian province, 1978–80 (Source: Fujian Economic Commission Xiamen Export Office, May 1980)

consideration. The Fujian provincial government formally announced these in December 1979 as the sites for the SEZ.[38] However, the potentially huge infrastructural costs of these sites led to their abandonment.

As the Xinglin SEZ was to concentrate on heavy industry, the sectoral policy shift in early 1979 towards light industry and the concomitant retrenchment of large-scale projects contributed both to the downfall of Xinglin as well as to the eventual focus on only one SEZ. The options of Langqi Island and Xinglin were shelved in the meantime. In May 1980, the State Council gave top priority to the development of Xiamen SEZ at Huli district, only two kilometres from the Dongdu Harbour development project, finally approving this in October.[39]

Although there is little open information available about the issues debated in the decision-making processes, we can nevertheless detect in the discussion of the location of the zones an element of competitive regional rivalry both between Xiamen and Fuzhou and between Xiamen and outlying areas. Fujian province is divided linguistically from north to south. Communications between the two parts are not easy. The decision to locate the SEZ in southern Fujian may have caused some resentment among the northerners. Six months after the central government announced the opening of a SEZ in Xiamen, the Fujian authorities indicated that a SEZ in Fuzhou was also on the agenda, suggesting not only intra-provincial tensions but also a thrust from below to expand the scope of the policy. These hints of intra-regional rivalry surfaced on several occasions at later stages of the policy process.

As well as competitive tensions between Fuzhou and Xiamen there was also evidence of pressure in southern Fujian for maximum extension of the zone. There were at least four different proposals concerning where the boundaries of the zone should begin and end. The central government option of Huli industrial zone was the smallest whilst the largest extended the scope of the zone to Xiamen municipality and Tongan county (see Figure 4.2).[40]

Although Fujian had been granted special privileges regarding its foreign economic relations, the pace of policy implementation as at the national level proceeded slowly over the next two years (see Table 4.1). In 1980 a Japanese joint venture was set up in Fuzhou whilst a large American tobacco company arranged a processing deal with a Xiamen state-owned cigarette enterprise. Other joint arrangements included the Quanzhou Sony television assembly shop, the Fuzhou Overseas Chinese plastics plant and the Huian stone-carving factory.

The slow pace of policy implementation was due in part to the newness of the policy and in part to foreign investors' concern about the stability of the new government. Moreover, the reductions in capital spending both locally and nationally in early 1981 were a significant constraint on the pace of construction of the SEZ. These cutbacks marked a downswing in the Open Policy at both national and local levels. At the end of March, Hu Ping, Deputy Director of the Provincial Planning Commission, announced that capital construction investments were to be reduced by over a third compared to the previous year.[41] Deng Xiaoping had in fact already underlined in April 1979 that the zones were to be self-financing. Although the provincial government contributed Y50 million to the infrastructural development of Xiamen in March 1981, this was nevertheless

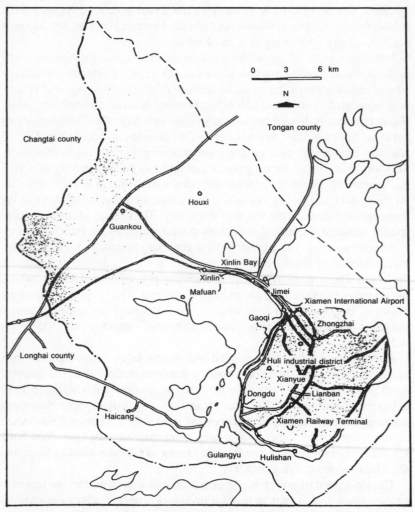

Figure 4.2   Xiamen municipality and Tongan county, (Source: *Xiamen SEZ, An Investment Guide*, Xiamen City 1986, p. 28)

limited by the policy of readjustment.[42] Xiamen was to find its own sources of funding, including foreign investors and Overseas Chinese.[43]

As well as these financial constraints, differences of opinion within the provincial leadership over the pace, aims and content of the SEZ policy also influenced the pace of implementation. These differences were both regionally and ideologically informed.

In the course of 1981 various proposals concerning the function of the

SEZ were made. In April, Ma Xingyuan, for example, announced at the Third Session of the Fifth Provincial People's Congress that Xiamen would be a comprehensive zone, specialising not only in export-processing but also in agriculture, aquatic breeding, tourism, construction and high-tech R&D.[44] However, at a work conference on Guangdong and Fujian provinces held in July 1981 it was proposed that Xiamen SEZ focus on export-processing and tourism.[45] In September 1981 various theorists suggested that Xiamen become an export-processing zone, tourist centre and trade zone.[46] There were also proposals for Xiamen to become a free port like Hong Kong.[47]

This debate over the functions and goals of the SEZ in Xiamen not only reflected differences within the local policy elite, comprising municipal and provincial government leaders informed by research and academic institutions, but also masked attempts by groups with particular regional interests to appropriate the benefits of the policy. Whilst 'some' felt that Xiamen should give priority to export-processing and simultaneously develop tourism, 'others' felt that Xiamen should become a free-trade zone giving priority to tourism and trade.[48]

The choice between the two hinged on differing conceptions concerning the regional role of Xiamen SEZ. Advocates of the first option saw Xiamen SEZ depending in the long term on foreign supplies of raw materials and in the interim on local supplies. Proponents of the second option, however, felt that Xiamen should handle the import and export business of south-west Fujian, serving as a major trade rather than industrial centre.[49] The issue at stake was Xiamen's dependence on outlying areas for its raw material supply, which would increase substantially with the construction of the zone.[50] This increase in raw material needs of the SEZ would, by putting pressure on existing supplies, lead to conflicts between the zone and industry outside the zone. This debate was taking place within the context of readjustment, when the importance of heavy industry, located primarily in Fuzhou, was declining.[51]

This debate suggests first, that there was already resentment brewing in the areas within South Fujian which had not been selected as 'special zones' with special privileges and second, that this resentment was fuelled by an expectation of 'losing out' under the policy. This debate over the policy direction of Xiamen SEZ continued into 1982.[52]

Ideology also informed the differences within the local leadership concerning the pace, content and form of the Open Policy. In early 1981 an article appeared in the provincial daily newspaper suggesting that the phenomenon of smuggling indicated the continued need for class struggle. Although the commentary endorsed the policies of the Third Plenum, it nevertheless called for their implementation 'within given limits'. This cautious approach as well as the emphasis in the article on 'political stability and unity' reflected divisions within the local leadership over the reforms and the Open Policy.[53] Moreover, the vocabulary used suggested that Maoists were still strong in Fujian province.

These tensions within the local leadership culminated at the Third Session of the Fifth Fujian People's Congress in April 1981 where there was heated discussion over the pace of implementation of Fujian's special policies and measures. Whilst some deputies felt that the policy had been adequately carried out in the last two years, many wanted a faster pace of implementation, reflecting the frustration felt by the reformist leaders.[54] In May 1981 there were reports that the Provincial Governor, Ma Xingyuan, and the Provincial Party Secretary, Liao Zhigao, who had been in power since the mid-1970s, were to be replaced. Xiang Nan, a technocrat in favour of reform and opening up and a close associate of Hu Yaobang, was destined to take over as provincial chief, with the reform-minded Hu Ping as vice-governor.[55]

By September the imminent downfall of Ma Xingyuan was secured. At a key conference convened by the provincial committee, discussion took place concerning the implementation of policies, including Overseas Chinese affairs, which redressed those wrongly accused during the Cultural Revolution and external economic links.[56] Ma Xingyuan was not present. At the Eleventh Session of the Fifth People's Congress in October 1981 the reform-minded Hu Ping was appointed vice-governor and Xiang Nan officially became the provincial party chief.[57] Although both Xiang Nan and Ma Xingyuan were elected as deputies to the Fifth National People's Congress, Xiang Nan's name appeared first on the list, indicating again that Ma Xingyuan was losing political ground.[58] This change in leadership paved the way for a new cycle in the Open Policy in Fujian province.

Cycle 2 — small steps forward: October 1981 to 1982

With Hu Ping as vice-governor headway could be made in implementing Fujian's 'special policies and flexible measures'. Construction on the Xiamen SEZ began in earnest in October 1981.[59] Xiang Nan announced policies 'even more preferential' than in other areas. For example, tax incentives were to be extended not only to joint ventures in the Huli export-processing zone but also to all joint ventures on Xiamen Island, and possibly even throughout Fujian province.[60] This extension of tax incentives to areas beyond the confines of Huli suggested not only pressure from below to expand the policy but also a pragmatic reasoning that in order to fund the zone, foreign capital would have to be drawn to other areas in the meantime.

One month later Hu Ping announced that Fujian hoped to draw Y1.4 billion in foreign investment over the next five years, contributing 25 per cent of the province's total budget.[61] At the same time Hu Ping gave details of the preferential treatment to foreign investors, hinting also at the future issue of special SEZ regulations.[62] Policies towards Overseas Chinese were improved.[63] Growing national criticism of the zones and in particular of Shenzhen SEZ, however, overshadowed this upswing in the policy in the winter of 1981. The issue triggering this spate of controversy over the zones concerned economic crime.

Smuggling had been on the increase since mid-1980. In January 1981 an article in the national press reported large-scale smuggling in Fujian, Guangdong and Shanghai during the previous year.[64] At the end of the month the Fujian provincial government issued a circular calling for an attack upon smuggling.[65] As this had little effect, the Fujian government convened an anti-smuggling meeting in mid-March.[66] Further calls for an anti-smuggling campaign were endorsed at the Fifth Fujian People's Congress in early 1981.[67]

By this time the problem of smuggling in Guangdong, Fujian and Zhejiang had come to the attention of the central government which then convened an anti-smuggling conference in August. This was followed by yet another provincial anti-smuggling conference in September.[68] At the same time a provincial meeting of Propaganda Department directors at all levels referred to the need to criticise 'bourgeois liberalisation'.[69] The attack upon economic crime soon translated into an assault upon the SEZs. Although Shenzhen bore the brunt of the criticism, Xiamen SEZ also felt the reverberations.

This growing central concern for the zones prompted visits by Wang Zhen, member of the Military Commission, and Bo Yibo, Vice-Premier of the State Council, to Fujian on separate occasions in November 1981. Whilst Bo Yibo called for the 'bold implementation' of Fujian's special policies, the response of Wang Zhen was more veiled. Nevertheless, his call for greater unity between the army, government and people might be interpreted as cautious support for the SEZs.[70] At the same time as these visits, local opponents of the zones and Open Policy latched on to the growing problem of economic crime to attack the Open Policy. Ma Xingyuan, and other leftist leaders, who had recently been demoted, were probably behind this attack. Similar attacks by leftists within the central leadership fuelled their efforts.

Articles appearing in the provincial press on the themes of self-reliance and imperialism betrayed similar concerns to opponents within the central leadership. References to the SEZs as a form of 'semi-colony' reflected the intensity of opposition within the province as well as influence from the leftists at the centre.[71] Underlying this view was a fear that all foreign direct investment would necessarily lead to the loss of China's national sovereignty and independence. These parallels in the ideological rhetoric at national and local levels suggest on the one hand the influence of factional networks linked to the Whateverists and ultra-leftists and on the other hand a potential merging of interests between possible losers under the new policies and leftist opponents.

Reports of particular cases of economic crime linked to the Open Policy appeared in the press. In May 1981, for example, leading Party cadres of a Xiamen district signed a barter contract with Hong Kong business-people to import 53 tons of polyester silk thread and 138 TVs. These TVs were then sold internally at prices fixed by the department itself and prefer-entially to different ranks of employees. This incident provided easy ammunition for the leftist opposition who were keen to link the issue of economic crime to the Open Policy.[72]

The controversy over the zones carried on into 1982, dampening the initial boost given to the policy in the autumn of 1981. The pervasiveness of the leftist ideological view as well as the intense press coverage had a deleterious effect on the development of foreign direct investment. Some cadres were reluctant to establish contact with foreign businesspeople for fear of being accused of 'national betrayal'.[73]

Although Chen Yun's cautious comment in early 1982 implied central government support for the zones, it was not until the Fifth Session of the Provincial People's Congress in March 1982 that the reformers began to regain control at the provincial level. During this meeting the question was raised of whether there was a conflict between economic crime and the Open Policy. Supporters of the Open Policy expressed their fear that an attack upon economic crime would hinder the implementation of 'special and flexible' policies. The opposition, however, maintained that economic crime was the direct result of the Open Policy.[74]

By thematically linking the Open Policy with the issue of economic crime, the opposition had been able to define the terms in which the Open Policy was discussed. Although the publicity given to instances of local corruption made it difficult for the advocates of the Open Policy to disentangle economic crime from the Open Policy, they were nevertheless able to manipulate the ideological themes to their favour. Whilst not denying the link between the themes, they presented the attack upon economic crime as necessary for the proper implementation of the Open Policy.[75] This represented a compromise on the part of the reformers to enable them to push ahead with the Open Policy.

Despite these continuing tensions within the provincial leadership progress was made in establishing the Open Policy. In March 1982 the Congress issued a 'Statute on the Establishment of SEZs in Fujian'.[76] One month later the People's Congress passed three sets of regulations concerning the registration and management of enterprises, land use and labour manage-ment in Xiamen SEZ.[77] These regulations closely resembled those adopted by Guangdong province over the previous two years but Fujian was offering greater incentives to foreign investors.[78] As Xiamen had only just begun to construct the zone, more attractive terms had to be offered to lure foreign investors.[79] The passing of these regulations indicated the growing strength of the reformers within the provincial leadership.

Following the publication of the State Council decisions on economic crime in mid-April 1982, the Provincial Party Standing Committee held a meeting to review its anti-smuggling campaign. Events at the national level once again intruded upon the policy process at the provincial level. The divisions between the reformers and the Whateverists and ultra-leftists intensified in the next few months, as reflected in the spate of contradictory articles in the local press on the links between the Open Policy and economic crime. Whilst some articles portrayed this as a 'manifestation of class struggle', reflecting the influence of leftists, others claimed there was no causal link between opening up and economic crime.[80] Statements by reform-minded provincial leaders such as Wang Yan confirmed the continuation of the Open Policy. In the next three months further cases of economic crime involving smuggling and speculation were exposed in the press.[81]

The campaign against economic crime continued to have a deleterious effect on the implementation of policy. Comments such as the following suggest that some officials were taking a cautious approach to their work: 'It is difficult to avoid making mistakes when doing business abroad. In the future it would be better to make fewer mistakes and even better not to make any at all.'[82]

Despite the intense political struggle both centrally and locally, some progress was made both in establishing and implementing the policy, though the pace was frustratingly slow for the reformers. Processing and assembly deals, which involved less risks on the foreign side than joint ventures and yielded quick profits, were particularly popular in localities which were home to Overseas Chinese.[83] As these deals were less controversial than the more intrusive equity joint ventures and wholly owned foreign enterprises, they tended to go ahead. Nevertheless, the campaign against economic crime had a braking effect on the pace of policy innovation and implementation. It was not until the Twelfth Party Congress in September 1982 that the situation improved, marking the onset of another cycle in the evolution of the Open Policy in Xiamen SEZ.

Cycle 3 — pushing ahead, but not too fast: September 1982 to 1983

The Twelfth Party Congress of 1982 not only witnessed the final downfall of Hua Guofeng, one of the mainstay opponents of reform and opening up, but also the victory of the reformers in the ongoing battle over the SEZs. Following the publication of the investigation into Shenzhen and Zhuhai, the SEZs not only were to enjoy greater autonomy *vis-à-vis* central government but also were to lead the country in domestic economic reform. These events had a positive impact on the policy process in Xiamen SEZ, contributing towards the cyclical upswing.

On his return from the Twelfth People's Congress, Zou Erjun, Vice-Director of Huli Management Committee, urged combating economic crime at the same time as promoting the Open Policy.[84] Whilst this showed a genuine concern amongst the reformers about the rise in economic crime, it was at the same time a small compromise with the leftist opposition, allowing the reformers to push ahead with new policies. The issue was mentioned briefly again in mid-November 1982 at the end of an article reviewing the progress of the zone. This argued that although the Open Policy would lead to some 'spiritual pollution', this could be prevented through political and ideological work.[85]

The more positive climate prevailing since the Party Congress enabled further advances in the Open Policy in Fujian province and especially Xiamen SEZ. In October 1982 state councillor Gu Mu called for greater autonomy for Xiamen. In the same month two more ports opened for exports.[86] Pressure from areas outside Xiamen to enjoy the same privileges regarding foreign economic relations increased over the next year. Jinjiang and Longxi districts (see Figure 4.3), for example, drew attention to their crucial role in the development of the SEZ, underlining both their potential for tourism as well as their strong Overseas Chinese links.[87] As these two districts accounted in 1982 for almost 70 per cent of export goods, they were clearly eager to obtain the benefits of the Open Policy too.

Attempts to appropriate the policy through its extension have involved not only Xiamen and other areas in South Fujian but also the northern capital of Fuzhou. In March 1983 the Governor of Fujian, Hu Ping, proposed the development of two economic centres in Fujian, namely Xiamen, along with the subcentres of Quanzhou, Zhangzhou and Longyan, and Fuzhou in the north of Fujian province, along with Nanping and Sanming (see Figure 4.4). This proposal was a compromise in that it attempted to satisfy the demands not only of the areas surrounding Fujian's two major cities but also of the northern capital of Fuzhou. Furthermore, this proposal contained elements of the Golden Triangle concept approved in 1985 which broadened the scope of the Open Policy to include both Quanzhou and Zhangzhou and outlying areas. However, at a conference on Xiamen SEZ held by the Fujian government in mid-September 1983 it was decided that Xiamen should be the catalyst for the development of Fujian's economy.[88]

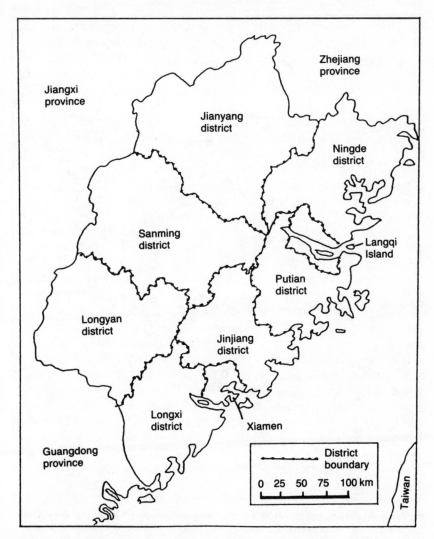

Figure 4.3 Fujian province: districts (Source: *China Business Review*, Sept.–Oct. 1980, p. 13)

Not only was there continued discussion about the geographical extent of the Open Policy but the goals and content of the policy concerning the development of Xiamen SEZ had still to be firmly established. During his visit to Xiamen at the end of October 1983, Zhao Ziyang proposed that Xiamen should concentrate on introducing technology and knowledge-intensive enterprises.[89] This not only marked a departure from the previous

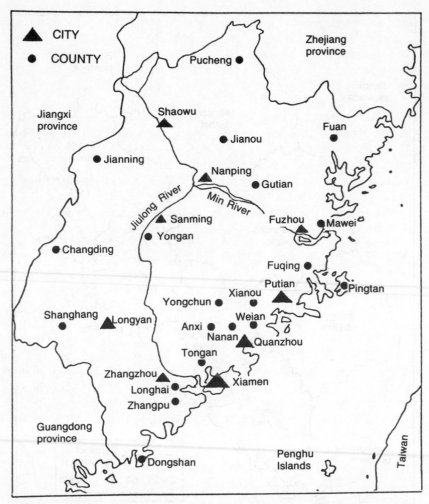

Figure 4.4 Fujian province: cities and counties (Source: FERTC, *A New Look of Fujian*, Fujian Economic Relations and Trade Commission Publishing House: Fuzhou, 1985)

more conventional goals of export-processing but also signalled the demotion of the proposal to develop Xiamen as a tourist centre. It also reflected a more general concern that the SEZs were attracting mainly small-scale, labour-intensive, non-productive enterprises.

Although the discussion concerning the geographical extension of the Open Policy suggested considerable support for the Open Policy in Fujian province, opposition to the Open Policy continued to be expressed in 1983.

The spring reorganisation of the provincial government had bolstered the power of the reformers, although some conservative leaders retained positions of influence.[90] In January 1983 the reform-minded Hu Ping replaced Ma Xingyuan as provincial governor, although Ma remained a party secretary.[91] Over 135 new officials, who were younger and more educated than their predecessors, were promoted to bureau director or deputy director.[92]

Articles in the local press on the key themes of self-reliance, independence and minimal debt pointed to continuing opposition. At the practical level opponents of the new policies deliberately delayed and obstructed implementation. This reluctance to implement the Open Policy was rooted in inter- and intra-institutional conflicts reflecting power struggles between the expectant losers and beneficiaries under the policy.

The launch of the spiritual pollution campaign in the autumn fuelled this simmering discontent amongst political leaders and cadres who had substantially lost out under the spring reorganisation and marked a downswing in the policy. Xiang Nan's statement that the 'special policies' in the economic sphere did not apply to politics, ideology or living standards showed that the campaign was already afoot in Fujian.[93] The implication was that any deviations in the ideological or political spheres at the local level were not to be tolerated. As in the economic crime debate the proponents of the Open Policy again took a conciliatory stance. Without denying the links between increased foreign economic relations and 'capitalist corruption', they called for more ideological and political work to eliminate 'spiritual pollution'.[94] At the same time they linked the slow pace of the policy to 'rigidity in thinking' and 'unliberated thought'.[95]

The intensity of the struggle at both national and local levels between the leftists and reformers raised doubts amongst foreign investors about the stability of China's leadership. Moreover, local officials, anxious about the possible outcome of this leadership struggle, were reluctant to make any major decisions in the field of foreign economic relations. Although the Fujian government agreed in September 1983 to increase Xiamen's autonomy, the pressure of the spiritual pollution campaign braked the implementation of this proposal.

Despite this downswing in the policy cycle there had been a significant expansion in Fujian's foreign economic relations since 1979. By 1983 Fujian had 68 foreign-invested enterprises involving more than US$ 60 million in foreign investment (see Table 4.6). Although the downswing in the policy cycle implied a temporary retreat, each whole cycle marked a step forward in the overall evolution of the Open Policy. Nevertheless, the pace of policy implementation in those first four years was still slower than desired by the reformers and lagged painfully behind Shenzhen, which by now boasted a total of 460 contracts for foreign direct investment. The spiritual pollution

Table 4.6   Annual foreign direct investment in Fujian province: 1979—90

	1979—83	1984	1985	1986	1987	1988	1989	1990
No. of projects								
EJV	21	113	206	70	140	496	436	432
CJV	46	116	182	34	60	188	123	94
WOFE	1	7	7	5	15	129	313	517
Total	68	236	395	109	215	813	872	1,043
Agreed FDI (US$m)								
EJV	34	121	242	53.5	78	245	270	284
CJV	23	65	130	9.5	19.5	75	56	72
WOFE	5	14	5	1.6	20	142	576	804
Total	62	200	377	64.6	117.5	462	902	1,160

Source: *Fujian Statistical Yearbook 1991* (in Chinese), pp. 317—19.

campaign had done little to encourage more foreign direct investment in Fujian. Deng Xiaoping's visit to Xiamen in early 1984 marked the start of a new cycle in the Open Policy.

Cycle 4 — striding ahead: 1984 to 1986

The visit by Deng Xiaoping to Xiamen SEZ in February 1984 breathed new life into the Open Policy, which had begun to flounder under the impact of the spiritual pollution campaign. By indicating central government support for the policy, Deng Xiaoping's visit served to dispel the intense controversy over the zones and to catalyse the policy process. The following two years witnessed an expansion and deepening of the Open Policy at both national and local levels.

During his visit to Xiamen in February 1984 Deng Xiaoping called for the more rapid and improved development of the zone. At the local level this was seen as central government supporting the zone specifically and the Open Policy in general. On his return to Beijing Deng Xiaoping proposed opening 14 coastal cities to foreign investment, including the northern provincial capital of Fuzhou. He also proposed the extension of Xiamen SEZ from the original small area of 2.5 sq km in Huli to cover the whole 131 sq km of the island (see Figure 4.2). The various proposals from local leaders in 1980 concerning the scope of the zone suggest that this idea of extending the zone to the rest of the island was locally conceived and centrally authorised. Xiang Nan's call in October 1981 for an extension of tax incentives to all joint ventures on Xiamen Island likewise suggested local support for an expansion in the scope of the policy.[96]

Although the extension of the zone indicated the consolidation of the Open Policy at central level, continuing opposition within the central leadership as well as differences amongst the proponents of the Open Policy may have accounted for the reticence in expressing further designs for Xiamen SEZ and the subsequent failure of Deng Xiaoping to secure free-port policies for Xiamen. Although Deng Xiaoping proposed in a speech to senior leaders on 24 February 1984 that Xiamen should become a free port, this was not made public until almost a year later.[97]

However, that the idea had not been totally swept under the carpet was apparent from an article published in October 1984 referring to the implementation of free-port policies in Xiamen.[98] In an interview at the end of 1984, Gu Mu, state councillor, denied that Xiamen and Hainan were to become free ports, suggesting that there were still differences of opinion over this within the central leadership.[99] Although details are not available, it is likely that the draft plan formulated by Xiamen People's Congress Standing Committee in July 1984, which was then submitted to the State Council, also contained proposals for making Xiamen a free port.[100]

Whilst Deng Xiaoping became identified with the idea of free port policies for Xiamen, other central leaders had different views about the strategy to be adopted by Xiamen SEZ. Zhao Ziyang, for example, emphasised that Fujian should become a technology- and knowledge-intensive centre, importing both new technology and management methods.[101] The influence of Zhao Ziyang's ideas was apparent in the report concerning the coastal cities given by Hu Ping to the provincial government in mid-April 1984.[102] Hu Ping stressed that the zones were to be 'windows' for technology, management, knowledge and foreign policies, with no mention of tourism, trade or free ports. Li Xiannian, the President of China and one of the more cautious reformers, called for developing both the mountainous and coastal parts of the province, revealing a sensitivity to the potential danger of growing intra-provincial regional disparities.[103]

These differences in policy strategy among the pro-Open Policy central leadership nevertheless had the advantage of allowing local leaders considerable leeway in their interpretation of policy. As pressures for the extension of the policy to other areas had already been considerable, it was not surprising that the provincial press interpreted Deng Xiaoping's statement regarding Xiamen SEZ, namely that it should develop more rapidly and better, as applying not only to Xiamen SEZ but also to Fujian province.[104]

The opening of Fuzhou city in April 1984 did not, however, resolve the ambiguity regarding the regional economic roles of Xiamen and Fuzhou. We can safely surmise that the choice of Fuzhou as a coastal city was in part a result of pressure from a constellation of political forces in Fuzhou seeking to become beneficiaries of the Open Policy. The report of a meeting of the Provincial People's Congress Party Committee stated only that the opening of Xiamen SEZ and Fuzhou ETDZ would stimulate both the two cities and the whole of Fujian province.[105] This implied on the one hand that the issue of the relative roles of Xiamen and Fuzhou had not been resolved and on the other hand a much broader interpretation of the function of both the SEZ and ETDZ. The suggestion in October 1984 that Xiamen SEZ and Fuzhou ETDZ should form a base for international financial activities introduced yet another policy goal for Xiamen. It also indicated that there were still tensions over the regional roles of Xiamen and Fuzhou.[106]

Provincial and municipal support for the extension of the Open Policy and Deng Xiaoping's call to improve the performance of the zone served to accelerate the process of policy-making in Xiamen SEZ. At the end of March 1984 a Provincial Party Committee and Government Work Group, including Hu Ping, Governor of Fujian and Ma Xingyuan, former governor of Fujian, visited Xiamen SEZ. The work groups examined law, planning, foreign economy, tourism, transport resources and finance.[107] As a result of this visit these various administrative organisations formulated new policies, offering preferential treatment to foreign investors.[108] In July 1984 Fujian People's Congress Standing Committee also issued six new regulations concerning entry formalities, management of the registration of enterprises, labour management, land use fees, technology introduction and intra-regional links.[109]

By mid-1984 the policy-making process had extended beyond foreign economic relations to other areas of the political economy, such as banking and transport. By now it was clear that the Open Policy not only had repercussions beyond its immediate sphere of operation but also hinged crucially on the success of other domestic reforms. Xiamen SEZ, therefore, was not only to lead the province in opening up but also to provide a model of domestic economic reform. Although the report on the zones in September 1982 served to expand their function as pioneers of domestic economic reform, this did not become local reality in Xiamen SEZ until 1984, partly because developments in Xiamen SEZ tended to lag behind Shenzhen.

So as to accelerate the pace of opening up and reform the provincial government granted Xiamen further autonomy. In fact, this had already been approved in September 1983 but was not implemented, partly because the spiritual pollution campaign put a brake on the policy process.[110] The new policies decentralised decisions concerning foreign economic relations from provincial to municipal levels.

The expansion of the zone in March 1984 as well as the granting of special privileges to Fuzhou in April 1984 had two effects on other areas in Fujian. First, they symbolised the official endorsement of the Open Policy and as such gave the 'green light' to go ahead. As a result some outlying areas took advantage of this favourable climate rapidly to expand their foreign economic ties. In 1984 alone 31 joint ventures were formed in areas such as Jianou, Shaowu, Longhai, Tongan and Changding (see Figure 4.4).[111] The mayor of the mountain city of Sanming, Yang Weijie, announced numerous incentives to foreign investors, including offers of cheaper labour than in the coastal areas.[112] This regional spread of foreign capital into rural and mountainous areas received support from provincial leaders such as Hu Ping.[113]

Second, in an effort also to reap the benefits of the Open Policy, other key cities such as Quanzhou, which had strong Overseas Chinese links, pressed for inclusion in the scope of the Open Policy. In early October Quanzhou municipal government adopted several measures to accelerate the implementation of the Open Policy, but also expressed the demand for greater authority from the provincial government to conduct business with foreign companies.[114] The establishment of policy by the Quanzhou government not only reflected the consolidation of pro-Open Policy groups within that government but may also have been related to the national plans for the South Fujian Golden Delta. In October 1984 Quanzhou was already being mentioned as a key port in Fujian, implying that it might soon come on the agenda as a recipient of the Open Policy.[115]

As the institutionalisation of the policy deepened and the web of beneficiaries of the policy expanded geographically, the process of policy establishment became increasingly informed by a wider regional, social and institutional constituency. Whilst previously central government may have deemed it wise to pay attention to the opinions of the provincial government, with the geographical extension and decentralisation of the policy, the provincial government simultaneously became more subject to the demands of lower-level organisations and interests.

Provincial input into the establishment of policy continued. In December 1984 the Fujian provincial government introduced further measures to improve the foreign investment climate. The areas covered in these policies, such as taxation, domestic sales and enterprise management reflected in part Chinese perceptions of the interests of foreign capital, such as tax incentives, as well as underlying tensions between foreign capital and the host country, such as domestic sales.[116]

The year 1985 witnessed a further expansion of the Open Policy in Fujian. In March 1985 the State Council approved the opening of the three Golden Deltas in China, including the South Fujian Delta, to foreign direct investment. Nine additional counties as well as the cities of Quanzhou and Zhangzhou opened to foreign capital (see Figure 4.5).[117] The scope of the policy was influenced both from above by overall national plans and from below by regional pressures.

The details of this policy expansion involved the interaction of both central and local policy elites. During his visit to Xiamen in January 1985,

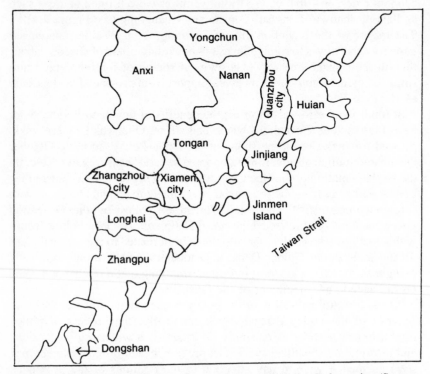

Figure 4.5   The open cities and counties of the South Fujian Delta region (Source: FERTC, *A New Look of Fujian*, Fujian Economic Relations and Trade Commission Publishing House: Fuzhou, 1985, p. 65)

Wan Li, Vice-Premier and member of the Central Committee member, stated that the boundaries of the South Fujian golden triangle should be drawn in accord with Overseas Chinese villages and potential projects rather than according to geographical position.[118]

Differences between central and provincial leadership were, however, also apparent. Whilst Wan Li saw the key areas in need of improvement as electricity and water supply, for which some central government funding might be provided, Xiang Nan, the provincial Governor, also sought central financial support for developing civilian aviation and banking.[119] This reflected frustration on the part of the provincial government with only 'special' policies and a concomitant desire for more central funding.

The regional extension of the Open Policy during 1985 was paralleled by the sectoral spread of the policy from production to finance. In June 1985 the State Council approved the right of Xiamen to borrow from abroad, issue bonds overseas and make spot transactions.[120] This new right reflected both the urgency of acquiring funds to develop the zone as well as plans to make Xiamen a financial centre.

The adoption of free-port policies for Xiamen SEZ in July 1985 provided further evidence of the close involvement of central government, and in particular of individual leaders, in the establishment of policy in Fujian. The first stage of this free-port plan was due to commence in early 1987.[121] These free-port policies permitted Xiamen not only to manage its foreign trade itself, but also to conduct direct trade with Taiwan.[122] As mentioned previously, this proposal was on the one hand the pet concern of Deng Xiaoping and on the other hand enjoyed the support of particular leaders within the local policy elite. Xiang Nan had revealed earlier in an interview that 'some' people in Fujian had proposed making Xiamen a 'free port'.[123]

These policy innovations in mid-1985 coincided, however, with a tightening of central control over the economy, triggered by the decline in foreign exchange reserves. In 1985 Fujian had a trade deficit of US$ 133 million compared with a surplus of US$ 153 million the previous year.[124] Moreover, only 14 per cent of the zone's output was exported that year, far short of the desired 70 per cent.[125] Fujian's foreign debt had doubled between 1984 and 1985 and again between 1985 and 1986. Moreover, by the end of 1986, 85 per cent of these debts were, contrary to the situation two years previously, financed by commercial loans.[126] Reports of 'blind imports', such as nylon-zipper production lines, also contributed to a reappraisal of the management of the Open Policy.[127]

Renewed criticism of the zones in the wake of the Hainan scandal served to dampen the pace of policy implementation and innovation. Attention focused on the failure of the zones, including Xiamen, to attract technology-intensive, export-oriented, productive enterprises. Reimposition of central control over the external economy braked progress in the opening of the South Fujian Golden Delta.

Although the Open Policy had made great strides in Fujian since 1984, opposition had not been quelled. The economic imbalances of mid-1985 as well as national criticism of the SEZs gave strength to the opposition in Fujian province, culminating in the dismissal of Xiang Nan in early 1986.[128] Press articles in 1985 referred, for example, to the interference of the opposition in joint ventures. At the same time statements regarding the need to form 'spiritual and cultural windows' in the zones and set up 'screens to keep out the negative influences' suggest not only that there was continued resistance to the policy but also that this resistance found expression in the ideological arena.[129]

This downswing in the policy cycle nevertheless permitted a reappraisal of the functions of the zone in the economy. Changes in the strategic conception of the zones at the central level fed into the formulation of policy concerning Xiamen SEZ. At a national SEZ work meeting held in January 1986 it was proposed that in the seventh five-year plan the SEZs should move up from being primarily an export-oriented economy to a 'window' for technology, management, knowledge and the Open Policy and look simultaneously outwards and inwards, like 'two fans'.[130] Zhao Ziyang's conception of the SEZs as sites to attract technology- and knowledge-intensive industry had gained a strong foothold, in part because of criticism concerning the 'parasitic' and non-productive nature of the zones.

These proposals also revealed that the relation between the coastal and inland areas in the Open Policy had become an issue within the central policy elite. In fact Li Xiannian had already hinted at the potential regional impact of the Open Policy. This concern for the regional implications of the Open Policy was echoed at the provincial and municipal levels. At a meeting of the People's Congress in May 1986, Hu Ping stated that technology imports and exports should be linked to assisting poor areas.[131] Furthermore, in July 1986 Xiamen SEZ issued seven documents offering preferential treatment to economic links between the SEZs and inland places.[132]

The imposition of macroeconomic control from mid-1985 onwards had begun, as at the national level, to have a deleterious effect on the level of foreign direct investment in Fujian. In 1986 the value of newly signed foreign direct investment agreements fell dramatically from US$ 376 million in 1985 to US$ 64.5 million in 1986 (see Table 4.6). Moreover, the tightening of central control over foreign exchange began to affect the newly founded joint venture bank in Xiamen.[133] This downswing in the policy cycle continued till mid-1986.

Cycle 5 — moving ahead, but at a tempered pace: mid-1986 to 1987

Whilst the tightening of central government control over the economy from mid-1985, particularly in the sphere of foreign trade, had brought imports under control, it at the same time had a deleterious impact on the level of foreign direct investment (see Table 4.1). The outcome of the restrictive measures fed back into the policy process. Pressure from foreign capital in early 1986 to improve the foreign investment climate prompted the central government to assess the current situation and devise new incentives.

From mid-1986 there was a resurgence of policy activity at the provincial level. Thirteen key industrial townships around Zhangzhou, Quanzhou and Xiamen were also granted preferential policies given in the South Fujian golden triangle to foreign direct investment.[134] This regional extension of privileges pointed again to provincial and municipal support from pro-Open

Policy leaders, as well as a lower level push for inclusion within the scope of the policy.

As regards foreign direct investment, Xiamen municipal government set up a committee to investigate complaints from foreign investors about arbitrary fees. Foreign companies were permitted to refuse payment if they thought fees were too high. Moreover, the municipal government readjusted its charges.[135] In mid-September Xiamen won further concessions including exemption from import duties for machinery and raw materials used for export, as well as tax exemption on exported finished products.[136]

These efforts to improve the investment climate were but a prelude to the more far-reaching regulations introduced in October 1986 to encourage foreign direct investment. In the wake of this central impetus the Xiamen government formulated new policies. The issues covered in the regulations included the right to 'hire and fire', Rmb funds, raw materials supply, prices of domestically sold goods and forex balance.[137] These topics embodied both some of the economic problems aggravated by the Open Policy such as materials supply, shortage of funds, as well as the political tensions arising between foreign capital and the Chinese state and foreign capital and Chinese labour.

As part of a set of new measures to improve the investment climate in October 1986 the Fujian government issued a regulation that approving departments should grant approval to foreign investors for letters of intent and contracts within one month from the day of receipt. This implied that lengthy and timely bureaucratic procedures due both to opposition and old regulations had impeded the progress of foreign direct investment.[138]

It also set up new institutions which addressed specifically the problems of foreign investors. Moreover, it simplified and decentralised procedures for the approval of foreign-invested enterprises.[139] As at the national level, a leading group for foreign direct investment was set up to act as an authority for foreign-invested enterprises facing difficulties. A management bureau for Sino-foreign joint ventures was also established to carry out the leading group's decisions.[140] Although foreign investors in Xiamen welcomed these new regulations, there were still some who doubted whether they would be implemented. The opening of Dongshan Island in the Taiwan Straits to tourism marked another step forward in the Open Policy.[141]

The launch of the anti-bourgeois liberalisation campaign in early 1987 cast a shadow over these recent attempts to improve the foreign direct investment climate. However, as there were no student demonstrations in Xiamen SEZ, the impact of the campaign was less severe than in other cities. In order to mitigate the potential effects of the campaign on foreign direct investment, particularly as a foreign direct investment symposium was underway in Fuzhou, Hu Ping underlined the continuation of the policy.[142]

At the same time there was a renewed effort to tighten control over investment expenditure, including Chinese investment in joint ventures, suggesting that the recentralisation measures adopted since mid-1985 had not worked sufficiently.[143] The gradual petering out of the ideological campaign as well as Zhao Ziyang's proposal to further open up, which included the development of Fujian as an export-oriented economy, served to curtail the downswing in the policy cycle.[144] Moreover, the concern amongst some central and provincial leaders to increase exports rapidly bolstered the emphasis given to attracting Overseas Chinese investment.[145]

Continuing central and local leadership support for the Open Policy as well as the gradual cooling of the economy led to more favourable results in trade and foreign direct investment. In the first nine months of 1987 Fujian province signed 174 new contracts involving US$ 56 million of foreign investment.[146] The export of electronic goods also increased substantially.[147] However, with the Thirteenth Party Congress approaching in October 1987, officials were still reluctant to take any major decisions.

Cycle 6 — One step forwards, and two steps backwards: 1987 to 1990

The victory of the reformers at the Thirteenth Party Congress gave a further boost to the Open Policy in Fujian province. However, the impending economic crisis which peaked in 1988 also took its toll at the local level. This was followed by the well-documented political crisis of 1989. Although Xiamen was relatively calm, the overall external perception of instability adversely affected the investment climate. An equally significant factor in this cycle was the enormous upsurge in Taiwanese investment, made possible by the relaxation of relations between China and Taiwan. This made it increasingly clear that the success of Xiamen SEZ hinged crucially on relations with Taiwan.

The more positive climate following the Thirteenth Party Congress in October 1987 contributed to an increase in the number of projects agreed in the early part of 1988. During that period Fujian approved 127 foreign-funded projects, well over half the total of the preceding year.[148] In fact Fujian had the highest increase in foreign investment in China in the first eight months of 1988, with the bulk of this coming from Taiwan. In Xiamen SEZ 80 new Taiwanese enterprises were agreed that year, compared to a total of 20 up till 1987.[149]

Characteristic of this new upsurge in foreign investment was the growing popularity of wholly owned foreign enterprises. In the first quarter of 1988 four times as many wholly owned foreign enterprises were approved as in the same quarter in 1987.[150] Indeed Fujian and Guangdong together took the lion's share of the 240 wholly owned foreign enterprises approved in 1988.[151]

Following the Thirteenth Party Congress, the reformers designated Fujian, like Guangdong and Hainan, an experimental area for overall reform.[152] In April the State Council granted Xiamen the same power as a province in economic management.[153] The Fujian provincial government and Xiamen SEZ took this opportunity to make further policy changes in favour of opening up. In line with the State Council's regulations issued in May, Fujian announced new regulations in mid-1988 on the management of labour in foreign-invested enterprises.[154] These regulations reiterated the right of foreign-invested enterprises to hire workers according to their needs and set their own wages, suggesting that there had been difficulties in doing so previously. At the same time Quanzhou followed suit with similar regulations.[155] So as to upgrade its existing enterprises and help them export, Fujian opted not only to invest Y5 billion and US$ 500 million in importing technology but also to sell or lease 88 enterprises to foreign companies at the forthcoming Foreign Trade and Investment Fair.[156]

Further innovations came when Xiamen announced new regulations in June 1988 permitting the free transfer of land in preparation for its first land auction. Maximum land tenure for industry was 40 years, for commerce and transport 50 years and for residences 70 years.[157] The investors were quick to spot the speculative profits that could be made in real estate. The introduction of new national regulations to encourage Taiwanese investment in July 1988 gave Taiwanese compatriots the right to buy and sell real estate.[158] Xiamen quickly followed suit and in August issued special preferential policies for Taiwanese investors. Fujian provincial government likewise announced plans to set up 10 Taiwanese investment zones.[159] By the end of 1989 Xiamen had leased 63 tracts of land, with overseas investors accounting for 60 per cent of these.[160]

National rectification in the autumn of 1988 had an adverse effect upon Xiamen. When in October 1988 the Ministry of Foreign Economic Relations and Trade imposed central control over the many export companies which had mushroomed under decentralisation, Fujian province had to follow suit and many companies were closed down. In Xiamen, for example, the 'rectification small group' revoked the right of 69 companies to import or export.[161] Similarly, in November 1989 when the State Council proposed further measures to screen and rectify foreign economic and trade companies, Xiamen SEZ also felt the reverberations.[162] The State Council decision in October 1988 to abolish the preferential foreign exchange retention rates of the SEZs adversely affected Xiamen.[163] Local leaders tried publicly to keep a 'brave face'. In an interview with a Hong Kong newspaper, Zhang Shoushan, Vice-Director of Fujian Foreign Economic Relations and Trade Commission adamantly maintained that Fujian's economy would not be affected by the current national rectification.[164] Contracts under negotiation would not be cancelled. Moreover, he denied rumours that the central government would withdraw Fujian's economic autonomy.

Whilst political unrest throughout the country in 1989 undermined the confidence of foreign investors, the democracy movement of 1989 had minimal impact on actual production in Xiamen. Some students demonstrated to mourn the death of Hu Yaobang but enjoyed little support from citizens or workers.[165] The university loudspeakers switched from their usual mixed repertoire of Chinese, Hong Kong and Western pop to news broadcasts from the BBC and VOA. A few students went on hunger strike for two days outside the Cultural Palace. In Fuzhou several demonstrations took place throughout May. In response to the declaration of martial law on 19 May, around 1000 students prevented the Beijing-bound train from leaving. The wave of protest spread to smaller cities in Fujian such as Nanping and Longyan. Inspired by events in Beijing some workers in Fuzhou set up a preparatory committee for forming an autonomous trade union.[166] However, the students remained a socially isolated group. Moreover, compared to Beijing, Xiamen University was a sea of tranquility, as in previous student demonstrations in 1979 and 1986.

In fact in the post-Tiananmen years it is rumoured that parents have encouraged their children to apply to Xiamen University rather than Beijing precisely because of its relative inactivity during the national crisis of 1989. Foreign investors I spoke to in a recent visit informed me that the political crisis had little effect on them. As one foreign manager said, 'we just carried on as normal'.[167]

Although existing foreign investors in Xiamen may not have lost confidence in the post-Tiananmen climate, new investors, as at the national level, were on their guard. To offset any potential negative effects, Fujian province began to offer foreign investors even greater incentives to invest their money. For example, the People's Insurance Company offered foreign investors a policy against war and strikes.[168] Also local officials doggedly emphasised the cheap labour costs and China's huge domestic market to lure Taiwanese investment.[169] In May the State Council approved the setting-up of two special Taiwanese investment zones in Haicang and Xinglin.[170] Taiwanese investors proved less anxious about the political instability than their Western counterparts and so accounted for 97 per cent of new investment in 1989.[171]

More troubling for local leaders than the democracy crisis was growing central interest in Pudong, Shanghai. Like their counterparts in Guangdong, provincial and SEZ officials interpreted this development as the onset of the demise of the zones. The national conference on SEZs held in February 1990 tried to allay concerns of local officials that central government was abandoning the SEZs in the current wave of enthusiasm for Pudong. Retrenchment and the withdrawal of previous privileges were also taking their economic toll. Li Peng reaffirmed the policy on the SEZs at this meeting.[172]

However, it was clear by mid-1990 that the SEZs had fulfilled their role in the first decade of reform and opening up. The attention of the central leadership was now focused squarely on Shanghai. In July 1990 the Vice-Mayor of Shanghai, Huang Ju, promised conditions not available in the zones. Shanghai was to become pivotal to the economic restructuring of China. Whilst the zones would focus on labour-intensive production, Pudong would become a manufacturing, service and financial centre.[173] Yao Yilin stated clearly that whilst the first decade had favoured Fujian and Guangdong, in the next decade priority would be given to Pudong.[174] Jiang Zemin expressed similar sentiments during his inspection visit to Guangdong's SEZs.[175] Careful to appease SEZ leaders, central leaders such as Jiang Zemin and Bo Yibo continued at the same time to endorse the correctness of the SEZ policy.[176]

Local leaders responded to central overtures to Shanghai by fiercely competing for foreign capital. Both Xiamen and Fuzhou, like other coastal cities, sent delegations to Hong Kong in anticipation of the Shanghai mayor's visit in June.[177] Promising better incentives than Shanghai they hoped to clinch special deals.

In the first half of 1990 Taiwanese investment began to pour in again to Fujian, doubling the amount in the first half of 1989.[178] The relaxation of the Taiwanese government's policy towards the mainland had facilitated this upsurge. In February 1990 the Taiwanese Ministry of Economic Affairs relaxed curbs on market survey trips to the mainland and allowed businesspeople to attend exhibitions.[179] Similarly, decentralisation of the visa application process for Taiwanese visitors also encouraged this upturn in investment. CITIC too opened advisory branches in Hong Kong to help Taiwanese investors. By June 1990 Fujian had approved 588 Taiwanese projects.[180] Previously, Taiwanese investors had come on an individual basis but from mid-1990 they came in groups or as trade associations with plans to develop whole regions or islands.

But from mid-1990 onwards foreign investment in Xiamen began to slow down.[181] Inadequate port facilities and the lack of direct shipping links with Taiwan increasingly deterred potential investors. This decline in foreign investment activity as well as the return of relative political stability at the central level prompted officials to innovate further.

Despite national rectification 1990 turned out to be a good year for Xiamen and Fujian. Fujian enjoyed a growth rate of 11.2 per cent, lower than Guangdong's 16.9 per cent but higher than the national average.[182] Foreign trade had reached US$ 3.17 billion, exports came to US$ 2.23 billion and more than one thousand contracts for foreign direct investment worth US$ 1.16 billion were agreed that year. By the end of 1990 foreign-invested enterprises in Fujian accounted for over a fifth of total provincial industrial output value, compared with 4.7 per cent in 1989.[183] Xiamen SEZ's trade volume reached US$ 1.1 billion, with 44 per cent of its exports being industrial products.[184] By now Xiamen had 506 foreign-invested enterprises in operation.[185] Out of the 262 foreign-invested enterprises Xiamen approved in 1990, 195 were wholly owned foreign enterprises.[186] However, the amount of actually realised foreign direct investment fell 65 per cent in 1990 compared with 1989.[187] Foreign-invested enterprises were by now playing a key role in Xiamen's economy. In 1990 they accounted for 80 per cent of Xiamen's industrial export earnings and 56 per cent of Xiamen's industrial output value (see Table 4.7). Furthermore, they now began to pay tax, handing over Y250 million in 1990.[188]

Cycle 7 — lurching outwards: mid-1990 to 1992

With the restoration of economic and political order at the national level, the time was ripe for a bolder approach again to opening up. The Fujian provincial government clearly felt the moment had come to stride ahead and to speed up the process of opening. From mid-1990 onwards we can observe a spate of policy innovations aimed at drawing in more foreign investment and increasing the role of market forces.

In August 1990 the Fujian government approved Xiamen's plan to develop industry, transport, tourism, foreign trade, commerce and services.[189] A month later it announced plans to turn Langqi Island into a Taiwanese investment zone, fulfilling its ambitions to make this area special.[190] By the end of 1990 Fujian had over 3700 foreign-invested enterprises, a quarter

Table 4.7 Contribution of foreign-invested enterprises to Xiamen's industrial output value: 1983–90 (Ym)

	1983	1984	1985	1986	1987	1988	1989	1990
Xiamen City	1,202.1	1,508.5	2,185.2	2,465.8	3,285.6	4,500	5,452	6,491
Foreign-invested enterprises (industrial)	14.2	75.3	404.6	439.7	967.7	1,946	2,633	3,650
% of FIEs IOV to IOV of Xiamen	1.2	5.0	18.5	18.0	29.4	43	48	56

Source: Compiled from: Xiamen Statistical Bureau, Interview, 1987; *Collection of Statistical Material on the Open Coastal Cities, SEZs, Unified Planned Towns 1989* (in Chinese), pp. 17–20; *Fujian Statistical Yearbook, 1990 and 1991*, p. 302/p. 325.

of these in Xiamen (see Table 4.8). In early 1991 the Fujian provincial government indicated that it was planning to open up more. At a conference in January the Acting Governor, Jia Qinglin, proposed more economic and trade links with Taiwan.[191] National leaders were also pushing Fujian to open its doors more. In January 1991 Peng Chong, Vice-Chair of the National People's Congress Standing Committee visited Fujian and called for greater opening up.[192] Discussions were underway for another foreign trade port in Fujian.[193] The Fujian government announced its plans to increase exports to US$ 3.5 billion by 1995 and absorb US$ 3.5 billion of foreign investment.[194]

This wave of enthusiasm gathered force in April 1991. At a meeting of National People's Congress deputies on the SEZs Xiamen officials expressed their intent to increase links with Taiwan and hurry up the construction of the Taiwanese investment zones in Haicang and Xinglin as well as the industrial parks of Caihu and Xiao Dongshan.[195] By this month Xiamen had already approved 262 projects, 60 per cent of which came from Taiwan.[196] More innovation came when Jia Qinglin announced that Fujian would set up bonded industrial parks and bonded capital goods markets. He also announced that both Xiamen and Fuzhou ETDZ would adopt free-port policies.[197] Efforts continued to improve the investment climate. Taiwanese and other foreign investors would be able to set up branch banks in Fuzhou and other coastal cities in Fujian. Fujian would also establish a financial market to serve the export economy.

These innovations were facilitated by the improving relations with Taiwan. On 30 April Taiwan announced that it would end the 'period of mobilisation for suppression of communist rebellion'.[198] This was the first time that Taiwan had shown a willingness to coexist peacefully with the mainland. Vice-Premier Wu Xueqian urged Taiwan to move faster in relaxing relations between Taiwan and China and reasserted the applicability of the concept of 'one country, two systems' to a reunified Taiwan.[199] The gradual relaxation in relations with Taiwan over the decade was reflected also in the fall in the number of troops stationed in Fujian.[200]

Direct links between Xiamen and Taiwan existed already by this time on an informal basis. A Panamanian flag shipping service, for example, operated between Xiamen and Kiaoshung every 10 days, which reduced shipping costs by 40 per cent compared to the cumbersome route via Hong Kong. However, this service was disbanded temporarily in spring 1991 as Taiwanese customs objected to containers bearing mainland Chinese emblems.

By mid-1991 over 337 400 tourists, mainly Taiwanese, had visited Xiamen, over twice the number in 1988.[201] Indirect trade between Taiwan and the mainland came to US$ 5.79 billion, a 40 per cent increase over the same period in 1990.[202] Taiwan exports raw materials and components,

Table 4.8 Cumulative foreign direct investment in Xiamen SEZ and Fujian province: 1980 to June 1992

	1980–3	1984	1985	1986	1987	1988	1989	1990	1991	1992
Number of FIEs agreed										
Xiamen	24	110	215	249	299	479	680	942	1,155	1,326
Fujian	68	304	699	808	1,023	1,836	2,708	3,751	na	na
Agreed investment										
Xiamen	91.69	386.24	794.52	847.25	949.05	1,311.16	1,870.66	2,386	2,972	na
Fujian	176.00	430.80	869.17	984.16	1,203.06	1,828.03	2,789.37	4,026	4,163	na
Agreed FDI										
Xiamen	37.06	186.73	428.75	456.33	513.01	668.65	1,182.65	1,636	2,156	na
Fujian	62.00	262.00	639.00	703.60	821.10	1,283.10	2,185.10	3,345	na	na
Realised FDI										
Xiamen	7.75	48.19	121.47	155.93	173.46	221.42	351.22	424	na	1,190
Fujian	21.55	69.83	187.65	249.14	300.53	430.70	759.50	1,049	na	na

Note: na = not available.
Sources: Xiamen Statistical Bureau, Interview, 1987; *Fujian Statistical Yearbook 1991* (in Chinese), pp. 319–21; HKWWP 22.1.1992 in SWB/FE/1293/B2/1 1.2.1992; XH 4.7.92 in SWB/FE/W0239/A/6 15.7.1992.

textiles, machinery, electrical components and plastic materials to China and imports medicinal herbs, feathers and fish from China.[203]

Xiamen continued to pave the way for greater Taiwanese involvement in the economy. In May 1991 work began on the construction of the Haicang and Xinglin Taiwanese investment zones.[204] In June 1991 the Bank of East Asia opened a branch in Xiamen which would provide advice to Taiwanese investors.[205] Outlying areas also made preparations to attract more Taiwanese investment. Longhai county, for example, set up Jiaomei industrial development district in July 1991, which succeeded in attracting Taiwanese investment.[206]

In May 1991 Jia Qinglin became the new governor of Fujian. Wang Zhaoguo resigned and was transferred up to Beijing to become head of the State Council Taiwan Office. Locally, it was rumoured that the centre wanted to keep a tighter control over Fujian and saw Wang as too closely aligned to local interests for comfort.

The spate of innovation continued. In June 1991 Fujian approved the setting up of Anping overseas investment development district.[207] In the same month the new governor urged local governments and departments to simplify their procedures, improve their efficiency and provide foreigners with preferential terms for developing land.[208] Work on the Hong Kong-funded Panlong industrial development zone began the same month.[209]

One of the most fascinating policy changes in Xiamen in this cycle was the decision that the government would no longer buy shares in foreign-invested enterprises in the zone. This effectively implied that all new foreign-invested enterprises would be fully foreign-funded.[210] Moreover, it implicitly acknowledged the difficulties in cooperating in joint ventures as well as financial constraints following the rectification policies of 1988. This policy change in fact endorsed a trend already afoot to promote wholly owned foreign enterprises. By May 1991 the number of wholly owned foreign enterprises already exceeded that of joint ventures, at 464 to 375. By the end of the year wholly owned foreign enterprises in Xiamen accounted for 65 per cent of total foreign investment according to Xiamen Foreign Executive Committee. Taiwanese investors have apparently preferred this form of investment as they perceived joint venture partners to be squeezing rents and concessions. Again Xiamen's desperation to acquire foreign capital has enabled foreign investors to achieve greater power in setting the terms of investment.

Encouraged by the tide of reform at the national level, the Xiamen government also expressed its commitment to more market regulation and a concomitant reduction in the role of planning.[211] In the spirit of this renewed shift towards the market, Fujian opened 10 land development zones for foreign investment covering an area of 13 sq km, revealing plans to open another 10.[212] Taiwanese investors were quick to seize the golden opportunities in real estate. US pressure to tighten up on textile quotas contributed towards this enthusiasm. A well-known Taiwanese textile company in Xiamen, for example, has expanded into this sector.[213] Speculation in real estate caused land prices to soar fivefold between 1988 and 1991.[214]

By mid-1991 exports from Xiamen came to US$ 582 million, well over half the amount again in the same period the year before.[215] Xiamen had approved a total of 1000 foreign-invested enterprises with a combined investment of over US$ 3 billion.[216] Of these 600 were in operation, contributing more than half the industrial output value of the city. Taiwanese investors boasted the grand sum of 417 ventures involving investment of US$ 1 billion, putting them squarely in the lead. However, Taiwanese investors have tended to transfer their labour-intensive production processes and older machines to Xiamen, in preference to introducing high tech. Taiwanese investment has also poured into non-productive sectors such as entertainment and real estate.

There is clearly a policy contradiction between, on the one hand, the goal of potential reunification and on the other hand, of technological modernisation. The flood of labour-intensive production from Taiwan also reflects the Taiwanese government policy of encouraging this in the recession period. The proposed plan of Taiwan's largest company, Formosa Plastics, to set up a factory in Haicang near Xiamen has caused the Taiwanese government considerable anxiety, both with regard to potential technology transfer as well as to the loss of jobs to the mainland. As Taiwan's petrochemical industry contributes almost 40 per cent of Taiwanese output value, the government has been pressurising this large company to invest instead in Taiwan.[217]

Although Taiwanese investors in theory no longer enjoy any special privileges, their familiarity with culture, language and the region have made them much more adept at working their way through the bureaucratic maze and indeed in operating factories. The relative upsurge in Taiwanese investment capital has penetrated deep into Fujian's rural areas, tying them more closely into the international capitalist economy. Foreign enterprises in Tongan county, for example, now contributed half of its output value.[218] The rapidly proliferating township and village enterprises have been quick to foster Taiwanese connections.[219]

Economic crime continued to be a problem in Fujian as in other parts of the country. The slight relaxation of relations with Taiwan not only encouraged more investment and trade but also provided an opportunity for more smuggling of luxury goods and even drugs. Cadres were not immune from these activities. A vice-mayor of Xiamen and the head of the Foreign Investment Bureau were arrested in the late 1980s on charges of corruption.[220] One story ran that Taiwanese investors had taped their conversation and sent this on to central leaders. In May 1991 Pintgang in Fujian was put under tighter administrative supervision as it had become a base for smuggling and illegal immigration across the Taiwan Strait.[221]

As at the national level, the Party was trying hard to improve its public image and bring cadres accused of corruption to justice. In Fujian, Wang Decai, a former director and party group secretary of Nanping Prefectural Public Security Bureau, was expelled from the Party and sentenced to 15 years in prison for accepting bribes in return for applications to leave the country.[222] The provincial government also began to restrict people from outside staying in Fujian.[223] In June six anti-smuggling officers from Xiamen ended up in Taiwan after chasing a Panamanian boat involved in smuggling.[224] In the same month police in Xiamen arrested drug traders caught trafficking drugs from Yunnan to abroad.[225] In September 1991 Fujian farmers were found to be involved in illegal emigration activities to the USA.[226]

Although Taiwanese investment has increased rapidly since 1988, the recession in Taiwan as well as regulations requiring them to declare their interests in China contributed to a fall in the rate of Taiwanese investment in 1991. Inadequate port facilities, the absence of direct shipping links with Taiwan and therefore relatively higher transport costs left Xiamen a less attractive option to rival Guangdong. The lower wages and rent relative to both Taiwan and Guangdong still could not offset these persisting constraints. Most production was labour-intensive, low-tech export-processing, with few externalities to the domestic economy. Fujian was now China's largest producer and exporter of footwear. The US threats to block China's above-quota exports were an added threat to the investment prospects for Xiamen. Moreover, the turnround in Taiwanese government policy to now actively helping Taiwanese investors disinvest in the mainland also did not augur well for the future.

In the light of these constraints, Xiamen municipal government bolstered its efforts to entice more foreign investment. In August 1991 it set up a Foreign Investment Commission to replace the Foreign Administration Bureau. According to Zou Erjun the commission would approve, administer and provide services for foreign-invested enterprises. In this way local leaders hoped to simplify further the investment process, making Xiamen even more attractive to Taiwanese and foreign investors.

National leaders continued to support Fujian in its efforts to chivvy along the process of opening up. Both Qiao Shi and Wan Li visited Xiamen and other key cities in Fujian province in the last quarter of the year, calling for more reform and opening up.[227] Wan Li had already visited Xiamen in 1981 and 1985 and so would have been well impressed by the progress made since 1988.

The idea of Xiamen becoming a free port came onto the agenda again in October 1991.[228] There was discussion of drawing a special zone administrative boundary and relaxing trade, financial and bonded business policies. The aim would be to make Xiamen the most open coastal city in China and pave the way for direct contacts with Taiwan. In December 1991 Xiamen celebrated its tenth anniversary. Jiang Zemin visited Xiamen on this special occasion, lending full central support to Xiamen's development.[229] A special meeting was held also this month to promote economic and technical cooperation with Taiwan.[230] Xiamen had approved 504 Taiwanese-funded projects out of a provincial total of 1200 with investment worth over US$ 1.17 billion.[231] Although Xiamen ranked second next to Shenzhen in terms of foreign trade volume in the five SEZs and fourth among cities with province-level economic decision-making power, the large gap between the two zones reflected the continuing constraints in trading directly with Taiwan.[232] Foreign-invested enterprises continued to play an important role in the economy, boasting 55 per cent of the industrial output value of Xiamen and 85 per cent of export volume.[233]

However, there were already indications that Xiamen SEZ was becoming increasingly frustrated by the hold of both the province and centre over its pace of development. An article appeared in the local daily in early December calling for greater legal autonomy for Xiamen on a par with the province.[234] Local officials felt the slow pace of legal change unnecessarily constrained on-the-ground initiative and held back the process of reform.

The visit of top leaders to Xiamen in December boosted the enthusiasm of local officials who embarked early in 1992 on a further round of policy innovation. In January Chen Guangyi, Provincial Party Secretary, announced plans to grant foreign trade enterprises greater autonomy and drew special attention to developing Fujian–Taiwan trade. He also encouraged foreign investment in sectors such as real estate, finance and commodity retail services.[235] Just after the spring festival a delegation from Xiamen set off for Hong Kong to seek new investment.[236] In the spring of 1992, the provincial government announced plans to open a special port for Taiwanese trade on Meizhou Island.[237] In June Fujian opened its fifth coastal port to foreign ships.[238] In the same month the provincial government granted inland mountain areas similar rights in opening up as the coastal cities, so extending the scope of the Open Policy.[239] In July Xiamen city government boldly announced its plans to catch up with the 'Four Little Dragons' of Hong Kong, Taiwan, Singapore and South Korea and set about hastening the implementation of its free-trade-zone policies.[240]

By the summer Fujian had approved 973 new foreign enterprises, almost double the amount in the same period in 1991.[241] The amount of foreign investment contracted and utilised increased threefold compared to the previous year. The main local paper in Xiamen was now reporting a new 'spring wave' of foreign investment.[242]

Whilst the Chinese government was doing its best to attract Taiwanese investors, the latter were becoming increasingly worried by US threats to impose tariffs on mainland products.[243] Moreover, the lack of any investment protection agreements had led many potential Taiwanese investors to adopt a cautious attitude.[244] Taiwanese investors were also constrained by their own government, which took an ambivalent position on mainland investment. On the one hand it welcomed the opportunities for trade and fast profits, but on the other hand, it was concerned about key industries transferring to China and too much dependency on a regime still perceived as hostile. However, the relaxation of some restrictions on mainland investment over the course of the year improved the investment climate for Taiwanese investors. In May, for example, the Taiwanese Ministry of Finance made tentative proposals to ease restrictions on indirect remittances between China and Taiwan.[245] Later in September the Taiwanese government hinted at direct shipping links on a trial basis in the near future.[246] The following month the Taiwanese Economic Ministry lifted the ban on state enterprises exporting to the mainland.[247]

The victory of the radical economic reformers at the Fourteenth Party Congress gave the official go-ahead to a further expansion of the Open Policy in Xiamen and the province. Inspired by the course of the congress, Shi Zhaobin, a delegate from Xiamen, boldly proclaimed that Xiamen would strive to achieve the income level of Hong Kong over the next 20 years.[248] Within days of the congress preparations were already underway to provide more incentives to Taiwanese investors, such as low-interest loans.[249]

Conclusion

The evolution of the Open Policy in Fujian province, and in particular Xiamen SEZ, has followed a similar trajectory to the national level. The slow change in the provincial leadership, however, constrained the pace of implementation up till the autumn of 1981. On the other hand Fujian's historic tradition of openness as well as its labyrinth of Overseas Chinese links have contributed not only to a heightened awareness of the potential benefits of the policy but also to a more 'outward-looking' and 'open' attitude towards contact with the outside world. Local leaders have often given rather vague policies from above a broader interpretation so putting policy practice ahead of policy rhetoric. As the extent of Overseas Chinese connections widens the net of potential beneficiaries, it also makes the benefits of the policy more immediately apparent and the policy itself more acceptable. Attempts to withdraw privileges relating to foreign economic relations encounter resistance from an expanding net of beneficiaries. The provincial government has indeed felt pressure from smaller cities to decentralise further the special rights and privileges enjoyed by Xiamen. The Open Policy thus creates its own web of interests. Whilst this has stimulated the expansion of foreign trade and foreign investment, it has also had unforeseen consequences such as a boom in consumer imports, and the inappropriate use of foreign exchange, as well as instances of economic corruption. As the new beneficiaries have an interest in retaining their newly acquired privileges, this in turn makes recentralisation more difficult with each cycle. The expansion of the Open Policy thus creates crucial problems of control.

Since 1988 the Taiwan factor has become an increasingly significant determinant in the fate of Xiamen SEZ. The continuing inflow of Taiwanese investment after Tiananmen served to mitigate the potential effects that sanctions might have had on Xiamen. Moreover, the recent upsurge in Taiwanese investment has raised expectations even further. The streets of Xiamen have changed beyond imagination within the last three years. As the taste for fashionable clothing, pop music, discos and karaoke grows, pressure to push open even more, particularly from the young, will continue to mount. But without a further relaxation of relations between Taiwan and China, and in particular the establishment of direct trade and communications, Xiamen will be inhibited from a genuine take-off, let alone fulfilling its ambition of attaining Hong Kong living standards within the next 20 years. Whilst the Fourteenth Party Congress has paved the way for further reform and opening in Xiamen SEZ, the ace card lies in the hand of Taiwan.

Notes

1. See Introduction, note 2; FEER carries occasional articles on Xiamen SEZ but books and articles on the SEZs tend to focus on Shenzhen — see, for example, Jao and Leung, 1986 and Crane, 1990.
   The fieldwork for this case-study was carried out in Xiamen SEZ and Fuzhou between 1987 and 1988 and in 1992. Over 60 enterprises, state departments, trade companies and labour institutions were interviewed. The names of officials interviewed as well as the names of specific companies are not revealed in this book.
2. See Fujian Jingji (FJJJ) (*Fujian Economy*), 1988, no. 4, pp. 21–3 — before the reforms Fujian was oriented to the domestic economy.
3. Ma Xingyuan took over as governor from Liao Zhigao in December 1979. Prior to that he had been provincial Party secretary and vice-chairman of the Provincial Revolutionary Committee, thus second in command to Liao (HK, SCMP 9.5.1981 in FBIS 13.5.1981 W3-4).

4. FFPS 16.10.1981 in FBIS 21.10.1981 02.
5. BJ, ZGXWS 22.11.1981 in FBIS 23.11.1981 01–2.
6. Fuzhou People's Broadcasting Station 11.1.1983 in FBIS 19.1.1983 01–2.
7. XH, BJ 25.3.1983 in FBIS 25.3.1983 01.
8. BJ, GMRB 10.11.1986.
9. FJRB (*Fujian daily*) 8.9.1981.
10. FJRB 13.7.1984.
11. FJRB 6.10.1984, p. 2.
12. FJRB 25.4.1985, p. 1.
13. FJRB 1.1.1981, p. 2.
14. ibid.
15. FJRB 10.6.1982, p. 1.
16. FJRB 10.6.1982.
17. ibid.
18. FJRB 23.9.1981.
19. Fuzhou People's Broadcasting Station 12.2.1987 in FBIS 18.2.1987 01.
20. XMRB (*Xiamen daily*) 14.2.1984; XMRB 22.2.1984; XMRB 10.5.1984;
    FJRB 14.6.1984.
21. FJRB 10.6.1982.
22. FJRB 26.3.1985, p. 1.
23. XMRB 4.2.1983.
24. See, for example, FJRB 6.10.1984, p. 2.
25. FJJJ 1988 no. 3. See p. 37 for details about differences of powers with regard
    to investment.
26. FJRB 17.4.1985, p. 1.
27. FJJJ 1987 no. 10 pp. 21–3.
28. FJRB 5.7.1985.
29. FJRB 18.10.1985.
30. Interview, May 1987. As pointed out in note 1, the names of officials and
    companies interviewed are in general not cited in the book.
31. Between January and September 1987 there was a 20 per cent increase in
    the value of foreign direct investment contracts in Fujian over the same period
    the previous year (see FJRB 16.10.1987 in FBIS 11.2.1988 pp. 18–19).
    In an interview the Deputy Mayor of Xiamen, Jiang Ping, stated that
    considerable progress had been made in foreign direct investment in the first
    half of 1987. Apparently the number of joint venture contracts signed in
    the first five months of 1987 was over a quarter of that in the previous year
    (see HK, SCMP 22.6.1987, p. 16).
32. According to Hu Ping, 'the state has decided to allocate $200 million in
    foreign exchange for us annually and we are now allowed to make certain
    decisions on the use of this money' see HK, WWP 5.2.1983 in FBIS
    16.2.1983 W 13.
33. FJRB 10.4.1985, p. 2.
34. See Shi Qinglin, 'The function of foreign exchange balance in the overall
    balance of the SEZ' in *Xiamen Tequ Diaoyan* (in Chinese) no. 4 (Dec. 1985),
    pp. 20–2.

35. Terry, 1980.
36. For a discussion of the 'one country two systems concept' see BJ, BYT 25.7.1987 pp. 27–8 and SH, SJJJDB 26.1.1987.
37. FJRB 26.9.1982.
38. Terry, 1980, p. 12.
39. ibid. Construction on the first phase of the Dongdu Harbour district project began in 1976.
40. See Chu, D.K.Y., 1986, pp. 21–38.
41. FFPS 31.3.1981 in FBIS 2.4.1981 01–2.
42. XH, BJ 24.3.1981 in FBIS 25.3.1981 01.
43. FFPS 25.3.1981 in FBIS 26.3.1981 01.
44. FFPS 2.4.1981 in FBIS 6.4.1981 01–3.
45. Almanac of Xiamen SEZ Editorial Board, 1986, p. 379.
46. FJRB 8.9.1981.
47. This was revealed by Xiang Nan in his briefings to the Hong Kong press (see HK, WWP 1.11.1981 in FBIS 5.11.1981 01–4).
48. FJRB 8.12.1981. Arguments against the latter option were that tourism and trade would neither draw significant amounts of foreign capital, nor introduce advanced technology or managerial methods. It was also argued that this would lead to mainly commercial activity and potential foreign exchange problems as tourism involved substantial imports which would render the domestic economy subject to fluctuations in the international market.
49. FJRB 20.10.1981, p. 3.
50. FJJJ 1988 no. 7, p. 18. Xiamen obtains 95 per cent of its raw materials from outside the island.
51. FFPS 31.3.1981 in FBIS 5.11.1981 01–2. Loss-making enterprises were also being encouraged to stop production.
52. Wang Yitu, the official in charge of Xiamen SEZ, underlined the importance of Xiamen as a port and proposed that Xiamen develop as a centre for four major activities, namely international trade, export processing, tourism and cultural/educational activities (see FJRB January 1982).
53. FJRB 14.1.1981.
54. FFPS 7.4.1981 in FBIS 9.4.1981 U1.
55. HK, SCMP 9.5.1981 in FBIS 13.5.1981 W3–4.
56. FJRB 5.9.1981.
57. HK, SCMP 2.11.1981 in FBIS 3.11.1981 01–5.
58. FJRB 16.10.1981 in FBIS 27.10.1981 01.
59. XH, BJ 15.10.1981 in FBIS 16.10.1981 05.
60. ibid.
61. HK, SCMP 2.11.1981.
62. ibid.
63. HK, WWP 1.11.1981 in FBIS 5.11.1981 01–4.
64. XH, BJ 18.1.1981 in FBIS 23.1.1981 L1.
65. FFPS 30.1.1981 in FBIS 3.2.1981 03–4.
66. FFPS 27.3.1981 in FBIS 31.3.1981 02–3.

67. FFPS 12.4.1981 in FBIS 13.4.1981 02.
68. FJRB 21.9.1981 in FBIS 1.10.1981 02–3.
69. FJRB 23.9.1981 in FBIS 5.10.1981 05.
70. FJRB 20.11.1981 in FBIS 27.11.1981 K8. The opinion of Wang Zhen was important because, as a member of the Military Commission, he was likely to influence the army. Hence when Deng Xiaoping visited the SEZs in early 1984 to quell the growing controversy, he took Wang Zhen with him.
71. FJRB 8.9.1981.
72. FJRB 14.10.1981.
73. FJRB 27.11.1981, p. 3.
74. FJRB 11.3.1982, p. 1.
75. FJRB 6.4.1982.
76. FJRB 11.3.1982, p. 1.
77. FJLT 20.6.1982.
78. See Foreign Languages Press, 1982.
79. For example, Xiamen SEZ offered 60 per cent share of profits for the foreign side compared with only 50 per cent in Guangdong. See Clarke, 1983, p. 10. Also in an interview Xiang Nan stated that whilst an apartment building built with Chinese and foreign funds in the three SEZs in Guangdong might be evenly shared, in Xiamen SEZ the profits might be 40 per cent for the Chinese side and 60 per cent for the foreign partner (see XH, BJ 15.10.1981 in FBIS 16.10.1981 05).
80. FJRB 14.5.1982.
81. FJRB 5.6.1982.
82. ibid.
83. FJRB 8.7.1982.
84. FJRB 26.9.1982.
85. FJRB 17.11.1982. In view of the low prestige of the Party after the Cultural Revolution it might have been somewhat optimistic, if not precarious, of the proponents of the Open Policy, to rely on political and ideological means to curb economic crime.
86. XH, BJ 24.10.1982.
87. XMRB 12.3.1983, p. 3.
88. Almanac of Xiamen SEZ Editorial Board, 1986, p. 349.
89. ibid., p. 379.
90. Clarke, 1983, p. 10.
91. ibid.; and Fuzhou Radio 11.1.1983 in FBIS 19.1.1983 01–2.
92. ibid.; and BJ, ZGXWS 9.3.1983 in FBIS 14.3.1983 01; XH, BJ 25.3.1983 in FBIS 25.3.1983 01; Fuzhou Radio 8.3.1983 in FBIS 18.3.1983 02–3; Fuzhou Radio 10.4.1983 in FBIS 14.4.1983 01–2.
93. FJRB 19.9.1983, p. 3.
94. FJRB 16.12.1983, p. 3.
95. XMRB, Oct. 1983.
96. XH, BJ 15.10.1981 in FBIS 16.10.1981 05.
97. HK, XWB 3.1.1985 in SWB/FE/7841/BII/1.

98. FJRB 6.10.1984.
99. HK, WWP 14.12.1984, p. 3 in FBIS 17.12.1984 W2.
100. FJRB 15.7.1984, p. 1.
101. FJRB 19.2.1984, p. 1.
102. FJRB 17.4.1984, p. 1.
103. FJRB 19.2.1984, p. 1.
104. ibid.
105. FJRB 22.4.1984, p. 1.
106. FJRB 6.10.1984, p. 2.
107. FJRB 30.3.1984.
108. The Provincial Transport Bureau, for example, decided to give Xiamen SEZ preferential treatment in importing materials for the construction of the zone (see FJRB 29.3.1984, p. 1). The customs also introduced more flexible policies. For example, imported goods could now be delivered first to the factory warehouse and then inspected (see FJRB 5.5.1984, p. 1).
109. FJRB 15.7.1984; also referred to in FJRB 24.2.1985 in SWB/FE/W133/C/1−9 27.3.1985.
110. In fact in October 1982 state councillor Gu Mu called for greater autonomy for Xiamen (see Almanac of Xiamen SEZ Editorial Board, 1986, p. 381).
111. FJRB 15.10.1984.
112. FJRB 6.7.1984.
113. FJRB 6.10.1984, p. 2.
114. ibid.
115. ibid.
116. FJRB 5.12.1984, p. 1.
117. UNIDO *Investment Promotion Meeting, 25−29 November 1985, List of Investment Proposals* 30.8.1985, p. 8. These comprised Tongan, Zhangzhou, Longhai, Zhangpu, Dongshan, Huian, Anxi, Jinjiang, Nanan, Yongchun and Quanzhou. For further details see Fujian Enterprises Investment Company brochure and Fujian Foreign Economic Relations and Trade Corporation brochure, p. 65.
118. FJRB 23.1.1985, p. 1.
119. ibid.
120. FJRB 25.11.1985.
121. Falkenheim, 1986, p. 39.
122. Moreover, Xiamen would be able to engage in transit trade and act as trade agent for inland areas (FJRB 25.11.1985).
123. HK, WWP 1.11.1981 in FBIS 5.11.1981 01−4.
124. CD 2.5.1987.
125. *China Trader*, 'Fujian Xiamen SEZ', February 1987.
126. See Fuzhou: FJLT, no. 9, 5.9.1987 in FBIS 5.9.1987.
127. Chen Jingcheng, 'Problems in technology absorption' in FJLT 5.7.1985, pp. 13−16.
128. HK, CM 1.12.1986 in FBIS 4.12.1986 K 13.
129. XMRB 16.5.1985.
130. FJRB 7.1.1986, p. 1.

131. FJRB 26.5.1986, p. 3.
132. FJRB 21.7.1986, p. 1.
133. HK, SCMP 27.10.1985 in FBIS 15.11.1985, p. 112.
134. FJRB 9.8.1986, p. 1.
135. *China Trader*, February 1987.
136. ibid.
137. FJRB 15.10.1986, p. 1.
138. FJRB 27.1.1986.
139. FJRB 22.8.1986; FJRB 14.10.1986, p. 1.
140. A materials supply company was also established to assist foreign-invested enterprises in obtaining raw materials.
141. HK, ZGXWS 11.12.1986 in FBIS 18.12.1986 01.
142. FJRB 5.2.1987.
143. FJRB 22.2.1987 in FBIS 9.3.1987 02.
144. Beijing Radio 12.4.1987 in FBIS 20.4.1987 01.
145. HK, ZGXWS 31.3.1987.
146. FJRB 16.10.1987.
147. FJRB 4.1.1988 in FBIS 8.3.1988 p. 25.
148. CEI 1.6.1988 in FBIS 88/132/44.
149. CEI 30.9.1988 in FBIS 88/190/36 and Wang Zhong, 'Xiamen City positively uses foreign investment to development the zone economy' in *Fujian Waimao Jingji (Fujian Foreign Trade Economy)*, no. 7, 1989, pp. 47–8.
150. CEI 1.6.1988 in FBIS/88/107/42.
151. XH 9.1.1989 in SWB/FE/W0016/A/7.
152. NFRB 7.11.1988 FBIS 88/218/27.
153. HK, MCED (in Chinese) 1990, 3, p. 24.
154. XH 22.6.1988; XH 18.5.1988.
155. CEI 1.6.1988 in FBIS 88/132/44.
156. CEI 1.8.1988 in FBIS 88/148/39.
157. HK, SCMP 27.6.1988 in FBIS 88/123/53.
158. CBR Sept./Oct. 1990.
159. HK, S 29.10.1988 in JPRS 88.080, p. 6.
160. XH 12.5.1990.
161. XMRB 19.2.1990.
162. XH 10.11.1989 in SWB/FE/0614/B2/8 10.11.1989.
163. HK, WWP 15.10.1988 in SWB/FE/0286/B2/5.
164. HK, S 27.11.1988 in FBIS 88/0347/B2/5.
165. Erbaugh and Kraus, 1990.
166. Lu Ping, Hong Kong Trade Union Education Centre, *A Moment of Truth* (Asia Monitor Resource Centre, 1990).
167. Interview, Xiamen SEZ, December 1991.
168. XH 26.6.1989 in SWB/FE/W0085/A/4.
169. CBR, Sept./Oct. 1990.
170. HKMCED (in Chinese) 1990, 3, p. 24.
171. ibid.

172. XH 9.2.1990 SWB/FE/0688/B2/1.
173. HK, SCMP 20.7.1990 in FBIS 90/139/46.
174. ZGXWS 6.6.1990 in SWB/FE/0785/B2/3.
175. XH 28.6.1990 in SWB/FE/0804/B2/3.
176. XH 26.11.1990 in SWB/FE/0933/B2/1.
177. HK, SCMP 28.5.1990.
178. CD 8.8.1990.
179. CBR Sept./Oct. 1990.
180. CD 8.8.1990.
181. According to a local official of Xiamen Foreign Executive Committee, applications for foreign-funded projects averaged 15—20 per month, compared with their peak of 25—30 per month in 1989.
182. XH, BJ 19.2.1991 in SWB/FE/0995 B2/5 13.2.1991.
183. See Fujian Statistics Bureau, 1991, pp. 330—1.
184. XH, BJ 11.9.1991 in SWB/FE/W0198 A/5 25.9.1991.
185. XMRB 15.4.1991.
186. ibid.
187. ibid.
188. XMRB 5.1.1991.
189. XH 13.8.1990 in FBIS 90/157/54.
190. CD 23.8.1990.
191. XH 16.1.1991 in SWB/FE/0973/B2/2 18.1.1991.
192. Fujian People's Broadcasting Station 27.1.91 in SWB/FE/0984/B2/2 31.1.1991.
193. XH 26.2.1991 in SWB/FE/1008/B2/2 28.2.1991.
194. XH 15.3.1991 in SWB/FE/W0172/A/1 27.3.1991.
195. XH 9.4.1991 SWB/FE/1047/B2/4 16.4.1991.
196. XH 30.3.1991 in SWB/FE/W0174/A/5 10.4.1991.
197. XH 23.4.1991 in SWB/FE/1055/B2/4 25.4.1991.
198. RMRB 11.5.1991 in SWB/FE/1070/A3/5 13.5.1991.
199. HK, WWP 10.5.1991 in SWB/FE/1070/A3/6 13.5.1991.
200. RMRB 15.5.1991 in SWB/FE/1075/A3/1 18.5.1991.
201. In 1988, 152 169 tourists visited Xiamen (Xiamen Statistics Bureau, 1989, p. 364).
202. Qingguo Jia, 'Changing relations across the Taiwan Strait, Beijing's perceptions' in *Asian Survey*, vol. XXXII, no. 6, July 1992.
203. Central News Agency, Taipei, 31.3.1992 in SWB/FE/W0255/A/11 8.4.1992.
204. SWB/FE/W0/179 A/4 15.5.1991.
205. XH 8.6.1991 in SWB/FE/W0184 A/7 19.6.1991.
206. XH 9.7.1991 SWB/FE/W0188/A/5 17.7.1991.
207. XH 8.6.1991 in SWB/FE/W0184/A/6 19.6.1991.
208. XH 17.6.1991 in SWB/FE/1102/B2/8 19.6.1991.
209. XH 11.6.1991 in SWB/FE/W0185/A/5 26.6.1991.
210. HK, WWP 30.6.1991 in SWB/FE/1116/B2/7 5.7.1991.
211. ibid.
212. XH 24.7.1991 in SWB/FE/W0190/A/2 31.7.1991.

213. Interview, Xiamen SEZ, December 1991.
214. ibid.
215. XH 2.8.1991 in SWB/FE/W0192/A/3 14.8.1991.
216. XH 11.9.1991 in SWB/FE/W0198/A/5 25.9.1991 A/5.
217. CBR, Sept./Oct. 1990.
218. XH 15.11.1991 in SWB/FE/W0208/A/7 4.12.1991.
219. On the increasing role of township and village enterprises (TVEs) in Fujian's economy see 'South Fujian opens to outside world' in *New China Quarterly*, May 1992 , no. 24 pp. 63–76. Quanzhou has set up planned parks for TVEs and now has 50 000 TVEs employing 500 000 people, 25 per cent of the rural labour force of Quanzhou.
220. Personal communication.
221. XH 3.5.1991 in SWB/FE/1065/A3/7 7.5.1991.
222. Fujian People's Broadcasting Station in SWB/FE/1071/B2/7 14.5.1991.
223. HK, WWP 14.5.1991 in SWB/FE/1074/B2/7 17.5.1991.
224. SWB/FE/1099 i 15.6.1991; ZGXWS, BJ 14.6.1991 in SWB/FE/1100/A3/5 17.6.1991.
225. ZGXWS, BJ 16.6.1991 in SWB/FE/1103/B2/8 20.6.1991. See HK, ZGXWS 25.7.1991 in SWB/FE/1137/B2/4 on use of Taiwan boats in smuggling in Fujian, Guangdong, Hainan and Zhejiang 30.7.1991.
226. XH 2.9.1991 in SWB/FE/1169/B2/15.9.1991.
227. XH 21.9.1991 in SWB/FE/1184/B2/2 23.9.1991.; XH 19.11.1992 in SWB/FE/1238/B2/3 25.11.1991.
228. HK, ZGTXS 7.10.1991 in SWB/FE/1203/B2/6 15.10.1991.
229. XH 18.12.1991 in SWB/FE/1260/B2/1 20.12.1991.
230. XMRB 13.12.1991.
231. LHP, Taipei in SWB/FE/1326/B2/1 11.3.1992 and XH 1.4.1992 in SWB/FE/W025/A7 8.4.1992.
232. ZGXWS 15.1.1992 in SWB/FE/W0214A/8 22.1.1992.
233. LHP, Taipei in SWB/FE/1326/B2/1 11.3.1992.
234. XMRB 7.12.1991.
235. XH 22.1.1992 in SWB/FE/1286/B2/8 24.1.1992.
236. XH 5.3.1992 in SWB/FE/1323/B2/2 7.3.1992.
237. CBR May/June 1992.
238. XH 17.6.1992 in SWB/FE/W0236/A/8 24.6.1992.
239. ZGXWS 27.6.1992 in SWB/FE/W0239/A/8 15.7.1992.
240. XH 10.7.1992 in SWB/FE/W0240/A/9 22.7.1992.
241. ZGXWS 17.7.1992 in SWB/FE/W0241/A/4.
242. XMRB 10.6.1992.
243. Central News Agency, Taipei 16.1.1992 in SWB/FE/1282/A3/8 20.1.1992.
244. Beijing Radio 15.10.1992 in SWB/FE/1514/C1/1 17.10.1992.
245. Central News Agency, Taipei 27.5.1992 in SWB/FE/1394/A1/4 30.5.1992.
246. Central News Agency, Taipei 21.9.1992 in SWB/FE/1497/A2/3 28.9.1992.
247. Central News Agency, Taipei 13.10.1992 in SWB/FE/1512/A1/2 15.10.1992.
248. XH 15.10.1992 in SWB/FE/1515/C1/7 19.10.1992.
249. Central News Agency, Taipei 19.10.1992 in SWB/FE/W0254/A/5 28.10.1992.

5

Towards a market-facilitating state

We have shown in the first part of the book how political forces have shaped the trajectory of China's Open Policy. But what has been the impact of opening up on the state itself? Given the pivotal role of the state in the policy-making process in state socialist countries such as China, the relationship between economic reform and the state is of crucial importance. To what extent has the drawing back of the bamboo curtain altered the structure, functions and social base of the state? Have these changes helped or hindered the process of reform and opening up? What is the nature of the new metamorphosing beast? These are some of the questions we address in this chapter.

The state in China comprises a complex of political, administrative and coercive institutions. Whilst the reformers have been extremely reluctant to tinker with the basic political system, apart from radical thinkers such as Zhao Ziyang, they have since the débâcle of Tiananmen become increasingly aware of the need to reform the administrative giant.[1] The idea of a new civil service organised along Weberian lines has entered top-level discourse on state reform.[2] At a national meeting on public administration in October 1991 Li Peng stated openly that economic reform and political reform must proceed simultaneously, which contrasted with the previous dominant view that economic reform did not require political reform.

Up till Tiananmen there was a general consensus amongst Chinese policy-makers as well as overseas academics that the state in the SEZs was fundamentally the same as elsewhere in China. The magic word 'special' in SEZs referred only to the economic policies prevalent in the zones. In his study of Shenzhen SEZ, Chang, a Hong Kong academic, wrote that

> As far as the Party organisation and state apparatus are concerned, the principle of governing is no more 'special' than elsewhere in China for the SEZs are not special 'administrative' zones. Party discipline, the state constitution and laws and state administration all remain the same.[3]

Top leaders not only perceived this to be the case but also felt, with the exception of Zhao and some followers, that economic reform should and indeed could proceed without political reform. We argue here, however, that whilst the state is still basically the same in the SEZs as elsewhere in China, the process of reform and opening over the past decade has altered the character and institutional fabric of the state. The crisis of Tiananmen forced these changes painfully to the surface.

The Chinese state is currently in a process of transition.[4] The introduction of market forces, both international and domestic, has spawned elements of a new 'market-facilitating' state. This has been most pronounced in the SEZs where the concentration of foreign capital is highest and domestic economic reform has proceeded furthest. Other parts of China in the throes of reform and opening up also harbour elements of this change, though to a lesser degree.

The key features of this market-facilitating state are as follows: first, it is entrepreneurial, that is, it both promotes entrepreneurship and engages itself in risk-taking, profit-seeking economic pursuits; second, it is legalistic, that is, it legally defines relations between economic actors in the market-place and settles economic disputes through the law; third, it is technocratic, that is, the state is run by technically and professionally qualified people; and finally it is regulatory, that is, it seeks to regulate the market at the macro-economic level whilst withdrawing through deregulation from the tangle of the microlevel.[5]

We can observe embryonic elements of this market-facilitating state in the structure, operational mode and social composition of the state. Before exploring this in detail, let us look first at the nature of the state in the pre-reform period. We confine our discussion to those parts of the state dealing with foreign economic relations.

The state and the external economy pre-1978

Since Liberation the Soviet model has wielded a strong influence upon the overall character of the Chinese state. The Party has been the chief policy-making body with a bulging bureaucracy in charge of administration and the army and public security organs serving national defence and domestic order. Apart from some short periods of decentralisation in 1958 and 1970, the Chinese state has been a highly centralised creature. Although the criteria governing recruitment to the state have fluctuated, 'redness' has tended to dominate, especially during the Cultural Revolution. These features also defined those organs of the state dealing with the external economy.

In the early 1950s the management of foreign trade was centralised under the Ministry of Foreign Trade. The Western embargo on trade with China prompted the setting up of the China Council for the Promotion of International Trade to negotiate non-governmental trade agreements. With the socialisation of all privately run trade companies in 1957 foreign trade fell wholly under state control.

The central ministry assigned import and export quotas to the provincial foreign trade bureaux, which in turn passed these down to the various import/export companies. Neither export-producing enterprises nor import/export companies were financially responsible for the outcome of their foreign trade activities. As in other sectors of the state, political criteria were important in recruiting staff. Although training in foreign trade and economics was provided in the 1950s and early 1960s, during the Cultural Revolution such 'bourgeois' subjects enjoyed little prestige.

The expansion of foreign economic relations since 1978 and the subsequent increasing demands on the foreign trade organs has brought into relief some of the shortcomings of the pre-existing foreign trade system. The following have been of particular concern to the reformist leadership. First, the Ministry of Foreign Trade exerted excessive and rigid control over its subordinate bodies. As a result export-producing enterprises had little control over the level or direction of exports.[6]

Second, there was inadequate integration between production and marketing. As foreign trade bureaux and production enterprises had minimal contact with their suppliers or customers, apart possibly from annual meetings at the Guangzhou Trade Fair, their marketing skills, knowledge about alternative suppliers and international prices and experience were severely constricted.

Third, there was no clear division of functions between the 'government and enterprise'. Administrative trade organs took decisions on economic matters concerning the trading companies. Moreover, a maze of innumerable formalities and procedures reduced efficiency.[7]

Finally, as a result of the Cultural Revolution the bulk of foreign trade personnel at the dawn of the Open Policy were poorly versed in the art of foreign trade, especially in relation to the international capitalist economy. With the rapid increase in foreign trade and other forms of external economic links since 1978 reform of this state sector became imperative.

Effects of the Open Policy on the state since 1978

With the opening of China and reform, the Chinese state has entered a period of transition. Elements of a new market-facilitating state, which is entrepreneurial, legalistic, technocratic and regulatory, are emerging. These coexist uneasily with institutions born out of the previously centrally planned system. At the same time there is a temporary vacuum where the pace of institutional adaptation and creation falls behind the changes in the economy. The Chinese state is not in retreat. On the contrary it is in a process of major restructuring, shedding some functions but taking on others. The web of the command planning state is receding whilst the web of the market-facilitating state is advancing.

How then do we know the Chinese state is going through this metamorphosis? We can identify elements of a market-facilitating state in the restructuring of state institutions, changes in their operational mode and social composition. These elements are more apparent in the SEZs such as Xiamen where the penetration of market forces has been greater than in non-zone areas. Let us look at each of these in turn, drawing on the case of Xiamen SEZ to illustrate our points.

Restructuring of state institutions

The Open Policy has stimulated the creation of new state institutions at both central and lower levels and prompted existing institutions to adapt to their new circumstances. This reweaving of the institutional fabric has proceeded apace with the spiral evolution of the Open Policy.[8]

So as to cope with the rapidly expanding foreign economic relations the reformist leadership created several new central institutions. These included the Foreign Investment Control Commission, which was to manage the introduction of foreign investment; the State Import and Export Commission which was to make policies concerning technology imports and new trading arrangements; and the General Administration of Customs, which was to formulate preferential customs policies as well as the China International Trust and Investment Company (CITIC) which was to facilitate the establishment of joint ventures.[9]

To encourage greater entrepreneurship the reformers split the tasks of the Foreign Trade Bureau between the Ministry of Foreign Economic Relations and the Foreign Trade Corporation, with the former concentrating on planning and policy formulation and the latter on actual foreign trade. The non-governmental China Council for the Promotion of International Trade also plays a key role in arranging trade negotiations between China and potential trading partners, mounting trade exhibitions and providing consultancy services.

Similarly, in Fujian province the Fujian Import/Export Office took over the policy and planning functions of the Foreign Trade Bureau as well as the allocation of foreign exchange within the province, thus usurping the administrative authority of the Foreign Trade Bureau.[10] At the same time the newly founded Foreign Trade Corporation, which was responsible for its own profits and losses, weakened the control of the Foreign Trade Bureau over the branches of the Foreign Trade Corporations.[11] The coexistence of the Foreign Trade Bureau, the Import/Export Office and the Foreign Trade Corporation meant there was considerable overlap in functions.

However, in March 1982, as part of a general reform of the State Council's organisations, the Commission for Import and Export Control, Ministry of Foreign Trade, Ministry of Foreign Economic Relations and the Commission for the Control of Foreign Investment merged to form the current Ministry of Foreign Economic Relations and Trade.[12]

Fujian province likewise followed suit when it set up the Fujian Foreign Economic Relations and Trade Commission to administer foreign trade. Similarly, the Xiamen SEZ Economic Relations and Trade Commission was set up in 1983 to administer and plan foreign trade, foreign investment and supervise overseas labour exports.[13] With the Xiamen Foreign Economic Relations and Trade Commission now directly responsible to Beijing, it enjoyed greater autonomy, in theory, from its provincial counterpart. Setting up a zone in Xiamen promised greater powers and more freedom from provincial constraints.

When the area covered by the SEZ expanded in March 1984 further institutional changes were set in motion. The Municipal Economic Commission, Commission of Foreign Economic Relations and Trade and Finance Office merged into a single Municipal Economic and Trade Commission, handling Xiamen's economy.[14] This enabled tighter institutional coordination to manage an increasingly complex economy, highlighting the intermeshing of domestic and external economies.

With the launch of the four SEZs in mid-1979 the reformers created SEZ Administration Offices in Guangdong and Fujian provinces. As the controversy over the SEZs heated up in 1981, supervision of the zones became a national concern. So in June 1982 the reformers set up the State Council's Office of SEZ Affairs under the leadership of the two reformers Gu Mu and Zhao Ziyang.[15] Following the support given to SEZs by reformist leaders at the Party Congress in September 1982, Gu Mu called for greater autonomy for Xiamen.[16] Central leaders were well aware that the concentration of power and resources with the provincial government was a significant constraint on the pace of opening up in Xiamen SEZ. Although in September 1983 the Fujian People's Government decided to increase Xiamen's autonomy, it was only after the visit of Deng Xiaoping in 1984 that Xiamen could have its own SEZ committee and so implement its autonomy from the provincial capital.[17] This was partly because the spiritual pollution campaign launched that autumn by the leftist opposition had cast a momentary shadow over the future of the zones. But also the provincial government was probably reluctant to cede power immediately. The relation of authority between this central office and the provincial SEZ Management Committees was not, however, well defined.[18]

As for foreign direct investment, the Ministry of Foreign Economic Relations and Trade assumed prime responsibility from 1982. However, the drop in foreign investment in 1986 as well as the growing complexity of institutions dealing with foreign capital underlined the need for greater coordination. So the reformers set up a State Council Leading Group for Foreign Investment in August 1986, again headed by state councillor Gu Mu.[19] This group comprised not only members of the State Council but also officials from a wide range of state institutions connected to the Open Policy.[20] As the Open Policy became more deeply entrenched, the cast of actors involved in the policy process likewise expanded. This group was to make policy recommendations to the State Council, arbitrate in the problems of foreign-invested enterprises, supervise both departments and regions in their use of foreign investment and draft legislation for foreign investment procedures.[21]

As at the national level several new institutions were born in Fuzhou and Xiamen to deal with the specific needs of foreign capital, so hastening the development of a market-facilitating state. Local leaders set up, for example, the Xiamen SEZ Foreign Investment Leading Group Office to plan and approve joint ventures in Xiamen SEZ and to facilitate relations between joint ventures and government.[22] They also set up a materials supply company to ensure that foreign-invested enterprises could secure guaranteed supplies of local raw materials. Although proposals for joint ventures require the approval of the Xiamen Economic and Trade Commission, three other state bodies are also permitted to negotiate joint venture contracts, namely the Xing Xia Corporation, the Xiamen Construction and Development Corporation and the Xiamen United Development Corporation. In October 1991 Xiamen SEZ set up yet another institution to coordinate and plan foreign investment projects.

As at the central state level, there has also been a proliferation of trading and investment corporations at lower levels. By breaking up the monopoly of the large national foreign trading corporations, the reformist leadership hoped to remove some of the rigidities inherent in a centrally and vertically integrated system. The mushrooming of these institutions has been most pronounced during upswings in the Open Policy when decentralisation was afoot. However, in downswings of the Open Policy, when the centre tried to reimpose control over the economy, the growth in these institutions halted and may even have contracted.

The first wave of new institutions began in 1980 when the reformers set up 17 new import/export corporations and experimented with foreign trade corporations in Beijing, Tianjin, Shanghai, Guangdong and Fujian.[23]

Provincial branches of new national specialist trading corporations such as the Fujian Footwear and Headgear Branch Corporation have surfaced. Cities such as Sanming, Putian and Quanzhou could for the first time since Liberation set up branches of sectoral and provincial foreign trading corporations. The success of these early initiatives spurred other provinces to set up foreign trade corporations as well. Similarly, CITIC set up provincial branches to facilitate the negotiation and financing of joint ventures.

Decentralisation of the economy in early 1984 accelerated this process further. By August 1984 there were over six hundred import/export companies under the Foreign Trade Corporation at provincial level and above, not to mention those in the SEZs, compared with 120 in 1978.[24] The following month industrial ministries and provinces received permission to set up medium and small foreign trade corporations. So by 1987 the number of such corporations rose to 1900.[25] Fujian boasted that by that time 208 local corporations authorised to export locally supplied products outside central control. Xiamen laid claim to 105 of these.[26] With foreign trade way out of control, the province, under directions from the Ministry of Foreign Economic Relations and Trade, reappraised this tangle of trading agencies.[27] By requiring all trading corporations to register in early 1986 the Ministry of Foreign Economic Relations and Trade managed to reduce this number. Technological trade corporations in Fujian, for example, fell from 100 to 18.[28]

Not only has opening up led to the creation of new institutions, but it has also fostered the emergence of a new part of the legal system to deal with external economic relations. The legal system has expanded partly in response to the concern of foreign capital for legal protection.[29] Since the passing of the Sino-Foreign joint venture law in 1979, the reformers have devised laws and regulations on taxation, patents, foreign exchange management, accounting, customs, entry and exit formalities and wholly owned foreign enterprises.

The Open Policy has also prompted the development of a legal structure dealing with foreign economic relations. Xiamen has set up a Foreign Economic Lawyers' Office which provides legal services for both Chinese and foreigners. It has also passed over 50 administrative and economic laws since opening up. However, like Shenzhen, Xiamen has been pressing central government recently for greater powers to pass its own laws.[30] The time needed for the provincial government and State Council to approve draft laws and regulations has impeded Xiamen's efforts to nurture a legal climate conducive to foreign investment.

With the growth of foreign investment and foreign trade, arbitration committees have sprung up to resolve disputes between Chinese and foreign parties. The China Council for the Promotion of International Trade has, for example, set up an arbitration committee for foreign economic relations.[31] These arbitration bodies, coupled with the expansion of legislation, promise a potential shift in the mode of conflict resolution. Conflicts in China have tended to be resolved through mutual negotiation, or what the Chinese call 'rule by man' rather than 'rule by law'.[32] Closer links with the capitalist world economy as well as the contract responsibility system have highlighted the need for more legal authority in tune with international law.

The implementation of the Open Policy has not only spawned a labyrinth of new state institutions at central and lower levels but has also led to *the adaptation of existing institutions*. As the degree and extent of opening has increased, a wider range of institutions has had to adapt. Financial and labour institutions, customs, the Party, army and other institutions have all had to adapt and expand parts of their structures and methods of operation to accommodate foreign capital. This phenomenon reflects the 'snowball effect' of the Open Policy whereby changes in one part of the economy and administration entail alterations in other parts of the overall system.

The banking system has had to adapt considerably to the new demands of foreign trade, foreign investment and foreign borrowing. The Foreign Exchange Control Bureau of the People's Bank of China not only is in charge of foreign debts but also regulates the foreign exchange transactions of foreign-invested enterprises.[33] The Bank of China has, for example, through its Trade and Consultancy Department, become involved in the formation of joint ventures. The opening up of certain areas to foreign capital has also prompted the decentralisation of certain banking functions. In July 1984 Chinese banks in the SEZs and the 14 coastal cities were granted greater power, putting them on par with provincial banks.[34]

The Ministry of Finance has also broadened its activities. It has not only had to devise regulations on finance and taxation for foreign-invested enterprises, but also determined their access to the domestic market.[35] It has also decentralised some of its functions. By November 1985 the number of financial institutions authorised to act as guarantors in China had increased to 41.[36] With the sprouting of foreign-invested enterprises the work of accountants and auditors has not only expanded but also altered in content.[37]

Tourism and trade have increased the work of the customs. Customs officers have not only to inspect a greater volume of goods, but also to deal with the unrelenting scourge of smuggling. In 1991 five Xiamen customs officers ended up in the hands of the Taiwanese as they furiously chased Filipino smugglers across the straits.[38] There are even reports that customs officials have cast a blind eye on some smugglers in return for pay-offs in consumer goods.[39] Drug-trafficking between Taiwan and Yunnan via Fujian has been a new phenomenon for customs officials in Xiamen to deal with.

Educational establishments in the zone have also adjusted their curricula to suit the needs of the special economic environment. The Lujiang University, for example, has set up specialist vocational courses for training secretaries, interpreters and technicians to work in the zone. Two electronics high schools have been set up to train people for the local electronics industry. Xiamen University has also expanded its foreign trade, law and management departments. The recruitment of labour through advertisements has also altered the role of newspapers, reflecting both the commoditisation of labour and the media.

The opening up of China has also contributed to changes within the Party.[40] Whilst the structures of the Party have not been directly affected, the methods of operation as well as the social basis of the Party betray some influence from the Open Policy. For example, as some foreign-invested enterprises have banned political meetings during production hours, the Party has had to devise other means for disseminating Party policy amongst both its members and the 'masses'. Both the reforms and the Open Policy have encouraged the Party to recruit younger, more educated candidates with scientific and technological skills.

The army, too, has had to make adaptations in its functions and scope of activities. In the SEZs and open coastal cities, the army has had to yield land to the construction of factories and the development of tourist spots. Under pressure to finance imports of military equipment, the army has converted its factories into export-oriented civilian production. With the demobilisation of the army, troops have been lending a hand in constructing the SEZs and factory sites.[41]

In sum, the implementation of the Open Policy has contributed to a restructuring of that part of the state dealing with foreign economic relations. We can see this in the creation of new institutions at central level, the proliferation of trading companies and investment corporations at provincial level and below as well as the adaptation of existing institutions. The snowball effect of the Open Policy has also served to extend the agenda of reform required for opening up from the foreign trade system to other state sectors.

However, the process has not been complete. Whilst the reformers have created new institutions to deal with foreign investment, there is still a lack of effective coordinating institutions at central and lower levels to ensure that the introduction of foreign investment follows unified plans. Similarly, there is no coordinating institution, either centrally or regionally, responsible for foreign borrowing.

The development of the legal system has come a long way since the early days of reform. But the pace of legislation has continued to lag behind the needs of foreign companies. The contractual joint venture law was, for example, only passed in 1988, ten years after opening up. Similarly, a law on wholly owned foreign enterprises was only drafted in mid-1986 and implementing regulations have still to appear. The broad, ambiguous nature of many of the laws and regulations allows considerable scope for interpretation and inconsistency at the local level.[42] Poor translations have added to the uncertainties of foreign investors. Following the move towards a socialist market economy at the Fourteenth Party Congress, leading academic and National People's Congress member Ma Hong called for the revision of existing laws which were formulated when the plan was more dominant in the economy.[43]

The immaturity of China's legal framework has been one of the chief obstacles to foreign investment, particularly US and Japanese. Although progress has been made in the development of economic legislation, Xiamen still lacks laws in the fields of auditing, real estate and management as well as in specific sectors such as agriculture, transport, communications, resources, market and financial services. Moreover, even where laws exist, the problem of enforcement has constrained their efficacy.[44]

This unevenness in the process of institutional restructuring is in part because institutional change tends to lag behind policy change and in part because institutional change has political reverberations. Clearly, the development of a legal system governing foreign economic relations requires time and expertise. As the forms of trade and foreign borrowing have become more diverse since opening up, this process of legislation has also become more complex. Moreover, the dearth of professionally trained lawyers as well as the lack of supervisory bodies ensuring the implementation of laws put significant constraints on the realisation of the 'legal state'.

As the restructuring of the state redistributes power and resources, resistance from potentially 'losing' institutions feeds into the process. The rise in importance of economic institutions has been paralleled by the decline in influence of ideologically oriented institutions. The latter have frequently formed the backbone of ideological campaigns directed against the Open Policy. Delays in the granting of import and export licences or the approval of joint ventures point not only to lengthy bureaucratic procedures but also to resistance by planning institutions whose powers are being eroded. Similarly, the adaptation of institutions such as the army, which has effectively yielded some of its resources and privileges for the construction of the SEZs, may also have fuelled resentment amongst some army members concerning their loss of power since the Third Plenum. As well as this restructuring of state institutions, we also find a change in the operational mode of the state.

Changes in the operational mode of the state

Whilst the changes in the institutional landscape provide the structural foundations for a potential market-facilitating state, the development of a more entrepreneurial and regulatory state requires crucial changes in the way state institutions operate. The reformers have attempted to create a more dynamic state institution which is responsive to market change by decentralising authority over foreign economic relations from central to lower levels, by setting up quasi-state institutions and recruiting professionally and technically skilled persons to state positions.

The proliferation of state institutions at provincial level and below has been accompanied by the decentralisation of some authority over foreign trade, foreign investment and foreign borrowing. By granting lower-level trading agencies as well as production enterprises greater authority in managing foreign trade, the central government hoped to stimulate local initiative and dynamism. Decentralisation has mainly been administrative − where power devolves to lower levels of the state machinery − although some economic decentralisation − where power devolves to economic units − has also occurred.

Central government has decentralised in varying degrees the authority to conduct foreign trade to the branches of national corporations under the Ministry of Foreign Economic Relations and Trade, to the provincial branches of the trade and industrial ministries as well as to the newly established provincial trading companies. The granting of 'special policies and privileges' to Guangdong and Fujian Provinces in July 1979 enabled these two provinces to export nearly all products without central approval.[45] Compared to other provinces, they enjoyed greater authority in devising and implementing provincial plans, more favourable terms and conditions in the allocation of funds, loans, foreign currency and tax relief, a greater degree of direct trading between provincial authorities and foreign partners and received permission to set up a SEZ.[46] This strengthened their economic independence *vis-à-vis* central government, enabling them to undertake construction projects and import technology that would otherwise have required central approval.

Following the success of the experimental General Foreign Trading Corporations set up in Beijing, Tianjin and Shanghai in 1980, the reformers extended the right to engage in foreign trade and approve contracts over the next four years to other areas in China including the inland cities of Wuhan and Chongqing. Some large industrial enterprises in coastal areas were even able to export their own products directly, so bypassing the corporations.[47] According to some estimates, bypassing the national corporations could halve the time required to fulfil an export contract. Although the central government has been willing to decentralise some authority over exports, it has been more reluctant to unleash control over imports.

The heyday for provincial and branch trading entities came in 1984. In January provisional regulations for the issuing of import licences were introduced, giving the go-ahead to decentralisation. Foreign Trade Corporations under the Ministry of Foreign Economic Relations and Trade, as well as those run by ministries and provincial authorities, could now import unrestricted items without central approval, leading to a fall in the percentage of imports through the trade ministry from 87 per cent in 1981 to 65 per cent in 1984.[48] In September 1984 the State Council approved the further decentralisation of the foreign trade system.[49] This involved a reallocation of functions within the state. The Ministry of Foreign Economic Relations and Trade and its regional branches would now focus on the administrative management of foreign trade, whilst foreign trade companies would independently engage in importing and exporting.[50]

Faced with a huge import boom and a disturbing decline in foreign exchange reserves the central government felt compelled to reimpose its control. So it recentralised foreign trade in 1985 and 1986, removing various foreign trade privileges from provincial and local organisations.[51] It increased the number of restricted import items and introduced an export licensing system. In January 1986 it required foreign trading companies to fulfil a set foreign exchange quota.[52] Trading and investment corporations wanting to borrow from abroad had now to obtain the approval of the People's Bank of China.[53] By 1987 provincial trading authorities accounted for 90 per cent of all exports and only one quarter of all recorded imports.[54]

Closely linked to foreign trade is the more thorny issue of foreign exchange decentralisation. To encourage provincial exports the central government introduced a system of foreign exchange retention in 1979.[55] With the formalisation of this system in January 1984 most provinces could keep 25 per cent of their foreign exchange earnings from planned exports for their own use. But some areas could keep more. The 'special' Guangdong and Fujian could retain 30 per cent whilst minority areas such as Ningxia could keep 50 per cent. The SEZs were even more privileged and could keep some of their above-plan export earnings. Xiamen, for example, could retain 100 per cent of its own foreign exchange earnings. Wanting production enterprises to export more, the central government introduced new regulations in January 1985, requiring foreign trade companies to share the retained foreign exchange equally with enterprises.

Why was the right to retain foreign exchange such a coveted privilege? With access to their own foreign exchange treasuries, provincial authorities had more autonomy to develop in their own way. They could undertake projects without central financing and approval. They had more incentive to export and could speed up the process of importing. Possession of some foreign exchange enables exporters both to have easier access to imported inputs and to reduce the administrative costs of applying for foreign exchange through regular channels. Local control over foreign exchange also provided opportunities for individual state cadres to line their own purses by reselling imported goods at higher prices. Thus the decentralisation of foreign exchange retention to both Fujian and Xiamen SEZ authorities has granted them greater power than previously in imports, the planning of the economy as well as technology introduction. The Overseas Chinese link in Fujian province also provides it with an extra source of foreign exchange through Overseas Chinese remittances.[56]

Allowing greater provincial access to foreign exchange stimulated the export industries, but it also contributed towards the import boom in 1984 and 1985. In response central government cut foreign exchange retention rates in the SEZs to 30 per cent. As the SEZs ended up with even more financial difficulties, the central government raised the rates again in early 1986. In 1991 central government again removed the foreign exchange privileges of the zones putting them on a par with the rest of the country.

The reformers also decentralised the authority to establish foreign-invested enterprises, extending this right over the past decade from the SEZs to the 14 coastal cities and to inland and border areas. In April 1984, for example, Tianjin and Shanghai could approve projects up to US$ 30 million, Dalian up to US$ 10 million and other coastal cities up to US$ 5 million.[57] Following Deng's visit to Xiamen in 1984 Xiamen Municipal Economic and Trade Commission could approve joint ventures with a total investment of up to US$ 10 million itself. However, for projects over this amount as well as wholly owned foreign enterprises Xiamen had to obtain central government approval. The provincial government had thus lost its authority over Xiamen SEZ to approve foreign investment. However, it is difficult to assess whether being answerable directly to central authorities always facilitates the realisation of Xiamen's autonomy. On the one hand, it enables Xiamen to bypass provincial authorities but on the other hand, it could make Xiamen more vulnerable to fluctuations in policy at central level.

In the 1990s cities bordering the Soviet Union, Vietnam and Laos have been able to approve some foreign investment.[58] Initially, the reformers cautiously confined wholly owned foreign enterprises to SEZs. In the decentralisation heyday of 1984 they extended the right to allow wholly owned foreign enterprises to the coastal cities.[59] They also permitted certain trust and investment corporations at provincial level to negotiate joint ventures, but still with final approval from the provincial branch of the Ministry of Foreign Economic Relations and Trade. The Fourteenth Party Congress held in October 1992 portends a further geographical decentralisation of the Open Policy, opening almost the whole of China to foreign investment.

This decentralisation of some authority over foreign economic relations to the branches of foreign trade corporations under the trade ministry to provincial trading and investment corporations as well as to the branches of industrial trading corporations indicates a change in the way the state operates. In particular, it fosters a more entrepreneurial state, able to respond more rapidly towards opportunities in the market-place. The implementation of these decentralisation policies, however, has been neither even nor smooth. The unevenness comes in part from various unintended consequences of decentralisation, such as the duplication of imports, the introduction of inappropriate technology and the rapid upsurge in consumer imports in mid-1985. Whilst the market-facilitating state unleashed local-level initiative, it could not regulate or coordinate the economic actions of the numerous new trading companies. By 1984 non-trade organisations accounted for almost 40 per cent of all trade activity in Xiamen whilst foreign-invested enterprises lay claim to 20 per cent.[60] Intense competition amongst different trading agencies meant in turn that national and provincial Foreign Trade Corporations could not procure goods for their export plans. Provincial and subprovincial trading companies and branches tended to pursue local rather than national interests. The increasing role of township and village enterprises both in the domestic economy and in foreign trade will make it even more difficult for the state to regulate foreign economic relations.

The response to these economic imbalances has been to apply the administrative medicine of the command state. However, by redistributing power and resources to provincial and municipal authorities and to the lower levels of national foreign trade corporations, decentralisation created its own web of interests. The provincial and municipal trading authorities are unlikely to cede their newly acquired powers readily. As decentralisation strengthened the position of the Fujian provincial government, for example, in relation to the central authorities and of Xiamen in relation to the Fujian authorities, the process of recentralising has become more complicated as lower-level authorities seek to defend their newly acquired privileges. Recentralisation then involved a conflict of interests between the centre and lower-level state institutions.

The spawning of new agencies, with no prior experience of central control, has made this process even more complicated. So attempts at recentralisation tended to leave some residue of power at lower levels. Lower-level trading and investment authorities still fared better in 1987 than in 1978, even though their wings have been considerably clipped compared to the heyday of 1984. The development of a market-facilitating state thus raises crucial issues of control — not only of the market-facilitating state over the market but also of the command state over the newly emerging market-facilitating state.

Closely linked to the decentralisation of authority over foreign economic relations has been the emergence of a layer of 'quasi-state institutions' mediating between the state and foreign capital. They are quasi-state in that they are set up and owned by the state but are supposed to behave like business enterprises. The reformers have founded these crossbreed institutions not only to encourage greater flexibility and initiative in the way the state interacts with market forces but also to promote a more profit-conscious state which is responsive to economic rather than administrative principles. These institutions are symptomatic of what Blecher describes as an emerging 'entrepreneurial state', whereby semi-autonomous enterprises are created to engage in profit-making activities.[61]

Although the state created these quasi-state institutions, their organisational structure as well as operational mode resemble those of a business enterprise. Responsible in theory for their profits and losses and enjoying some leeway in the use of their earnings, they should relate to higher authorities and their subordinate enterprises according to economic rather than administrative principles. Compared to other state trading entities, they display greater initiative and innovation in their economic activities.

CITIC was one of the first such hybrid institutions to sprout at the national level. By 1981 there were already 22 CITIC branches in 16 provinces and municipalities. Although CITIC supposedly operated as a business entity, employing methods and techniques common in the capitalist world, it also enjoyed the status of a government ministry directly accountable to the State Council.[62] As it answers directly to the State Council, it would seem in theory to have equal power to the Ministry of Foreign Economic Relations and Trade, at least until mid-1989 when its administrative status was demoted.

Although it is difficult to assess to what extent CITIC and its branches as well as provincial investment corporations behave like business enterprises, there is considerable evidence of greater innovation and initiative in their economic activities than in other state institutions.[63] Compared to other state trading companies, these investment and trust corporations have a much wider scope of business ranging from the establishment of joint ventures to the issuing of bonds overseas. As CITIC disposes of its own funds and is able to raise its own money through overseas bonds and commission, it enjoys greater financial autonomy than other trading entities.[64]

The most prominent quasi-state institution in Xiamen SEZ is the Xiamen Construction and Development Corporation, set up in January 1981 by the Xiamen municipal government and the Administration Committee of Xiamen SEZ.[65] Its activities are broad, including the establishment of joint ventures, import/export business and leasing. Xiamen Construction and Development Corporation has been involved in around half of all joint ventures in Xiamen SEZ and is a shareholder in about one-third of these. It is thus an important and relatively accessible source of finance for state-owned enterprises seeking to import technology or set up joint ventures with foreign companies. As its name suggests, it is a crossbreed institution, harbouring features of both a state organ and an economic enterprise. Although the Xiamen Construction and Development Corporation enjoys considerable financial autonomy compared with other state organs, it is not totally autonomous. According to informal sources, the municipal authorities clamped down on Xiamen Construction and Development Corporation in early 1987, monitoring carefully any further loans it made to state-owned enterprises for technology imports or joint venture projects.

Partly to facilitate trade with Taiwan and partly to manage the infrastructural development of Huli District, Xiamen Construction and Development Corporation set up a joint venture, namely the Xiamen SEZ United Development Corporation, in October 1983 along with the Trust and Consultancy Company of the Bank of China and five Hong Kong banks.[66] As there are no governmental trade relations between Taiwan and China, Xiamen United Development Company, as a non-governmental enterprise, was better equipped to manage business with Taiwan. Xiamen United Development Company is in theory at least an independent economic entity, responsible for its own profits and losses. Other quasi-state institutions include the Xing Xia Company, Xiamen Investment and Enterprises Company and Xiamen International Trade and Trust Company.

Although the structure of these quasi-state institutions resembles on the surface that of a business enterprise, with the highest level of authority being, in theory at least, the board of directors, there is some evidence to suggest that the recruitment of leaders follows a similar pattern to state institutions. For example, as in state-owned enterprises, there can still be considerable duplication of posts both within and between organisations. Liu Shouming, for example, was in 1988 both chairperson and executive director of the Fujian Foreign Trading Corporation, whilst the director of Fujian Foreign Economic Relations and Trade Commission was also chairperson of the quasi-state Fujian Investment and Enterprise Corporation.[67] The occupation of key posts in these organisations by leading political figures in the province – who are highly likely to be Party members – implies the continued involvement of outside administrative bodies, casting a shadow over their supposed independence.

To the extent that these political figures are reform-minded, their connections with other parts of the state administration could also help to smooth over any hiccups between these new institutions and state bodies they may have to deal with. On the other hand, as they are politically rather than professionally qualified, the potential tendency to seek administrative solutions to economic problems might be greater. Moreover, the competing interests of external administrative bodies may constrain the economic transactions of these companies.

The expansion of China's foreign economic relations has prompted the emergence of an intermediary layer of quasi-state institutions mediating between the state and foreign capital. The rise of such quasi-state institutions has accompanied the ebb and flow of decentralisation policies. Whilst these quasi-state institutions are supposed to operate like business entities, there is a need for further research to find out how much they relate to subordinate companies and enterprises according to economic rather than administrative principles. As the comparable industrial corporations have been criticised for evolving more often into 'administrative' rather than economic organisations, these quasi-state institutions dealing with foreign economic relations might also inherit features of the command state.[68]

The emergence of the quasi-state institutions also raises key issues of control. As they dispose of considerable funds, earned in part through fees charged to their clients, and do not require the approval of the Ministry of Foreign Economic Relations and Trade for some of their activities, they have greater room for manoeuvre than other state organs. Although these institutions may have proven more dynamic than their administrative counterparts, their business initiatives have also contributed towards the periodic imbalances in the economy.

We can observe the development of a more entrepreneurial state not only in the rise of quasi-state institutions but also in the emergence of voluntary trade associations set up by local businesspeople and Overseas Chinese. Some members of the Fujian Provincial Federation of Industrialists and Businessmen and Fujian Provincial Federation of Returned Overseas Chinese set up the Sanlian Economic Development Company, a non-governmental economic entity, to attract foreign investment, introduce advanced technology and conduct foreign trade.[69] Similarly, the Fujian Overseas Chinese Investment Company also appeared in March 1984.

Whilst the quasi-state institutions share similar features to other such bodies in the rest of China, the voluntary associations are distinctive in that they reflect the interests of a particular social group, namely, Overseas Chinese. On the one hand, this may be linked to deliberate policies of both central and local government to tap this lucrative source of foreign capital; on the other hand, it is an expression of mutually recognised interests based on family and historical ties. The potential political implications of these associations are far-reaching, particularly with respect to the issues of reunification and Overseas Chinese policy.

The rise of voluntary trade associations to engage with the external economy forms part of a more general trend in the Dengist era. Domestic economic reform has cultivated a myriad of new economic and social associations and during the upheavals of mid-1989 even some short-lived political ones. During a recent research visit to a small town in Zhejiang province, where economic reform was well underway, almost one hundred such associations had emerged.[70] Out of these, 20 were economic, such as trade associations, and 42 were scientific and technical. The economic associations are an attempt not only to protect members against the vagaries of the market but also to represent their interests *vis-à-vis* the state. On the one hand, they are a response to new needs arising out of marketisation; on the other hand, they are a response to the shortcomings of existing institutions.

In so far as these associations are voluntarily formed, we can see how socio-economic changes translate into the organisational sphere. Economic reform and opening up has created new social categories such as private entrepreneurs and traders and rich farmers. The introduction of market forces has sown the seeds of a new form of civil society.[71] Following the upheaval of mid-1989 top leaders became ultra-sensitive to the political potential of these new associations and ordered them all to register with the Civil Affairs Office. Aware too that institutional change has lagged behind economic change, the Party and the state have sponsored the emergence of such associations. In this way it can both monitor and respond to changing needs at the local level and, more importantly, incorporate these new associations into the policy-making process.

Changes in the social composition of the state

The shift towards more entrepreneurial and regulatory state involvement in the economy has also been facilitated by changes in social composition. Opening up has cultivated a layer of technical and professional cadres. Qualified staff are needed not only to make decisions about what technology to transfer but also to facilitate the process of technology absorption. The expansion of foreign trade has required more people with negotiation skills who are in touch with the workings of international trade. Similarly, foreign-invested enterprises need trained managers familiar not only with domestic business but also with Western or Japanese business culture. Lacking suitably qualified personnel, Xiamen has had to import technicians from other provinces. In 1984 Huli Management Committee recruited 260 special-ised, technical cadres from Beijing, Shanghai, Tianjin and Nanjing, some of whom took up positions as managers and supervisors in joint ventures.[72]

The employment patterns in local foreign trade institutions suggest that professional qualifications have become a significant recruitment criterion. A young manager in the quasi-state Fujian Investment and Enterprise Corporation told me that 80 per cent of the staff had college or university education.[73] Moreover, he pointed out that 'there are many opportunities with this organisation to continue training, even abroad. Sometimes banks in Japan and Australia offer scholarships to study abroad.' The percentage of tertiary educated employees in the intermediary organisations I interviewed in Xiamen was also relatively high. Although compared to 1978 there were more young people with university education and language skills in the General Foreign Trade Corporation in Fujian, newly founded organisations are more able to adopt professional criteria in recruitment.[74] Young graduates too are keen to work in these organisations. As a recent business studies graduate told me, 'wages are higher than in universities or state-owned enterprises and there are more opportunities to go abroad.'[75]

The importance of these new skills at the same time heralds the demise of political qualities and activity as criteria for recruitment to the state. In the Cultural Revolution 'redness' was a greater virtue and quality than 'expertise'. In the Dengist reform period the 'colour of the cat' is not so important. The beneficiaries of the newly emerging market-facilitating state are the technocratic cadres whilst the losers are the politicocratic cadres. Nevertheless, the changes in the structure and operational mode of the state involve the creation of new sources of power such as access to foreign exchange and foreign goods, overseas business trips and opportunities to study abroad. Party membership is still an asset, especially for those going for trips abroad or receiving training overseas. So the politicocratic cadres can minimise their losses by using their positions to take advantage of these new opportunities.

To foster these technical skills the government has offered retraining courses for those whose education was forfeited during the Cultural Revolution. It has also introduced new subjects into the curriculum such as English language, economics, foreign trade, computers and management studies. At the same time Xiamen has set up various courses to train young people in relevant skills such as Japanese, English languages, catering, hotel management, tourism, business studies and foreign trade.

The reformers have simultaneously encouraged younger, more-educated people to join the Party and older, less-educated cadres to retire early. Key policy-making think-tank organisations are increasingly staffed by young, Western-educated economists and social scientists.[76] Although in the aftermath of Tiananmen these young technocrats came under suspicion and political criteria gained weight in the selection of cadres, since 1991 Deng Xiaoping has emphasised the critical role of science and technology in modernisation and urged China's young intellectuals overseas to return to the flock. In May 1992 Shenzhen went so far as to send a recruitment team to the USA to persuade overseas students to return and work in the zone.[77]

Although the reformist leadership has been keen to recruit technocrats to the state administration and Party, the time-lag in training as well as the reluctance of politicocrats to make way for the better-educated and technically skilled technocrats has constrained its efforts. To accelerate the 'technocratisation' of the state, the Ministry of Foreign Economic Relations and Trade laid down in early 1987 that Party and government officials could not work for both trade companies and government and Party institutions at the same time.[78] This reflects not only the commitment of certain central leaders to the reform of the state but also the unwillingness of the politicocratic cadres, who owe their positions of authority to political rather than economic credentials, to cede some of their power over economic decisions.

Politics thus rudely permeates the emergence of the market-facilitating state. The losers under the market-facilitating state may obstruct, delay or reinterpret the Open Policy to their favour, whilst the beneficiaries will try to push the Open Policy forwards. The 'experts' have not found it easy to make their voices heard. Some leading scientists have complained that their opinions are often neglected.[79]

The state has not only been recruiting younger, more professionally and technically qualified people to the state, but has also resurrected former capitalists to positions of power. The rationale for this is clearly that these people possess particular business skills and more importantly an understanding of the international capitalist economy which is in short supply. Wang Guangying, who was a successful joint owner of a chemical works in Tianjin before 1949, was elected vice-mayor of Tianjin in 1980 and appointed chairman of the board of directors of Everbright Industrial Corporation in Hong Kong.[80] Similarly Rong Yiren, the head of CITIC, was a former Shanghai capitalist, whose experience with the capitalist world would presumably facilitate the development of a profit-conscious enterprise. The appointment of former capitalists to power might add to dissatisfaction amongst both former revolutionaries as well as those cadres who came to power during the politically charged period of the Cultural Revolution. These cadres then form part of the social base of opposition to reform and opening up.

To summarise, we have shown here how the Open Policy has affected that part of the state dealing with foreign economic relations. The creation of new institutions at the central level, the mushrooming of trading entities at the provincial level and below, as well as the adaptation of existing institutions, provide the structural conditions for greater flexibility and entrepreneurship.

However, the restructuring of the institutional terrain is not a sufficient condition for the state to take maximum advantage of market opportunities. The post-Mao era has also witnessed a change in the way parts of the state behave in the sphere of foreign economic relations. The emergence of a layer of quasi-state institutions acting according to economic principles such as profit-maximisation exemplify a new entrepreneurial mode of operation on the part of the state. The strong Overseas Chinese links in

Fujian province have been a significant factor stimulating greater economic entrepreneurship in the form of voluntary trade associations. The promotion of both former capitalists and technically skilled personnel to positions of authority has aided the development of an entrepreneurial state.

Although the nurturing of a market-facilitating state has brought greater initiative at the local level, it has also created its own problems of economic imbalance, uncoordinated imports and exports as well as a predominance of small-scale, non-productive investment. Moreover, the redistribution of economic power to a proliferation of lower-level institutions has strengthened the independence of local-level authorities, raising key issues of central political control. As the development of a market-facilitating state is both politically and economically complex, its future will continue to parallel the spiral evolution of the Open Policy. Although we can observe these changes in the character of the state in all parts of China where reform and opening up are underway, the process has been most advanced in the SEZs, as exemplified in Xiamen.

Implications for China's Open Policy

But what then do all these changes mean for the process of opening up? The market-facilitating state is not fully fledged and the command state still rears its gargantuan head. The current transitional character of the state has ambiguous effects on the implementation of the Open Policy. The proliferation of institutions due to decentralisation combined with the continued existence of command institutions has not only created an impression of overlapping bureaucracy amongst foreign investors but has also confused lines of authority both for Chinese cadres as well as for foreign companies. The Chinese manager of a Hong Kong electronics company complained that 'each department has many leaders. The division of responsibility is not clear. Sometimes the leaders do not agree with each other.'[81] Moreover, the institutional vacuum means that neither cadres nor foreign companies are sure about what to do. The American manager of a wholly owned enterprise in Xiamen pointed out that 'there are times when there are no clear regulations about what to do, so we just go ahead'.[82] Periodic fluctuations in the development of the market-facilitating state have exacerbated this.

Similarly, the conflict between 'losing' and 'winning' state institutions can also create confusion about the axes of power as losing institutions attempt desperately to hold on to their former powers. When the Fujian Foreign Trade Bureau was losing its power to the new Import/Export Office and Foreign Trade Corporation in 1980, a foreign journalist reported the frustration of a local cadre: 'Overlap authority exists to such an extent between the Foreign Trade Bureau and its new rivals that a provincial spokesman confessed, "It is the provincial authorities that decide who gets what".[83]

To the extent that the market-facilitating state is only partially developed, there is a disjuncture between the existing institutional framework and the needs of the Open Policy. We can observe this in bureaucratic delays. Although Xiamen SEZ has considerable autonomy in approving joint ventures, continued central control over some aspects of joint venture operations can in turn constrain the pace of construction and production. In the words of an official from an electronics company, 'even after six months we still had not got approval for our domestic sales'.[84]

In the wake of Deng's visit to Xiamen in 1984 certain institutions came under fire for the unnecessary bureaucracy which inhibited Xiamen's progress in opening up. The provincial newspaper reported that bureaucrats in the Department of Industry and Commerce had 'become preoccupied with their own rules and regulations'.[85] But if bureaucrats were to stop applying old rules no longer compatible with the changes, they must have been quite daunted at having to decide individually when to ignore which regulations. Vagueness over the validity of existing rules meant there was considerable leeway for interpretation and dispute.[86]

The immaturity of the legislative system as well as the continued presence of non-professionals in key positions has also affected the operations of foreign-invested enterprises. The vice-mayor of Tianjin, for example, vented his frustration in an article: 'The managers and staff members of the Chinese side in some Sino-foreign joint ventures have directly affected the venture's management due to their poor professional ability.'[87]

Reform and opening up have also led to unexpected changes in state behaviour. Although the state may give the appearance of becoming more entrepreneurial, diverse factors may be at work, which are not wholly in the spirit of reform. We can detect on the one hand 'defensive' entrepreneurship where the state innovates to hold on to power it is losing. White cites the example of the Shanghai Textile Bureau which set up a financial allocation centre to preserve its powers.[88] Similarly, when in early 1987 the Ministry of Foreign Trade proposed the agency system whereby it contracted with lower-level trade bodies for imports and exports, it effectively ensured a continuing hold.

We can also detect 'parasitic' entrepreneurship. Individual cadres use their positions to line their own purses. For example, an official in Fujian was sentenced in in 1991 for forging exit visas and educational certificates for people to go overseas.[89] With the central government propagating a philosophy of 'getting rich quick', state cadres too are keen to jump on the bandwagon. The children of many top leaders were the first to set up lucrative businesses overseas. This corruption on the part of some state officials frustrated those who could ill afford to bribe. When workers and staff joined students in the 1989 marches, it was largely to vent their anger at this growing corruption.

In response to the unrest in 1989 the state has been desperately trying to clean up its public image, both at home and abroad. It set up corruption hotlines to ferret out deviant officials and unearth scandals. Discipline and inspection teams have travelled the country trying to promote 'clean and honest government'.[90] Cadres are no longer allowed to run businesses at the same time. Political criteria again became important in recruiting and promoting cadres. In 1991 some top leaders, such as Chen Yun, were proposing that Party members should publicly disclose their own financial situation.[91]

Although decentralisation has stimulated microlevel initiative, it has also inadvertently given rise to what the reformers call 'localism' and 'departmentalism'. Given a taste of power, state institutions have tended to pursue local and departmental rather than national and general interests. Since the mid-1980s the central leadership has been trying to stamp out the 'three irregulars', that is, collecting fees, imposing fines and pooling funds.[92] In May 1992 Fujian provincial government resolved to abolish 602 of the 695 road checkposts as departments and counties were arbitrarily collecting charges.[93]

Local governments and departments have acted this way for various reasons. On the one hand they interpret the market as 'grabbing what you can while you can', but at the same time the revenue of the state has declined over the past decade. The State Statistical Bureau reported that since reform and opening up there has been a distribution of income away from the state towards the individual. The state share of national income fell from 31.6 per cent in 1978 to 14.5 per cent in 1990, compared to a rise in individual share from 49.3 per cent to 61.7 per cent.[94] Given the immaturity of tax policy, let alone the difficulties in enforcing existing regulations, departments seek arbitrarily to boost their own resources by squeezing the private sector. This in turn reduces the confidence of foreign investors. An employee I interviewed in a wholly owned enterprise in Xiamen complained bitterly about the erratic charges they had to pay to different administrative bodies.[95]

These deviant forms of entrepreneurship, namely defensive, parasitic and localistic, have raised crucial problems of control and legitimacy for central government. Furthermore, they have also impeded the progress of reform and opening up by undermining attempts to develop a more legalistic culture and a more competitive economy. Institutional creativity may be bureaucratically or politically driven rather than economically driven. One of the largest electronics joint ventures in Xiamen, for example, is actually fully state-owned. The state bought out the bankrupt Hong Kong partner. The manager of a local inland joint venture in the same sector complained to me about the 'unfair' competition it faced from this company which had full government support in its production and sales.[96]

The coexistence of elements of both a new market-facilitating state and the former command state has contrary to the wishes of the reformers actually bloated rather than reduced the size of the state. State personnel rose from 15 million in 1979 to over 34 million in 1991.[97] When the reformers tried to separate administrative from executive tasks, the former administrative organs just set up new bodies with a new cortège of staff. A *People's Daily* article reports that a county in an unnamed province had between 1989 and 1991 set up or reorganised 148 leading groups. Moreover, there was an uncontrollable spate of organisations upgrading themselves so as to obtain new powers and resources.[98]

All this in turn had increased the expenditure of the state. According to the Ministry of Finance expenditure on state administration rose from Y40.4 billion in 1980 to over Y140 billion in 1991.[99] In one province, where the number of administrative personnel had tripled over the past decade, the administration consumed Y2.6 billion of the Y3.3 billion of local revenue collected in 1990.

Faced with declining state revenues the central government has renewed its efforts to streamline the state, proposing cuts in staff, the number of state bodies and institutional expenditure.[100] In the run-up to the Fourteenth Party Congress proposals to cut State Council staff by a third, substantially alter the functions of the State Planning Commission and even abolish political departments in party and government organs, enterprises and schools, which had been fiercely resisted previously, showed the seriousness with which top leaders were treating state reform.[101] These financial constraints on the government have in turn spurred along the idea of creating a slimmer, rational-legal civil service.[102] Employees in government departments such as the Ministry of Foreign Economic Relations and Trade were reportedly fearful about their jobs. Without a well-established social security system, the streamlining of state departments as well as reform of state-owned enterprises will clearly pose a serious political problem for the radical reformers.

State cadres have already responded to these imminent changes by securing positions in other organisations. Those with some technical or professional skills will clearly find this easier than those with primarily political credentials. There are reports, for example, of a 'new craze' amongst state cadres for establishing businesses, which is in part an attempt to secure future employment as government streamlining proceeds.[103] Similarly, during a research visit to Shenyang in the north-east of China in September 1992 it was apparent that newly founded social and economic associations provided a welcome safety net for senior cadres whose posts were under threat from state and enterprise reforms.

The transitoriness of the institutional framework can thus have an adverse effect on the Open Policy. The overweight state administration has frustrated rather than facilitated foreign investment and trade. Nevertheless, to the extent that the market-facilitating state does gain a foothold, the downswings in the Open Policy spiral become more institutionally cushioned.

Conclusion

The process of reform and opening up has led to a redefinition of the state in post-Mao China. The introduction of market forces, both domestic and foreign, has stimulated the emergence of a 'market-facilitating state', which is more entrepreneurial, regulatory, legalistic and technocratic. We can observe this in the restructuring of the state, changes in its operational mode as well as its social composition. Although we have focused on that section of the state dealing with the external economy, similar changes are occurring in other parts of the state concerned with the domestic economy. Moreover, we can see this redefinition of the state in varying degrees in all parts of China, where reform and opening up are underway, though the process has proceeded furthest in the SEZs, where the concentration of foreign capital is greatest.

The ongoing nature of these changes implies that the state is in a process of transition. As a result the state assumes a polymorphic character, whereby features of the former institutional complex coexist with the seeds of a new matrix. State cadres who owe their positions to political credentials cohabit the corridors of power with the new 'professional-technocratic' strain of state employees. Whilst the 'old-style' command institutions continue to operate according to administrative logic, the new institutional generation responds to the economic imperatives of the market-place. At the same time there is a temporary vacuum where the pace of institutional change lags behind the transformation of the economy. In particular, the web of the command planning state is receding whilst the web of the market-facilitating state is advancing.

Conflict and cooperation between potential 'winners' and 'losers' within the state has contributed towards the ebb and flow of the market-facilitating state. During upswings in the Open Policy the market-facilitating state gathers momentum whilst in the downswings the command state reasserts itself. As each new cycle in the Open Policy expands and consolidates China's foreign economic relations, the roots of the market-facilitating state likewise become deeper and stronger. So we can observe an 'institutional' spiral shadowing the Open Policy spiral.

As the web of the market-facilitating state advances, the institutional environment for opening up becomes more favourable. Whilst the political unrest in 1989 prompted the reassertion of control by the command state, the move towards a socialist market economy announced at the recent Fourteenth Party Congress heralds a greater role for the market-facilitating state.

Notes

1. For further discussion of divisions within the leadership over political reform see Barnett, 1992 and Dittmer, 1990.
2. See XH, BJ 12.10.1991 in SWB/FE/1205 B2/6−7 17.10.1991 and XH, BJ 18.10.1991 SWB/FE/1208 B2/4 21.10.1991.
3. Chang, 1986, pp. 108−9; policy-makers in Xiamen also shared this view — in an introductory pamphlet to Xiamen SEZ published by the Fujian FERTC, it was stated: 'Xiamen SEZ, neither a political zone nor a special administration zone like Hong Kong ... is a so-called SEZ because it practises the SEZ policy, special economic management system and special flexible measures.'
4. For a collection of recent analyses on the state in China see White, 1991 and in particular Howell, 1991, ch. 5, pp. 119−46.
5. For a discussion of deregulatory aspects of post-Mao reform policy, see Lampton, 1987, ch. 1.
6. Similarly import/export offices operated in accordance with national plans devised by higher planning authorities.
7. Zheng Tuobin, 1987, pp. 31−3.
8. See Chapter 1 above.
9. See World Bank, 1988, p. 101.
10. Terry, 1980.
11. ibid., p. 15.
12. SH, CJYJ 3.10.1987 in FBIS 19.2.1988 pp. 38−43.
13. For details of this organisation see Fujian FERTC (1985), p. 89.
14. GD, NFJJ no. 6, 1986.
15. Chan, Chen, and Chin, 1986, pp. 87−104.
16. XH, BJ 24.10.1982.
17. See Almanac of Xiamen SEZ Editorial Board, 1986 and Annals of China's SEZs (Guangdong People's Publishing House, 1990), p. 522 (in Chinese).
18. Whilst some reports indicate that the national office was not intended to supersede the authority of the local SEZ management committees, on the other hand, investments over US$ 2 million had to be negotiated with the central office under Gu Mu.
19. See CBR (Jan./Feb. 1987), p. 10.
20. Institutions involved included, for example, the State Planning Commission, State Economic Commission, Ministry of Foreign Economic Relations and

Trade, Bank of China, Ministry of Finance, China Customs Administration, China Foreign Exchange Administration Bureau, State Council Special Economic Zones Office.
21. XH 9.10.1986 in SWB/FE/8389/C1/4.
22. Similarly, in Fuzhou three service organisations were set up, namely the Fuzhou Coordination and Leading Group for Foreign Invested Enterprises, the Fuzhou Foreign Invested Enterprises Materials Supply and Service Company and the Fuzhou Foreign Economic Relations and Consultation and Service Company.
23. NCNA 4.2.1981 in SWB/FE/W12/A/19.
24. Zheng Tuobin (China Economic Studies, Summer 1987), p. 30.
25. HK, SCMP 30.5.1987.
26. *China Trader* (February, 1987).
27. ibid.; and BJ, GJJB 16.1.1986 in SWB/FE/8182/C1/3.
28. Interview, Fujian FERTC, June 1987.
29. The development of the contract system, particularly in the agricultural sector, has been a significant factor in the expansion of the legal system.
30. XMRB 7.12.1991.
31. RMRB 5.5.1986 in SWB/FE/8262/C1/5. This committee was a development of the Foreign Trade Arbitration Commission which was established in 1956.
32. For examples of the increasing use of the legal system for the resolution of conflicts in foreign-invested enterprises, see XH 3.12.1986 in FBIS 6.1.1987, p. 86 and XH, BJ 10.3.1987 in FBIS 11.3.1987, p. 72; on the inadequacy of the current legislation see, for example, LW 24.11.1986 in FBIS 6.1.1987; BJ, GJMYWT, no. 1, January 1987, pp. 8–13; Cohen, 1988; Peele and Cohan, 1988.
33. See HK, MB 2.10.1984 in SWB FE/8384/BII/5–6 8.10.1986 on debt management; see XH 25.4.1987 in SWB/FE/W1440/C/1–3 13.5.1987 regarding these foreign exchange regulations.
34. In December 1984, for example, the Shanghai branch of the Bank of China announced that it would provide loans on a trial basis to Chinese investors seeking to set up foreign-invested enterprises with foreign companies (see XH 10.12.1984 in FBIS 14.12.1984 03).
35. CD 28.1.1987 in FBIS 5.3.1987 pp. 54–5.
36. HK, SCMP 8.11.1985 in FBIS 8.11.1985 W1.
37. Beijing, *Guoji Maoyi* (International Trade), no. 4, 27.4.1985, pp. 34–7 in FBIS 30.7.1985 pp. 121–9
38. ZGXWS, BJ 14.6.1991 in SWB FE/1100/A3/5 17.6.1991.
39. See, for example, HK, WWP 25.3.1991 in SWB/FE/1035/B2/1 2.4.1991 FBIS 2.4.1991; ZGXWS 8.4.1991 in SWB/FE/1047/B2/3 16.4.1991; RMRB 26.5.1991 in SWB/FE/1095/B2/7 11.6.1991.
40. See Saich, 1991.
41. This has been the case in Xiamen SEZ.
42. Khan, 1991, p. 27.
43. XH 6.11.1992 in SWB/FE/1534/C1/5 10.11.1992.
44. See HKMCED 6, 1986.

45. ZGXWS 14.10.1981 in FBIS 15.10.1981 K8.
46. *Sino-British Trade Review*, June 1981.
47. See Horsley, 1985.
48. See World Bank, 1988, pp. 101−3.
49. CD 14.10.1984.
50. See World Bank, 1988, p. 21 for Ministry of Foreign Economic Relations and Trade's report on reform of the foreign trade system approved by State Council on 15.9.1984.
51. See Denny, 1987.
52. BJ, GJSB 16.1.1986 in SWB/FE/8182/C1/3−7 13.2.1986.
53. *Financial Times* 13.8.1986.
54. See Denny, 1987.
55. See World Bank, 1988, p. 20.
56. It is difficult, however, to estimate precisely the contribution of remittances to Fujian's economy.
57. In July 1985, however, the privileges of 10 of the coastal cities were restricted again.
58. HK, WWP 31.5.1991 in SWB/FE/1089/B2/5 4.6.1991; Kyodo News Agency, 22.6.1991 in SWB/FE/W0186/A/3 3.7.1991; and XH 9.7.1991 in SWB/FE/W0188/A/6 17.7.1991.
59. According to Chen Nai-Ruenn, *Foreign Investment in China: Current trends* (US Dept. of Commerce 1986), p. 24, two WOFEs were set up in Shanghai in 1984, two in Fujian and one in Guangxi province.
60. Almanac of Xiamen's SEZ Editorial Board, 1986, p. 94. Although it is not clear what 'non-trade organisations' refers to, it probably refers to production enterprises and possibly investment corporations.
61. See Blecher, 1991.
62. See Rong Yiren, 1986.
63. For example, in order to secure supplies of timber and obtain forestry experience, CITIC set up a forestry company in the USA. Similarly, CITIC took a 10 per cent equity share worth US$ 79 million in an aluminium smelter being built in Australia.
64. CITIC, for example, has issued since 1982 bonds worth US$ 600 million overseas and in 1986 issued bonds worth HK$ 400 million (see XH 20.1.1987 in FBIS 25.2.1987).
65. Interview, Xiamen Construction and Development Corporation, April 1987.
66. Topper, H., 'Xiamen SEZ: poised for take-off' in *China Business Review* (November, 1988), p. 16.
67. See Terry, 1980; and Fujian Foreign Trade Centre, *Fujian Foreign Trade* (1986) and Fujian Investment and Enterprise Corporation, *A Brief on Fujian Investment and Enterprise Corporation* (1986).
68. See, for example, BJ, RMRB 9.11.1981 in FBIS 16.11.1981 K 6−8.
69. CD 2.5.1987.
70. See White *et al.*, 1991.
71. On the concept of civil society see Keane, 1988 and Wood, E.M., 'The uses and abuses of civil society' in *Social Register*, 1991. On civil society

in China, see note 70; and Kelly and He Baogang, 1992; He Baogang, 1992; Gold, 1990; Pye, 1991.
72. FJRB 26.3.1985, p. 1.
73. Interview, Fujian Investment and Enterprise Corporation, June 1987.
74. Interview, Fujian Foreign Trade Corporation, June 1987.
75. Interview, Xiamen, December 1991.
76. On the increasing importance of these research institutes see Breslin, 1990, pp. 115–34.
77. XH 12.5.1992 in SWB/FE/1380/B2/6 14.5.1992.
78. BJ, GJSB 16.1.1986 in SWB/FE/8182/C1/3–7 13.2.1986.
79. XH, BJ 17.3.1987.
80. XH 21.6.1983 in FBIS 23.6.1983 K34.
81. Interview, Xiamen 1987.
82. ibid.
83. Terry, 1980, p. 15.
84. Interview, April 1987.
85. FJRB 14.6.1984.
86. The customs were also implicated as being particularly zealous in applying their own regulations, even though these may not have been conducive to the progress of the Open Policy (see FJRB 19.2.1984).
87. TJRB 13.10.1986, p. 2 in FBIS, 5.11.1986 R1–6.
88. White, 1991, p. 11.
89. Fuzhou People's Broadcasting Station 3.5.1991 in SWB/FE/1071/B2/7 14.5.1991.
90. XH, BJ in SWB/FE/1144/B2/3–4 7.8.1991 — refers to Ministry of Foreign Economic Relations and Trade.
91. HK, CM 1.7.1991 in SWB/FE/1119/B2/5 9.7.1991:
92. XH 10.6.1991 in SWB/FE/1096/B2/2 12.6.1991.
93. ZGXWS, BJ 28.5.1992 in SWB/FE/1401/B2/4 8.6.1992.
94. RMRB, 20.1.1992 in SWB/FE/W0219/C1/4 26.2.1992.
95. Interview, Xiamen, 1987.
96. ibid.
97. XH 27.10.1992 in SWB/FE/1525/B2/5 30.10.1992.
98. XH 24.11.1991 in SWB/FE/1241/B2/3 28.11.1991.
99. XH 17.10.1992 in SWB/FE/1515/C1/14 19.10.1992.
100. See ZGXWS, HK 5.12.1991 in SWB/FE/1250 B2/1 9.12.1991.
101. HK, JJRB 15.9.1992 in SWB/FE/1494/B2/2 24.9.1992; XH 25.9.1992 in SWB/FE/1498/B2/1 29.9.1992; HK, CM 1.9.1992 in SWB/FE/1483/B2/6 11.9.1992.
102. HK, WWP, 11.12.1991 in SWB/FE/1258/B2/5 18.12.1991.
103. LW, 10.8.1992 in SWB/FE/1504/B2/3 6.10.1992.

6
The fate of labour

The opening up of China, and in particular the introduction of foreign direct investment has brought about dramatic changes in labour policy, institutions and relations. For a government which professes an ideological commitment to the interests of the working class the changes are profoundly significant. As the primary goal of capitalism is to increase profits, which is achieved in Marxian terms through the extraction of the surplus value of labour, the introduction of foreign direct investment presents an ideological and political dilemma for a socialist state.

To what extent should the government relinquish certain socialist traditions and principles such as equality, full employment and the abolition of exploitation for the sake of 'modernisation', 'growth' and 'efficiency'? Whose interests does the state serve in foreign enterprises and China's export-processing zones? What should be the role of the trade unions in these foreign concerns? And to what extent are Chinese workers the 'master' of the enterprise? These are some of the issues which academics and policy-makers in China and abroad have debated since the reformers pushed open China's doors.

We focus our attention here on the nature of labour policy in foreign-invested enterprises, with particular reference to recruitment, terms and conditions of employment and remuneration. We explore the responses of trade unions to these policy changes and consider the implications for state-labour relations. As the new nation-states in East Europe and the former Soviet Union open their arms to foreign investment, the experience of China can provide many pertinent lessons about policy and institutional change.

Setting the scene: labour reforms in the post-Mao era

The post-Mao emphasis on the goals of economic growth and modernisation has contributed towards a heightened awareness of enterprise efficiency. In the eyes of the reformers the centralised, administrative system of labour allocation and remuneration has contributed to the poor performance of state-owned enterprises. The allocation of labour according to a centrally determined plan has led to overstaffing, a mismatch between skills and job requirements as well as job dissatisfaction. Whilst the 'iron rice bowl' of permanent state workers guaranteed job security, it also weakened the power of managers to alter the size and quality of the workforce in line with production needs. Moreover, the centrally administered system of wage management, the policy of low wages as well as the weak link between wages and work performance contributed to low labour productivity.[1] As part of a strategy to enhance the microlevel efficiency of the enterprise, the post-Mao leadership has sought to introduce numerous changes in the recruitment, employment and remuneration of labour.

Instead of this centralised, administrative labour system the reformist leadership has sought a more flexible system of labour allocation and remuneration, which ultimately and implicitly steers towards the development of a labour market. According to this scenario employer and employee would sign a contract covering terms and conditions of employment, which either side could terminate in accordance with the stipulated terms.[2] The employee would exchange their labour power for a given wage (or other forms of remuneration) relative to the prevailing conditions of supply and demand.[3] In return for the more efficient allocation of labour as well as the aspired increase in labour productivity, the reformists are prepared to tolerate a certain level of unemployment, job insecurity and increased wage differentials.[4]

To achieve greater 'flexibility' in the labour system the reformist leadership has sought to reduce the role of the state, decentralise allocation decisions and grant enterprises greater autonomy in the employment and remuneration of labour.[5] Although the state was to remain responsible for overall national labour plans, it was to play a more indirect role at both central and local levels in the allocation process. This entailed changes in the allocation of particular categories of labour, namely graduates of tertiary institutions and demobilised army members, which were previously guaranteed and assigned jobs through the central labour bureau in Beijing.

The reformers also set up new institutions to recruit labour, such as the Labour Service Corporations and exchange centres for skilled workers and professional and technical staff. The Labour Service Corporations have since their appearance in 1979 played a significant role both in the local recruitment of labour and the promotion of the collective and individual sectors.[6] By January 1987 there were around 45 000 Labour Service Corporations, providing jobs for over 10 million. Whilst the Labour Service Corporations have in practice served mainly to provide employment, the 'talent exchange centres' have aimed to increase the circulation of professional and technical staff. By 1984 Shenyang, Liaoning, Beijing and Guangdong all laid claim to service centres for the exchange of such personnel.[7]

The reformers have also increased the power of enterprise managers to recruit employees, though within the limits of centrally given quotas. As early as 1980 job vacancies began to be publicly advertised on an experimental basis for unemployed youth.[8] Some enterprises had even started to set selection exams to ensure that potential recruits were suitably qualified.[9] There have also been proposals to assess the technical and professional competence of potential leaders as well as their popularity through exams and democratic elections.[10]

The reformers have tried to grapple with overstaffing by expanding the collective and individual economies. By improving the conditions of employment with respect to wages, labour insurance, welfare and political rights compared with the state-run economy they have tried to enhance the social status of these economies.[11]

As well as diversifying the institutional base dealing with labour recruitment, the reformers have launched a cautious attack upon the much coveted life-tenure system. The labour contract system, pioneered in Shenzhen SEZ, has boldly challenged the iron rice bowl. Shenzhen could comfortably take the lead in this reform as it had no pre-existing workforce which could resist the reform.[12] The contract system was deemed to have the advantage of allowing greater flexibility in both the size and quality of the workforce. By setting limits on the period of employment as well as permitting managers to dismiss employees, the contract system was intended to increase managerial control over the size and quality of the workforce. In this way enterprises would be able to adjust their workforce more readily in response to market or technological changes. Moreover, the threat of unemployment would motivate workers to work harder, leading to increases in labour productivity.

As well as making changes in the terms of employment the reformers have also tinkered with wage remuneration policies. The post-Mao era has witnessed the revival of 'material incentives' to raise labour productivity. This has entailed changes in the type and composition of the wage. The reformers have reintroduced piece-rate and floating wages to forge a closer link between individual work performance and remuneration.[13] Moreover, there have been experiments in linking wages to the economic performance of the enterprise rather than to figures defined in state plans.[14]

The reformers have also sought to develop a new social security system.

One proposal has been to increase the total wage payable to the staff or worker whilst reducing the amount of subsidies for housing and welfare.[15] As the contract system reduces the socio-economic commitment of the enterprise towards its workforce, reform of the welfare system becomes crucial. Welfare provision has become a shared responsibility between the enterprise, local government and newly formed insurance agencies. Ultimately, these changes in the welfare system imply a functional shift in the nature of the Chinese enterprise and in particular a diminution in its role as a unit of social reproduction.

Although these policies have led to greater flexibility in the labour system, the pace of change has been frustratingly slow for reformers. The system of administrative direct allocation still predominates. The proliferation of Labour Service Corporations has led to a diversification of the channels of labour allocation. However, the continued subordination of these companies to various state institutions, as well as their primary function of job creation, has not provided a radical challenge to the dominant system of unified, administrative allocation. Although enterprise managers do enjoy greater power in the selection of new recruits than previously, the dismissal of workers is still extremely difficult to implement. However, the rapid development of the private economy has increased considerably the opportunities for labour mobility.

Progress in the introduction of the contract system has also been limited. Although the labour contract system was generalised in 1983 to most enterprises and areas, it was not until October 1986 that all state-owned enterprises, government institutions and people's organisations were required to implement the labour contract system when employing new workers.[16] However, this still applied only to new workers and not to existing workers in state-owned enterprises.[17] By 1991 only 14 per cent of the 103 million employees in state-owned firms had signed contracts with their employers.[18] Similarly, although there has been some headway in forging a closer link between individual work performance and wage remuneration, the results have been much slower than desired by the reformers. In the run-up to the Fourteenth Party Congress in 1992 the minister of labour called for the implementation of the contract system for all staff and workers.[19]

Nevertheless, reform of the labour system has advanced furthest in areas with a concentration of foreign capital, such as the SEZs.[20] The Chinese leadership and policy-makers have closely followed the types of labour policy adopted in foreign-invested enterprises and heralded them on occasions as models for emulation in state-owned enterprises.[21] We can observe their implicit experimental nature in their gradual spread from Shenzhen SEZ to Guangdong and then to the whole of China in 1986.

Opposition from both policy-makers and policy recipients as well as a lack of detailed and clear planning have contributed towards the slow pace of reform. For example, the introduction of the labour contract system has required complementary policy changes in other areas such as housing and medical care, which the reformers did not anticipate or provide for sufficiently.[22] In 1991 the reformers admitted that worker resistance had made it very difficult to implement the contract system, in part because of the failure to develop a complementary welfare system.[23] On the basis of this experience they have tried once again since 1991 to push the contract system whilst at the same time elaborating the social security system and reforming wages.

Similarly, the initial failure to impose national limits on bonuses coupled with the greater financial autonomy of the enterprise have led to large increases in wages. In 1991, for example, the total wages income of China's employees rose 16.6 per cent over 1990, with growth rates highest in foreign-invested enterprises.[24] This has caused resentment amongst workers in less 'profitable' enterprises, fuelling pressure on managers to raise bonuses.[25] In May 1991 the Minister of Labour, Ruan Chongwu spoke strongly in favour of linking wages with performance to a reporter in Hong Kong: 'There should be a wage gap. Whoever works better, gets more; whoever works worse, gets less. That will create competition.'.[26] By the end of 1991 Labour Ministry officials were hinting at the state's intention to withdraw from decisions concerning promotion and wage increases within the enterprise, concentrating instead on macrolevel wage management.[27] Throughout 1992 the Ministry of Labour has put forward more proposals for reforming labour administration, wage distribution, regulations for dismissing workers and social insurance.[28] These initiatives reflect a determination on the part of the more radical reformers to shift towards a labour market.

At the ideological level political opponents of reform have expressed concern about the compatibility of a labour market with socialism. In addition they have interpreted the development of an employer/employee relationship implicit in the labour contract system as indicative of capitalist relations of production. More conservative reformers have shared some of these doubts.

At the politico-institutional level state labour bureaux have been reluctant to devolve major decisions to lower-level authorities or enterprises.[29] The contract system has aroused concern not only amongst new workers who fear the threat of unemployment but also amongst employing units which fear that they will not be able to attract sufficient employees. Reformers, too, are sensitive to the potential socio-political consequences of disturbing the delicate balance of relations between the state as guarantor of employment and the worker as fulfiller of national production plans.[30]

Managers likewise have preferred to avert major tensions in the enterprise by, for example, not specifying time periods in the contract or distributing bonuses equally amongst workers.[31] To the extent that enterprises are expected to bear responsibility for their losses, managers may be equally reluctant to tamper too much with the status quo.

In brief, the recruitment, employment and remuneration patterns in China betray an uneven blend of reform and pre-reform systems. As pointed out by White, the changes that have occurred do not as of yet imply a definitive shift towards a labour market.[32] The centralised, administrative system of labour allocation with guaranteed, life-long employment in the state sector still predominates. The slow pace of implementation has its roots not only in the policies themselves but also in a combination of politico-institutional and social factors. In the next section we examine the nature of labour policy in foreign-invested enterprises and the SEZ.

Labour policy in foreign-invested enterprises

In order to attract foreign capital and in particular to acquire advanced management techniques, the reformist leadership has been keen to grant foreign-invested enterprises considerable autonomy in their operations, in theory as much as they enjoy in their respective countries.[33] Foreign-invested enterprises are allowed not only to 'hire and fire' their employees but also to determine wages. The circulation and exchange of labour in foreign-invested enterprises are to proceed according to the principles of supply and demand in the labour market rather than administrative fiat. These policy changes have occurred within the context of an overall reform of labour policy in China. Policy-makers have taken a keen interest in labour practices and policies in the foreign-invested enterprises with an eye to transferring some of these experiences to the often loss-making state-owned enterprises. What then are the features of labour policy in foreign-invested enterprises?

Hiring and Firing

Unlike their state-owned counterparts, foreign-invested enterprises have since their inception been permitted to hire and fire employees according to their 'production needs'. The Sino-foreign joint venture law of July 1979 states: 'The employment and dismissal of the staff and workers of a joint venture shall be provided for in accordance with the law in the agreement and contract of the parties to the venture.'[34]

The reformers have referred to the hiring and firing of employees as one of the rights of foreign investors.[35] The reformers have reiterated these rights on several occasions, reflecting on the one hand their commitment to these policies and on the other hand the problems in their actual implementation. Article 15 of the 'Provisions of the State Council of the PRC for the Encouragement of Foreign Investment' codified the rights yet again in October 1986:

> Enterprises with foreign investment may, in accordance with their production and operation requirements, determine by themselves their organisational structure and personnel system, employ or dismiss senior management personnel, increase or dismiss staff and workers. They may recruit and employ technical personnel, managerial personnel and workers in their locality.

Despite the official sanctioning of the right of foreign investors to hire and fire, the actual implementation of this principle and in particular the dismissal of employees has been much harder to achieve. State labour institutions have continued to be involved in the allocation of labour to foreign-invested enterprises. In the early years of foreign investment in China, local Labour Service Corporations assigned staff and workers to foreign enterprises. If they were not satisfactory, the foreign-invested enterprises could send them back, although this was not an easy process. The shortage of technically, linguistically and professionally skilled people meant there was no guarantee that a suitably qualified replacement could be found.

Since 1984 foreign-invested enterprises have been able to interview and select candidates, though these were still filtered through the Labour Service Corporation. Advertising for labour was already underway in go-ahead provinces such as Fujian. By 1987 one sixth of staff and workers in foreign-invested enterprises in Xiamen had been recruited through adverts placed by the Labour Service Corporation.[36] In July 1984 Xiamen local government issued new regulations on labour management which gave SEZ enterprises the rights autonomously to decide their own labour plans and the size and composition of their workforce.[37] SEZ enterprises could recruit staff and workers by themselves, but for labour from rural areas or the interior they would still need the approval of Xiamen Labour Bureau. The emergence of a labour market was thus to be geographically confined, in part for fear of the political and economic effects of uncontrolled migration from rural and inland areas.

As foreign-invested enterprises still had difficulty finding suitable personnel, in November 1986 the Ministry of Labour allowed them to recruit technical and managerial staff from other provinces.[38] With the respective labour personnel department still mediating this process, labour allocation through administrative means continued to predominate. Further relaxation came in May 1988 when the State Council allowed joint ventures to hire from outside the province without approval from the Labour Bureau.[39] So although there have been attempts to increase labour mobility, the labour administration has tried to retain some control over recruitment processes. But why have the foreign-invested enterprises faced difficulties in pursuing this new recruitment policy? First, the hire and fire principle assumes that a labour market already exists. Although various measures have been adopted to increase labour mobility, the mechanisms and institutions required to facilitate such mobility are still relatively immature. For example, up till October 1986 foreign-invested enterprises in Xiamen could officially only recruit from within the zone. China has not yet developed a labour market. The administrative system of labour allocation in the state sector as well as the infamous *hukou* (residence permit for the cities) have limited labour mobility. Moreover, the potential loss of control and regional imbalances incumbent upon massive rural—urban migration flows has also encouraged state officials to keep a tight rein over labour mobility.

Second, the hire and fire principle, which not only presupposes the existence of a labour market, but also implies the commoditisation of labour, raises particular ideological dilemmas for a socialist state committed not only to full employment but also to the 'dictatorship of the proletariat'. The Chinese press has abounded with discussions about whether labour in a socialist commodity economy is also a commodity and, moreover, whether the commoditisation of labour under socialism is the same as under capitalism.[40] As an official from the Labour Service Corporation in Xiamen put it: 'Is labour in a joint venture a commodity or not? If if it isn't a commodity, then why do we talk about employers and employees?'[41] These issues have been of concern not only to opponents of reform but also to conservative elements within the reformist leadership.

Third, the hire and fire principle also challenges the socialist principle of guaranteed employment, hence the implicit social contract between the state and the workforce. The official sanctioning of the right of foreign-invested enterprises to dismiss managers and staff and workers marks a radical departure from previous practice, where reeducation was the major form of disciplining.[42] Reluctant to shed labour, government officials have frequently put pressure on foreign companies to retain staff and workers of partner state-owned enterprises. The manager of a ceramics joint venture in Xiamen SEZ recounted, for example: 'We had to take on most of the staff and workers of the Chinese partner factory but our advanced technology doesn't require such a large workforce. I don't know where they all are at the moment.'[43] Similarly, when Xiamen SEZ was first being set up, foreign companies came under pressure from the Labour Service Corporation to employ displaced farmers. In the words of the foreign manager of a wholly owned foreign enterprise:

In the beginning the Labour Service Corporation wanted us to employ the farmers who had lost their land in the construction of the zone. But we wanted to employ people from Xiamen city. We thought they would be more adapted to factory routine and discipline. We have since regretted this. We found the farmers from Huli worked much harder. The city boys look down on the people from the countryside. We've had to break up fights between the city lads and farmers from Huli.'[44]

On a return visit to Xiamen in 1991 I found that this factory now recruited nearly all its workers from rural areas, reporting total numbers to the Labour Service Corporation.

Foreign enterprises have also found it difficult to dismiss or transfer employees. In a plastics joint venture I interviewed the foreign side had tried in vain to replace the Chinese manager.[45] However, as the manager concerned was related to a leading cadre in one of the Chinese partner organisations, production came to a virtual standstill for almost a year and the foreign side was eventually forced to consider selling its shares. Other Overseas Chinese companies also complained about the difficulties of dismissing employees because of the procedures that had to be gone through.[46] The legacy of past traditions as well as an ideological preference for 'reeducation' rather than outright dismissal have combined to make the dismissal of employees in joint ventures extremely difficult.

Finally, Chinese units have been reluctant to release skilled workers and technical and professional staff. On the one hand, they tend to 'hoard labour' as a strategy to cope with unanticipated production demands from above. On the other hand, they have themselves been short of such technically qualified staff, particularly in the wake of the Cultural Revolution.[47] In the early days of a wholly owned foreign enterprise in Xiamen, an American manager recounted the problems they faced employing an electrician:

We needed an electrician. We were not allowed to hire one and all the best ones were employed by the government. We found an electrician from Xian but weren't allowed to hire him. After discussion we were allowed to hire him but not keep him because he was from Xian. Eventually we were able to hire him, but only temporarily. When we asked what temporary meant, the Labour Service Corporation said 'for the rest of his life'.[48]

Similarly, the foreign manager of a Sino-Danish joint venture told me the difficulties he had in retaining his personal secretary:

My secretary is a former doctor. He wants to transfer from his old unit to here. But he has then to move out of his flat and we don't provide accommodation. We wrote to the mayor of Xiamen to let him stay where he is. The hospital unit argued that joint venture employees are paid higher wages.[49]

Finally this person was able to transfer and retain the flat. But some joint ventures have had to pay a fee to the original work unit which can be as high as Y10 000.[50] In response to this reluctance of state-owned enterprises to part with their technical and mangerial personnel, the reformist leaders yet again issued a regulation in May 1988: 'When they [joint ventures] recruit personnel from other enterprises, relevant departments and units must not obstruct by collecting irrational payments, taking back living quarters etc.'[51]

Given the limited supply of technical personnel and higher wages in foreign-invested enterprises and the SEZs, state-owned enterprises and inland areas are clearly anxious about losing such staff. It is not surprising that adjustments of administrative restrictions on geographical mobility have been slow. By 1987 inland areas were already openly expressing concern about the transfer of technical and professional staff to the coastal areas. This 'brain drain' made it even harder for them to bridge this regional economic and technical gap.

Although the state has tried to maintain control over the supply of labour to foreign companies, as these have increased in number and rural people have flowed into the cities, existing labour institutions have found it more difficult to cope. Indeed most of the fears about rural migration into the zones have been borne out. Rough estimates put China's floating population at 50 million.[52] The labour bureau has found it more and more difficult to monitor this rural influx. The outcome has been that foreign companies have increasingly recruited labour though private channels, particularly unskilled workers from the rural areas. One foreign investor I interviewed in December 1991 said: 'Now we don't bother to go through the Labour Service Corporation. We just let them know how many workers we've got.'[53] Unable to deal with the mounting workload Labour Service Corporations have turned a blind eye to this development. In Xiamen SEZ word-of-mouth and kinship ties have become an important method of recruitment in foreign-invested enterprises in Xiamen SEZ. In a wholly owned foreign plastics factory the managerial staff as well as several of the workers stemmed from Huian county, which was the birthplace of the owner of the company. Similarly, in a wholly owned foreign electronics enterprise, the Chinese director was a close relative of the Hong Kong owner.[54] To the extent that personal connections or *guanxi* form the basis for recruitment, the market for labour becomes distorted and inappropriate allocation of labour continues to be a problem.

This practice of employing rural labour captured the national limelight when a wholly owned foreign factory in Guangdong suffered an enormous fire, killing 71 people and injuring 48. Most of these workers came from outside Guangdong, not only because rural workers were prepared to work for lower wages but also because the local population was moving more and more into the commercial sector. Following this catastrophe, the Guangdong Labour Bureau tightened up on recruitment of workers from outside the province.[55] This example illustrates well the growing inability of the existing organisations to deal with an increasingly fluid rural labour force. Foreign-invested enterprises who are quite ready to bypass the system to meet their production needs are thus pushing the development of a labour market at a pace much faster than the state can cope with.

Parallel to this rural influx has been the rise of a putting-out system. Restrictions on the employment of rural workers in the city coupled with the shortage of suitable urban workers have prompted some enterprises early on to contract out work to the rural areas. One clothes factory in Xiamen SEZ began in 1987 to put out part of the production process to female workers in nearby rural areas who had already been trained in the factory. In this way the company was able to reduce production costs, as the worker bore the expenses of electricty, rent and lunch, and fees to the Labour Service Corporation could be bypassed. In view of some of the tensions on the shopfloor between rural and urban workers, skilled and unskilled, and workers and supervisors, contracting out work to rural women in households was a way to gain greater control over the workforce. It also extended the web of commodity relations, in this instance of labour, into rural areas.

In brief, on the one hand we find foreign-invested enterprises unable to recruit or dismiss workers because of pressure from the state to retain control over labour. On the other hand, we find state labour institutions increasingly unable to cope with the rising demand for labour from foreign-invested enterprises as well as the influx from rural areas. In practice we are seeing greater labour mobility, particularly of the unskilled rural workforce, but an increasingly inadequate institutional framework to shape this process. In this limbo between market and administratively led labour recruitment, we will continue to see sporadic but weak attempts by the state to seize the reins.

Smashing the iron rice bowl

The labour contract system has its origins in Shenzhen SEZ. Although the basic content of this policy has been generalised to state- and collective-owned enterprises and other areas of China, the pace of its implementation has clearly been much faster in the SEZ and foreign-invested enterprises than in the state or collective sectors. For example, in October 1981 the Hong Kong joint venture Xinghua Electronics Company in Shenzhen was already practising the contract employment system.[56]

Xiamen SEZ has also ventured ahead with the labour contract system. All workers and staff in Xiamen SEZ are employed on a contract basis. The terms of the contract cover employment, dismissal and resignation, the length of the contract, production and work tasks, wages, bonuses, hours of work and holidays, labour insurance, welfare, labour protection and discipline.

Although the introduction of the contract system in foreign-invested enterprises and SEZs has proceeded relatively rapidly and smoothly, in part because of the lack of a pre-existing workforce to offer resistance in some of the zones, there have been attempts to mitigate the implicit insecurity of contract employment. Cadres have been able to retain their permanent posts in state organs as a safety valve should the contract not be renewed in the joint venture. This effectively nullifies the intended effects of the contract system. For example, in a wholly owned foreign enterprise electronics factory in Xiamen SEZ, a Chinese director and manager informed me that he had kept his post in the local electronics bureau.[57] Cadres were able to utilise their positions to mitigate the potential risks of contract employment.

Although the labour contract system was supposed to enhance labour mobility, joint ventures still had to submit the contract to the Labour Bureau, implying a continued, though less direct state involvement than previously. Similarly, although foreign-invested enterprises in Xiamen SEZ have the right to dismiss employees under certain conditions, they must first give one month's notice to the trade union and SEZ Labour Service Corporation. Although this process constrains the flexibility of joint ventures, it also protects workers' rights.

There is thus a contradiction in the regulations, on the one hand between a commitment to protect the interests of the workers and on the other the desire to strengthen the power of the enterprise over its workforce. In practice the dismissal of employees in foreign-invested enterprises has proven difficult to implement. Some political cadres in the trade unions and Labour Service Corporations have felt ideological unease at smashing the iron rice bowl. These measures too have not proved popular with the workforce. Although the regulations to a certain extent provide some protection for the workers, they also seek to protect the enterprise's interests from the negative effects of increased labour mobility made possible through the contract system. Workers who have received training from the enterprise but fail to work for the stipulated period afterwards are required to compensate the firm for the training costs according to the contract.

Down with egalitarianism

The Sino-foreign joint venture law of 1979 allowed the board of directors the right to determine wage scales, the form of the wage and bonuses.[58] One year later the 'Provisions for Labour Management in Chinese—Foreign Joint Ventures' laid out explicitly that the wages of the staff and workers in joint ventures should come to 120—50 per cent of the real wage of staff and workers in state-owned enterprises in the same locality and industry.[59] Lower and upper ceilings on the joint venture wage have limited, however, the room of manoeuvre of joint ventures. Local regulations have tended to provide greater flexibility for foreign investors. Labour regulations issued in Fujian in 1984, for example, gave no details about wage limits. However, the Fujian Economic Relations and Trade Commission wrote in a brochure for foreign investors that minimum salaries could range between Rmb 120—80 with no limits on upper salaries.[60] Stricter supervision of employees as well as payment according to the socialist principle of 'to each according to his work' portended greater managerial control over the workforce. Moreover, by granting the board of directors the right to determine the wages of senior managerial and technical staff, the way was paved for greater wage differentials within the enterprise based on professional rather than political criteria.

Although the government allowed foreign-invested enterprises greater autonomy to decide on the form of the wage, it offered little guidance as to how to do this. As a result foreign-invested enterprises vary considerably in their wage scales, levels and bonus systems.[61] So the experience of Shekou industrial zone in setting wages and determining the form of wages became the initial model adopted by the SEZ. Shekou has taken the lead in adopting new wage policies not only because it was the first zone to be established but also because its management by the Hong Kong-based China Steamship Merchants' Navigation Company has permitted greater innovation. Moreover, as part of the rationale for the establishment of the SEZ is related to future reunification, the adoption and adaptation of policies and practices in Hong Kong would help realise the concept of 'one country, two systems'.

Although the wage system in Shekou industrial zone has passed through numerous stages, the system adopted in October 1983 has been the most influential. According to this the total wage of a worker in Shekou consisted of a basic wage, work post (*zhiwu gongzi*) and floating wages. Workpost wages were an attempt to link the wage to particular skills and tasks whilst the floating wage sought to link the wage to the performance of the enterprise. After this reform the average monthly wage of workers in Shekou was Y170 a month, compared to Y131 in Shenzhen SEZ.[62] Of this 30 per cent was floating wages, 35 per cent basic wages and 35 per cent workpost wages.

At a forum held by the Secretariat and State Council attended by representatives of the SEZ, open coastal cities and Hainan in April 1984, leaders urged all the SEZs to popularise Shekou's management experience.[63] The following month Shenzhen put forward further reforms of the wage system, reducing subsidies and raising wages.[64] In August 1985 top leaders hailed Shenzhen SEZ as the model of labour reform for the rest of China.[65]

Although some estimates put wages in foreign-invested enterprises in China at around half of those in Hong Kong, average wage levels have tended to be higher in foreign-invested enterprises than in state-owned enterprises and higher in the SEZs than non-zone areas. In 1989, for example, the average annual wage of staff and workers in industrial state-owned enterprises came to Rmb 2055 whilst in joint ventures and wholly owned foreign enterprises it amounted to Y2669 and Y3567 respectively.[66] Moreover, in some foreign-invested enterprises, particularly in Shenzhen SEZ and Shekou industrial zone, workers have received part of their wages in foreign currency, raising further the total real wage.

However, although money wages in foreign-invested enterprises appear nominally higher than in state-owned enterprises, workers may not necessarily enjoy higher standards of living. In particular, state-owned enterprises provide numerous subsidies such as rice coupons, heating, home leave and other benefits such as housing. According to a report in *Workers' Daily*, welfare subsidies in state-owned enterprises amounted to 54 per cent of the average annual basic wage.[67] The actual wage received in a foreign-invested enterprise has to satisfy a wider range of needs than in a state-owned enterprise. What was previously received as an entitlement has now to be purchased as a commodity — where it is available. Moreover, the higher wages enjoyed by workers in the SEZs is offset by the higher cost of living and higher inflation rates in the SEZ.

In Xiamen the advantages of the state sector such as job security, housing and other social benefits have proven more attractive to some categories of workers than the higher wages in the foreign-invested enterprise. Initially, workers were keen to work in foreign-invested enterprises as nominal wages were higher.[68] But the stricter discipline, longer effective working hours, as well as the lack of security regarding both the length of the contract and welfare provisions have led not only to high labour turnover but also to an unwillingness amongst some workers to work in such enterprises.[69] With flats in Xiamen commanding prices of US$ 30 000 on the private market and rents for one room spiralling to Y400 or more a month, the offer of accommodation in a state-owned unit, even with the housing reform, is still a very attractive option. According to the Labour Service Corporation there has been a tendency in recent years for workers to drift back from foreign-invested enterprises to state-owned enterprises. From interviews in some factories it was apparent that most of those who had resigned had done so to obtain permanent posts. Work in a foreign-invested enterprise is thus likely to be more attractive to young, unmarried workers but less appealing to older, married workers concerned about welfare provisions and job security.

The experience of Xiamen SEZ underlines the deep-rootedness of the implicit social contract between the state and urban workforce.[70] In return for guaranteed job security and welfare provision, labour complies in meeting production requirements. By not meeting the social needs of the workforce the foreign-invested enterprise effectively removes one of the 'carrots' that a state-owned enterprise wields to seek compliance. This leaves management with less to offer whilst wielding the newly acquired stick of dismissal and non-renewal of contracts and bonus disparities.

The pressure in foreign-invested enterprises to respond to the requirements of the international market, especially regarding punctual delivery and high quality, puts a strain on relations between labour and management. Concerned to meet orders, the Chinese manager is compelled to enforce stricter discipline on the shopfloor, so increasing the potential for conflict. In Xiamen, however, tensions between labour and foreign capital have, up till now, been expressed in labour turnover rather than in voluntary industrial action.[71] As long as the alternative of life-long employment in a relatively privileged state sector exists, certain categories of workers will opt with their feet out of foreign-invested enterprises to state-owned enterprises. However, as the contract system spreads to state-owned enterprises, this attraction is likely to wear off and the stimulus of higher wages in both the recruitment and management of labour will become more effective.

Difficult though it is to compare wages in foreign-invested enterprises and state-owned enterprises, some foreign investors consider the overall wage levels in the SEZs too high, claiming that productivity is much lower than in Hong Kong, Thailand or the USA.[72] The reformers have responded to these perceptions by providing for lower labour costs in the regulations issued in October 1986 to encourage foreign direct investment.[73]

In Xiamen SEZ there has clearly been a tendency to restrain the level of wages, at least for workers. According to the State Council regulations, wages in foreign-invested enterprises in Xiamen SEZ can exceed state-owned enterprise wages by 120–50 per cent. However, there is some ambiguity in practice as to whether this implies a foreign-invested enterprise wage one-fifth to a half more than state-owned enterprise wages or one-and-a-fifth to one-and-a-half times the state-owned enterprise wage. Moreover, it is not clear whether this refers to the wage actually received by the worker or the wages paid by the foreign-invested enterprise.

According to the Labour Service Corporation official interviewed in Xiamen SEZ the average wage in a foreign-invested enterprise in 1986 was only 26.14 per cent higher than a state-owned enterprise, suggesting the former interpretation of the figures.[74] However, whilst the figure quoted by the Labour Service Corporation official was the average wage, a local academic has claimed that the differences between wages in foreign-invested enterprises and state-owned enterprises could be as much as 10 times, particularly for managerial staff and directors.[75]

Whatever the reality of the actual wages received, the statement by the Labour Service Corporation reflects on the one hand a desire to make labour more competitive than in other SEZs, and on the other a fear on the part of local leaders and policy-makers of the potential political consequences of large wage differentials. Policy-makers and academics in Xiamen SEZ had already expressed concern about such discrepancies which could lead to resentment amongst workers in state-owned enterprises, particularly as the rise in the cost of living in the zone has affected all workers, regardless of where they worked.[76] Policy-makers were also concerned about the inflationary effects of high wages in foreign-invested enterprises. In other parts of China, foreign enterprises have met resistance in increasing wage differentials both from workers and officials. For example, the foreign managers of a joint venture in Tianjin widened salaries and abolished some living and service facilities. Employees protested by slackening their work pace and the joint venture had to renege on this wage policy[77]. A survey of workers carried out by the All-China Federation of Trade Unions in 1992 pointed to the wide gap in incomes between state-owned enterprise workers and both private businesspeople and workers in foreign-invested enterprises as a factor in their low 'enthusiasm' for work.[78]

Unlike state-owned enterprises, foreign-invested enterprises can determine their own allowance system. Again there has been little guidance from above as to how this 25 per cent Labour Service Corporation fee should operate in practice. In fact the reformers have been groping in the dark in their attempts to develop a welfare system and have eagerly awaited local innovations for inspiration. The allowance system adopted in the SEZs and foreign-invested enterprises has largely been the result of trial and error rather than deliberate planning. The system which emerged in Guangdong and was later adopted in Xiamen is as follows: foreign-invested enterprises in Xiamen SEZ and Guangdong have to submit 25 per cent of the total wages of the Chinese staff and workers to the Labour Service Corporation each month for the employees' pension funds, funeral expenses, medical expenses after retirement and unemployment fees. In Guangdong this 25 per cent did not have to accord with standards used in state-owned enterprises for labour insurance, medical expenses and government subsidies.[79] The enterprise also pays 5 per cent of the total wage bill towards the workers and staff welfare fund, which is used for the collective welfare, medical and health care and for hardship allowances. The external-isation of the welfare functions in the foreign-invested enterprise reflect an attempt to alter the character of the enterprise in China and in particular to emphasise its role as a unit of production rather than social reproduction. So we can see that the reformers have allowed foreign-invested enterprises to determine wage levels, the form of the wage and bonuses. However, ideological, political and economic factors have constrained the exercise of this 'right'. Ideological factors such as a preference for non-material rewards have affected both the distribution of bonus according to individual work performance and the raising of received wages as an incentive to higher productivity. The tendency of managers both to raise bonuses and to distribute these equally, regardless of differences in individual performance, has been common both to state-owned enterprises and foreign-invested enterprises. This behaviour is in part a response to the pressure from workers themselves, some of whom may not favour such increased inequalities. An official of an electronics joint venture I interviewed in Xiamen commented: 'Egalitarianism is common in state-owned enterprises. Although now we are a joint venture, it is still difficult to change the previous situation completely ... Traditional thinking can influence joint venture affairs.' This has been particularly common where the Chinese partner is an already existing state-owned enterprise. This suggests the reproduction in joint ventures of patterns of behaviour common to state-owned enterprises, so constraining the pace of reform.[80] Some foreign-invested enterprises have circumvented this by paying workers in individual sealed wage packets so that no worker knows what the other is being paid.[81]

Although foreign-invested enterprises have the 'right' to determine wage levels, most of the foreign investors in joint ventures interviewed in Xiamen SEZ expressed frustration at their inability to raise wages as a reward for good work or as an incentive to higher productivity. This suggests not only that the foreign investors exert little control over the issue of wages but also that administrative authorities continue to play a decisive role in the joint venture.

Political factors have also affected the distribution of the total wage between the worker and the state. Some foreign investors have expressed the desire to reduce the amount of the wage paid in subsidies and to the Labour Service Corporation and to increase the amount received by the individual worker, hoping that this will improve labour productivity.[82] Chinese leaders in joint ventures have been reluctant to increase the wage received by the worker as it could lead to political tensions both within the joint venture and between workers in joint ventures and state-owned enterprises. First, the differentials between a worker or cadre in a joint venture and a state-owned enterprise would become too wide, thus in the long-term affecting the 'enthusiasm' of state-owned enterprise workers in the same sector and locality and leading potentially to calls for higher wages.

Second, if workers did receive the total wage, the wage gap between contract workers and permanently employed workers and cadres within the same enterprise would also widen and create a further source of friction. In fact, tension has already emerged between contract workers and permanent workers in state-owned enterprises where the former are receiving higher wages, although receiving possibly less benefits.[83] An official from a joint venture cigarette factory in Xiamen, for example, recounted:

> The contract workers in the export-processing joint venture workshop were paid on a piece-rate basis. They were young and new and earned more than our older, permanent workers. Things got so bad that we had to let the older workers work in this workshop so they could increase their earnings.

The move the factory took negated the intended effects of the contract system.

Third, large increases in wages for joint venture workers might also lead to demands for higher salaries amongst other social groups such as intellectuals. Higher wages for workers in some joint ventures in Guangdong had also drawn the resentment of local teachers who were earning less than their former pupils.[84]

The practice of egalitarianism has proved, however, to be double-edged. Whilst on the one hand there has been a reluctance to implement the principle of 'from each according to his work' and in particular to dampen wage levels, on the other hand there has been a demand for parity in wages between Chinese and foreign directors of joint ventures.[85] The latter demand has not been met, in part because of objections from foreign companies and in part because of the potential effects of higher wages on foreign directors in state-owned enterprises.

Ambiguity and paucity of detail have also constrained the right of foreign-invested enterprises to determine wages. The type of policies eventually adopted in the zones were primarily the result of trial and error based on the experience of Shekou. Moreover, the failure to consider linkages between policies and thus prepare a coordinated set of complementary reforms in the spheres of housing, welfare and social insurance also affected the feasiblity and potential acceptability of these wage reforms. The commoditisation of labour required the parallel commoditisation of other services previously provided by the enterprise.

Changes in the institutional landscape

What then has been the institutional response to these changes in labour policy? New institutions such as the SEZ Labour Service Corporation and the Sino-foreign employees' exchange centre have sprung up whilst existing institutions such as the trade unions have adapted their structures and methods.[86] The Labour Bureaux in SEZs have created special SEZ Labour Service Corporations to deal with the employment and training of Chinese staff and workers.[87] The form of a corporation reflects a desire to provide flexibility in dealing with the needs of foreign-invested enterprises and to separate policy planning from practice. Although the Labour Service Corporation enjoys some autonomy, it is still answerable to the Labour Bureau. The Labour Service Corporation charges the foreign enterprise a negotiable fee, which is used for the welfare of the workers. In Xiamen SEZ, for example, the wholly owned foreign enterprise pays the Labour Service Corporation HK$ 100 per month per person whilst the joint venture pays Y44.60, rates considerably lower than in Shenzhen.[88]

What is particularly interesting is that the Xiamen SEZ Labour Service Corporation performs certain functions akin to those of a trade union. In the words of the Labour Service Corporation official interviewed, 'our main function is to act on behalf of labour and personnel in foreign-invested enterprises.' So the Labour Service Corporation deals with the recruitment of employees to foreign-invested enterprises, arranges the contracts, provides training and negotiates wages. It also assists with the drafting of labour plans and the transfer of potential employees in foreign-invested enterprises from their original units. It ensures that employees have residence permits, graduation certificates and unemployment cards. In the negotiation of contracts the Labour Service Corporation is responsible for the detailing of provisions concerning labour, welfare and social security whilst the trade union supervises the process to ensure that the contract abides by the law and is in the interest of the workers.

As the Labour Service Corporation coordinates relations between capital and labour, it also mediates in labour disputes. Between 1983 and 1986 the Xiamen SEZ Labour Service Corporation resolved 30 disputes. The Labour Service Corporation also takes on the responsibility for discharged workers or workers whose contracts have terminated, providing unemployment benefit and help with finding new work. The role of the Labour Service Corporation was particularly crucial in wholly owned foreign enterprises which were less likely to have a trade union and also did not have the benefit of a Chinese partner to deal with administration. In wholly owned foreign enterprises the work of the Labour Service Corporation takes on a more general, coordinating role.

The Labour Service Corporation functions like the trade union in part because some foreign-invested enterprises ban trade union activity in production hours. But unlike the trade union, the Labour Service Corporation is not a mass organisation, does not constitute a body of elected representatives and does not carry out political or ideological work. It is instead an administrative organ in the form of a corporation. Moreover, it does not explicitly claim to represent the interests of the workers.

As well as the creation of a new institution to deal with the recruitment and management of labour in the SEZ, the trade unions have adapted their functions and mode of operation. The local trade union officials I interviewed pointed out several ways in which the functions of a trade union differed in a foreign-invested enterprise to a state-owned enterprise.

First, as well as purporting to defend the 'rights and interests' of the staff and workers, the trade union also has to support foreign businesspeople and defend foreigners' legal interests. As an official said: 'In a dispute the role of the trade union is different to in a state-owned enterprise as the trade union must pay attention to the interests of foreigners.'

Second, it has to coordinate relations between labour and capital within the enterprise. The trade union intervenes in labour disputes and in particular facilitates relations between Chinese workers and foreign management and workers. It also has to represent workers in labour-related issues on the board of directors. Within joint ventures trade unions have the right to attend board meetings as non-voting delegates in matters concerning award, punishment, wages and labour protection.[89]

Third, although trade unions have an educational role in state-owned enterprises, in foreign-invested enterprises they put particular emphasis on educating staff and workers about the Open Policy. This involves not only explaining the advantages of the Open Policy and the SEZ to the staff and workers but also persuading staff and workers to adapt to the different hours and stricter discipline in joint ventures. Moreover, the trade union has also to educate workers in foreign affairs discipline, such as not divulging state secrets or changing money.

Fourth, the trade unions in foreign-invested enterprises are responsible for implementing each government policy, thus in effect performing the work of the Party. Although the trade unions have served primarily as channels for the dissemination and implementation of Party policy rather than as organs for pursuing workers' interests, within state-owned enterprises they have shared Party-related work with Party members and Communist Youth League members.

Fifth, the trade unions have to deal specifically with the needs of contract workers. As all workers in joint ventures are contracted, whilst most in state-owned enterprises are permanent, the role of the trade union in handling matters relating to contract workers is more prominent. If a foreign-invested enterprise does not have a trade union, then the Labour Service Corporation or the trade union of the relevant industrial department handles the dispute. So the trade union ensures that workers' interests, such as wages, social security and welfare are covered in the contract.

Finally, the trade union has to encourage workers to make proposals about improving production. Although the union also does this in state-owned enterprises, the importance of this function is much greater in foreign-invested enterprises where the relation between labour and foreign management resembles that of 'employer' and 'employee'.[90]

Not only have the functions of trade unions in foreign-invested enterprises expanded but their methods of operation have also changed in several ways. Trade union cadres in joint ventures have at the same time as carrying out their trade union activities had to participate in production. This is closely related to the change in the system of payment of trade union staff in foreign-invested enterprises. In a state-owned enterprise full-time trade union staff are in practice paid out of the welfare funds. In many foreign-invested enterprises in the SEZs employers have refused to pay the salary of the trade union chairman. As a result most trade union workers are part-time, conducting their activities in the evening.[91]

As there are fewer trade union cadres employed in joint ventures, the work of a trade union cadre has intensified. Due to the ban on political activity during production hours in these enterprises, trade unions have had to hold their meetings outside production hours. Moreover, in order to maintain contact with the union's members, trade union cadres have increased their visits to the homes of workers. Trade unions have also experimented with different ways of organising labour, including such innocuous pursuits as general knowledge competitions. Finally, trade unions have also had to widen their channels of information dissemination. In 1984 Xiamen trade union began its own newspaper which was put on public sale three years later.

Not only are the methods of operation used by trade unions in foreign-invested enterprises different to those used in state-owned enterprises, but the nature of the conflicts also differs. The main types of conflict arising in joint ventures have concerned the disciplining of employees, the provision of welfare facilities and the negotiation of contracts.

First, whilst state-owned enterprises discipline unsatisfactory workers through collective criticism or reeducation, joint ventures have the right to dismiss workers and impose financial penalties. The following case recounted to me by a trade union official illustrates well the role of trade unions:

A waitress in a foreign-managed hotel laid the table and put the table near the door. The manager told her to move the table further inside. She was about to go off for lunch and so refused to do so. The manager wrote down her name and said he would reduce her bonus and cut one month's wages. She came to us and we then went to discuss this with the manager. We said they had reduced the wages too much and that the worker had a child. We told the waitress that the customer should come first. We stopped the manager cutting her wages.

Second, the provision of welfare facilities such as kindergarten and crèches has also been a source of contention in Xiamen. Hardly any of the foreign-invested enterprises have provided such facilities. This is in part related to the age structure of its workforce which has tended to lie between 16 and the early 20s. Moreover, as the contract system provides the possibility of not renewing the contracts of pregnant or married women, pressure from below for such facilities has not been great.

Finally, conflicts also arise over the signing of contracts. For example, a trade union official in Xiamen SEZ recounted a case where the trade union intervened in the negotiation of compensation money:

> The worker contacted us because when he was signing the contract, one clause stated that if he left, he would have to pay Y 10 000 to the factory, which for a Chinese worker is an unrealistic amount. So we found the manager, discussed this with him and eliminated the clause.

Although not all joint ventures have trade unions, they are nevertheless bound by law to provide an office for the trade union in the enterprise and give financial support to trade union activities. Moreover, whilst the joint ventures cannot interfere in trade union activity in the enterprise, at the same time the latter are not permitted to hold meetings during production hours. As in state-owned enterprises the goals of the trade union are subordinate to the needs of production, as seen in:

> Party Organisations, Communist Youth League organisations and trade unions are not allowed to organise activities interrupting production in the enterprises [i.e. wholly owned foreign enterprises] or to infringe on their legitimate interests. The trade unions should play a positive role in facilitating regular production in the enterprises. These measures have freed foreign businessmen from worries.[92]

Changing loyalties: relations between state, labour and capital

What then are the implications of opening up for relations between the state, labour and capital? How have the trade unions responded to their increasing contradictory role in foreign-invested enterprises? And how has the Party-state dealt with the ideological dilemma posed by the new labour policies in foreign-invested enterprises?

The restrictions placed on the activities of trade unions in foreign-invested enterprises have weakened the formal channels for the articulation of workers' interests within the enterprise. We can observe this in various phenomena. Trade unions in Xiamen SEZ are not permitted to carry out their activities during production hours, unlike in state-owned enterprises and other administrative units where workers and staff regularly attend political meetings organised by the trade union or Party. Although trade unions can still hold meetings after work or during lunch breaks, the prohibition against meeting during working hours makes it more difficult to organise labour. As this regulation refers to all political meetings, it also constricts the role of the Party.[93] However, the trade union head in joint ventures is often the Party secretary. As one Party official stated, 'to the foreigners we say they are the trade union official, but for us they are the party head.'[94] Also the managers of joint venture personnel departments are often Party members. Moreover, if there are at least three Party members in a joint venture, these are supposed to form a Party cell.

Although joint ventures are supposed to cooperate with trade unions and permit them to establish offices, there are still many foreign-invested enterprises without unions. In 1987 only 30 per cent of the approved 7700 foreign-invested enterprises in China had trade unions.[95] In Xiamen SEZ only 60 out of 150 joint ventures and 1 out of 11 wholly owned foreign enterprises had them.[96] By mid-1990 the situation had improved, with over 70 out of Xiamen's 100 wholly owned foreign enterprises having unions.[97] Moreover, changes in the payment system of union workers, as previously mentioned, have also reduced the number of fully employed union members in foreign-invested enterprises. These changes in the remuneration of union staff have led trade unionists to take on other jobs. Instances of trade union chairmen also working as head of personnel in foreign-invested enterprises in the SEZs clearly complicate the work of the unions as the interests of these chairmen are now split between the defence of workers' interests and those of the enterprise. Although the actual power of trade unions in state-owned enterprises may be weak *vis-à-vis* the Party and management, the absence of unions in certain foreign-invested enterprises reduces further any possibility of formally channelling workers' demands.

Even if a foreign-invested enterprise does have a trade union, the regulations do not require or explicitly permit workers' congresses to be organised. Officially almost 85 per cent of state-owned enterprises in Xiamen had workers' congresses, which the unions organised, but none of the joint ventures had such organisations.[98] Even though the workers' congresses in state-owned enterprises may be empty vessels in many instances, they at least offer the potential for some degree of workers' democracy.[99] As the joint ventures have neither workers' congresses nor elections of factory directors, the channels open to labour for criticism or complaint against management are sharply circumscribed compared to state-owned enterprises.[100]

The position of the trade union on the board of directors also suggests a subordinate role for the union in the enterprise. Although the trade union can represent the interests of workers in matters concerning wages and the distribution of bonus and profits, it nevertheless has no voting rights on the board. However, the position of the union in a state-owned enterprise may in fact be no better. Moreover, there is evidence that unions do not always attend these meetings, in part because of the problems of funding full-time union staff.[101] Even if historically the trade unions have subordinated the interests of the workers in the enterprise to overall national policy, the constriction of the avenues of union activity in foreign-invested enterprises further reduces the potential bargaining power of the unions and ultimately labour.

These changes in the structural presence of trade unions within the enterprise have become an issue at the national level in the discussion of the Open Policy. Conservative opponents of the SEZs, and more generally of the policy of opening up, have queried why foreign-invested enterprises are able to prevent trade unions and the Party from operating, when unions are active in foreign capitalist countries.[102] Underlying this criticism is a concern that the introduction of foreign capital will lead to a deterioration of the conditions of workers and to exploitation reminiscent of the pre-independence days. To the extent that trade unions make a social contract with the foreign-invested enterprise, as has been the case in state-owned enterprises, there is some justification to this fear.

If joint ventures are perceived to be models of economic efficiency, then it might well be concluded by analysts in China and abroad that their success is in part due to the restrictions on the channels of organisation and mobilisation of labour and in particular to the curbing of the power of the trade unions and Party. This would lend further support to the current assumptions that the inefficiency of domestic enterprises is partly due to the fusion of the 'political' and the 'economic'. With the granting of greater autonomy to enterprises as well as the introduction of the factory-director responsibility system, the need for trade unions and workers' congresses has already come under challenge.[103]

At the same time, however, there is a contradiction between the labour reforms in state-owned enterprises and the new conditions of labour in foreign-invested enterprises. Whilst greater worker participation in the form of workers' congresses is seen as a prerequisite for better production relations and, ultimately, increased production in state-owned enterprises, in foreign-invested enterprises less worker participation is seen as essential to better production. The weaker position of formal labour institutions such as the trade unions and workers' congresses in foreign-invested enterprises reflects not only the relative power of foreign capital to lay down the terms of its operation, but also some foreign investors' perception of trade unions as agencies of conflict in China.[104] Some foreign investors assume that the trade unions will necessarily be in conflict with capital, will represent the interests of workers and have the potential to disrupt production. As a union official in Xiamen stated:

> Foreigners are afraid of trade unions because the trade unions might be against them or organise strikes and so endanger their profits. Also they are afraid that trade union activities will interfere with production. The trade union doesn't view it this way. Everyone should consult together.

In China the trade unions may claim to represent the workers, but historically their primary goal has been to ensure the implementation of Party policy and the fulfilment of production plans in particular.

Since Liberation trade unions have found themselves in the contradictory position of having to implement Party policy and defend workers' rights. Their obligation now to defend the interests of capital has added a new dimension to this paradox. So the trade union faces a dilemma. If it defends the interests of capital, it must necessarily be ignoring the interests of labour. But if it protects the interests of labour, it must ultimately be acting against capital.

The somewhat ambivalent role of trade unions in labour disputes in foreign-invested enterprise has highlighted this catch-22 situation. The statement of this trade union official betrays this dilemma:

> The unions help workers understand through study sessions that in observing contracts they are acually helping make China's Open Policy a success. Most workers know that the policy designed to build a strong and prosperous China, conforms to their ultimate interests.

According to the Trade Union Federation in Shenzhen, which represents 20 000 workers in 88 foreign-invested enterprises, over 24 disputes had occurred between 1978 and mid-1985, all of which had been resolved through the trade unions. In one instance the union intervened in favour of labour. The management of a Hong Kong-owned toy company in Shekou forced workers to work an extra four to six hours a day in the summer of 1983 to meet a rush order. The union then intervened, demanding that the management abide by the labour contract. According to the contract extra hours could only be worked if absolutely necessary and required the consent of the workers.[105] In another instance the trade unions intervened in favour of capital. Workers in a Japanese factory demanded a longer spring festival holiday even though management had already granted five days instead of the statutory three. The unions in this case refused to back the workers.[106] In a Sino-Hong Kong printing and dyeing factory in Shenzhen, where workers had reportedly been 'slack in their work and defiant of discipline', the trade union mediated between foreign capital and labour to secure the compliance of the workforce. The union set up training programmes to help the workers 'respect the legal rights and interests of overseas investors'.[107] In 1987 the number of labour disputes in foreign-invested enterprises in Shenzhen rose to almost 50, suggesting a possible increase in worker resistance.[108]

However, the extension of working hours has occurred not only in foreign-invested enterprises but also in the domestic enterprises run on contract or lease.[109] Some enterprises had apparently insisted at the time of contract signing that the workers agree to work overtime, whilst others had apparently dismissed workers who refused to work overtime. Tensions arising between labour and capital have highlighted the increasingly contradictory role of trade unions as protector of workers' interests and defender of national policy. As a local trade union official so aptly stated:

> The trade unions are there to help, not to oppose foreign-invested enterprises. Foreign trade unions want to increase wages whereas here we want to increase production and solve any problems through consultation. In China the goals of trade unions and foreign-invested enterprises are the same.[110]

The orientation of the trade unions towards production and the concomitant declared identity of interests with the foreign-invested enterprise is not surprising in the light of the historical role played by the unions in post-liberation China. There has been a constant tension since 1949 between the role of the trade union as implementer of national policy and defender of workers' interests. Despite the efforts of union leaders such as Li Lisan and Lai Ruoru to attain some degree of autonomy for the trade unions, since liberation the unions have subordinated the interests of the workers to overall national and Party policy.[111] With the restoration of the unions in 1978 the relationship between the Party and the trade union has again become the focus of attention. As of yet the principal stated goal of the trade union has still been to organise workers for production.[112]

The adoption of the contract responsibility system and the rapid mush-rooming of the private economy as well as the introduction of foreign capital have thrown the contradictory role of the trade unions into sharper relief. The political crisis of mid-1989 spawned for the first time since Liberation the spontaneous rise of new autonomous trade unions both in Beijing and other cities. In 1956, in fact, the increase in wage differentials across sectors and jobs due to wage reforms contributed in part to calls for trade union autonomy, though none emerged then.[113] These new unions challenged the legitimacy of the official trade unions. Moreover, their voluntary character posed an alarming threat to the Party-state, which had kept a tight control over society through corporate-type institutions. With the socio-economic structure of society changing under reform and the Open Policy, the old institutional fabric was becoming increasingly redundant. The politico-institutional system of social control lagged tortoise-like behind the rapidly changing socio-economic base.

The initial response of the Party-state has been to clamp down on these precocious beasts. Their leaders were quickly arrested, tried and imprisoned. Compared to the student demonstrators, the worker leaders received much harsher treatment. For the reformers the threat to production was of far greater concern than the intellectual demands of students, whose links with the economy and society were less direct. Following Tiananmen, the official trade union has reiterated the need for continuing Party leadership over the union.[114] The following quote from an article by Ni Zhifu, President of the All-China Federation of Trade Unions, illustrates this well: 'The trade unions must always maintain a high degree of unanimity with the Party and Central Committee in political and ideological affairs and in action.'[115]

What then are the implications of the Tiananmen experience for future labour organisation, particularly in foreign-invested enterprises? There are two possible scenarios as follows:

1. The trade union will opt for defending the interests of the workers and perhaps assume a more conflictual role in the foreign-invested enterprise. The events of Tiananmen abruptly warned the official trade union of the dangers of not heeding workers' grievances. To salvage some legitimacy the official unions will have to pay some heed to the voices from below. Given that there have always been elements within the official union movement in favour of prioritising workers' interests, these may press for such a strategy.

2a. In the short term labour will resort increasingly to other informal means to express their discontent. This could take the form of spontaneous stoppages, go-slows, resistance to demands for higher productivity or higher labour turnover. A survey carried out by the All-China Federation of Trade Unions revealed that a lack of 'labour enthusiasm' amongst workers became manifested in low rates of attendance and low labour productivity.[116] Furthermore, a confidential report of the All-China Federation of Trade Unions cited in *Asian Labour Update* stated that over 50 000 workers had been involved in various forms of protest including strikes between July 1989 and December 1990.[117]

    Given the current clamp-down on voluntary organisations in the political sphere, it is likely that workers will resist sporadically and individually. Moreover, as long as trade unions are absent from foreign-invested enterprises, so nullifying an otherwise potentially useful channel of conflict expression and resolution as well as worker control, this scenario is likely to be reinforced. As workers resort in this vacuum to more informal means to express their grievances, the process of conflict management assumes an element of unpredictability.

2b. In the long term we could see the reemergence of voluntary worker associations, perhaps in the form of autonomous trade unions or perhaps in the guise of workers' committees as in the former Soviet Union.[118] Underground workers' organisations still operate in China. In January 1992, for example, the 'Preparatory Committee of Free Trade Unions of China' published its manifesto.[119] Clearly, to the extent that trade unions are not able to salvage their legitimacy, the more there will be pressure from below for alternative channels and forms of representation.

The introduction of foreign investment has led to a redefinition of the relationship between the state and labour. As a socialist state purporting to represent the interests of the working class, the state has an ideological commitment to the defence of the interests of labour. Yet the introduction of foreign capital necessarily involves the exploitation and oppression of workers. Supporters of the SEZ maintain in accord with Lenin that some exploitation of workers is a necessary and inevitable trade-off for the introduction of foreign capital. Opponents of the SEZs, however, find the notion of exploitation of workers difficult to reconcile with a 'socialist' China.[120] The willingness of the state to prohibit trade union activity during production hours not only reflects the predominance of national interests but also the ideological contradiction in the relationship between the state and labour.

The changing relationship between the state and labour has also surfaced in the issue of the status of workers in foreign-invested enterprises, and in particular, in wholly owned foreign enterprises. As wholly owned foreign enterprises are still capitalist in nature, labour—capital relations within such enterprises are the same as those between employers and employees. However, this raises the question of whether workers in wholly owned foreign enterprises are the real 'masters' as should be the case, in theory at least, in a truly socialist state. According to Zou Erkang, former mayor of Shenzhen SEZ, workers in wholly owned foreign enterprises forfeit this position in favour of the national interest, as seen in:

As a class, the working people are the masters of the state. But in those [wholly owned foreign] enterprises, the workers pay a price for being hired labourers. That means they allow the investors to exploit part of their surplus labour. They make these sacrifices for the sake of the long-term interests of the working class and the country.[121]

The introduction of the factory-director responsiblity system in state-owned enterprises, however, also effectively undermines the ideological position of workers as 'masters' in the enterprise. This issue of workers being 'masters' of the enterprise is indeed an ideological one, in the negative sense of this concept.[122] A survey conducted by the All-China Federation of Trade Unions amongst 210 000 workers in 400 enterprises revealed that over a third of workers did not believe themselves to be 'masters of the enterprise' whilst half thought their status in the enterprise was too low.[123]

Some studies suggest that in practice the Party and trade unions have had a tight control over workers in the enterprise. Walder, for example, demonstrates how Party clientelism, personal-instrumental ties and the socio-political division of the workforce combine to create a particular institutional culture of authority which enables the Party-state to control labour.[124] The particularism of this culture allows workers, however, some leeway in negotiating individually better deals for themselves.

Given that foreign-invested enterprises operate as units of production rather than units also of social reproduction, unlike their state-owned enterprise counterparts, the political and economic dependence of the worker on the foreign-invested enterprise is far less pronounced and the economic base of particularistic social control weakened. By June 1991 only one-third of Guangdong's foreign enterprises had party organisations. Their role in facilitating foreign capital is clearly reflected in the following excerpt from a Guangdong radio broadcast in June 1991: 'They conscientiously have kept an effective grip on the ideological education among party members and other workers and staff members, and helped them adopt a correct attitude towards cooperation with foreign businessmen.'[125] These new conditions as well as the ideological contortions illustrated in the quote above not only reduce further the probability of greater worker control in practice, but also make this rhetoric appear increasingly farcical.

These changes in labour policy, institutions and state—labour relations in turn have consequences for the course of the Open Policy. Compared with other nearby Asian countries such as South Korea and the Philippines, the relations between labour and managment are relatively stable. The phenomenon of some Philippines investors shifting their plants to China indicates that the perception of labour relations as stable in China has contributed positively towards the investment environment.[126] Despite Tiananmen foreign investment has continued to flow into China. Foreign investors in China have expressed concern more for the apparent low level of labour productivity and the difficulties of dismissing labour than labour unrest.

However, to the extent that the constriction of the formal channels for the articulation of workers' interests leads to spontaneous, voluntary worker action, the balance of labour—management relations becomes more precarious. If foreign-invested enterprises are in the future able to realise their autonomy to dismiss 'unsatisfactory' workers or shed labour according to production needs, the possibility of industrial labour action might increase. Political instability at the enterprise level could in turn have an adverse effect on the investment climate, particularly for those foreign investors attracted to China by the cheap source of labour.

As at the Fourteenth Party Congress radical reformers clearly expressed their commitment to enterprise reform and in particular to cutting the labour force, without rapid changes in the social welfare system we can predict increasing unrest in the workplace. Over the past two years there have already been several reports of attacks by workers upon cadres, managers and buildings when job losses have been announced.[127] Potential opposition towards abolishing the three 'irons', that is, the iron rice bowl (permanent job), ironclad wages (fixed wages) and iron armchair (life-long jobs for cadres) will become increasingly worrisome for China's top leaders as they steer China towards a socialist market economy.

Whilst the current relative stability of labour relations, even after Tiananmen, contributes towards the creation of a more favourable investment climate in China, the issue of exploitation in foreign-invested enterprises has provided ideological ammunition for the opponents within the leadership to the Open Policy. Although it has not been the main platform on which the leftist opposition has challenged the reformist leadership, it has nevertheless been one of the criticisms levelled against foreign-invested enterprises and in particular wholly owned foreign enterprises.

Moreover, as the role of the Party and trade unions in foreign-invested enterprises is in theory circumscribed compared to state-owned enterprises, opponents of reform and opening up could find support at lower levels amongst dissatisfied Party and trade union members as well as some members of the workforce. On the other hand, technocratic cadres as well as the managerial staff in foreign-invested enterprises are likely to provide the social base of support for the reformers in their efforts to change mangement practices, so pushing the Open Policy forwards.

Conclusion

The opening up of China has prompted changes in the policies concerning the allocation, employment and remuneration of labour. These in turn have affected the institutional fabric of the labour system as well as the relations between the state, labour and capital. The setting up of foreign-invested enterprises has brought into sharper relief the contradictory role of the trade unions as promoter of enterprise interests and defender of workers' interests. The labour policies adopted in foreign-invested enterprises have pre-empted labour reforms in the state-owned enterprises. Political, ideological and economic factors have, however, constrained the implementation of labour policies in foreign-invested enterprises.

The occasional spontaneous and voluntary eruption of worker resistance in foreign-invested enterprises as well as the sprouting of autonomous trade unions during the democracy protests of 1989 have further complicated the situation. As most foreign-invested enterprises up till now do not have trade unions, hence sharply circumscribing the formal avenues for the articulation of workers' interests, we can predict that these spontaneous, informal expressions of worker dissatisfaction as well as attempts individually to negotiate better deals will become more frequent. To the extent that official trade unions continue to lose their legitimacy, and official channels of conflict resolution become redundant, the prospect of new forms of voluntary worker association emerging becomes greater. The changing nature of state restrictions on autonomous activity will in turn condition their structure and character. Whether the autonomous trade unions of the 1989 Democracy Movement will provide the image of the future for these associations, we have yet to see.

Notes

1. White, 1987a, p. 130.
2. White, 1987c, p. 367.
3. ibid.
4. Efficient is used to mean both economically and socially.
5. As pointed out by White, 1987a, p. 132, the term 'labour market' is ideologically sensitive in China as in Marxist terminology 'labour market' is associated with capitalism. To avoid this, reform economists have preferred until recently to use the terms 'flexibility' and 'circulation'.
6. XH 30.9.1982 in FBIS 2.10.1982.
7. CD 8.6.1984.
8. In 1982 it was proposed at a Ministry of Labour forum that the public advertising of posts become generally permitted (see XH 11.1.1983 in SWB/FE/7237/BII/4).
9. RMRB 25.6.1982 in SWB/FE/0478/BII/3. In Hunan, 1505 unemployed youth sat an exam for the selection of 200 workers in a Zhuzhou textile mill (Hunan People's Broadcasting Station 23.9.1981 in SWB/FE/6854/BII/12).
10. Hunan People's Broadcasting Station 30.1.1983 in SWB/FE/7249/BII/9.
11. NCNA 23.11.1981 in SWB/FE/6891/BII/1.
12. Other factors might have been that most workers in SEZs were first-time employees. Moreover, by virtue of being a SEZ, it had some legitimacy for trying out new policies.
13. In May 1983 Guangzhou announced that all enterprises would implement

the floating wage system (see GZRB 2.5.1983 in SWB/FE/7331/BII/12).
For a discussion of the floating wage system, see BJ, GMRB 17.4.1983
in FBIS 28.4.1983 K5.

14. Guangdong People's Broadcasting Station 12.3.1983 in SWB/FE/7249/BII/19.
15. CD, 3.2.1983, p.1 in FBIS 3.2.1983.
16. XH 2.9.1986 in SWB/FE/8356/BII/6.
17. ibid.
18. XH, BJ 28.3.1991 in SWB/FE/W0173 3.4.1991.
19. LW, HK 2.3.1992 in SWB/FE/1332/B2/1 18.3.1992.
20. For example, by May 1983 Guangzhou had already decided to extend the
    contract system gradually to all staff and workers.
21. See interview with Liang Xiang, Mayor of Shenzhen in Guangdong, 6.6.1983
    in FBIS 8.6.1983. Moreover, the SEZs have frequently been deployed as
    laboratories for potential future domestic reforms, as, for example, the
    contract bidding system.
22. White, 1987c, p. 377.
23. HK, AFP 15.5.1991 in SWB/FE/1074 B2/3 17.5.1991.
24. ZGTX, HK 3.5.1991 in SWB/FE/W0179 15.5.1991 A/2.
25. RMRB 12.7.1991 in SWB/FE/1135/B2/4 27.7.1991.
26. HK, AFP 15.5.1991 in SWB/FE/1074 B2/3 17.5.1991/2.
27. HK, DGB 2.12.1991 in SWB/FE/1255 B2/4 14.12.1991.
28. Beijing People's Broadcasting Station, 11.2.1992 in SWB/FE/1303/B2/3
    13.2.1992; XH 24.4.1992 in SWB/FE/1370/B2/3 2.5.1992; HK, JJDB
    2.11.1992 in SWB/FE/1533/B2/2 9.11.1992.
29. White, 1987c, p. 377.
30. ibid., pp. 369−71.
31. ZGXWS 21.1.1983 in SWB/FE/7249/BII/8; BYT 10.2.1983, pp. 10−12
    in FBIS 25.2.1983.
32. White, 1987b, p. 120.
33. See Howell, 1992.
34. Foreign Languages Press, 1982, pp. 1−8.
35. NCNA 7.6.1982 in SWB/FE/7046/C1/2.
36. Interview, Labour Service Corporation (LSC) 1987.
37. Fujian: FERTC and China Council for the Promotion of International Trade,
    A New Look of Fujian (1985), p. 51.
38. This still had to be mediated through the respective labour personnel
    department, thus reflecting the continued predominance of the administrative
    labour allocation system.
39. XH 18.5.1988 in SWB/FE/W0029/A/6.
40. See GMRB 2.8.1986 in SWB/FE/8351/B2/3 and JJRB 18.4.1987 in
    SWB/FE/8569/B2/9.
41. Interview, LSC, Xiamen, April 1987.
42. ibid.
43. Interview, Xiamen SEZ, April 1987.
44. Interview, Xiamen SEZ, May 1987.
45. Interview, Xiamen SEZ, June 1987.
46. Interviews, Xiamen SEZ, May−July 1987.

47. See Walder, 1986a, p. 15.
48. Interview, Xiamen SEZ, June 1987.
49. Interview, Xiamen SEZ, May 1987.
50. Interview, Xiamen SEZ, LSC, 1987.
51. XH 18.5.1988 in SWB/FE/W0029/A/6.
52. GMRB, BJ 29.11.1991 in SWB/FE/1259/B2/7 19.12.1991.
53. Interview, Xiamen SEZ, 1991.
54. Interview, Xiamen SEZ, 1991.
55. ZGXWS, HK 23.7.1991 in SWB/FE/1134/B2/5 26.7.1991.
56. This company also enjoyed the right to promote, reward and dismiss any staff or worker (Guangdong 22.10.1981 in SWB/FE/W1162/B1).
57. Interview, Xiamen SEZ, 1987.
58. NCNA 7.6.1982 in SWB/FE/7046/C1/2.
59. Foreign Languages Press, 1982, pp. 22 and 225.
60. See note 37.
61. For examples of different wage systems in foreign-invested enterprises, see Shum and Sigel, 1986, pp. 201–26.
62. For a discussion of the differences between national and SEZ labour regulations, see Moser, 1985.
63. NFRB 11.6.1984 in FBIS 17.6.1984, p. 2.
64. Guangdong People's Broadcasting Station 11.10.1984 in FBIS 15.10.1984.
65. BYT 25.8.1985 pp. 10–12 in FBIS 12.9.1985. Shenzhen's experiments with contracting out or inviting bids for capital construction as well as the system of hiring cadres through elections was also being taken up in other parts of China.
66. State Statistical Bureau P.R. China (1988–91), 1990, p. 139.
67. GRRB 5.5.1991 in SWB/FE/1078 B2/6 22.5.1991.
68. Interview, Xiamen SEZ, Labour Service Corporation, 1987.
69. According to the *Almanac of Xiamen SEZ, 1986*, the annual number of staff and workers employed in foreign-invested enterprises in Xiamen SEZ 1985 was around 8000 (p. 405) whilst the average staff and workers employed in these enterprises came to almost 6000 (p. 406), suggesting turnover during the year.
70. See White, 1987a, p. 149.
71. Interview, Xiamen SEZ, Labour Service Corporation, 1987.
72. According to the foreign partner of the Sino-US joint venture Beijing Jeep Corporation, workers in Beijing required 88 hours to assemble one vehicle compared to 32 hours in Ohio, USA (see FEER 12.6.1986, p. 132). However, it is difficult to compare productivity levels across countries. This low productivity though might be related to low wages. According to interviews carried out by Walder, workers have responded to low wages, especially during the Cultural Revolution, by working slowly or doing only the minimum (see Walder, 1986, ch. 6).
73. In the new regulations the stipulation that wages in foreign-invested enterprises should be at least 120 per cent of those in comparable Chinese state-owned enterprises was continued so as to ensure minimum protection of workers' interests. The upper ceiling was removed.

74. Interview, LSC, Xiamen SEZ (May 1987).
75. Zhong Xingyang, 'We must pay attention to resolving the contradiction between two types of wages in Xiamen SEZ' in *Xiamen Tequ Diaoyan* (Xiamen SEZ Research) (in Chinese) (December 1985).
76. ibid.
77. See Hendryx, 1986.
78. ZGXWS, HK 9.3.1992 in SWB/FE/1335 B2/4 21.3.1992.
79. See Article 11 of 'Interim provisions for labour and wage management...' in Foreign Languages Press, 1982.
80. See Howell, 1992 on 'sinification' of foreign-invested enterprises.
81. Interview, Fuzhou, Fujian, July 1987.
82. In a Sino-foreign electronics joint venture in Xiamen SEZ, the level of wages for workers proposed by the foreign general manager was considered too high by the chairman of the board of directors. At the board meeting, the chairman apparently said, 'the general manager decides the level of wages with the approval of the Chairman'.
83. Interview, Xiamen SEZ, June 1987.
84. See FBIS 21.7.1980, pp. 130–4.
85. See Cohen and Harris, 1986, pp. 10–13; Chiang, 1983.
86. China's first Sino-foreign employees' exchange centre was set up in June 1992 in Beijing — see XH 17.6.1992 in SWB/FE/W0236/A/9 24.6.1992.
87. According to the regulations on SEZs in Guangdong, approved by the central government in August 1980, each SEZ in Guangdong is to have a Labour Service Corporation (see Foreign Languages Press, 1982, p. 198).
88. Interview, Xiamen SEZ, July 1987.
89. XH 13.6.1985 in FBIS 14.6.1985.
90. Interview, TUs, Xiamen SEZ and Fujian, July/August 1987; and Beijing, 1992.
91. HK, S, 27.4.1986, p. 5; and interview Xiamen SEZ, TU, 1987.
92. See Chu Baotai, 1986, p. 80 for a similar attitude:
    A foreign investor need not worry about the union being unproductive towards the management or the Chinese employees being insubordinate to the foreign managers. Experience proves that with the guidance of their trade unions, the Chinese staff and workers in joint ventures are highly conscientious, disciplined and industrious employees working for the interest of the venture.
93. Nevertheless, the Party may continue to operate in the enterprises through informal mechanisms — see Howell, 1992.
94. Interview, Xiamen SEZ, 1988.
95. XH 14.4.1987 in SWB/FE/8545/B2/11.
96. Interview, Xiamen Municipal TU, April 1987.
97. CD 30.7.1990.
98. Interview, Xiamen Municipal TU, April 1987.
99. XH 14.6.1985 and XH 13.6.1985 in FBIS 14.6.1985. See also XH 4.9.1991 in SWB/FE/1172/B2/5 9.9.1991 — a TU survey showed that only 20 per cent of Beijing's workers' congresses were healthy.
100. In June 1983 directors and managers of factories and enterprises in Shenzhen

SEZ were required to be elected. It is not clear whether this referred also to foreign-invested enterprises; however, this seems unlikely. See NFRB 16.6.1983, p. 1 in FBIS 21.6.1983.

101. HK, S 27.4.1986.
102. HK, MB 22.6.1985 in SWB/FE/7986/BII/5; XH 13.8.1985 in FBIS 15.8.1985 pp. 6—8.
103. FJRB 11.1.1985, p. 3.
104. Interview, Xiamen SEZ, TU, 1987.
105. ASWJ 14.6.1985.
106. XH, BJ 14.6.1985 and XH 13.6.1985 in FBIS 14.6.1985; there is some evidence that the contractual conditions of workers in wholly owned foreign enterprises have been less favourable than in joint ventures — see Shudang (ed.) 1984, *Investigation into Shenzhen SEZ and Economic Development Zone* (Nankai University Publishing House: Tianjin), p. 69.
107. Moreover, in 1986 the Shenzhen Municipal Federation of TU received 976 complaints from workers, of which 791 were successfully resolved. Strikes have occurred over issues such as wage increases, behaviour of foremen, holidays and overtime (see Leung Wing-Yue, 1988, pp. 155—71).
108. XH, BJ 14.4.1987.
109. Gongren Ribao 4.3.1987 in SWB/FE/8520/B2/4.
110. Interview, Xiamen SEZ, TU, June 1987.
111. Lee Lai To, 1986.
112. ibid., p. 148. At the Ninth Trade Union Congress the importance of improving production relations in enterprises was underlined.
113. See Harper, 1969. pp. 104—6.
114. RMRB 28.6.1991 in SWB/FE/1121 B2/1 11.7.1991.
115. ibid.
116. 21.3.1992 B2/4.
117. *Asian Labour Update*, October 1991, p. 13 (Asia Labour Monitor Resources Centre).
118. Clarke and Fairbrother in *Capital and Class*, 1993, pp. 7—18.
119. *Asian Labour Update*, April 1992, p. 11 (Asia Labour Monitor Resources Centre).
120. HK, MB 22.6.1985 in SWB/FE/7986/BII/5; XH 13.8.1985 in FBIS 15.8.1985, pp. 6—8.
121. Zou Erkang, 1985—6, p. 81.
122. See Macridis, 1983, for a discussion of negative understanding of ideology as used by Marx.
123. ZGXWS, HK 9.3.1992 in SWB/FE/1335 B2/4 21.3.1992.
124. Walder, 1986.
125. Guangdong Radio 18.6.1991 SWB/FE/1107 B2/4 25.6.1991.
126. Interviews, Xiamen 1987—8.
127. ZGXWS, HK 29.5.1992 in SWB/FE/1406 B2/3 13.6.1992; XWB, HK 16.4.1992 in SWB/FE/1360 B2/5 21.4.1992.

Conclusion

Since the Third Plenum in 1978 China's Open Policy has traversed six cycles in its development. During cyclical upswings new ideas are generated, policies are established and the pace of implementation gathers speed. In cyclical downswings the proposal of new ideas is inhibited, the establishment of new policies stalled and the pace of implementation slows down. With each cycle the Open Policy spins its web deeper and further.

The incremental accretion of these cycles creates a spiral pattern of development. The policy of opening up has not proceeded in textbook, linear fashion with neatly defined stages of policy generation and implementation. Nor has it evolved in repetitive cycles of advance and retreat. On the contrary each cycle has integrated China more closely into the international economy and made retreat to a zero position increasingly difficult.

The spiral course of the Open Policy has both a political and an economic logic. From our analysis of the Open Policy over more than a decade we found that a combination of interests has shaped its evolutionary course. As well as the perennial struggle within the top echelons of the party, lower-level institutional, socio-economic and regional interests have also crucially influenced the content, scope and direction of the Open Policy and in particular its pace of implementation. Pressure from particular regional governments to extend the scope of the policy as well as demands from foreign capital for greater concessions have, for example, fed into the process of policy generation. Understanding how policy 'is made' in China requires the analyst to look beyond the confines of the policy elite, to the policy implementers and recipients. The most salient economic factor has been the tension between the reformers' goals of microlevel dynamism and macrolevel stability. Whilst decentralisation of some authority over foreign economic relations stimulates lower-level initiative, it also leads to economic imbalances. Recentralisation in turn reimposes macroeconomic control but at the same time dampens microeconomic dynamism. This economic dilemma also has a political dimension. The decentralisation of some authority over foreign economic relations shifts resources and power from central government and ministries to provincial and municipal authorities, branches of ministries and production enterprises, especially in the coastal areas. Growing economic complexity breeds a new array of socioeconomic interests. Reluctant to cede their newly acquired privileges, the beneficiaries of the Open Policy hamper attempts to restore macroeconomic balance. The process of opening up becomes highly politicised. The tensions between potential and/or actual beneficiaries and losers of the policy not only contribute towards these periodic policy fluctuations but also redefine the political and economic context in which the Open Policy evolves.

The opening up of Xiamen SEZ in Fujian province has followed a similar spiral trajectory to the national level. Whilst political and economic events at the national level, such as the spiritual pollution campaign and the overheating of the economy in mid-1985 have affected the course of the Open Policy in Xiamen, specific regional factors have also played a role. Of particular relevance is the positive impact of Overseas Chinese connections on the acceptability of the Open Policy. Although there has been opposition to the Open Policy from particular institutions, sectors of the economy and socio-economic groups, which have perceived themselves as actual or potential losers under the policy, there has nevertheless been considerable popular support for opening up. This is in part because the extent of Overseas Chinese contacts has both heightened awareness of the potential benefits of opening up and contributed towards a more 'outward-oriented' mentality. The Taiwanese factor has since the late 1980s become increasingly relevant, but until direct relations are established the full import of this will not be felt.

Popular support for the Open Policy has in turn encouraged provincial leaders to interpret national policies concerning the province and SEZ more broadly, so extending the geographical and social web of beneficiaries. This has likewise fuelled impulses by other cities and counties in the province to push ahead with opening up. This support from below, which has broadened as the policy has become more deeply rooted, has contributed significantly towards the expansion of the policy. As a result the strength and influence of the opposition has waned and the possibility of retrenchment has become increasingly remote.

It would be unwise to make too many generalisations on the basis of one case study, as China is a large country with diverse peoples, traditions and local histories. Nevertheless, the forward movement of the Open Policy spiral suggests that the Open Policy has been a popular policy, both nationally and in Fujian province. Moreover, it might be argued that its very popularity has contributed to the periodic economic imbalances as regional, individual and departmental interests have outpaced national priorities. With the deepening of external economic relations, the prospect of a return to the isolationist approach becomes increasingly unlikely, in part because of the potential socio-political consequences, particularly from the actual and expectant beneficiaries of the policy, and in part because of the influence of external actors.

The process of opening up to the international economy has also altered the politico-economic context within which policy is made. Changes in the external economy have prompted changes in other parts of the domestic politico-institutional and economic fabric. We observed this snowball effect in changes in the state and labour policy and institutions.

Along with the reforms the Open Policy has contributed towards a redefinition of the state, in its administrative, coercive and even political capacity. The overall direction is towards the emergence of a 'market-facilitating state', compatible with the idea of a 'socialist market economy' which was sanctioned at the Fourteenth Party Congress. In this process of transition the state has assumed a 'polymorphic' character, whereby the 'old-style', command Leninist institutions coexist with new state forms established in the context of reform and opening up. At the same time the rapid pace of economic change in post-Mao China has left a temporary institutional vacuum. This process of redefinition in turn affects the course of the Open Policy. To the extent that the market-facilitating state gains a foothold, a more favourable politico-institutional context for opening up to the capitalist world economy is created.

The emergence of a market-facilitating state has ramifications not only for the future course of the Open Policy but also for the relation between the state and society. Although the expansion of the legal system has chiefly been in response to the domestic economic reforms, particularly the contract responsibility system, and the demands of foreign companies, there has also been pressure from within the leadership for a general strengthening of the legal system in the realm of polity. Peng Zhen, in particular, has sought to make Party policy legally binding. Thus the Party and government could in the future be expected to be accountable in law for their activities. Moreover, as individual economic actors such as private entrepreneurs seek redress through the law, there is a strengthening of the sense of both 'individual' and 'economic' rights. This might lead to a sharper definition of the notion of citizenship in China. Discussions in intellectual circles about issues such as 'human rights' already portend a clearer legal delineation between the state and citizen.

Opening up and reform have likewise engendered changes in the associational realm of civil society. The rise of new socio-economic groups such as traders, private entrepreneurs and factory managers in foreign enterprises has fostered new interests and needs which the state is increasingly unable to meet. These groups have begun to set up new economic associations to further their own interests in the market and *vis-à-vis* the state. The sprouting of numerous voluntary professional, social and economic associations provide new channels of interest articulation separate from the Party.

Following the political crisis of Tiananmen the state has responded by exerting control over existing associations: banning undesirable ones, requiring others to register and regularising their activities. It has also initiated new associations to mediate between market and enterprise. To the extent that the socio-economic landscape becomes increasingly complex, the state will come under pressure to alter existing channels of interest expression and create new ones. Given that institutional change tends to lag behind economic change, the expanding institutional vacuum will frustrate the articulation of new interests, sowing the seeds of further unrest.

Whilst reformers have been increasingly willing to reform the state administration, they have been less eager to tamper with the political system. Although Zhao Ziyang tried to push political reform, the Tiananmen crisis undermined any attempts to alter the political fabric. However, the reformers realised that the legitimacy of the Party had weakened considerably, even before the Tiananmen débâcle. So the reformers have tried to address some of the issues raised by pro-democracy demonstrators. They have tried to 'clean up' the image of the Party and state administration, recreate the image of the Party, incorporate the language of the opposition into their own rhetoric and indeed incorporate new emerging interests. At the same time, the coercive apparatus of the state has come down firmly on any opposition, softening at times in response to international pressure. As is apparent from the Fourteenth Party Congress, the Party does not intend any major reform of the political structure, particularly if it is not at the helm.

The process of opening up has also prompted changes in labour policies, institutions and relations. The overall direction of the new policies has been towards the development of a labour market. Foreign-invested enterprises in China have offered labour in state-owned enterprises the 'image of their own future'. The reformist leadership has had to dilute certain socialist principles and accept some degree of exploitation of the workforce, inequality and job insecurity as an inevitable trade-off for more rapid modernisation. The rhetoric of the 'worker and peasant state' has become increasingly empty.

With the endorsement of enterprise reform at the Fourteenth Party Congress we can expect more attempts to close down loss-making state-owned enterprises, tighter management practices and greater labour mobility. This in turn will favour the realisation of the autonomy granted to foreign-invested enterprises in labour management. At the same time, however, without a rapid development of a social security system, unemployment will lead to serious social problems and unrest. Any further increase in China's floating population will put enormous pressure on China's cities.

These changes in labour policy have also prompted readjustments in the institutional fabric of the labour system. The introduction of foreign direct investment has brought into sharp relief the increasingly contradictory role of the trade union as dual defender of the interests of production and the workforce. The trade unions, where they exist in foreign-invested enterprises, have responded in ambiguous ways to conflicts, either coming out in support of the workforce or defending the interests of foreign capital. To the extent that trade unions take on the interests of workers, we might predict a more conflictual role on the part of the unions than hitherto witnessed. The conspicuous absence of trade unions in many foreign-invested enterprises as well as the crushing of the new autonomous unions after 4 June portends, however, more frequent instances of voluntary, spontaneous worker action. However, when Hong Kong passes into the hands of China in 1997, the experience of trade unionists is likely to influence at least Guangdong and may keep open the possibility of organised worker action.

What then are the implications of these findings for the future development trajectory of China? The Fourteenth Party Congress was a major landmark as radical reformers committed China to 100 years of opening up and reform. However, much will depend on the fates of the gerontocratic elite and the issue of succession. Should Deng Xiaoping depart before Chen Yun, conservatives will seize the opportunity to promote a cautious approach to the economy, with the bird safely in the cage. However, should Deng survive Chen Yun, we can expect a quicker pace of reform and opening up. Deng will continue to groom a younger generation of reformers to ensure the realisation of a socialist market economy.

Opening up and reform have created a much more complex economy than existed pre-1978. Forms of ownership have diversified, channels of circulation have multiplied and economic decision-making has been diffused to lower levels. The Fourteenth Party Congress promised a continuation of this trend. The leaders in Beijing have to heed a new and larger net of interests bred by these dramatic policy changes. The Open Policy has enjoyed considerable support from below. Intellectuals have appreciated the opportunities for overseas study, academic exchange and exposure to new ideas. Foreign-invested enterprises and trade companies have provided avenues of advancement outside the state. Sections of the army have welcomed the opportunity to modernise military hardware and strengthen China's combat capacity. The new rural workers of the township enterprises have begun to gain experience in trading with the external market. City dwellers have appreciated the choice of consumer goods, even if their purses do not stretch so far. China's urban youth have begun to identify with the symbols of global capitalism, such as jeans, disco music and karaoke. The inland areas of China aspire towards the growing prosperity of the 'gold coast'. Reform and opening up have raised expectations. Turning the clock back is not a politically feasible option.

However, the path of reform and opening up will not be smooth. Growing socio-economic, institutional and regional inequalities will fuel discontent. The scramble to 'get rich quick' will leave those with less resources in terms of money, initiative, connections, way behind on the developmental ladder. Privatisation, marketisation and increased external links are breeding a new social group in China, akin to the comprador bourgeoisie of pre-liberation days. As the gap between 'rich' and 'poor' widens, China will increasingly resemble other Third World countries. Continuing economic imbalances will also frustrate the expectations of expectant beneficiaries. The popularity of the Open Policy not only pushes the policy forwards but also dilutes the influence of the opposition, making the possibility of retrenchment increasingly remote.

Rising discontent will find expression in increasing crime, social disorder and deviance. Dissatisfaction amongst the actual and expectant losers under reform and opening up could put pressure on the central government to extend the scope of the Open Policy, pushing it further and faster forwards. But this dissatisfaction may also become expressed in opposition to the Open Policy and reform, which will serve to constrain the pace of opening up. The crushing of the democracy movement in the summer of 1989 and the subsequent repression will stifle organised opposition in the near future. It is likely therefore that the Open Policy will continue to evolve in a spiral fashion, though the constituencies of support and opposition may alter as the Open Policy encounters and creates new problems.

The collapse of Eastern Europe and the disintegration of the Soviet Union have challenged both the credibility of socialist theory and practice as well as the legitimacy of national unity. As the economic base and ideological superstructure become increasingly out of joint, the reformers will have to struggle hard to find a new rhetoric to 'cement together' the increasingly complex and diverse social fabric. Failure to do so will undermine their own legitimacy to rule. As the tide of ethno-nationalism spills over into China's minority border areas, disintegration will pose an increasing threat to those at the wheel in Beijing. 'Splittism' and 'regionalism' will be the dominant worries of the government over the next decade.

China's future hinges not only on the interplay of domestic socio-political forces but also on the rapid shifts in the New World Order. The unification of Hong Kong in 1997 and Macao in 1999 will bolster the regional strength of the South, challenging the political centrality and power of Beijing. With direct links between Taiwan and China imminent, an end to the Asian 'cold war' will be in sight. China's efforts to secure its economic dominance in the Far East and Pacific promise a greater role in the politics of this region. As China's coastal economy becomes more closely intertwined with the international economy, foreign capital will be increasingly able to squeeze concessions and influence the course of opening up. With a large economy, a solid industrial base and a strong sense of history, China is unlikely to fall into a dependency trap. However, greater integration into the international economy will mean that Chinese leaders will be less immune to the voices from outside.

The relation between reform and opening up is also a crucial factor in the future course of the Open Policy. Since 1982 it has become increasingly clear that the pace and extent of opening up is contingent upon the degree, quality and success of reform. There is a mutual dialectic between reform and opening up. The design of a strategy for opening up should thus be formulated as an integral part of an overall package to reform the economy. Furthermore, this should involve a clear specification of the economic and political objectives of the policy as well as some analysis of the potential contradictions between these goals. At the policy level there is thus a need to formulate particular policies regarding foreign trade, foreign direct investment and foreign borrowing in conjunction with other domestic economic reforms.

Linked to this need for synchronisation between the Open Policy and domestic reform is the issue of the relation between economic and political liberalisation. The changes in the economic base due to the introduction of domestic and international market forces have highlighted the increasing redundancy of old-style Leninist economic and political institutions. This has led not only to the creation of new institutions and the adaptation of existing economic and political state bodies but also to the growth of voluntary, economic associations linked to particular professional or sectoral interests. In the long term this could imply greater plurality in the political arena. However, it would be unwise to draw too broad conclusions about an implicit deterministic relation between economic and political liberalisation, as the cases of Britain and Chile well show. Although this diversification of the associational landscape may not lead immediately to greater political pluralism, it nevertheless redefines the political context in which the Open Policy and reforms evolve.

China was one of the first so-called socialist countries to embark on a full-scale reform of its economy. It is now one of the few states with a declared Communist Party still at its helm. Its Communist Party, unlike those of the former Soviet Union and Eastern Europe, has retained political control whilst at the same time initiating radical economic change. The disintegration of the Soviet Union and the concomitant economic disorder suggests that radical economic change is best brought about with a stable and unified government. However, the Tiananmen episode also tells us that dramatic changes in the socio-economic base will find echoes in the political superstructure. Sooner or later political reform will come onto the agenda. Resisting this could be disastrous for the reformers. The current leadership would be wise to pre-empt political chaos by making concessions to these new interests, creating new channels for the expression and resolution of conflict and taking control over the process of political change. A failure to do so would rebound and threaten the success of economic reform itself.

Paradoxically, the process of transition from command planning to a market economy still requires a central role for the state. At the political level the state functions to manage new competing and conflicting interests. At the economic level the state steps in to regulate the potential anarchy of market forces. At the same time reform and opening up change the structure and very nature of the state itself.

Transition also requires ideological manoeuvring, a skill in which the Chinese Communist Party has shown itself to be weak. The ability to adapt ideology is crucial, both for the continuing legitimacy of the party as well as the need to 'cement together' an increasingly diverse and atomised socio-economic base. Disillusionment amongst the youth with the Party and socialism after both the Cultural Revolution and Tiananmen have left an ideological vacuum which the Party has been slow to fill. In the meantime the youth have turned towards music, dance, religion and materialism.

Appendix: Chronology of key events in Open Policy 1979−86

Cycle 1 − period of innovation: December 1978 to 1981

Dec. 1978   Cyclical upswing takes off. Shekou industrial zone established. Special export zones under discussion. Cutbacks in large-scale imports, especially in heavy industry. Processing/assembly and compensation trade promoted. Regional experiments in decentralisation of foreign trade in Beijing, Shanghai and Tianjin.

Feb. 1979   22 contracts with Japanese firms suspended.

March 1979   Baoan and Zhuhai become municipalities as preparation for establishment of SEZs. Fujian authorities express interest in establishing SEZ. Li Qiang, Minister of Foreign Trade, announces China will accept foreign loans.

April 1979   Deng Xiaoping endorses SEZ proposals.

July 1979   Location of four SEZs in Shenzhen, Zhuhai, Xiamen and Shantou announced. Law on Sino-foreign joint ventures promulgated. Export of labour permitted. Guangdong and Fujian provinces granted 'special privileges and flexible measures'. Gu Mu and Rong Yiren indicate possibility of setting up wholly owned foreign enterprises.

Sept. 1979   China accepted UN loan of US$ 15 million.

Nov. 1979   Shenzhen granted municipal status.

Dec. 1979   China receives aid loans from Belgium and Japan.
             Guangdong government draws up draft regulations for
             establishment of two SEZs.

April 1980   Eight ports opened on Yangtse River to foreign trade.
             China joins IMF and World Bank. Guangdong province
             officially uses term 'Special Economic Zone'.

Aug. 1980   National regulations also use term 'Special Economic
             Zone'.

Sept. 1980   First statute concerning SEZ in Guangdong issued.

Feb. 1981   Cyclical downswing sets in. Reimposition of central
             control over economy. Further project cancellations
             involving Japanese, German and US companies.

March 1981   Seven more cancellations involving Japanese and
             German investment announced. Import restrictions on
             luxury consumer goods introduced.

April 1981   New directives introduce central control over exports.

Aug. 1981   State Council convenes Anti-Smuggling Conference.
             SEZs come under closer central scrutiny.

Cycle 2 – pushing ahead but not too fast: early 1982 to mid-1983

Feb. 1982   Cyclical upswing takes off. Proposal discussed to grant
             11 provinces, cities and autonomous regions more auto-
             nomy regarding foreign economic relations.

March 1982   SEZs continue to be criticised.

July 1982   Imposition of customs duties on raw materials imported
             for export-processing and assembly. Restrictions imposed
             on rights of lower-level authorities to export.

Sept. 1982   Results of investigation into Shenzhen and Zhuhai pub-
             lished. Victory for reformers. SEZ to be model for reform.

Early 1983   Storm over SEZ abates somewhat.

Feb. 1983   Hu Yaobang visits Shenzhen SEZ.

March 1983   SEZ in Shanghai proposed (but not approved). Proposal
             to make Hainan a first-level government.

April 1983   Joint ventures in Shenzhen SEZ permitted to sell some
             of their products domestically. Indications that there may
             be a foreign trade deficit by the end of the year.

July 1983   Reimposition of central control over investment expendi-
             ture and technology imports.

Sept.1983   Duties on imported raw materials and components lifted.
             Wholly owned foreign enterprises in SEZs permitted to

set up enterprises on trial basis outside SEZs.

Oct. 1983   Spiritual pollution campaign launched. Some foreign investors withdraw their contracts.

Cycle 3 – striding ahead: 1984–6

Feb. 1984   Cyclical upswing takes off. Deng Xiaoping visits the SEZs and indicates his approval.

April 1984   State Council forum approves following proposals:
* Open Policy to be extended to 14 coastal cities and Hainan Island.
* Economic and technological development zones to be set up in some of these cities. These will focus on technology/knowledge-intensive industries and will enjoy more privileges than the coastal cities but less than the SEZs regarding foreign economic relations.
* Xiamen SEZ to be extended to cover whole of island.
* Relaxation of tax and marketing policies for foreign-invested enterprises.
* Discussions about possibility of Xiamen and Hainan becoming free ports.

July 1984   Shenzhen introduces economic management system reforms.

Aug. 1984   Decentralisation of foreign trade announced.

Sept. 1984   Decentralisation of foreign trade approved by State Council. Amount of foreign exchange kept by exporters increased.

Oct. 1984   Wuhan granted provincial status in economic management with limited privileges in foreign direct investment.

Jan. 1985   Proposal that Open Policy bed extended to Pearl River Delta, Yangtse River Delta, Liaoning and Jiaodong Peninsula. Proposal amended to 'three golden triangles' of Yangtse, Pearl and South Fujian River Deltas.

March 1985   Governor of Liaoning refers to likelihood of increasing trade with Soviet Union and Eastern Europe.

April 1985   Shenzhen criticised as aberration.

May 1985   Zhao Ziyang indicates China will open up further.

Mid-1985   Onset of cyclical downswing. Hainan scandal involving resale of 89 000 vehicles to inland areas revealed. Economic imbalances in foreign trade and foreign exchange reach peak. SEZs under renewed criticism. Deng Xiaoping comments that SEZ only an experiment.

July 1985	Reimposition of central control:

- Import duties on imported luxury consumer goods introduced.
- Recentralisation of foreign trade and foreign exchange management.
- Privileges of SEZs reduced.
- Mayor of Shenzhen, Li Xiang, replaced by Li Hao.
- 10 out of 14 coastal cities to be frozen. Shanghai, Tianjin, Dalian and Guangzhou to be main focus. Xiamen SEZ to adopt certain free-port policies.

Sept. 1985 Deng Xiaoping claims SEZs are successful experiment. Gu Mu suggests possible opening of Jiaodong and Liaodong Peninsulas and reveals plan to open coastal belt from north to south.

Dec. 1985 Meeting held by State Council to discuss future course of SEZs. SEZs claimed a success.

Jan. 1986 Renminbi devalued. Tight central control over foreign trade maintained but some reforms proposed such as 'separation of government from enterprise'. Ministry of Foreign Economic Relations and Trade requires foreign trade companies to register with it. Financial support for SEZs resumed. Regional allocation of foreign exchange reduced. Period of operation of joint ventures extended from 30 to 50 years. Discussion begins about relaxation of restrictions on wholly owned foreign enterprises and drafting of a wholly owned foreign enterprise law.

May 1986 Zheng Tuobin, Minister of Foreign Trade, announces possibility of further reforms in foreign trade and foreign exchange later in year.

Cycle 4 – moving ahead but not too fast: mid-1986 to 1987

Aug. 1986 Cyclical upswing takes off. State Council grants nine window institutions right to raise funds abroad. Zhao Ziyang reveals more concessions to foreign investors in pipeline.

Sept. 1986 Spiritual civilisation resolution issued.

Oct. 1986 State Council issues 22 Articles to promote FDI. Provincial governments issue similar regulations. Reforms in China's foreign exchange structure announced. Import restrictions on cars lifted in Hainan.

	Proposal to set up SEZ in Wuhan. Deng Xiaoping indicates Open Policy will continue into next century. Ji Chongwei proposes opening up of China to East Europe and Soviet Union.
Dec. 1986	Student demonstrations take place.
Jan. 1987	Cyclical downswing sets in. Anti-bourgeois liberalisation campaign launched. Tightening of central control over investment expenditure. Li Peng warns of project cancellations. Decentralisation of authority to approve WOFE to provincial authorities proposed. Some branches of Bank of China permitted to borrow abroad. Contract responsibility system introduced by MoFERT. System of import/export licences introduced.
March 1987	12 supplementary regulations for encouragement of FDI issued.
April 1987	Anti-bourgeois liberalisation campaign dies out.
May 1987	Rong Yiren of CITIC indicates Open Policy will be expanded.
Aug. 1987	Announced that Hainan Island will become a SEZ with more liberal policies than the other SEZs.

Cycle 5 — riding high, falling fast: 1987 to mid-1990

Oct. 1987	Thirteenth Party Congress takes place. Onset of new cycle. Further relaxations of restrictions on domestic sales of foreign-invested enterprises approved. Shenzhen to undertake more reforms.
Jan. 1988	Zhao Ziyang reveals coastal development strategy. Taiwanese investment takes off this year.
May 1988	State Council approves new regulations concerning hiring rights of joint ventures. Hainan granted more preferential policies.
June 1988	Foreign banks in the SEZs allowed to conduct business in Rmb.
July 1988	New regulations issued granting special privileges to Taiwanese investors. Shenzhen sets up bonded industrial zone. MoFERT announces new regulations decentralising foreign trade. New regulations restricting joint venture domestic sales introduced. Signs already of problems in the economy.
Sept. 1988	Shenzhen Party Secretary warns about abuse of power amongst Party and state cadres.

Oct. 1988	Preferential foreign exchange retention rates withdrawn from SEZs. Rectification of domestic economy begins. Article criticising Zhao's coastal development strategy published.
Dec. 1988	Tian Jiyun affirms continuity of Open Policy and calls for more foreign direct investment, especially wholly owned foreign enterprises.
Feb. 1989	Zhao visits Shenzhen to encourage local officials.
April 1989	Hu Yaobang dies. Students demonstrate.
May 1989	Student demonstrations spread all over China, calling for democracy, end to corruption and inflation. Factory and clerical workers join in.
4 June 1989	Tiananmen massacre results in international sanctions. Zhao Ziyang put under house arrest, democracy activists imprisoned.
July 1989	Propaganda Department launches anti-bourgeois liberalisation campaign.
Autumn 1989	Growth in foreign direct investment seriously affected.
Nov. 1989	Ministry of Foreign Economic Relations proposes increasing exports and further rectifying foreign trade companies.
Jan. 1990	Improvements in legislative framework made to attract foreign investment. State Council announces 'all-round open strategy' aimed at diversification of foreign trade and investment. China diversifies trade relations throughout year.
April 1990	Li Peng visits Shanghai.
June 1990	Yao Yilin announces Pudong, Shanghai to be focus of Open Policy. Economic situation beginning to improve. China has trade surplus and inflation is down.

Cycle 6 – on track again: mid-1990 to 1992

July 1990	Economy continues to improve. Taiwanese government issues list of products suitable for investment in China.
Sept. 1990	Central work conference declares satisfaction with rectification. Provincial leaders protest at attempts to recentralise outlined in eigth five-year plan.
Nov. 1990	James Baker invites Qian Qichen to the USA.
Dec. 1990	China has first trade surplus since 1984. Ten-year development programme promises expansion of Open Policy to inland border areas and further restructuring of foreign trade system. Heilongjiang opens SEZ.

Feb. 1991	Guangxi sets up Overseas Chinese investment zone. 11 foreign trade ports open on Mongolian, former Soviet and Laos borders. Mao craze sweeping through parts of China.
March 1991	Hu Qili reappears at National People's Congress. Sino-Soviet economic cooperation protocol signed.
April 1991	State Council approves 26 high-tech zones. Zhu Rongji and Zou Jiahua become vice-premiers. Central leaders touring provinces in first quarter to reassure people about reform and opening up. Douglas Hurd, Britain's Foreign Secretary, visits China.
May 1991	Li Peng meets Gorbachev in Moscow.
June 1991	State Council approves plan to open up Yunnan border to trade with Vietnam.
Aug. 1991	Anti-Gorbachev coup. Struggle between hardline conservatives and more moderate reformers intensifies. Reformer Li Ruihuan under pressure to leave Propaganda Department.
Sept. 1991	Article appears on distinguishing between socialism and capitalism. Deng speaks out against too much emphasis on anti-peaceful evolution. British Prime Minister, John Major, visits China.
Oct. 1991	Li Peng calls for more reform and opening.
Nov. 1991	Sino-Vietnamese relations normalised. State expenditure still too much. Cuts in import tariffs announced. Regulations on country-of-origin of exports amended in line with international practice.
Jan. 1992	Chen Yun expounds his views at Central Advisory Commission. Struggle within central leadership intensifies in run-up to Fourteenth Party Congress. Tian Jiyun urges expanding markets in developing countries and Eastern Europe.
Jan./Feb. 1992	Deng Xiaoping makes historic trip to South; calls for more and faster opening up and reform; commits China to 100 years of reform and opening up.
Feb. 1992	USA lifts ban on high-tech exports to China. House of Representatives adopts bill on China's MFN status.
Mar. 1992	South Korea and China sign non-governmental trade agreement.
Mar./June 1992	Military trips to SEZs organised. Battle between conservative ideologues and radical economic reformers intensifies.
April 1992	Deng Xiaoping meets Chen Yun. Border gates along Sino-Vietnamese border open.

May 1992	Chen Yun endorses correctness of development of Pudong but continues to have doubts about SEZs.
June 1992	Jiang Zemin makes key speech to Central Party School calling for implementation of Deng's remarks. Central Document number 4 circulated calling for further expansion of Open Policy. MoFERT announces further measures to liberalise trade.
July 1992	MoFERT allows foreign investment in previously forbidden sectors such as insurance and finance.
Aug. 1992	South Korea and China normalise relations.
Sept. 1992	Shenzhen stock riots. Tarim oilfields opened to foreign investment.
Oct. 1992	Fourteenth Party Congress meets; formally sanctions idea of 'socialist market economy'; calls for more and faster reform and opening up. Victory for radical economic reformers. No major political reform promised.

Bibliography

Primary sources

Official publications

Almanac of Xiamen SEZ Editorial Board (1984), *Almanac of Xiamen SEZ, 1984* (China Statistics Publishing House: Xiamen).

Almanac of Xiamen SEZ Editorial Board (1986), *Almanac of Xiamen SEZ, 1986* (China Statistics Publishing House: Xiamen).

Foreign Economy and Trade Yearbook Editorial Board (1991), *Foreign Economy and Trade Yearbook, 1991* (China Statistics Publishing House: Beijing).

Foreign Languages Press (1982), *China's Foreign Economic Legislation*, vol.1 (Foreign Languages Press: Beijing).

Fujian Foreign Economic Relations and Trade Commission and CCPIT Fujian Sub-Council (1985), *A New Look of Fujian* (Fujian Foreign Economic Relations and Trade Publishing House: Fuzhou).

Fujian Foreign Trade Centre (1985), *Fujian Foreign Trade* (Fujian Foreign Trade Centre: Fuzhou).

Fujian Statistics Bureau (1989, 1990, 1991), *Fujian Statistical Yearbook, 1989, 1990, 1991* (China Statistics Publishing House: Fuzhou).

Fujian Survey Department, Fujian Province Civil Affairs Department (1983), *Volume of Maps of Fujian Province* (Fujian Province Maps Publishing House: Fuzhou) (in Chinese).

State Statistics Bureau P.R. China (1988—91), *Statistical Yearbook of China, 1987, 1988, 1989, 1990* (Longman: Hong Kong).

Xiamen, Longxi Jinjiang Statistics Bureaux (1985), *South Fujian Golden Triangle and Xiamen, Zhangzhou and Quanzhou Development Zones, Outline of Social Economy* (China Statistics Publishing: Xiamen) August (in Chinese).

Xiamen City Statistics Bureau (1989), *Xiamen's Foreign Economy Statistics Yearbook* (China Statistics Publishing House: Xiamen) (in Chinese).

Xiamen City Statistics Bureau (1990a), *Collection of Statistical Material on the Open Coastal Cities, SEZs, Unified Planned Towns 1989* (China Statistics Publishing House: Xiamen), May (in Chinese).

Xiamen City Statistics Bureau (1990b), *Xiamen Statistical Yearbook 1989 and 1990* (Xiamen Statistics Publishing House: Xiamen) (in Chinese).

Xiamen City Statistics Bureau (1991), *Collection of Statistical Material on the Open Coastal Cities, SEZs, Unified Planned Towns 1990* (China Statistics Publishing House: Xiamen), May (in Chinese).

Xiamen, Fuzhou and Quanzhou City Statistical Departments (1990), *South Fujian Golden Triangle: General Survey of Social Economy* (China Statistics Publishing House: Xiamen), September (in Chinese).

Xiamen Municipal Committee Policy Research Office and Xiamen City Economic and Trade Commission (1989), *Manual for Use in Foreign Economic Work in Xiamen SEZ* (Minjiang Publishing House: Xiamen) (in Chinese).

Newspapers and periodicals

Asian Labour Update
Asian Wall Street Journal
Beijing Guoji Maoyi Wenti
Beijing Jingji Guanli
Beijing Review
China Business Review
China Daily
China's Foreign Trade
China Trader
Far Eastern Economic Review
Financial Times
The Guardian
Fujian Jingji
Fujian Waimao Jingji
Fujian Luntan
Fujian Ribao
Guangdong Nanfang Jingji
Hong Kong Macao Economic Digest (in Chinese)
Hong Kong South China Morning Post
Hong Kong Standard
New China News Analysis
Nanfang Ribao
The Observer
Shanghai Shehui Kexue
Shenghuo Chuangzao
Sino-British Trade Review
The Times (London)
Xiamen Ribao
Xiamen Tequ Diaoyan
Agence France Presse
China News Agency

Secondary sources

Auster, E.R. (1987), 'International corporate linkages: dynamic forms in changing environments' in *Columbia Journal of Business*, vol. XXII, no. 2, Summer, pp. 3–6.

Bachmann, D. (1986), 'Differing visions of China's post-Mao economy: the ideas of Chen Yun, Deng Xiaoping and Zhao Ziyang' in *Asian Survey*, vol. XXIV, no.3, March.

Bachmann, D. and Yang, D.L. (1991), *Yan Jiaqi and China's Struggle for Democracy* (M.E. Sharpe: New York).

Barnett, A.D. (1981), *China's Economy in Global Perspective* (The Brookings Institution: Washington, DC).

Barnett, A.D. (1985), *The Making of Foreign Policy in China* (Westview Press: Boulder).

Barnett, A.D. (1992), 'Will China follow the USSR?' in *China Business Review*, vol. 19, no. 2, March-April.

Bauer, E. (1986), *China Takes Off — Technology Transfer and Modernisation* (University of Washington Press: Seattle).

Blecher, M. (1991), 'Developmental state, enterpreneurial state: the political economy of socialist reform in Xinji muncipality and Guanghan county', in White, G.W. (ed.), *The Chinese State in the era of Economic Reform* (Macmillan: London), pp. 265–94.

Breslin, S. (1990), 'The foreign policy bureau' in Segal, G., *Chinese Politics and Foreign Policy Reform* (Kegan Paul International: London).

Brown, D.G. (1986), *Partnership with China: Sino-foreign joint ventures in historical perspective* (Oxford University Press: Oxford).

Bucknall, K. (1989), *China and the Open Door Policy* (Allen & Unwin: London).

Burns, J.P. (1989), 'China's governance: political reform in a turbulent environment' in *China Quarterly*, no. 119, September, pp. 481–518.

Cannon, T. (1988), 'Opening up to the outside world' in Benewick, R. and Wingrove, P., *Reforming the Revolution: China in transition* (Macmillan: London).

Chamberlain, H.B. (1987), 'Party—management relations in Chinese industries: some political dimensions of economic reform' in *China Quarterly*, no. 112, December, pp. 631–61.

Chan, T., E.K.Y. Chen and S. Chin (1986), 'China's special economic zones: ideology, policy and practice' in Jao, Y.C. and Leung, C.K., *China's SEZs: Policies, problems and prospects* (Oxford University Press: Oxford).

Chang, C.Y. (1986), 'Bureaucracy and modernisation: a case study of the special economic zone in China' in Jao, Y.C. and Leung, C.K., *China's SEZs: Policies, problems and prospects* (Oxford University Press: Oxford).

Chen Jilin (1984), *Fujian's Economic Geography* (Fujian Science and Technology Publishing House: Fuzhou) (in Chinese).

Chen Jingcheng (1985), 'Problems in technology absorption' in *Fujian Luntan*, 5 July 1985, pp. 13–16 (in Chinese):

Chen Nai-Ruenn (1986), *Foreign Investment in China: Current trends* (US Dept. of Commerce: Washington, DC), March.

Cheng Chu-yuan (1990), *Behind the Tiananmen Massacre* (Westview Press: Boulder).

Cheng, Y.K. (1978), *Foreign Trade and Industrial Development of China* (Greenwood Publications: Westport).

Chiang, J. (1983), 'What works and what doesn't' in *China Business Review*, Sept./Oct., pp. 26–9.

Child, J. (1987), 'Enterprise reform in China — progress and problems' in Warner, M. (ed.), *Management Reforms in China* (Frances Pinter: London).

Chu Baotai (1986), *Foreign Investment in China: Questions and answers* (Foreign Languages Press: Beijing).

Chu, D. (1985), 'The Trends and Patterns of Foreign Direct Investment in China', *Working Paper*, no. 2 (Centre for Contemporary Asian Studies, University of Hong Kong), October.

Chu, D.K.Y. (1986), 'The special economic zones and the problem of territorial containment' in Jao, Y.C. and Leung, C.K., *China's SEZs: Policies, Problems and Prospects* (Oxford University Press: Oxford), p. 24.

Clarke, C.M. (1981), 'Leadership divisions' in *China Business Review*, March/April, pp. 43—6.

Clarke, C.M. (1983), 'The shakeup moves down', *China Business Review*, Sept./Oct.

Clarke, S. and Fairbrother, P. (1993), 'The Workers' Movement in Russia' in *Capital and Class*, no. 49, Spring, pp. 7—18.

Clay, E.J. (1984), *Room for Manoeuvre: An exploration of public policy in agriculture and rural development*, Heinemann Studies in Development and Society (Heinemann: London).

Cohen, J.A. (1988), 'An American perspective on China's legislative problems' in *China Business Review*, March/April, pp. 6—8.

Cohen, J.A. and Harris, C.H. (1986), 'Equal pay for equal work' in *China Business Review*, Jan./Feb.

Cowan, C.D. (1964), *The Economic Development of China and Japan* (Allen & Unwin: London).

Crane, G. (1990), *The Political Economy of China's SEZs* (M.E. Sharpe: New York).

Daniels, J.D., Krug, J. and Nigh, D. (1985), 'US joint ventures in China: motivation and management of political risk' in *California Management Review*, vol. XXVII, no. 4, Summer, pp. 46—58.

de Keijzer, A.J. (1977), 'Sino-European trade: an overview' in *Contemporary China*, vol. 1, no. 5, February.

Denny, D.L. (1987), 'Provincial trade patterns' in *China Business Review*, Sept./Oct., pp. 18—22.

Denny, D.L. and Suris, F.M. (1977), 'China's foreign financial liabilities' in *China Business Review*, March/April.

Dernberger, R.F. (1975), 'The role of the foreigner in China's economic development: 1840—1949' in Perkins, D., *China's Modern Economy in Historical Perspective* (Stanford University Press: Stanford), pp. 19—49.

Dittmer, L. (1990), 'Patterns of elite strife and succession in Chinese politics' in *China Quarterly*, no. 123, September, pp. 405—30.

Eckstein, A. (1966), *Communist China's Economic Growth and Foreign Trade* (McGraw-Hill: New York).

Erbaugh, M. and Kraus, R. (1990), 'The democracy movement in Fujian and its aftermath' in *Australian Journal of Chinese Affairs* (23), January, pp. 145—60.

Falkenheim, V. (1986), 'Fujian's open door experiment' in *China Business Review*, Jan./June, pp. 38—42.

Ferdinand, P. (1990), 'Regionalism' in Segal, G., *Chinese Politics and Foreign Policy Reform* (Kegan Paul International: London).

Fitzgerald, E.V.K. (1985), 'The problem of balance in the peripheral socialist economy: a conceptual note' in *World Development* vol. 13, no. 1.

Gold, T.B. (1990), 'The resurgence of civil society in China' in *Journal of Democracy*, vol.1, no.1, Winter.

Goldenberg, S. (1988), *Hands across the Ocean: Managing JVs with a spotlight on China and Japan* (Harvard Business School Press, Cambridge, MA).
Gomes-Casseres, B. (1987), 'JV instability. Is it a problem?' in *Columbia Journal of World Business*, vol. XXII, no. 2, Summer, pp. 71−101.
Goodman, D.S. (1984), *Groups and Politics in the P.R. China* (University College Cardiff Press: Cardiff).
Goodman, D.S. (1989), *China's Regional Development* (London RIIA/Routledge: London).
Gu Shudang (ed.) (1984), *Investigation into Shenzhen SEZ and Research on Economic Development Zones* (Nankai University Publishing House: Tianjin) (in Chinese).
Guo Zhemin, Zhong Xingxiang, Xu Jinshui and Zhuang Zhijie (eds) (1986), *Outline of the SEZs* (Fujian Educational Publishing House: Fuzhou), May (in Chinese).
Hajime, H. (1976), 'Trends in Beijing's foreign trade' in *Issues and Studies*, June, pp. 37−78.
Han Minzhu (1990), *Cries for Democracy* (Princeton University Press: Princeton).
Harding, H. (1984), 'Competing models of the Chinese communist policy process: toward a sorting and evaluation' in *Issues and Studies*, vol. XX, no. 2, February.
Harding, H. (1987), *China's Second Revolution Reform After Mao* (The Brookings Institution: Washington, DC).
Harper, P. (1969), 'The Party and the unions in communist China' in *China Quarterly*, no. 37, Jan./March, pp. 104−12.
He Baogang (1992), 'Democratisation: anti-democratic and democratic elements in the political culture of China' in *Australian Journal of Political Science*, vol. 27, pp. 1−13.
Hendryx, S.R. (1986), 'Implementation of a technology transfer JV in the P.R. China: a management perspective' in the *Columbia Journal of World Business*, Spring, pp. 57−66.
Henley, J. and Nyaw, M.K. (1986), 'Introducing market forces into managerial decision-making in Chinese industrial enterprises' in *Journal of Management Studies*, vol. 23, no. 6, November, pp. 635−56.
Henley, J. and Nyaw, M.K. (1988), 'The system of management and performance of joint ventures in China: some evidence from Shenzhen special economic zone' in *Working Paper Series*, 88/15 (University of Edinburgh: Edinburgh).
Holmes, L. (1986), *Politics in the Communist World* (Clarendon Press: Oxford).
Horsley, J.P. (1985), 'The regulation of China's foreign trade' in Moser, M.J., *Foreign Trade, Investment and the Law in the PRC* (Oxford University Press: Oxford), pp. 6−35.
Horsley, J.P. (1988), 'The Chinese workforce' in *China Business Review*, May−June, pp. 50−5.
Hou, C.M. (1965), *Foreign Investment and Economic Development in China: 1840−1937* (Harvard University Press: Cambridge, MA).
Howe, C. (1978), *China's Economy — A Basic Guide'* (Basic Books: New York).
Howell, J. (1989), 'The political dynamics of China's open policy', D. Phil thesis, Sussex University, May.
Howell, J. (1990), 'The impact of China's open policy on labour' in *Labour, Capital and Society*, November, pp. 288−324.
Howell, J. (1991), 'The impact of the open door policy on the Chinese state' in White, G.W. (ed.), *The Chinese State in the Era of Economic Reform* (Macmillan: London) pp. 119−46.
Howell, J. (1992), 'The myth of autonomy: the foreign enterprise in China' ch. 7 in Smith, C. and Thompson, P., *Labour in Transition: The labour process in Eastern Europe and China* (Routledge: London).

Huang Fangyi (1987), 'China's introduction of foreign technology and external trade' in *Asian Survey*, vol. XXVII, no. 5, May, pp. 577—94.

Hussein, A. (1983), 'Economic reforms in Eastern Europe and their relevance to China' in Feuchtwang, S. and Hussein, A. (eds), *The Chinese Economic Reforms* (Croom Helm: London), pp. 91—120.

Jao, Y.C. and Leung, C.K. (1986), *China's Special Economic Zones: Policies, problems and prospects'* (Oxford University Press: Oxford).

Jencks, H.W. (1991), 'Civil—Military relations in China: Tiananmen and after' in *Problems of Communism*, May—June.

Kamm, J. (1989), 'Reforming foreign trade' in Vogel, E.F., *One Step Ahead in China: Guangdong under reform* (Harvard University Press: Cambridge, MA).

Keane, J. (1988), *Civil Society and the State: New European perspectives* (Verso: London).

Kelly, D. and He Baogang (1992), 'Emergent civil society and the intellectuals in China' ch. 3 in Miller, R. (ed.), *The Development of Civil Society in Communist Systems* (Allen & Unwin: London).

Khan, Z.S. (1991), *Patterns of Foreign Direct Investment* in China World Bank Discussion Papers, no. 130, (World Bank: Washington, DC), September.

King, F.H.H. (1969), *A Concise Economic History of Modern China: 1840—1961* (Praeger: New York).

Kirkby, R. and Cannon, T. (1988), *Regions for Development: Policies for all eventualities* (Unpublished paper), May.

Kleinberg, R. (1990), *China's Opening to the Outside World: Experiment in foreign capital* (Westview Press: Boulder).

Kokubun, R. (1986), 'The politics of foreign economic policy-making in China: the case of plant cancellations with Japan' in *China Quarterly*, no. 105, March, pp. 155—69.

Kraus, W. (1985), 'Joint venture-Erfahrungen in und mit der VR China' in *Asien*, no. 16, July, pp. 5—31.

Laaksonen, O. (1988), *Management in China During and After Mao* (Walter de Gruyter: New York).

Ladany, L. (1988), *The Communist Party of China and Marxism 1921—1985: A self-portrait* (C. Hurst: London).

Lampton, D. (1987), *Policy Implementation in Post-Mao China* (University of California Press: Berkeley).

Lansbury, R.D. (1987), 'The workers' congress in Chinese enterprises' in Warner, M. (ed.), *Management Reforms in China* (Frances Pinter: London), pp. 149—62.

Lardy, N. (1992), *Foreign Trade and Economic Reform 1978—1990* (Cambridge University Press: Cambridge).

Lasek, E. (1983), 'Imperialism in China: a methodological critique' in *The Bulletin of Concerned Asian Scholars*, vol. 15, no. 1, pp. 50—64.

Lee Lai To (1986), *Trade Unions in China 1949 to the Present* (National University of Singapore: Singapore).

Leftwich, A. (1983), *Redefining Politics: People, resources and power* (Methuen: London).

Leung, C.K. (1986), 'Spatial redeployment and the special economic zones in China: an overview' in Jao, Y.C. and Leung, C.K., *China's SEZs: Policies, Problems and Prospects* (Oxford University Press: Oxford).

Leung, H.M. and Thoburn, J.T. (1991), 'Contractual relations, foreign direct investment and technology transfer: the case of China' in *Journal of International Development*, vol. 3, no. 3, pp. 277—91.

266   *Bibliography*

Leung Wing-Yue (1988), *Smashing the Iron Rice Pot: Workers and unions in China's market socialism* (Asia Monitor Resource Centre: Hong Kong).
Lieberthal, K. and Oksenberg, M. (1988), *Policy-Making in China: Leaders, structures and processes* (Princeton University Press: Princeton).
Lin Yuru (ed.) (1990), *Annals of China's SEZs* (Guangdong People's Publishing House) (in Chinese).
Liu Guoguang (1992), 'Several problems concerning development strategy of China's SEZs' in *Chinese Economic Studies*, vol. 25, no. 3, Spring.
Liu, W.H. (1986), 'Construction of a post-Mao macroeconomic model and foreign trade' in *Issues and Studies*, vol. 22, nos. 1 and 2, Jan. and Feb.
Lu Ping (1990), *A Moment of Truth* (Asia Monitor Resource Centre).
Lukes, S. (1972), *Power: A radical view* (Macmillan: London).
Lyles, M.A. (1987), 'Common mistakes of JV experienced firms' in *Columbia Journal of World Business*, vol. XXII, no. 2, Summer, pp. 79–85.
MacDougall, C. (1982), 'Policy changes in China's foreign trade since the death of Mao, 1976–1980' in Gray, J. and White, G.W., *China's New Development Strategy* (Academic Press: London), pp. 149–71.
Macridis, R.C. (1983), *Contemporary Political Ideologies: Movements and regimes* (Little, Brown: Boston).
Moser, M.J. (1985), 'Law and Investment in the Guangdong SEZs' in Moser, M.J., *Foreign Trade, Investment and the Law in the P.R. China* (Oxford University Press: Oxford), pp. 143–78.
Nathan, A. (1973), 'A factional model for Chinese politics' in *China Quarterly*, no. 53, Jan./March, pp. 34–66.
Nelson, J.M. (1984), 'The political economy of stabilisation: commitment, capacity and public response' in *World Development* vol. 12, no. 10, pp. 983–1006.
Ng Sek Hong and Lansbury, R.D. (1987), 'The workers' congress in Chinese enterprises' in Warner, M. (ed.), *Management Reforms in China* (Frances Pinter: London), pp. 149–62.
Oke, S. (1986), 'China's relations with the world economy: trade, investment and contemporary developments' in *Journal of Contemporary Asia*, vol. 16, no. 2, pp. 237–46.
Oksenberg, M. (1971), 'Policy-making under Mao: 1949–1968: an overview' in Lindbeck, J.M.H. (ed.), *China: Management of a revolutionary society* (University of Washington Press: Seattle), pp. 79–115.
Oksenberg, M. and Goldstein, S. (1974), 'The Chinese political spectrum' in *Problems of Communism*, vol. XXIII, no. 2, March/April, pp. 1–13.
Papageorgiou, D. Michaely, M. and Choksi, A.M. (1991), *Liberalising Foreign Trade*, vol. 1 (Blackwell: Oxford).
Pearson, M. (1991), *Joint Ventures in the PRC: Control of FDI under socialism* (Princeton University Press: Princeton).
Peele, T. and Cohan, M.A. (1988), 'Dispute resolution in China' in *China Business Review*, Sept./Oct., pp. 46–9.
Phillips, D.R. (1986), 'SEZs in China's modernisation: changing policies and changing fortunes' in *National Westminster Bank Quarterly Review*, February, pp. 37–50.
Pomfret, R. (1991), *Investing in China* (Harvester Wheatsheaf: Hemel Hempstead).
Pye, L. (1981), *The Dynamics of Chinese Politics* (Oegelschlager, Gunn and Hain: Cambridge, MA).
Pye, L. (1986), 'The China trade: making the deal' in *Harvard Business Review*, July–Aug., pp. 74–80.

Pye, L. (1991), 'The state and the individual: an overview interpretation' in *China Quarterly*, no. 127, September, pp. 443–66.

Remer, C.F. (1968), *Foreign Investment in China* (Howard Fertig: New York).

Rong Yiren (1986), 'China's open policy and CITIC's role' in *Journal of International Affairs*, vol. 39, no. 2, Winter.

Rosen, S. and Zou, G. (eds) (1992), 'The Chinese debate on the new authoritarianism, winter 1990–1991' in *Chinese Sociology and Anthropology*, Spring.

Ruggles, R. (1983), 'Environment for American business ventures in the PR China' in *Columbia Journal of World Business*, Winter, pp. 67–73.

Saich, T. (1991), 'Much ado about nothing: party reform in the 1980s' in White, G.W. (ed.), *The Chinese State in the Era of Economic Reform* (Macmillan: London), pp. 149–74.

Schaffer, B.B. (1981), *To Recapture Public Policy for Politics* (Institute of Development Studies, University of Sussex: Falmer), October.

Schram, S. (1984), 'Economics in command? Ideology and policy since the Third Plenum 1978–1984' in *China Quarterly*, no. 99, September.

Schurmann, F. (1966), *Ideology and Organisation in Communist China* (University of California Press: Berkeley).

Segal, G. (1990), *Chinese Politics and Foreign Policy Reform* (Kegan Paul International: London).

Shi Qinglin (1985), 'The function of foreign exchange balance in the overall balance of the SEZ' in *Xiamen Tequ Diaoyan* (in Chinese), no. 4, December, pp. 20–2.

Shirk, S. (1985) 'The politics of industrial reform' in Perry, E.J. and Wong, C. *The Political Economy of Reform in Post-Mao China* (Council in East Asian Studies, Harvard University: Cambridge, MA).

Shum, K.K. and Sigel, L.T. (1986), 'Managerial reform and enterprise performance: assessing the experiment in Shenzhen and Zhuhai' in Jao, Y.C. and Leung, C.K., *China's SEZs: Policies, Problems and Prospects* (Oxford University Press: Oxford).

Skinner, G.W. and Winckler, E.A. (1969), 'Compliance succession in rural communist China: a cyclical theory' in Etzioni, A. (ed.), *Complex Organisations, A Sociological Reader*, 2nd edn (Holt, Rinehart and Winston: New York), pp. 410–38.

Sklair, L. (1985), 'Shenzhen: a Chinese "development zone" in global perspective' in *Development Change*, vol. 16, pp. 571–602.

Social Register: The retreat of the intellectuals (1991), eds R. Miliband, L. Panitch and J. Saville (Merlin Press: London).

Solinger, D. (1986), 'Industrial reform: decentralisation, differentiation and the difficulties' in *Journal of International Affairs*, vol. 39, no. 2, Winter, p. 115.

Somerville, C.T. (1987), 'The economic reform spiral in China: 1978–1986' in *Journal of Economics and International Relations*, vol. 1, no. 2, Summer, pp. 181–93.

Stoltenberg, C.D. (1984), 'China's SEZs: their development and prospects' in *Asian Survey*, vol. XXIV, no. 6, June.

Su Wenming (1985), 'The open policy at work', *China Today (10)* (Beijing Review Publications: Beijing).

Sung Yun-Wing (1991), *The China–Hong Kong Connection: The key to China's open door policy* (Cambridge University Press: Cambridge).

Takahara, A. (1987), 'The politics of wage reform in post-revolutionary China', PhD Thesis, IDS, University of Sussex.

Teiwes, F.C. (1984), *Leadership, Legitimacy, and Conflict in China* (Macmillan: London).

Terry, E. (1980), 'Decentralising foreign trade' in *China Business Review*, Sept./Oct., pp. 10–23.

Townsend, J.R. (1974), *Politics in China* (Little, Brown: Boston).

UNIDO (1985), *List of Investment Proposals* (Investment Promotion Meeting, 25–9 November).

Vogel, E. (1989), 'Special economic zones: experiment in new systems' in Vogel, E. *One Step Ahead in China: Guangdong under reform* (Harvard University Press: Cambridge, MA).

Walder, A. (1986), *Communist Neo-traditionalism: Work and authority in Chinese industry* (University of California Press: Berkeley).

Walder, A. (1987), 'Wage reform and the web of factory interests' in *China Quarterly*, no. 109, pp. 22–41.

Warner, M. (ed.) (1987), *Management Reforms in China* (St. Martin's Press: New York).

White, G.W. (1987a), 'The changing role of the Chinese state in labour allocation: towards the market?' in *Journal of Communist Studies*, vol. 3, no. 2, June, pp. 129–53.

White, G.W. (1987b), 'Labour reforms in Chinese industry' in Warner, M. (ed.), *Chinese Management Reforms* (Frances Pinter: London), pp. 113–26.

White, G.W. (1987c), 'The politics of economic reform in Chinese industry: the introduction of the labour contract system' in *China Quarterly*, September, pp. 365–89.

White, G.W. (ed.) (1991), *The Chinese State in the Era of Economic Reform* (Macmillan: London).

White, G.W., Howell, J., Zhe Xiaoye, Wang Ying and Sun Baoyang (1991), 'Rise of civil society in China', UNRISD Research Report, pp. 1–168.

Womack, B. (1987), 'The party and the people: revolutionary and post-revolutionary politics in China and Vietnam' in *World Politics*, vol. XXXIX, no. 4, July, pp. 479–507.

Wong, K.Y. and Chu, D.K. (1985), *Modernisation in China: The case of the Shenzhen SEZ* (Oxford University Press: Oxford).

Wood, E.M. (1991), 'The uses and abuses of civil society' in Miliband, R., Panitch, L. and Saville, J., *Socialist Register 1990: The retreat of the intellectuals* (Merlin Press: London), pp. 60–84.

World Bank (1988), *China: External trade and capital* (World Bank: Washington, DC).

Wu, F.W. (1982), 'The political risk of FDI in post-Mao China: a preliminary assessment' in *Management International Review*, 22, pp. 13–23.

Xiamen Municipal People's Government Industrial Research Office and Xiamen SEZ Research Institute (ed.) (1987), *Xiamen SEZ, Research into Foreign Investment* (Minjiang Publishing House: Xiamen) (in Chinese).

Xiamen SEZ Industrial Economics Research and Survey Editorial Commission (1987), *Research into Xiamen SEZ's Industrial Economy* (Xiamen Municipal People's Government Industrial Research Office: Publications Office, Xiamen), March (in Chinese).

Xue Muqiao (1986–7), 'Price fluctuations and changes in people's livelihood in China in the past six years' in *Chinese Economic Studies*, vol. XX, no. 2, Winter, pp. 55–63.

Yasheng Huang (1990), 'Origins of China's pro-democracy movement' in *Fletcher Forum of World Affairs*, vol. 14, Winter, part 1, pp. 30–9.

Yu Guangyuan (ed.) (1984), *China's Socialist Modernisation* (Foreign Languages Press: Beijing).

Zamet, J.M. and Bovarnick, M.E. (1986), 'Employee relations for multinational companies in China' in *Columbia Journal of World Business*, vol. XXI, no. 1 Spring, pp. 13–19.

Zhang Fengqing (1987], 'An attempt to analyse the constraining factors and policies upon the development of Xiamen's exports' in *Fujian Waimao Jingji*, no. 5, pp. 16–18 (in Chinese).

Zheng Tuobin (1987), 'The problem of reforming China's foreign trade system' in *Chinese Economic Studies*, Summer, pp. 27–49.

Zhong Xingyang (1985), 'We must pay attention to resolving the contradiction between the two types of wages in Xiamen SEZ' in *Xiamen SEZ Research*, no. 4 December (in Chinese).

Zou Erkang (1985–6), 'Special economic zone typifies open policy' in *Chinese Economic Studies*, vol. XIX, no. 2, Winter.

Zou Siyi (1983), 'The problem of export strategy' in *Chinese Economic Studies*, vol. XVI, no. 3, Spring.

Zweig, D. (1991), 'Internationalising China's countryside: political economy of exports from rural industry' in *China Quarterly*, no. 128, December, pp. 716–41.

Index